THE NEW DOWNTOWNS

THE NEW DOWN

Rebuilding Business Districts

LOUIS G. REDSTONE, FAIA

New York
St. Louis
San Francisco
Auckland
Düsseldorf
Johannesburg
Kuala Lumpur
London
Mexico
Montreal
New Delhi
Panama
Paris
São Paulo
Singapore

McGRAW-HILL BOOK COMPANY

Sydney
Tokyo
Toronto

TOWNS

Library of Congress Cataloging in Publication Data

Redstone, Louis G
  The new downtowns.

  Includes index.
    1. Urban renewal—United States.   2. Central
business districts—United States.   3. Cities and
towns—Planning—United States.   I. Title.
HT175.R43   309.2'62'0973   75-43849
ISBN 0-07-051369-4

234567890   HDHD   785432109876

*The editors for this book were Jeremy Robinson and Gretlyn Blau,
the design and layout were done by Naomi Auerbach,
and the production supervisor was Teresa F. Leaden.
It was set in Optima by York Graphic Services, Inc.*

It was printed and bound by Halliday Lithograph Corporation.

Note: Permission to use any photograph in this book should be sought
from the owner (photographer) cited in the credit.

In this Bicentennial Year of 1976, I dedicate this book to citizens of all countries for whom a well-rounded urban environment could mean the fulfillment of the good life.

To my wife Ruth.

Contents

Part Four   *Projects in Planning and Initial Implementation Stages 255*

Part Five   *Preservation and Restoration of Historic Buildings*
in the Central Business District Area 297

Foreword

by Charles A. Blessing, FAIA

Director of City Planning, Community and Economic
Development Department, City of Detroit
Past President of American Institute of Planners

The constructive and beneficial impact of this book on the leaders of central business district planning of America's cities, the design professions, and the general public should be immediate, dramatic, and encouraging. The very magnitude and dynamism of the rebirth of America's central business districts, as revealed in the many innovative case studies presented by Mr. Redstone in this book, will come as a surprise to all who are surfeited with the reports in the media of decline and decay and virtual hopelessness of the core city and its central business district. All should take to heart the simple and straightforward answer of an enlightened civic leader of a major central city. After listening patiently to an economist's predictions of doom, he gave an answer which is reinforced and confirmed by the overwhelming evidence of successful central-city renewal presented in this book: "All these dire predictions will come true only if we, who have been thrust into positions of leadership in the city, allow it to happen—only if we don't care whether these predictions come about, only if we give up and fail to apply initiatives to rejuvenate the heart of the city."

Two worldwide trends have created a paradox in the American city during the industrial-automotive age over the past 100 years. The first is the seemingly irreversible worldwide thrust of urbanization, which has already made most nations of Europe and America predominately urban. Thus the United States census of 1970 revealed that 80 percent of the total population is urban, with prospects that 90 percent may be urban by the year 2000. In most industrialized nations the situation is the same. The second trend, already far advanced in the United States, is a corollary to urbanization. This is the seemingly contradictory suburbanization and decentralization of urban populations and services, homes, jobs, shopping, and cultural activities to fragmented suburban locations. The result of this second trend has been the threatened collapse of many traditional functions of the central city and its heart—the central business district. Thus it is constantly emphasized that everyone who works in the CBD goes home at five o'clock after work, leaving an uninhabited, unloved, untended, dangerous core area—even less attractive, more insecure, and more disorganized in social and security terms. This threatened collapse of the CBD may well be too heavy a price for society to pay for the realization of the heralded new multifunction satellite city, with the core eroding and threatened with collapse of its traditional retail and office residence and entertaining functions, even though maintaining its banking, finance, and government roles.

If there were no perspective on this threat beyond the experience of the cities of the United States, one might give way to acceptance of the inevitable demise of the central core city and its functions. However, examination of what is happening in cities throughout the world suggests that it is precisely this continued vitality, even exuberance, of the heart of the city in countless great cities of Europe,

Asia, Africa, and South America which raises the insistent question: *why* here in America, the home of the skyscraper and all the products of the industrial revolution, electronic information retrieval, visual/verbal telephones, and many other innovations, *why* should our CBDs fade away when in most of the rest of the world the central city becomes ever more dominant, more exciting, and in many respects more beautiful and humane?

This timely, meticulous, and incisive work by Louis Redstone should reassure all central-city planners, urban designers, and architects that man's trait of adaptation has often taken and should again today take the age-old pattern of looking more carefully and analytically at the lessons of the past. It is indeed surprising that to date, so few American cities have transformed their principal downtown shopping street into a pedestrian galleria of the magnitude, vitality, and beauty of the great gallerias of 100 years ago in Milan and Naples or into a more modest arcade such as the Burlington Arcade in London; the Galeries St. Hubert in Brussels, the oldest merchant gallery in Europe; or the marvelous nineteenth-century galleries of the Palais Royal in Paris. The surprising historic American arcades in Providence (1828), Cleveland, and Los Angeles have long pointed the way to the downtown enclosed shopping center.

The work here presented is current—the latest innovations in CBD updating in more than fifty cities in the United States and in many other countries. It should be supplemented by study of each ensuing year's experience. One reason for qualified optimism about the future of the CBD as the continuing most vital central area of the region is the acknowledgment in public statements by the builders of many great regional shopping centers that the next step in the evolution of the shopping center will be the truly modern, efficient, beautiful, and comprehensively planned shopping center in the central business districts of America's cities, great and small.

It is said that man's most characteristic trait is his adaptability to change and to new conditions, second only to his ability to imagine—to create, to anticipate a better future. It is the ability to respond to this newfound urban condition that is so significantly documented by Mr. Redstone in this book, which is of basic importance to all concerned with improving the lot of the city and its urban inhabitants.

One fact should be emphasized: The great world cities, outside the United States, continue to thrive at the center—Paris, London, Moscow, Tokyo—with constant pressures to intensify the core. Their problems, generally, are not much different from ours—automobile traffic congestion, air pollution, obsolescence, and decay. In spite of these problems, in Paris, as only one example, living near the Place de la Opéra or minutes away from Notre Dame Cathedral in the very heart of the city of Paris seems preferable for the middle-and upper-income population than moving to the suburbs.

On the other hand, in city after city in the United States it has been true for many years that the urban dweller has sought relief from the burdens of the central city—social, financial, and environmental—by escaping to the ever-widening ring of suburbs, away from the effects of aging, obsolescence, and so-called invasion by those less fortunate, less wealthy, and less prepared to cope with the demands of the city.

The answer to this exodus—to the draining of vitality from the core of the central city and the fragmentation occasioned by the fantastic fact of the construction of 10,000 regional shopping centers in the United States alone in the years since the construction of the first regional center, Northland, in 1953 (the center is located in the adjoining city of Southfield on Detroit's northwest side)—is central to the very continued existence of the central city itself and to the idea of the role of the city throughout its long history as the seat of civilization, the center of commerce and culture and human services of all kinds. Perhaps there is no more crucial issue in the total spectrum of environmental planning in this nation today.

So it is that Mr. Redstone's survey of outstanding success stories in the recovery of vitality in the central core area is of paramount relevance and importance today. More than fifty outstanding examples of CBD design as a basis for a return to health and beauty and competitive stature to compete successfully with all the decentralizing forces of the regional shopping center are the subject of this survey. Others are not documented, but all are important to the future of the central city and its CBD as the true heart of the total metropolitan urban environment.

Overview

Much has been written on the sad state of affairs of the cities, the continued deterioration of the central business districts, and the generally discouraging outlook for any basic reversal in this trend. Some analysts are so pessimistic as to even question the necessity of a "city" in our new, emerging patterns of living! I strongly believe that the central city, with all its facilities, constitutes the heart of the urban organism. It serves not only the city within the legal boundaries but also the larger regional contiguous suburbs. We might compare its healthy condition to that of the human body, wherein the normal functioning of each part contributes to the well-being of the whole. This book is written to present an appraisal of actual happenings in cities of various sizes in the United States and in some other countries.

While as recently as a decade ago almost all the planning was in the "paper" stages—whether sponsored by government or private interests—the seventies show the dynamic beginnings of implementation of many imaginative and meaningful projects. This book will present some of the most significant examples of different approaches used to provide for the specific needs of each community. Examples will range from large, extensive transformations of entire core areas in the central business district in the large metropolises, as well as the smaller cities, to minimal improvements such as closing streets and creating malls for pedestrian use, using crossover connecting bridges, limiting auto traffic, and creating a more attractive atmosphere by means of landscaping, street furniture, special lighting, protective canopies, etc.

What are the necessary ingredients to make the city become again the center in people's lives? Amazingly enough, many major American cities have the basic fundamental requirements to make this transformation. They have the museums, libraries, theaters, universities, government and financial centers, and other recreational amenities. It seems that the biggest gap is the lack of housing near this center for all income groups who will become the supporting "backbone" for downtown activity. The demand for such places to live, whether in apartments, condominiums, etc., exists among a large number of city workers who prefer to be near their places of work, as well as near the center of activities. These include professionals, librarians, single people, couples without children, retirees, etc. They become the stable force which would make all the facilities economically viable. New housing construction would automatically fill in the empty and/or deteriorated areas existing in most cities, thereby reverting the downtown to a vibrant life. Also, these residential areas would become the supporting link for the various urban activities.

Nearly everyone in the professional diciplines agrees that cities must have people who live as well as work there. They all agree that what is needed is a continuous day and night activity in a *secure,* relaxed, and socially conducive atmosphere. I have emphasized the word "secure" because this seems to be the stumbling block in keeping people in the city as well as in bringing them back. There is no question that a well-populated area with a mix of different income groups will of itself create a positive feeling of security and become a great force against lawlessness. A good example of this is the city of Toronto, where the mixture of housing, business, and attractive events brings people to the center city and creates a lively and exciting atmosphere. I realize that in regard to American cities, the bringing of large numbers of people downtown, although an important element, may not be a cure-all for security problems. This book is not the place to delve into the many aspects connected with this universal urban problem. However, there is no question in my mind that a well-trained police force with a good understanding of social problems, coupled with closer cooperation and communication between the citizens and the law-enforcing agencies, would go a long way toward eliminating the critical stumbling blocks in the revival of the cities.

The question can be asked: Why make such an effort to bring people back to the city? I, for one, am convinced that people need the cultural, recreational, and educational facilities which only the city has available. Experience has shown that if exciting programs—art, theater, sports, etc.—are offered, people from miles away flock to take advantage of them. These are not usually available in the neighboring suburbs and small communities. One can only imagine how much better and more varied such programming would be, given a steady and continuous support from the residents of the central area. This in turn could generate a still greater influx from the outlying areas.

Another important element which needs to be considered in the revitalization of our cities is the development of a particular individuality and "special image." The desire for new and interesting "happenings," which the different character of each city can provide, would be an additional attraction for visitors and tourists as well as a source of pride for the local community.

Perhaps not all American cities can compete on the same level with the old, historic European cities. However, American cities have made their own contribution, not only in American history, but in industrial and technical fields as well.

To envision and create such a special image requires great ingenuity, not only on the part of the planners, but also on the part of the city's business, industrial, political, and financial leadership. All this, together with a broad base of citizen support, would guarantee the success of such a project. An example of what happens to such a project when total support is lacking comes from my own experience in Detroit. In 1965 an imaginative citizen, Walter C. Shami, headed a project for an "international village," which was planned for a downtown redevelopment area. The village was to include ethnic shops (reflecting the many nationalities that make up Detroit's population), variety stores, specialty shops, art galleries and studios, restaurants, movies, a theater, and an outdoor amphitheater. The project was approved by a federal agency for major funding, but lacked additional minor funding from local private sources. It is a sad commentary that the local business and industrial leaders were too shortsighted or unwilling to raise the additional sum (less than $1 million) to consummate a project which would have given that special attraction and boost to Detroit—an image which, in combination with the already available good convention facilities, would have made Detroit a tourist mecca! Now, years later, it is more evident than ever, how much such a project would have contributed to the city's revival.

Throughout the United States, in cities of all sizes, each faced with similar problems of the decline of the CBD, there are all-out efforts to confront these critical problems. In a number of cities, many redevelopment projects are already being implemented. In others, far-reaching plans, extending for a decade or more, are being started in stages, each completed stage serving as an impetus to the next. What is encouraging is to see the number of small and medium-sized cities which are forewarned by the general downward trend and are initiating immediate reconstruction and restoration projects in their central business cores.

It goes without saying that financing is one of the major considerations, and the larger and more complex the project, the more difficult and the more time-consuming it becomes to bring it to fruition. The most successful and "speedy" implementations are those in which the local citizens—merchants, bankers, developers, in cooperation with the local government authorities—take the initiative and responsibility for financing.

Where federal assistance and state and local commissions are involved, the process of implementing is a long and involved affair, requiring approval of every phase of the plan and involving the establishment of budgets which are seldom in agreement with those of the city departments and interested developers. Whether the CBD projects are small or large or are privately or governmentally (or both) assisted, many difficult obstacles must be overcome. Among these are the condemnation of property by the courts, the moving of long-established tenants, traffic rerouting, and sometimes the strong and nearsighted opposition of the local merchants to a new, competing development. These are only a few in a quick overview of the problems involved.

Although the diagnosed causes of the deterioration of the CBDs are similar, the solutions differ for each city. No community should look for set rules or try to emulate solutions that have worked for other cities. In some cities, as stated earlier, proposals are being made to redevelop a number of blocks, creating either open or enclosed malls with only service traffic allowed. Other plans call for constructing pedestrian malls above the street level, thus permitting the existing car and bus traffic to operate with minimum change. Some cities plan enclosed shopping and mall areas which are interconnected with already existing major department and other stores. A number of cities situated on rivers and lakes are in the process of developing the great potentials which the waterfront can add to the city's enrichment. By combining housing, recreation, and shopping, a stable core, so necessary for the quality and ongoing progress of the area, is created.

Other cities are in the process of utilizing air rights over railroad rights-of-way, expressways, main streets, etc., making it possible to bridge the wide gaps which divide one part of the city from the other. (In some cities, these gaps have been referred to as the "38th parallel.")

On a more modest scale, skyway bridges are used to interconnect department stores, office and commercial buildings, and parking structures at the second-floor level.

These are only a few of the techniques being used. Other concepts are presented in the individual case studies in this book.

The hopeful beginnings in many parts of the country should not lull us into the complacent belief that the directions of the planning and the choices made are always the best ones for attaining the ultimate goal: the city's revival. A number of cities embark upon the construction of huge sports arenas, stadia, and convention halls, with related service buildings and civic plazas. These developments do create some additional activity, bringing spectators and visitors into the city and thereby giving additional support to the existing commercial areas and encouraging the building of some new ones. Whatever benefits this type of planning brings, it only partly achieves the major goal of vital, exciting urban living. However, if the city is not to serve as a part-time location for business and sports, the planning must incorporate sufficient housing for all income groups which will provide a stable economic base for dynamic and exciting shopping complexes.

Because shopping is such an important part of the lives of both families and individuals, architects and planners have seen fit to create a pleasant environment for the purpose not only of buying goods but also of satisfying the human social needs of communication.

The need for a fresh approach to the revitalization of downtown means a complete rethinking by planners and architects. For one thing, the geographic area of planning has to be large enough to include long-range plans for all major functions; also, the complex has to relate to the contiguous areas—it cannot be an isolated, detached "island." We are witnessing many instances of self-contained complexes occupying as many as three and four square blocks in the CBD! However, because they are detached from the surrounding areas, they are not a complete answer to the problem of urban revitalization. These projects need to be planned as part of a continuous program of linking them to the adjoining existing or new structures.

An important new element which may greatly influence the acceleration of the downtown revival is the transportation problem caused by the worldwide energy crisis. All current planning, including that now being implemented, will have to take into account rapid-transit systems, local people movers in the downtown areas, and underground shopping concourses interconnecting various main buildings. Although rapid transit, when completed and accepted by the public, will lessen the need for parking spaces, present planning still needs to make ample provision for either underground or multistory parking structures.

The intent of this book is to spur and encourage the renewal of the deteriorating central business district in cities of all sizes. With this in mind, I realize that I can touch upon only the most vital elements contributing to the initiation and implementation of a very complex process. I am well aware that there are many aspects which could have been elaborated upon, and even some which no doubt warrant a separate chapter or even an entire book!

I decided that my direction should be to highlight the especially effective and successful procedures which were used in the four cities presented in Part 1. Each city was selected to illustrate a special technique. Jacksonville, Florida, provides an example of how a legal change can be effected by combining the city and county governments. This was the first step for the implementation of the urban renewal planning. Kalamazoo, Michigan, illustrates the leadership of the private business sector in initiating and financing the CBD area.

The city of Toronto was chosen to show how a citizens' task force can play an advisory and often decisive role in the final city government planning.

Cincinnati was selected to point up the decision-making process in the planning stages. Final decisions were made by a group which included the professional consultant, the developers and business people, and the elected and political officials.

In all these cases, the emphasis is on the current, up-to-date procedures. As tempting as it was to go back into the detailed history of each city's earlier efforts—some successful, some frustrating—I felt that this would not be a sufficiently supporting factor for the main goal of my book. The same approach is used in Part 3, which is intended to acquaint the reader with a variety of case studies. For the reader who is specifically interested in certain projects, this part provides the opportunity to pursue inquiries further to the source directly, whether public or private. This could involve, for example, details of land acquisition, tenant relocation, legal aspects, special legislation (state, county, and local), tax structure, public transit, and financing.

It may be of interest to many communities that they can have an available professional resource provided by The American Institute of Architects. Known as the Regional Urban Design Assistance Team Program (RUDAT), the national AIA headquarters in Washington assigns a team of architects at the request of the local community and its closest AIA sponsoring chapter.

The program is intended to serve as a catalyst for community action on design and planning problems and provides a fresh and objective look at a city's needs, assets, and options for change.

Team members serve as volunteers, agreeing not to accept commissions resulting from their studies and receiving only reimbursement for expenses.

At the time of this writing, RUDAT visits had been made to twenty-five communities since 1967. During 1975, active inquiries from ten other cities were under consideration.

City revival remains one of the most perplexing and challenging problems of our times. It will continue to require the expertise of the various related professional fields, in both the physical and the social planning. It is my hope that this book, with its case studies of projects already implemented, will encourage other cities to start their own exciting, new happenings!

Louis G. Redstone

Acknowledgments

In preparing this material, encompassing a wide variety of professional disciplines, I am indebted greatly to the many architectural, landscape design, and engineering firms involved in urban planning and renewal; to the executive directors and staffs of the city planning departments of the many cities presented in this book; to the heads of the federal and state urban renewal agencies involved in many of the projects; to the developers representing individuals, industrial corporations, financial institutions, and business leaders; to the National Endowment for the Arts; and to the many experts and consultants in the related fields of graphics, street furnishings, lighting, people-mover and rapid-transit systems, construction, and implementation. I am also indebted to the city planning departments and architects in Canada, Australia, Germany, Japan, Israel, France, and Yugoslavia.

In all cases the cooperation in assembling the graphic and descriptive material was generous and enthusiastic. This response was especially forthcoming from individuals and groups connected with historic preservation and renovation projects, whether a single project or a neighborhood sector.

A special word of appreciation goes to my secretarial assistant, Gloria Barnabo Tonelli, and, above all, to my wife Ruth, whose assistance in the three-year research which this complex subject required and whose awareness of the importance of, and necessity for, urban revival helped to make this book a reality.

Louis G. Redstone

Part One

Initiating CBD Renewal: Various Approaches

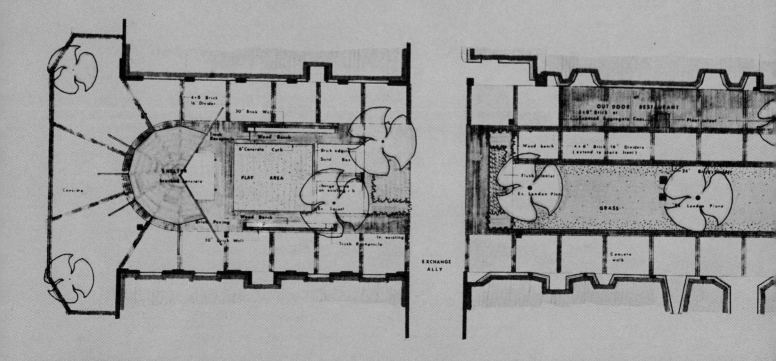

No poll is required to establish the fact that something is wrong with a life-style which has produced great facilities for commercial, governmental, recreational, educational, and cultural events, only to leave them to limited uses in the frantic flight from the city!

The search of the city dweller for "greener pastures" has not brought the complete fulfillment of a well-rounded life in suburbia, while at the same time the exodus has undermined the economic basis of, and has contributed to a defeatist mood toward, efforts to revitalize the city. Although the new shopping centers satisfied the marketing needs of some suburbanites, many others felt deprived of the cultural and recreational amenities which city life can offer. It stands to reason that because of the economics involved, no such extensive facilities can be expected to be provided in most of the suburbs. What, then, should our cities be doing to re-create the exciting urban experiences that afford people enjoyable and pleasurable social contacts? The first consideration—a prerequisite for any action program—is the true and sustained desire on the part of all segments of the population, from workers to government and business leaders, to support the revitalization plans. In many instances these plans cannot be limited to the city's borderlines, but should be coordinated with neighboring communities. In addition to the obvious benefits of such things as joint public transit, law-enforcement facilities, and vital utility amenities, such coordinating efforts might break down the borderlines between safe and unsafe areas. The results could greatly spark the revitalization of the urban central business district. The elements that influence the effective renewal of the urban central business district will vary with the size of the city, the ethnic makeup, the economic complexion, and the use density of the downtown residential areas.

In order to get an idea of how cities of various sizes initiated and implemented plans for their CBDs, it may be well to examine the procedures used in a city of moderate size, such as Jacksonville, Florida, and those employed in a smaller urban center, such as Kalamazoo, Michigan. Some aspects of the redevelopment of a large city are illustrated by the Toronto experience. Also of interest is the unique approach used in Cincinnati in successfully implementing the CBD revival.

Jacksonville illustrates the use of procedures for redevelopment involving a combined structure of city and county governments, relying for its implementation on public (federal, state, or city) and private financing.

In the case of Kalamazoo, the initiative for, and implementation of, CBD improvement came solely from the private sector and concerned citizens. This city claims the honor of having the first pedestrian mall built in the United States.

The effectiveness of citizen participation in formulating and implementing policies of city government is illustrated by the Toronto experience.

Jacksonville

Jacksonville, Florida (population approximately 200,000), after a number of years of continuous political effort, consolidated the city and Duval County governments. In 1968 the newly formed government set up a number of goals, among which were the following:

1. Create a new single county wide local government based on a check and balance "Mayor-Council" governmental structure.

2. Provide for a structure that allows easy electorate pinpointing of responsibility, thus leading to greater citizenry understanding and participation.*

In line with the above, the Jacksonville Downtown Development Authority was established on June 30, 1973. The Authority was charged with counteracting the findings which the new city government presented them, as follows:

A. Property values and environmental qualities in downtown Jacksonville have deteriorated for various reasons; and

B. Such deterioration in values and environmental qualities is detrimental to the public interest in having a viable core city area around which the life in the community, in all aspects, may center; and

C. Steps which could remedy existing conditions, halt further deterioration, and revitalize the downtown area of Jacksonville, would further this public interest; and

D. There exists a need for the redevelopment of the Jacksonville downtown area, to be planned, coordinated and implemented with the assistance of the Jacksonville Downtown Development Authority, as provided in Article 28 of the Charter.

The boundaries of the downtown central business district are then described in detail.

The Jacksonville Downtown Development Authority consists of seven members, appointed by the mayor and confirmed by the council. Each member serves a staggered term of four years. Each must be at least twenty-five years old and must have been a resident of the city for at least two years prior to appointment. No officer or city employee is eligible for appointment. Members do not receive a salary or benefits, but they are reimbursed for traveling expenses and other actual expenses incurred in the performance of their duties. The Authority elects its chairperson, vice chairperson, and secretary to serve for one year. It must hold regular monthly meetings and special meetings upon call of the chairperson or any three members.

The Authority is charged with the following specific powers and duties:†

1. To make or cause to be made studies and analyses of economic changes taking place in the Jacksonville downtown area and of the importance of the impact of metropolitan growth upon that area;
2. To prepare, in coordination with the planning board, a plan or plans for the development and redevelopment of the Jacksonville downtown area, and to submit them for review and approval by the planning board and the council;
3. To implement any plan of development in the downtown area which has been approved by the council and by the planning board.
   a. Coordinating development and redevelopment by public and private enterprise;
   b. Encouraging private development and redevelopment in a manner consistent with the plan;
   c. From time to time proposing such revisions in the plan as appear to the authority to be appropriate and in the best interest of the city;
   d. Constructing, acquiring, repairing, and operating any public development or project covered by the plan, or coordinating any of the foregoing among other governmental agencies, as the (city) council may provide from time to time;
4. In coordination with the planning board, develop long-range plans designed to halt the deterioration of property values in the . . . downtown area, and encourage property owners to implement the plans to the fullest extent possible;

*Urban Action Clearinghouse, Case Study 4, published by Chamber of Commerce of the United States, 1968.
†Excerpted from the Ordinance Code of the city of Jacksonville, chap. 28, paragraphs B–E, establishing the Jacksonville Downtown Authority.

5. To acquire by purchase or the exercise of power of eminent domain, which must be in the best interest of the public, for public purposes only subject to approval by the council . . . any land and any other property, real and personal, and any rights and interests therein which it may determine to be reasonably necessary in furtherance of its other powers . . . and to grant and acquire licenses, easements and options with respect thereto; provided however that the compensation paid to owners of land and any other property, real and personal, or any property right . . . shall include reasonable reimbursement for relocating an existing business; and provide further that any property leased to private interests shall not be exempt from ad valorem taxes.

6. To improve land, construct, reconstruct, equip, improve, maintain, and repair parking facilities, parks, plazas, malls, walkways and other public facilities and any necessary or desirable appurtenances thereto within the . . . downtown area;

7. To fix, charge and collect fees, rents and charges for the use of any project, any part thereof, and any facilities furnished thereby, and of any property under its control, and to pledge such revenue to the payment of revenue bonds issued by it;

8. To accept grants and donations of any type of property, labor, and other things of value from public and private sources, and to expend public funds for public purposes in the downtown area as a part of and in cooperation with any private project;

9. To enter into contracts in furtherance of its duties and in the exercise of its powers, and to contract and otherwise cooperate . . . with Federal and State agencies;

10. To grant to and receive from the city conveyances of property interests, grants, contributions, loans, and other rights and privileges;

11. To issue bonds of the authority, payable solely from revenues, to pay all or a part of the cost of one or more projects authorized by this article or to refund any bonds issued under this article. The bonds shall be offered for public sale and shall be awarded to the bidder whose bid produces the lowest net interest cost, calculated in the manner the authority may prescribe in accordance with sound financial practices. Notice of sale of the bonds shall be published at least twice in a newspaper published in and having a general circulation in Duval County; the first publication shall be at least fifteen (15) days prior to the date set for opening bids. The authority shall reserve the right to reject any and all bids. The bonds may be issued by the authority only upon approval by ordinance of the council. Notwithstanding any provisions of any other law or laws to the contrary all revenue bonds, including refunding bonds, issued pursuant to this article shall constitute legal investments for saving banks, banks, trust companies, executors, administrators, trustees, guardians, and other fiduciaries, and for any board, body, agency or instrumentality of the state, of any county, municipality, or other political subdivision of the state; and shall be eligible as security for deposits of state, county, municipal and other public funds; and

12. To borrow money and to issue notes for any purpose or purposes for which bonds may be issued under this article and to refund the same; to issue notes in anticipation of the receipt of the proceeds of the sale of bonds.

The authority shall prepare and submit its budget for the ensuing year to the city council on or before June 1 of each year, setting forth its estimated gross revenues, and estimated requirements for operations and maintenance expenses, debit service, and depreciation. A copy of the budget shall be published once in a newspaper of general circulation in the city during the month of June. The council and the mayor of the city shall approve or disapprove the budget in the manner provided in the charter of the city for budgets of independent agencies.

Section 28.107.   Except as the council may provide, the authority shall utilize the central services of the city, and shall pay for them on a cost accounted basis. The authority may utilize such other services of the city as may be mutually agreed upon from time to time and may pay for them on a fair and reasonable basis. The authority shall purchase all supplies, contractual services, capital improvements, and professional services in compliance with the same ordinances and regulations which apply to the city when making such purchases.

Section 28.109.   All instruments in writing necessary to be signed by the authority shall be executed by the chairman and secretary, or by such officer, agent or employee of the authority as it may by resolution designate. The authority shall provide for the examination of all payrolls, bills, and other claims and demands against the authority to determine before the same are paid that they are duly authorized, in proper form, correctly computed, legally due and payable, and that the authority has funds on hand to make payment.

The establishment of a downtown development authority or a renewal agency is only the starting point. It is important to understand that between the starting point and the implementation there is often a long procedural interval, frequently extending from five to twelve years. This estimate applies mostly to larger cities with a population over 500,000 in which the project depends also on state and federal grants and loans. In smaller cities where private enterprise and financing are involved, implementation could begin within two to three years from the time the plans are approved by the local authorities. The experiences of cities of various sizes in initiating and implementing urban renewal projects are presented in Part 3.

Kalamazoo

Kalamazoo, Michigan, a city of 85,500 residents, is located midway between Chicago and Detroit. Like many small American urban centers, the business community was experiencing, in the mid-1950s, transition pains in its key industries, which were starting to diversify. It is interesting to note that at the time the business recession was affecting Kalamazoo, suburban shopping-mall competition in the city was not a factor. It is to the credit of concerned business leadership that it realized the necessity of implementing a drastic plan of action to prevent deterioration of the central business district. In 1957 these leaders raised the funds to commission Gruen Associates to prepare a long-range plan. Gruen's report, entitled *Kalamazoo—1980* and published in March 1958, stated:

1. We must think in terms of comprehensive long-range planning for Kalamazoo rather than in terms of temporary stop-gap measures.
2. Further, we cannot and must not take the defeatist attitude of merely saving Kalamazoo's downtown, but must take active and positive steps to retain it as the heart of the entire metropolitan community.
3. Goals for downtown Kalamazoo:
   a. The most productive use of land.
   b. The fusion of governmental, commercial, and cultural activities into a vital entity serving all elements of the community.
   c. The provision of easy access to downtown.
   d. Minimizing demolition necessary for implementing the plan.
   e. Separation of pedestrian and vehicular activity.

The Gruen plan called for the redevelopment to be implemented in three phases:

Phase One. The construction of a one-way peripheral loop street around the downtown area using existing street patterns. The area inside the loop was to be devoted primarily to pedestrian use through a series of walking malls constructed in former street rights-of-way. Parking lots were planned to be strategically located within a five-minute walk from the center of town.

Phase Two. The perimeter road was to be expanded outward, and the pedestrian area was to be enlarged considerably.

Phase Three. The final elements of the Gruen plan included new buildings in the peripheral areas, the upgrading of existing buildings, extensive landscape treatment, and completion of the circulation system.

Merchant groups and business leaders next took the initiative in starting the plan. The city authorities (mayor, city manager, city planning director, and heads of various city departments) all agreed on starting phase one—a two-block mall, later enlarged to a third block, plus additional parking facilities.

General construction of the project in 1959–1960 cost approximately $90,000, exclusive of accessory projects, i.e., telephone and utilities. The cost was divided equally between abutting property owners and the city through special assessments. The expense was comparatively low because the mall was designed and constructed using "in-house" talent from the parks and recreation department, with assistance from public works, traffic engineering, and other departments. Merchants assisted in the areas of design and the preparing of timetables and procedures, and the first two of the three blocks were remodeled from curbline to curbline in 1959. Ten thousand automobiles per day were rerouted around construction as workers changed a street into a park. The third block was completed the following year; sidewalks were left intact, and trees, grass, flowers, and shrubs appeared where cars had once traveled. New fountains, street furniture, sculptures, and many other innovative parklike properties were introduced. Ten years later, in 1970, this historic mall got a face-lifting; all surfaces (including sidewalks) were replaced, and new lights, planters, benches, flowers, bushes, and structures were added. In 1974 a fourth block was added, extending the mall.

To ensure continued success of the Kalamazoo Mall concept, a regulations ordinance was passed, and a mall advisory board, responsible to the city planning commission, was established to make recommendations on mall conduct and decor. Also, the Downtown Kalamazoo Association was organized by central-district businesspeople for the purpose of promoting sales of goods and services and sponsoring community events. The confidence and efforts of the initiators were reflected in a 25 to 50 percent business increase in locations on or adjacent to the mall. In the first year of operation over twenty-five new downtown buildings were constructed, and the community found a new source of pride.

To make the mall work, major problems of access, mobility, and parking had to be solved. The city government was persuaded to take on an aggressive parking-expansion program. Since land in perimeter downtown Kalamazoo was not yet at a premium, the task was easier than it might be today.

A proposal to finance other phases of the Gruen plan through urban renewal was voted down in 1963 by the citizens in public referendum—because most feel a dislike of interference in local affairs by the federal government. Further action was delayed for about five years. Meanwhile, a new city manager was appointed, and a group called the CBD Master Plan Steering Committee was assembled under the leadership of a downtown merchant and the city planning commission chairperson. This committee enlisted the help of the city manager (James Caplinger), the mayor, two city commissioners, the chairperson of the mall advisory board, the mall redevelopment board, the county board of commissioners, the Metro Transit Board and the merchant's association, both county and city planning directors, and the head of the county chamber of commerce.

The group expanded as needed to incorporate city department heads for technical advice. Heading the consultants was Ralph Stephenson, who had been familiar with the project from its very beginning. This group tackled both short-term and long-term planning.

Their first project, as mentioned earlier, was a complete renovation of the existing three-block Kalamazoo Mall. The ten-year-old pedestrian area received a new surface, street furniture, and lights—all in all, a whole new image. This process sparked new enthusiasm. The city and the merchants participated on a fifty-fifty basis for the renovation, and downtown improvement momentum was again apparent. While the mall renovation was in progress, a dynamic young chamber of commerce executive, Rodney Benson, came to Kalamazoo. Along with a strong city administrator and a participating downtown merchants' group, he added drive to spearhead further development.

KALAMAZOO MALL
Kalamazoo, Michigan

DESIGNER: Kalamazoo Department
of Parks and Recreation
CONSULTANTS: Larry Harris, Landscape
Architect, and Robert O'Boyle
and Gordon Rogers, Architects

Location plan. (1) Kalamazoo Mall; (2) Kalamazoo Center; (3) city parking ramp; (4) mall extension; (5) new bank construction; (6) private parking ramp expansion; (7) Upjohn Pharmaceutical Research building; (8) Eleanor Street extension.

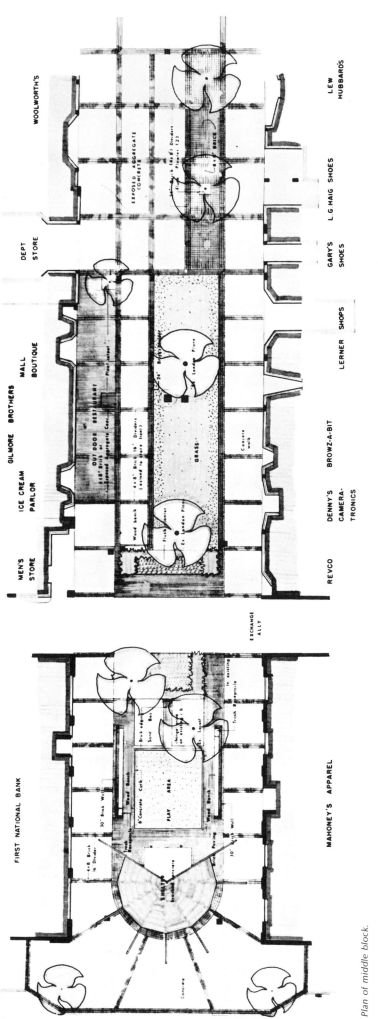

Plan of middle block.

View of mall showing decorative pool.

View of mall showing street furniture.

One of the most impressive results of Kalamazoo downtown planning has been the creation of Kalamazoo Center, which is an up-to-date attempt to curb CBD deterioration by removing antiquated, nonfunctional buildings in the heart of the city and replacing them with a multifunctional structure. The center is a one-block complex comprised of a large meeting-hall facility (city-owned), a hotel, an enclosed public mall, office space, a restaurant, stores, a discotheque, a health club, and open spaces, funded privately and through local donations. This downtown "magnet" will do several things to augment the already enthusiastic efforts of the merchants, the city, and the chamber of commerce. A larger convention market can be tapped, and new jobs will be added downtown. The economic spinoff from this type of project is self-evident.

KALAMAZOO CENTER
Kalamazoo, Michigan
ARCHITECT: Michael Severign of
Elbasani Logan & Severign

ABOVE: *Model of Kalamazoo Center complex. (Photographer: Gene-O-Smith Studio.)* LEFT: *Center completed 1975. (Photographer: Robert Maxwell, courtesy of Kalamazoo Gazette.)*

Credit for initiating Kalamazoo Center goes to the city manager, the chamber of commerce executive director, and many individuals and groups, including the merchants' group. Together, these people, sparked by a young clothing-store merchant, Roger Kooi, persuaded Inland Steel Development Corporation of Madison, Wisconsin, to invest in the private venture in the block. David Carley, president of Inland Steel Development Corporation, and his longtime friend and employee, Dr. Elton Ham, a resident of Kalamazoo, helped put the project together.

Kalamazoo Center proved several things:

1. A project coauthored to fill both the social and the profit motive of a community is welcomed.

2. A substantial amount of financing can be secured from the private sector to support such a project (in Kalamazoo, over $3 million was raised through donations for the city's portion alone).

3. Undercapitalized developers cannot survive the rigors of such projects.

4. The private partner and the public partner must continuously maintain defendable cost-benefit ratios for approval of the taxpayer.

5. Citizen participation is a time-consuming, but critical, factor.

6. Leadership must be knowledgeable and understanding of all phases of a project.

The Kalamazoo Center project is a natural continuation of the initial thrust of the "mall spirit" of 1957. The idea exists as a cooperative effort of intent and has been contributed to by professionals, amateurs, merchants, citizens, politicians, and administrators.

The planning process in Kalamazoo presently encompasses many downtown projects, all designed to beautify and stabilize the core city. Primary programs are:

1. Establishment of a new residential trend in the downtown area, specifically involving senior citizens and luxury apartments.

2. Development of an expanded transportation center incorporating rail, bus, taxi, and shuttle service in the central city.

3. Mall extension in low-density retail areas.

4. Expansion of professional office space, as well as additional retail and service expansion.

5. Ongoing beautification projects involving murals, landscaping, and refacing of buildings.

6. Additional parking construction.

The above program serves as another step in a continuous revival effort. Judging by its past accomplishments, Kalamazoo, with its dynamic leadership and its strong public support, can look forward to a viable urban environment.

Toronto

The city of Toronto provides an example of successful citizen participation in planning. There the impact of the high level of citizen involvement has influenced the decentralization of the city-planning function. Site-planning branch offices have been set up in neighborhoods, bringing together the planners and the local residents in the planning process. Working committees or task forces consisting of representatives of varied community interests have been established to work toward consensus agreements on development issues. In this way, organized citizen groups have real control over the future of their neighborhoods.

In addition to being concerned about their neighborhoods, many people fear the "Manhattanization" of downtown Toronto. Recognizing this, the city council in the summer of 1973 passed a two-year holding by-law requiring all new proposals for buildings over 45 feet in height and 40,000 square feet to be reviewed by the council before granting approval. Meanwhile, permanent legislation is being sought to better control the form of Toronto's future downtown growth.

Concern about the form and direction of the downtown core is important in that the core is viewed as a focal point for the Toronto community at large. Whereas many cities, especially in North America, have witnessed a decline in the importance of their downtown areas, Toronto's remains vibrant and continues to prosper.

COME TO THE PUBLIC MEETINGS ON

METRO CENTRE

Toronto, Ontario, Canada. Sample of public-meeting announcements for serious discussions on the core-area problems. (Photograph courtesy of Metropolitan Toronto Library Board.)

■ THE CITY OF TORONTO WILL SOON BE NEGOTIATING WITH METRO CENTRE DEVELOPMENTS LIMITED TO COME UP WITH DEVELOPMENT AGREEMENTS WHICH WILL DEFINE PLANS FOR THE OVERALL DEVELOPMENT OF THE METRO CENTRE PROJECT.

■ A PUBLIC DISCUSSION OF WHAT WILL GO INTO THESE DEVELOPMENT AGREEMENTS IS URGENTLY NEEDED SO THAT CITY COUNCIL CAN ARRIVE AT POLICIES IN THE BEST INTEREST OF THE COMMUNITY.

■ *THE METRO CENTRE SUB-COMMITTEE STRONGLY URGES YOU TO ATTEND THESE MEETINGS AND MAKE YOUR VIEWS KNOWN.* THE QUESTIONS BELOW ARE SIMPLY SOME SUGGESTIONS FOR THE KINDS OF THINGS YOU MIGHT WANT TO DISCUSS AT THE MEETINGS.

THURSDAY AUGUST 22 Committee Room 3 CITY HALL 8 p.m.	HOUSING AND LAND USE IN METRO CENTRE ● What are the best sites for housing in Metro Centre? ● Who should live there? 　● how much family accommodation should be included? 　● what proportion should be subsidized for low and moderate income people? 　● should there be provision for non-profit and/or co-operative housing? ● Should there be a mixed use community where housing is mixed with commercial and perhaps light industrial uses (that would be compatible with housing)?
THURSDAY SEPTEMBER 5 Committee Room 3 CITY HALL 8 p.m.	TRANSPORTATION TO METRO CENTRE ● What emphasis should there be on providing access to Metro Centre with improved public transit? ● Should the capacity of the downtown road system be increased to provide access to Metro Centre? ● How would this improved road capacity affect your neighbourhood?
THURSDAY SEPTEMBER 12 Committee Room 1 CITY HALL 8 p.m.	METRO CENTRE AND THE CITY ● How should Metro Centre relate to the waterfront and to the central business district to the north? ● How should the road system in Metro Centre be designed to best relate to the rest of the City? ● How should the public transit system in Metro Centre be designed to best relate to the rest of the City? ● What input should the public have in making decisions on Metro Centre?

This concern by a large number of individuals and groups sparked the formation of a citizen's task force. This task force was charged by the city council to make a series of comprehensive policy recommendations and to look into all aspects of movement and transportation in the central area of the city.

In order to establish the area to be studied, it was agreed that the core of the city included the central business and shopping districts—the dense concentration of mainly nonresidential activities—used daily by people from all over Metro and beyond. It was also agreed that the residential neighborhoods, which form a horseshoe around the inner core area, were by virtue of proximity affected by the activities of the inner core area to a greater degree than other residential areas of the city and should therefore be included in the study area. The inner core area is composed of three distinct but highly interrelated subareas: the Central Waterfront–Metro Centre area, the Downtown area, and the Midtown area. (See the map of the core area.)

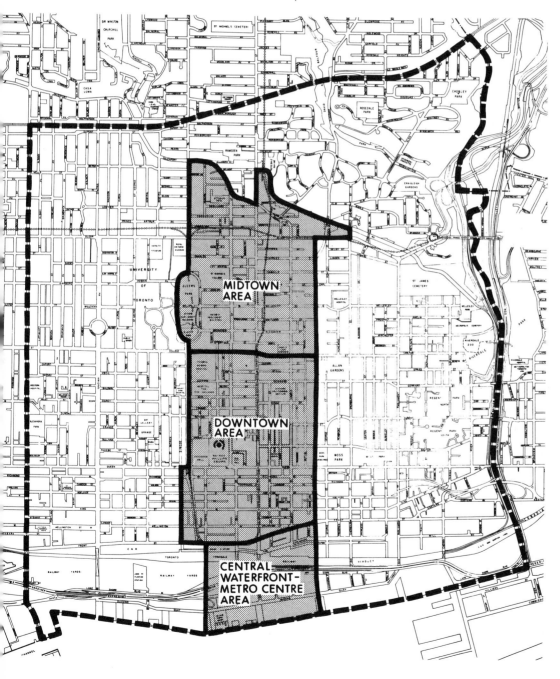

Toronto, Ontario, Canada. The core area studied by the task-force committee.

CORE AREA   INNER CORE AREA

At present, the Central Waterfront–Metro Centre area contains a mix of industrial and transportation uses. It has almost no residential populations and relatively little employment. But as current proposals for Harbour Square and Metro Centre indicate, there could be a tremendous increase in the residential population and both an increase and a change in the type of employment located there. The kind of development which occurs in the Central Waterfront–Metro Centre area will obviously have important implications for the core area. It will, for example, determine whether the present barrier between the Central Waterfront and the rest of the city will be overcome or only reinforced. It will also determine whether the recent trends toward high-rise luxury apartments and toward increasing concentrations of office uses in the inner core will be continued. The traffic generated by these developments could overload downtown streets or public transit facilities. Although this area was not analyzed in great detail, a number of general principles were developed which should guide development there, as well as in other parts of the core area.

The downtown area is the primary employment center of the core area and, like the Central Waterfront–Metro Centre area, has a low residential population. There have been marked increases in the amount of office space as well as in the density of development in this area in recent years. This dense office development has created pressure on transportation facilities.

The task force soon recognized that its work covered a much broader scope than just transportation problems and that it would need specialized studies in order to make meaningful recommendations on the following: land use and population, congestion, residential neighborhoods, and environmental quality. The city council recognized the need for these studies and provided assistance. The process followed by the task force deserves some comment. After exploring and defining the issues, the task force divided itself into four subcommittees to expand on the issues of land use, congestion, residential neighborhoods, and environmental quality. Each subcommittee was responsible for generating public discussion on its assigned subject. Three methods were used:

1. Large general public meetings.
2. Distribution of a questionnaire which asked people to suggest ways of improving the core.
3. Meetings with various planning groups working in the core residential areas (five area groups were involved).

Three of the subcommittees published working papers based on a consensus of their members. The fourth, on land use, was unable to report because of a division of opinion between those members representing essentially "residential" interests and those representing "business" interests. The major differences concerned the degree to which the commercial development of the core should be permitted to expand. Underlying this was a difference of opinion on the role of the core—on whether it was a national and international center to the exclusion of its role as a center to serve more local interests. The setting of the limits of the growth of the core and the relationship of this growth to the stability of downtown residential neighborhoods were also matters of disagreement. These disagreements were dealt with by having the staff assigned to the task force consolidate the divergent points of view into a single set of recommendations, which were considered, debated, and approved by the task force as a whole.

Following the publication of the working papers—including the points of view of both sides of the land-use subcommittee—the staff prepared draft-consolidated recommendations using the working papers as a base. These were published in December 1973 for consideration by the city council.

The affairs and documents of the task force were always public, and the recommendations, although in preliminary form, were reported in the press. Of special interest were the subjects of the agendas for the public meetings, which were conducted at almost weekly intervals during the summer of 1974. (See the sample of public-meeting announcements, page 12.) The experience of this task force would indicate that, given the opportunity, people will devote a great deal of their own time to participating in policy formulation and giving advice to government.

The task-force format is an effective method which argues forcibly for a continuing and expanded role for citizens in both the policy-setting and implementation phases of municipal government.*

Cincinnati

The success of Cincinnati's planning for the central business district revival came about as the result of its unique planning-process approach. At the heart of the Cincinnati planning process was the working review committee. The professional consulting members of the collaborative team were architect Archibald Rogers, of the Baltimore firm of Rogers, Taliaferro, Kostritsky, Lamb; transportation consultants Alan M. Voorhees and Associates; and economic consultants Hammer and Company.

Following are some comments from *Design & Environment* magazine.†

> This committee, consisting of 18 men, represented the city administration, the city planning commission, the downtown development committee and civic interests at large. Meetings of this committee took place every two weeks with Archibald Rogers presenting specific proposals and alternatives at each meeting. The ultimate plan document best describes the extraordinary process whereby agreement was reached on the redevelopment of downtown Cincinnati.
>
> To assure a process that would act logically on a hierarchy of decisions, an ever-increasing level of detail, a step-by-step ladder of planning decisions, was proposed. . . . This ladder of planning decisions consisted of: decisions as to the objectives of the plan, its strategies, its broad design concepts, and, finally, the detailed design illustrating these concepts and setting dimensions for the elements of the downtown plan.
>
> To make effective this decision-making ladder, it was decided that clear choices had to be presented at each stage for action by the working review committee. At each stage, the alternatives were to be developed from the preceding decisions. While at each stage the planning consultants were to give their technical recommendations, the Committee was free to accept or reject or modify these technical recommendations in arriving at its own recommendations to the city council.
>
> Since the working review committee, as a small working group, could not give a direct voice to every downtown interest, it was decided to conduct a downtown interview program and a metropolitan area attitude survey. The interview program covered many of the individual downtown enterprises. These surveys were designed to give the planning consultants and the committee insights into the specific aspirations and needs of a cross-section of the downtown enterprise and users so as to guide the committee in its role as community representative.

*Material resource based on the "Chairman's Prologue" and the report of the task-force committee for the city of Toronto, December 1973.

†Excerpted from an article by Ann Ferebee, "Successful Cincinnati," *Design & Environment* magazine, Winter 1972.

A useful publication called "Cincinnati: No Pause in Progress," prepared by the city's department of urban development, explains the effect of this process: what happened was that all the elements of the community were represented in the planning and decision making. This meant that the plan was approved as it was being developed.

Recommendations made by the working review committee went to the city planning commission and to city council. . . . Since representatives of both groups also sat on the working review committee, recommendations went smoothly through both the planning commission and the city council. Ultimately the city council passed more than 250 ordinances which allowed the Cincinnati department of urban development to implement the recommendations of the working review committee. The city planning commission and department of urban development both provided data to the outside planning consultants who incorporated it in their presentations to the working review committee.

The Cincinnati decision-making process distinguished and structured three areas of judgment. Technical judgments were made by Archibald Rogers and other professional consultants. Value judgments were made by developers, property owners and businessmen, whose interests were championed by Dennis Durden, advisor to the downtown development committee. Elected political officials also made value judgments on a city-wide scale. Because businessmen and politicians, making value judgments, could vote on proposals prepared on the basis of technical judgment by a highly competent professional team, the remarkable Cincinnati planning process was highly successful.

Special credit for the initiating of this planning process, in addition to Archibald Rogers, should be given to Mark Upson, chairman of the review committee; Peter Kory, director of Cincinnati urban development; and William C. Wichman, city manager.

Part Two
Elements of CBD Redevelopment

Goals and Concepts

It is encouraging to see in the mid-1970s the implementation of many plans and meaningful projects for CBD revival. Some of these plans have lain dormant for long periods or have been periodically revamped throughout years of political indecision. Some plans were spurred on by the 1967 racial upheavals, which pointed up the inexorable direction of continuing deterioration of city living.

The realization of the possible downfall of the urban centers exploded suddenly in the consciousness of every citizen. The present feeling of urgency has permeated every level of our population—concerned citizens; suburbanites; political, business, and civic leaders; architects; city planners; and the man on the street!

Urban redevelopment is a complex matter by anyone's measure. Every step is interwoven with set conditions, codes, zoning, economic feasibility, financing, and often frustrating political experiences. There is a great challenge to implement new concepts and to initiate some immediate short-range phases, while always looking toward achieving the long-range goals.

The ultimate goal to which nearly every major city aspires is to create an environment conducive to a lively, satisfying day/night variety of "people activities." To achieve this goal, the elements of the plan must include the following: the extension of facilities to attract people in the after-business hours, e.g., theater, sports, music, and special events; the diversification of new jobs and an increase in employment opportunities; the provision for residential units for various income groups (close to places of employment); the building of a balanced mix of new office, shopping, and recreational facilities; the provision for multilevel parking structures for private and public developments; the preservation and restoration of buildings of historical heritage, thereby adding character to the city and creating interest for visitors; and the provision for protected pedestrian walkways (whether elevated, at ground level, or underground) linking the major shopping, office, and municipal buildings.

As I have stated previously, a comprehensive plan of the CBD must be developed as a total concept. In the following pages I shall describe the various elements that could be materialized as first steps in order to improve the CBD environment and, at the same time, lend a much-needed credibility to the intentions of the planning agencies. The urgent need for immediate improvements, spurred by the pressure of involved citizen groups, has compelled those in charge of replanning the central business district areas to direct their attention and efforts to projects which could be accomplished in a relatively short period.

One such element in a continuous chain of improvements is the creation of the pedestrian mall. However, though the construction of the pedestrian mall seems to be the easiest to achieve, it should be construed only as a minimal step toward a total concept of CBD replanning.

Pedestrian Malls

In deciding on the type and scope of the mall, certain research data must be gathered and analyzed. This includes a thorough economic feasibility study: Will the additional investment warrant upgrading the area by closing the street and providing an attractive pedestrian parkway? Will the majority of merchants be willing to invest in upgrading their stores? What will be the effect on the CBD traffic system of the rerouting of traffic around the mall area? To what extent will the city be willing not only to subsidize the building of parking structures but also to keep the parking rate at an acceptable minimum? Also, in planning the more extensive mall development occupying a number of blocks, consideration must be given to incorporating local people-mover systems which would be ultimately connected with proposed rapid-transit systems.

Regardless of the favorable statistics showing increased merchant activity and sales growth averaging 10 to 20 percent, pedestrian malls should be considered only the first step in the continuous upgrading process required to keep up with the rapid social changes of our times. The mall ultimately should lead to a continuous expansion from the limited and isolated "commercial island" to become a part of future phases of the revitalized CBD.

It is well to note that the introduction of pedestrian malls as a CBD magnet may not always have the anticipated positive results. Much depends on the size of the city; the individual character of the area; the effect on traffic patterns, parking, and service areas; the overall control of the type of establishments; and general security arrangements.

Many large cities in the United States and Canada have had various degrees of success with the pedestrian mall. In some instances the malls are operated on a seasonal basis, especially where severe climate is a factor. Toronto has been experimenting with malls since 1971. The first area to be converted to a pedestrian mall was Yonge Street, between Bloor Street and St. Mary's Street. The conversion was accomplished in twenty-four hours, and the mall operated for seventeen days and was successful in increasing business and the people's enjoyment of the new environment.

Another section along the same street, several blocks away, between Gerrard Street and Dundas Street, was converted the following summer and was in operation for seven weeks. This particular area contained a number of massage parlors and pornographic movie houses. It also became a gathering place for hippies and transients who made the street mall their habitat. Added to this situation was the problem of constant littering of the area with promotional leaflets. At that time there was no legal jurisdiction to enforce controls. All these negative factors created a bad image for Yonge Street Mall.

A third section on Yonge Street was opened in 1973, and the operation was continued successfully for ten weeks during the summer of 1974. The better type of business establishments attracted a large cross section of people. The mall was scheduled to last for twelve weeks, but was cut short by two weeks because of a Toronto transit strike. This strike necessitated the opening of the mall section for the increased auto traffic on Yonge Street, a most important north-south traffic artery.

Alderman David Smith, who is the coordinator for the malls, is not discouraged with the termination of the Yonge Street Mall experiments. He is a supporter of the pedestrian-mall idea, but not the temporary type and not in areas like the section of downtown Yonge between Gerrard Street and Dundas Street, which gave the whole Yonge Street experiment its negative image.

A similar experimental approach was used in Grand Rapids. There, during early studies, temporary malls were placed in the immediate vicinity of the CBD district. Most of these failed within several months because of inadequate parking, the fact that traffic was allowed to interfere with pedestrian areas, and a lack of loading facilities. The experience gained from the installation of the temporary malls helped solve the traffic and parking problems.

The retail area under study in the central business district is a core which centers on Grand River. There is indication of a need for a pedestrian-oriented shopping mall which will be closely tied to an expanded convention facility and civic center.

With the elimination of unnecessary through traffic and the introduction of improved street pedestrian paving, planting, furniture, and building renovations, the area will become more inviting, and this should lead to an eventual increase in retail sales.

According to one proposal, the main thoroughfare, Monroe Street, will be permanently closed for five blocks, and this newly formed island will be completely devoted to the pedestrian. The existing open space, Campau Square, will become a mall, and all shopping will relate to this area.

Contiguous to this area are the existing civic center and the riverfront, which will be integrated with the shopping core. Pedestrian drop-off points and bus stops, at the ends of the closed streets, will take the shopper into connecting malls and arcades which front the major retail facilities. Servicing would be accomplished with loop roads or along closed streets.

The recommended mall concept, however, will not be enough to generate a revitalization of the downtown. The character and momentum of the concept must have a continuity in the developing of other, related areas within the central business district. (See the photograph of the Grand Rapids riverfront.)

Grand Rapids riverfront, Grand Rapids, Michigan. Master plan for riverfront development. (Architects: Wold Bowers DeShane Covert, Inc., Landscape architects: Johnson, Johnson & Roy, Inc.)

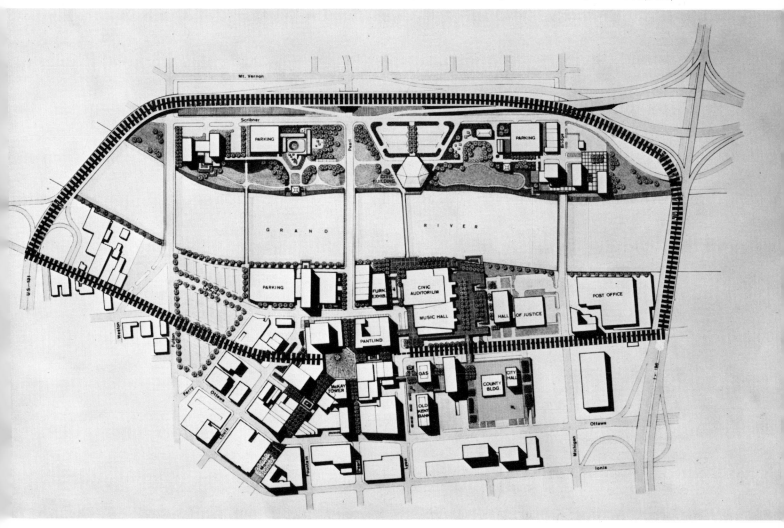

One of the earliest examples of private investment renewal in a public right-of-way, Central Plaza in Canton, Ohio, marks the rebirth of the old public square in the heart of downtown. It provides an illustration of how a simple concept, carefully matched to a limited budget, can change the face of an automobile-dominated business district.

Features of the development are fountains, two small buildings in the center of the avenue for an art display and information center and a snack shop, and an outdoor café type of plaza with underground refrigeration, which can be used for ice skating in the winter. Four lanes of traffic are retained for cars, buses, and taxis.

In Malden, Massachusetts, a pedestrian mall with a new Government Center serving as a magnet is planned to revitalize a deteriorated part of the CBD. Malden is located 5 miles north of Boston and has a population of approximately 60,000.

The basic concept of the downtown plan was to channel through traffic around downtown, rather than through the middle on the main shopping street. Thus a ring road was created around the downtown area, the main shopping street was developed as a pedestrian mall, and parking was located in peripheral areas. The prime commercial area already was located at the east end of Pleasant Street, whereas the west end of Pleasant Street was badly deteriorated. As a result, the new Government Center was at the west end of the Pleasant Street Mall. Currently, a new major office and residential project is planned, and a number of structures are being rehabilitated.

Doxiadis Associates, Inc., has served as prime architect for the Government Center and has designed a pedestrian overpass connecting the Government Center and Pleasant Street to the new Massachusetts Bay Transportation Authority (MBTA) station, which will connect Malden to Boston by rapid transit (ten minutes).

Although I have referred to a large number of pedestrian malls as the beginning of more ambitious projects, there are significant exceptions to this "rule." In the city of Baltimore, the Lexington Street Mall, which is two blocks long, serves as a pedestrian corridor between Charles Center and the major retail district to the west. It will serve as an essential link in the city's pedestrian system, which will ultimately incorporate the Inner Harbor redevelopment into a continuous downtown pedestrian environment unencumbered by automobile traffic. The mall will be restrictive to vehicular traffic and will provide free-flowing access for the heaviest pedestrian flow in the city. The 45,500 square-foot area will be landscaped to create an environment which will attract shoppers and sightseers. The design elements include reddish brick paving, tree plantings, all new lighting similar to that used in Charles Center, movable planters with seasonal flower arrangements and evergreens, benches, bollards, and special street signing. Special care was taken to ensure that merchants were able to conduct their business without undue interruptions during the construction period. It was planned that car and truck deliveries for stores lacking rear delivery access be accommodated at all times via a 12-foot wide, one-way westbound path and that thirty-minute truck parking areas be designated on Lexington Street at Howard Street, Park Avenue, and Liberty Street. Also, a traffic coordinator was on the scene and was available to merchants each day to ensure continuous access to each store during business hours and at other times when delivery and service access were required. It is interesting to note that although the planning for the mall was seventeen years in the discussion stage, construction actually took less than a year!

Central Plaza, Canton, Ohio. Plaza with snack shop and outdoor café. Underground refrigeration allows an ice-skating rink in winter. [Architects: Tarapata, MacMahon & Associates, Architects (Now Tarapata, MacMahon, Paulsen Corp.).]

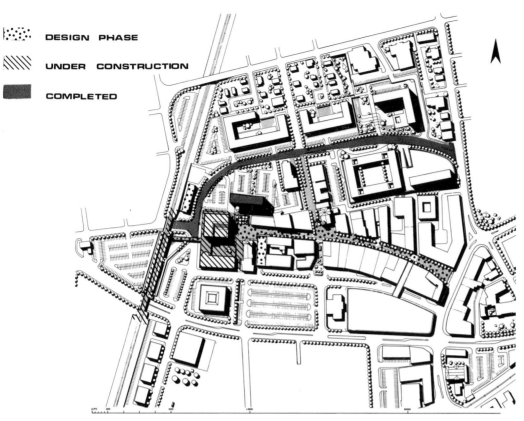

- DESIGN PHASE
- UNDER CONSTRUCTION
- COMPLETED

LEFT: *Site plan of pedestrian mall and Government Center.*

BELOW: *Section through Government Center complex showing link to Pleasant Street Mall. (Architects for the master plan and the Government Center: Doxiadis Associates, Inc. Associate architects: Robert J. Lynch, Inc. Landscape architects for mall: Sasaki, Dawson & DeMay, Inc.)*

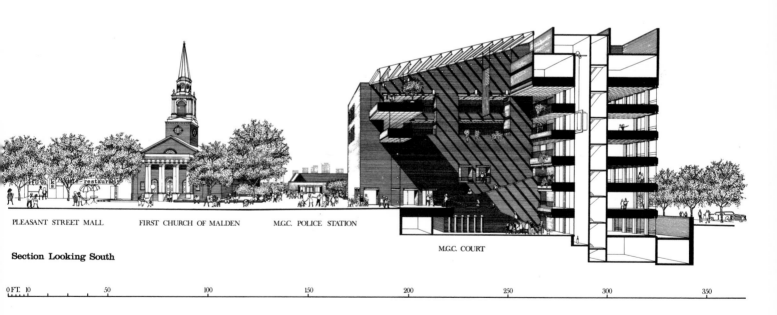

PLEASANT STREET MALL   FIRST CHURCH OF MALDEN   M.G.C. POLICE STATION   M.G.C. COURT

Section Looking South

0 FT. 10   50   100   150   200   250   300   350

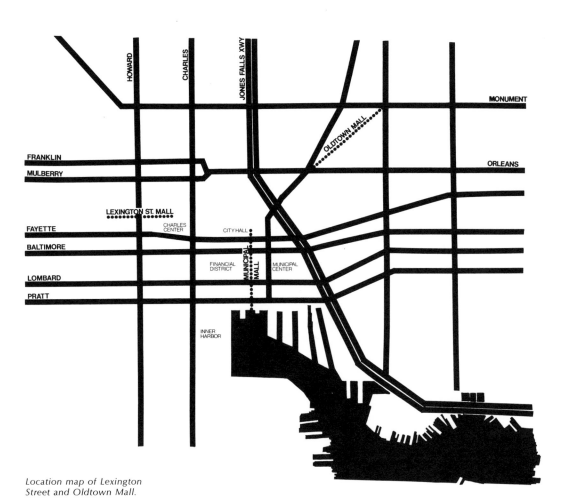

*Location map of Lexington
Street and Oldtown Mall.*

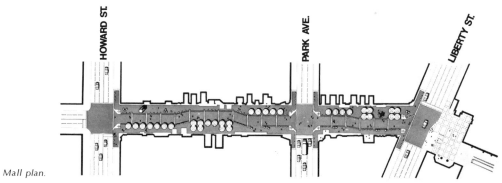

Mall plan.

View from Charles Center.

24

Baltimore also is now completing the Oldtown Mall in the east-side urban renewal area, on what was formerly Gay Street. The area is one of the original Baltimore settlements, and Gay Street has been a retail street for over 150 years. Several of the buildings predate the Civil War. Many of the existing shops have been in this location for several generations, and the merchants were anxious to continue in business here without interruption. The urban renewal plan for Oldtown rerouted vehicular traffic around Gay Street and provided service and public parking at the rear of the existing buildings, thereby permitting the creation of an exclusively pedestrian environment for the mall.

One small group of buildings has been razed to make room for a central parking lot and to permit a widening of the mall to 70 feet, creating a central court. This area, called Oldtown Square, forms a central focus for the mall and for the surrounding residential areas. Oldtown Square, separated from the parking lot by planters and a screen wall, contains a fountain, a clock tower, a platform for performances and public gatherings, benches, trees, flags, and a kiosk sheltering pedestrian amenities.

All commercial buildings along the mall are to be rehabilitated by the owners according to renewal ordinance provisions and subject to the Housing and Community Development approval. Guidelines were written into the renewal ordinance for the restoration of the building fronts to their original character on upper floors, while permitting more freedom in the design of storefronts as may be required by each commercial use. Flat signs are limited to lower portions of buildings, and only nominal projecting signs are permitted. Merchants are encouraged to provide soft, retractable awnings.

The several examples of mall development presented above are intended only to point out various approaches and methods of implementation and some of the problems to be anticipated. Case studies of a number of malls in other cities are presented in Part 3.

Oldtown Mall, Baltimore, Maryland. Mall plan. (Architects: O'Malley & Associates, Inc. Developer: Baltimore Department of Housing and Community Development.)

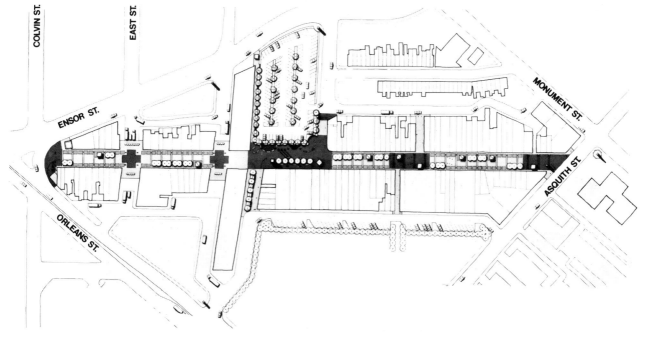

Downtown Regional Centers

Even though the concept of the pedestrian mall is the most attainable because of the time and economic factors, many cities are able to circumvent this minimal step and plan for large, significant projects with a strong impact on the center-city environment. Generally this happens in cities where private enterprise is supported by both government and civic efforts. These concepts range from single megastructures encompassing one or two city square blocks to a complex of a number of buildings which are interrelated aesthetically and interconnected physically by pedestrian parkways, skywalks, escalators, ramps, elevators, and underground shopping concourses. An encouraging factor for a more rapid implementation is the emerging confidence of the commercial developer in the idea of bringing the regional shopping-center concept to the CBD core.

An example of such a complex is Broadway Plaza, which covers a 4½-acre square block in downtown Los Angeles; it was designed by Charles Luckman Associates and was completed in 1973. It includes the Broadway department store, a Regency Hyatt hotel, an office building with a retail center, parking, and interconnecting enclosed plazas. Philip Hawley, chairman of the Broadway division of Broadway-Hale, comments, "We believe in the viability of the downtown economy and its ability to support a major department store. After years of expanding into the suburbs, we realized downtown Los Angeles has been overlooked."

Another important development in Los Angeles, having a different design approach, is Atlantic Richfield Plaza. It covers an entire square block and consists of twin fifty-two-story towers and a two-level block-wide subterranean shopping center. The parking structure is located one-half block away. Five of the eleven parking floors are located underground. The complex is expected to draw from the downtown Los Angeles work force of 250,000 persons.

Architect Albert C. Martin explained that a total-environment concept provided the framework for the planning and design of Atlantic Richfield Plaza. "Our objective was to relate the open plaza area, the towers, and the bank to one another. For example, the twin steel-frame towers, in spite of their height, were not allowed to overwhelm the site. We also utilized the landscaped open spaces to balance the strong vertical masses and the bold bank structure." (Case studies of the above projects are included in Part 3.)

A third major complex in downtown Los Angeles, located near the music center, is the Bunker Hill project, designed by John Portman & Associates. This creates another cohesive link in strengthening the CBD core area.

As important as these new projects are for the new downtown Los Angeles core, the most hopeful sign for its vigorous future is that the cultural center—with the music center nearby—the convention center, and the two major sports stadia are already there to bring the public to varied and interesting events taking place downtown. This variety and choice of activity make for a rich experience, not only for the local population, but also for the convention participant and the large number of tourists who contribute to a viable economic base.

Megastructures

Different concepts for encompassing multifunction uses are applied in a number of cities. Single megastructures, occupying an entire block (the site varying from 3 to 7 acres), combine multiple uses—shopping, office, hotel, residential, and parking facilities. This type of building will contribute to the downtown environment mainly if it allows ample space for walkways and plazas which could be eventually tied in with neighboring buildings, either existing or planned for the future. (See the discussion of Water Tower Place in Part 3.)

Park Centre, in Cleveland, Ohio, covers an entire city block and was financed by the FHA. Designed by architects Dalton · Dalton · Little · Newport, the complex consists of twin twenty-two-story towers, each with 500 apartments. A two-level shopping center, with one level underground, provides a number of eating places, a theater, and recreational facilities. Parking is provided on four floors over the shopping center. (See the case study in Part 3.)

Underground Concourses

Underground interconnected passageways between commercial buildings and street crossovers were originally intended to protect pedestrians from the weather as well as to enable them to get around faster and more easily. It was only a natural sequence that these passageways should be utilized as shopping concourses, since they not only are an economic asset but also offer the impulse buyer a large variety of enjoyable experiences. It goes without saying that the feeling of security is strengthened by the constant activity and liveliness of the area.

Tunnels have been used to connect adjacent buildings for a number of years. In the city of Houston, over the past twenty years, a tunnel system connecting a large number of buildings and parking garages (approximately thirty-five) was developed by the owners of the properties. Some of the tunnels include retail space. The Houston City Planning Department is proposing a continuation of the system, with three new tunnels in the planning stages.

Probably Montreal provides the most outstanding example of a downtown regional center. There the favorable factors of unified ownership of large tracts of land, extreme weather conditions, and the need for more downtown boutiques, specialty shops, restaurants, theaters, etc., have created an exciting underground world connecting the downtown hotels, office buildings, banks, and department stores and the main railroad station. The underground complex, designed by Vincent Ponte, is still being expanded as a tie-in with the added mass-transit development.

The shopping promenades in the heart of Montreal are shown on page 28. The southern portion of this complex consists primarily of the Place Bonaventure shopping promenade and a subway station. The upper levels of the Place Bonaventure structure contain a trade mart, a very large exhibition hall, and a 200-room luxury hotel at the rooftop level.

The middle group of blocks contains the Central Station of the Canadian National Railways, along with considerable retail space, a large hotel, and office buildings. The railroad station handles approximately 150 trains per day.

The northern grouping consists of the Place Ville Marie complex. All these components are connected by an extensive network of enclosed passageways, many of which also double as retail arcades. Stations of another subway line are located on blocks to the north of Place Ville Marie, with access by open air.

Retail space in these two allied complexes totals approximately 400,000 square feet, exclusive of the promenades and passageways. Layouts of the promenade levels at Place Ville Marie and Place Bonaventure are shown on page 28. Shop fronts have a uniform or coordinated design, and the quality of displays is controlled where necessary by the ownership corporation. Merchandise is varied and of high quality, and the arrangement of the promenades provides an exciting and agreeable shopping or strolling experience. In Place Ville Marie, the promenades are 20 feet wide,

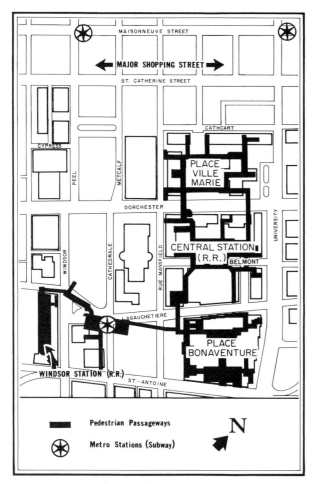

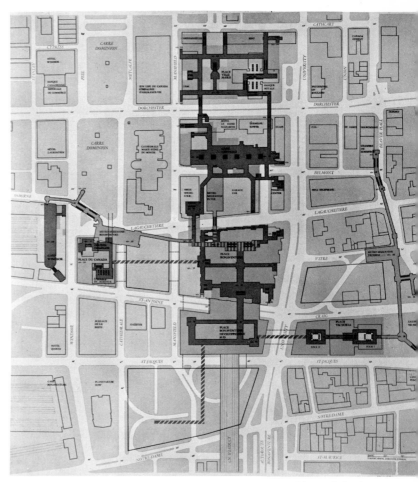

and ceiling heights are moderate. The promenades at Place Bonaventure are somewhat more spacious.

Stores, shops, and boutiques selling clothing and accessories account for one-third of the establishments in the Place Ville Marie shopping promenade. A great majority of the merchandising effort is directed toward women shoppers, as evidenced by the large number of boutiques, shoe shops, and gift shops specializing in merchandise of interest to women. A substantial number of other establishments serve food and drink or provide services to the resident office population and to shoppers and visitors. The shops are smaller than those normally found in a regional shopping center. Some boutiques are quite small indeed, and some of the specialty shops have as little as 400 square feet. In addition, there is a high ratio of display frontage to total retail area.

Facilities such as the movie theater and the supermarket are located off the most heavily traveled promenades. The supermarket plays a specialized role, catering to prelunch traffic, for example, and selling small quantities of sandwich ingredients and similar merchandise. It does a low dollar amount of business per sale, but has a very high volume of patronage.

Many of the well-known shops on West St. Catherine Street, Montreal's prestige shopping street, have branches in the Place Ville Marie shopping promenade, even though the main store is but a short distance away. Many of the shops represented at Place Ville Marie also have stores in Place Bonaventure. Annual sales volumes of shops in the Place Ville Marie shopping promenade are generally in excess of $150 per square foot, with sales above $200 per square foot being prevalent.

Another local factor that contributes to the success of the complex is a tendency for Montrealers to dine out fairly often. The restaurants in the complex thus capture considerable evening traffic as well as lunchtime patronage. The result is that the restaurants in Place Ville Marie are able to generate sales volumes which put them into a competitive position with other retail operations. . . .

Place Bonaventure contains approximately sixty-four retail establishments. Most of

ABOVE LEFT: *Montreal, Quebec. Major shopping areas, enclosed walkways, and transportation facilities. (Architect for underground layout: Vincent Ponte. Graphic drawing: Economic Research Associates.)*
ABOVE: *Place Bonaventure, Montreal, Quebec. Weather-protected pedestrian system in downtown Montreal. (Photographer: Arnott and Rogers Ltd.)*

these are located on the shopping-promenade level. There is a lower level providing access to the subway station which contains several service-type establishments, some shops, a small supermarket, a cafeteria, a post office, and the only discount store in the two projects. The shopping-promenade level contains a wide range of shops and boutiques. Most prevalent are those devoted to women's clothing and to gift items. Men's clothing is represented to a greater degree in Place Bonaventure than in Place Ville Marie. Place Bonaventure is younger than Place Ville Marie, and sales volumes are not at the unusually high level experienced by the latter. However, sales rates are equivalent to, or better than, those in suburban regional shopping centers, and management expects further increases. In addition to retail establishments at the two major shopping promenades, there is considerable retail space located at the railroad station and in passageways connecting the major complexes. . . .

Montreal has rigorous winters, and its network of underground passageways facilitates and encourages pedestrian movement at the Place Ville Marie shopping promenade. While winter is the peak season, pedestrian traffic in the promenade is heavy throughout the year because of the design of the promenade and its relationships to patterns of circulation and commercial activity in the heart of downtown. Daily population of the Place Ville Marie complex is estimated at between 22,000 and 25,000 workers. On an average summer day, when pedestrian traffic is lower than in wintertime, an average of 150,000 pedestrians pass through the shopping promenade. Many of these visits are accounted for by persons passing through more than once. . . .

Trade at Place Bonaventure is less intense than at Place Ville Marie, which is closer to the traditional shopping street. The working population of the Place Bonaventure building itself numbers approximately 4,000. The shopping promenade does not at present capture extensive suburban trade, but an attempt is being made to achieve more of this through upgrading merchandise lines and through promotional activities. Other changes that management has made to improve the functioning of the promenade include the gradual elimination of dead-end arcades and the diversification of eating establishments to cover the full range of the potential market.*

The study of this successful experience of Montreal has been helpful in the Philadelphia Transportation Mall and in the Market Street East project. This downtown renewal project includes a network of several levels of shopping concourses. The requirements concerning size of stores, mall width, type of merchandise, and other details will have to conform to the requirements and habits of Philadelphians. A detailed description of the Philadelphia project is presented in Part 3.

A good example of how downtown Brooklyn is utilizing and combining its existing underground transit facility with shopping concourses is the Hoyt-Schermerhorn Mezzanine project. The plan includes the utilization and renovation of the existing subway mezzanine into a lively retail pedestrian corridor. The corridor, one level below grade throughout, is planned to connect, with a stepping-up connection, to the town square.

This retail development is located partly under a 1,750-unit housing project (Benjamin Thompson & Associates, architects; New York State Urban Development Corporation, sponsor). An important element in this redevelopment is the construction of a new municipal garage connected with a retail corridor to the mezzanine and the Abraham & Straus department store. Altogether, this mezzanine makes three new connections into below-grade retail complexes. (See the photographs of Brooklyn, New York.)

*The description of the Montreal underground complex is excerpted from the Economics Research Associates report, *Market Support for Retail Space in the Market Street East Transportation Mall Complex,* prepared by John K. Haeseler and Robert B. Shawn for the Philadelphia Redevelopment Authority in January 1972.

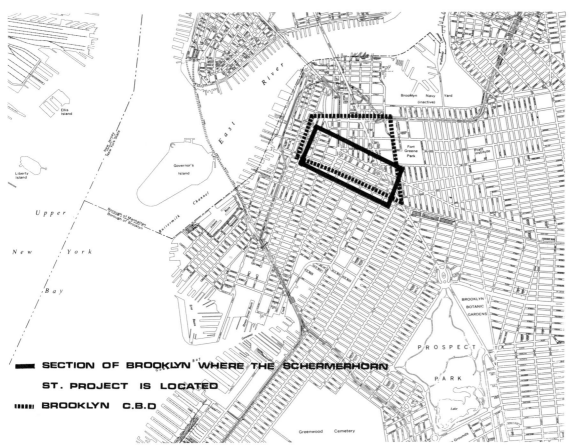

Brooklyn, New York. LEFT: *Schermerhorn Street project location plan.* BELOW: *Schermerhorn Strèet project showing location of Hoyt Street–Schermerhorn Street mezzanine.* RIGHT, ABOVE: *Hoyt Street retail transit pedestrian corridor showing location of Schermerhorn subway mezzanine.* RIGHT, BELOW: *Section through subway mezzanine, showing building 2—West Elevation. (Architects: Benjamin Thompson & Associates. Developers: New York State Urban Development Corporation, New York, New York.)*

■■ SECTION OF BROOKLYN WHERE THE SCHERMERHORN
ST. PROJECT IS LOCATED

▥▥▥ BROOKLYN C.B.D

▦ - HOYT SCHERMERHORN ST. MEZZANINE

▨ SCHERMERHORN ST. HOUSING

▥▥▥▥ HOYT ST. PEDESTRIAN CORRIDOR

■▪■ FULTON ARCADE

SCHERMERHORN STREET PROJECT   BROOKLYN, NEW YORK

URBAN DEVELOPMENT CORPORATION
NEW YORK, NEW YORK

BENJAMIN THOMPSON & ASSOC.
CAMBRIDGE, MASSACHUSETTS

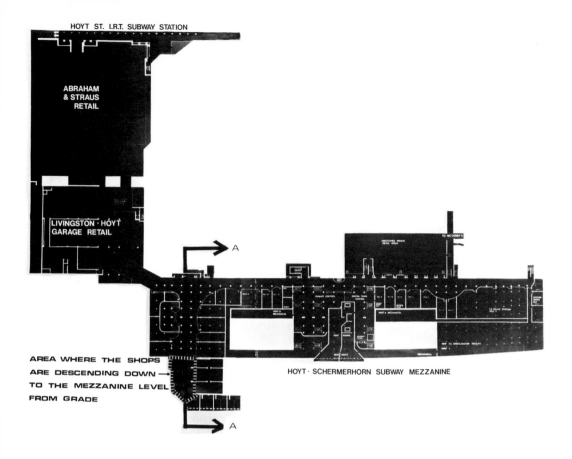

HOYT ST. I.R.T. SUBWAY STATION

ABRAHAM & STRAUS RETAIL

LIVINGSTON · HOYT GARAGE RETAIL

A

AREA WHERE THE SHOPS ARE DESCENDING DOWN → TO THE MEZZANINE LEVEL FROM GRADE

HOYT · SCHERMERHORN SUBWAY MEZZANINE

A

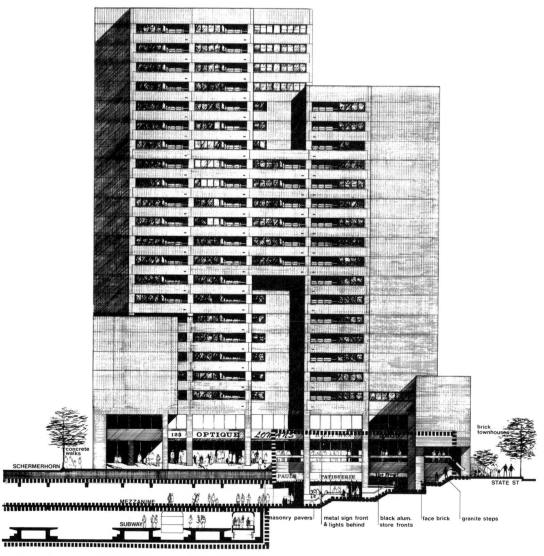

123 OPTIQUE

concrete walks

brick townhouses

SCHERMERHORN

PAULS PATISSERIE

STATE ST

MEZZANINE

SUBWAY

masonry pavers | metal sign front & lights behind | black alum. store fronts | face brick | granite steps

The retail connection occurs at the ground level and the mezzanine level (one level below grade). The city transit authorities will complete the concourse area and the store façades facing the concourse. The rental area is planned to be leased to a developer who will be responsible for the retail subleasing.

The project received a first award in the 1973 Progressive Architecture Award programs. Project participants were the Office of the Mayor, New York City; Office of Downtown Brooklyn Development, Richard M. Rosan, chairman; Reed Coles, executive assistant; Jeaninne Kahan, transportation planner; and Felix John Martorano, urban designer.

Drawings and graphics are by Felix John Martorano. Robert Votava has been project director since 1973. The architect for project implementation is Benjamin Thompson & Associates.

In Japan, the underground shopping centers had their early start as part of the main railway and subway stations. Because of the lack of building sites and the enormous cost of land, the underground concourses expanded into two- and three-level shopping malls, similar to regional enclosed malls in the United States. They are complete with fountains, excellent graphics, plantings, and unusual storefront displays. Escalators move the large numbers of commuters and shoppers quickly and efficiently. Tokyo and Osaka provide prime examples of this.

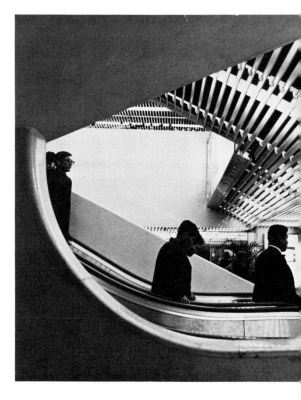

UNDERGROUND SHOPPING CENTER (HANKYU SANBANGAI)
Umeda, Osaka, Japan

ARCHITECTS: Takenaka Komuten Co., Ltd.
PHOTOGRAPHER: Kuniharu Sakumoto

In Vienna, at a city intersection at one of the busiest and most hazardous main thoroughfares, an underground four-way crossover is designed as a shopping center with emphasis on quick eating places, boutiques, and service shops.

Zurich, Switzerland, has a two-way underground crossover at a busy downtown intersection with numerous restaurants and special boutiques.

The advantages of utilizing the underground passageways between major buildings in the CBD area for retail shopping concourses will no doubt encourage city authorities and developers to consider this as a realistic approach. Underground passageways serve as protected pedestrian walkways and at the same time generate income for the city as well as for the tenants. Examples of several planned underground concourses are included in the case studies in Part 3. (See the discussions of the concourses in Oklahoma City, Houston, Philadelphia, and Toronto.)

The continuous expansion of the Rockefeller Center concourse system is another example of extensive use of underground concourses. This system interconnects all the center's twenty-one buildings, and two neighboring buildings, with nearly 2 miles of below-street passageways. It provides direct access not only to each building but also to the Independent subway station on the Avenue of the Americas. It is lined with more than 100 shops, restaurants, and stores which provide a variety of services, and thus it constitutes a large underground shopping center.

Three blocks have been recently added to the system beneath the Avenue of the Americas in conjunction with Rockefeller Center's three new skyscrapers. The project includes additional direct access to a subway mezzanine. The Transit Authority provided additional turnstiles and stairways to the station platform below. Special attention is given to the renovation and the decor of the mezzanine station by the Rockefeller management, which handles an estimated 17 million passengers a year!

An interesting proposal to tie into the existing underground concourse with a fifty-one-story Olympic Tower building, which includes condominium apartments, would have added another dimension of convenience for the walk-to-work city dwellers. The plan had to be abandoned because of the high cost of relocation of the underground utilities.

Rockefeller Center, New York. View of one of the underground areas.

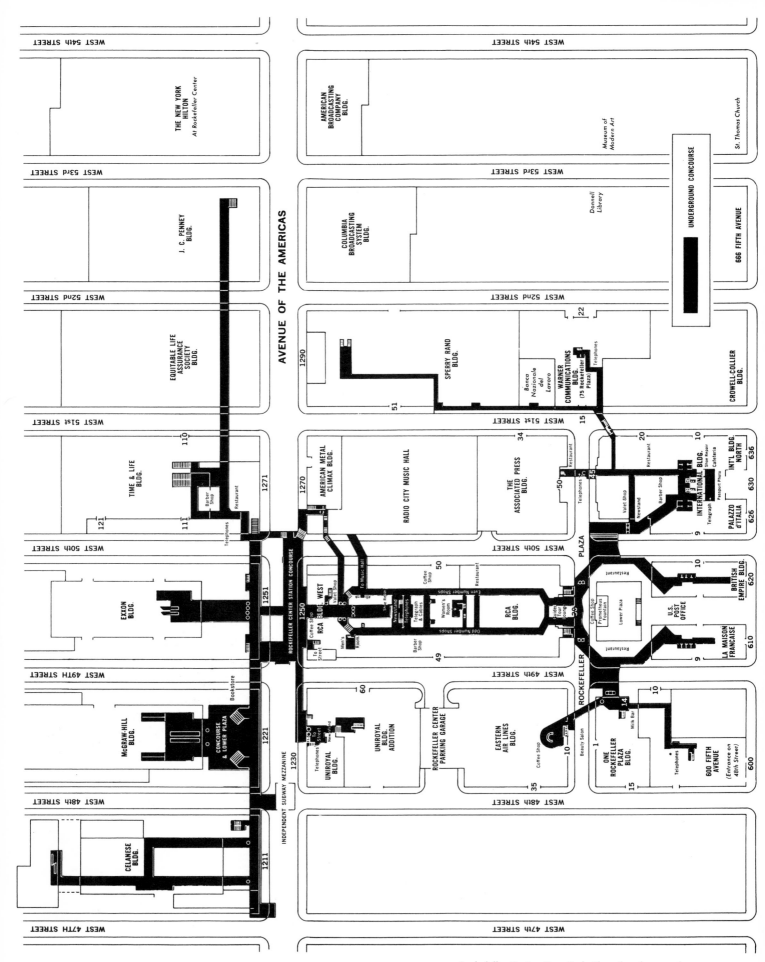

Rockefeller Center, New York. Plan of underground concourse.

Walkway Systems and Skyway Bridges

Elevated walkway systems are a comparatively recent development in the provision of a pedestrian linkage to the various major buildings in the most active area of the central business district. Minneapolis was one of the first cities to implement the concept successfully, and it is still being expanded there. The compactness of the downtown, plus its northern climate, demands that a weather-protected pedestrian level possess maximum continuity and directness, especially along its primary routes. These second-level passages not only offer protection from bad weather but also afford the pedestrian a safe and pleasant means of circulating within the CBD, completely separated from motor vehicles and their pollutants. Primarily, the skyway plan consists of mid-block crossings which connect with interior arcades through buildings to form one continuous system. They also connect with a series of strategically located enclosed courts which provide comfort and beauty and provide for year-round activities. Some of these spaces are two stories high and are accessible from both street and second-story levels. To carry out this plan, changes in zoning laws require new rules to incorporate skyways into building construction.

The first two bridges, which were designed by Cerny & Associates, won for them the 1970 bridge competition from the American Institute of Steel Construction. Both these bridges are in the vicinity of Marquette Avenue between South Fifth Street and Eighth Street.

Minneapolis, Minnesota. Proposed skyway system. (Architects: Minneapolis Planning and Development Department.)

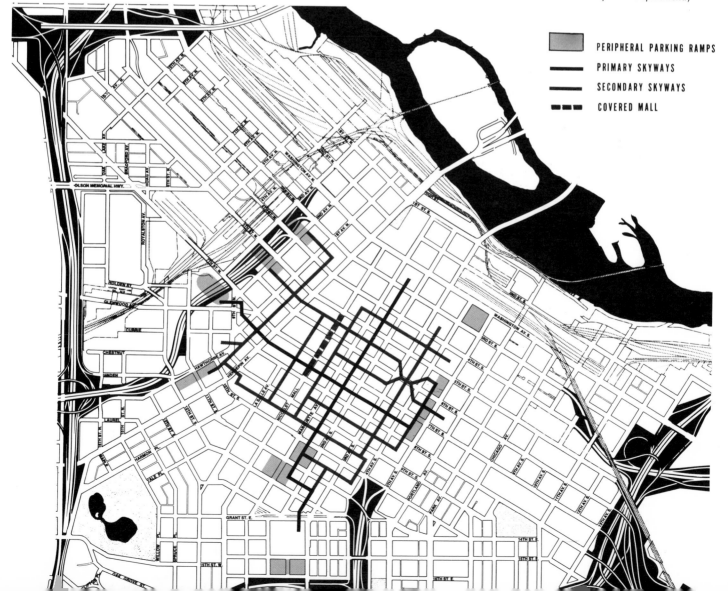

PERIPHERAL PARKING RAMPS

PRIMARY SKYWAYS

SECONDARY SKYWAYS

COVERED MALL

The bridges span some 80 feet across the street and interconnect a variation in elevations on the second-story concourse level. Another city-block project including four pedestrian bridges on the four respective sides of the project is the Investors Diversified Services, Inc., or the IDS Center. This development is in the 100 percent retail block in the CBD and includes four buildings in the block, one of which is a fifty-seven-story office tower. The entire project has 2 million square feet of usable space. A total of 255,000 square feet of retail space is located on the concourse level, first floor, and skyway level. The two major tenants are IDS and Dayton-Hudson Corporation. The architects for this complex are Philip Johnson and John Burgee, with associate architect Edward F. Baker. (See Part 3.)

While Minneapolis started its skyway system with several bridges financed by private enterprise, St. Paul was first with a preplanned publicly financed system, made possible by the fact that it was a renewal project consisting of many new

Minneapolis, Minnesota. Existing skyway system. (Architects: Minneapolis Planning and Development Department.)

buildings. The twin city of St. Paul is in the process of completing its overall skyway plan, for which the city received an AISC Award as well as a HUD Merit Award for the urban design concept. The area includes twelve blocks comprising 43.3 acres, or about one-fifth of the total downtown. The outstanding integrating feature of this urban design is the skyway. The skyway design involves consistency in form, material, and color, and a complete system of directional and identification graphics. The street-level environment achieves order and scale through the consolidation and redesign of all the various elements that serve the street, including bridges. All items are steel, composed of square and rectangular shapes and painted a rich, dark brown. These techniques provide identity and consistency amid diverse buildings.

It is interesting to note the financing of the pedestrian system. In the twelve-block Capital Centre renewal project, where most of the buildings are replaced with new construction, skyway systems through new buildings are paid for 100 percent by the Housing and Redevelopment Authority, except for project boundary street bridges, where the HRA pays 50 percent and the abutting property owners share the other 50 percent. In the twelve-block Capital Centre, the standard width of the bridges and concourses within the buildings is 12 feet. The Authority pays the developer for the 12-foot width and for the nodes (courts) at concourse intersections within the building. (In 1973 the cost was $35 per square foot.) The Authority also pays for a predetermined number of escalators and stairs which serve the system from ground level. Also installed at public expense, for concourse continuity, is a system of graphics, furniture, and plantings.

This entire system—second-level concourse, bridges, and also ground-level access from public sidewalk to vertical facilities (serving the second level)—is in a public easement. However, the Authority does not reimburse the developer for the ground-floor access space, nor does it pay for construction of the concourse system in existing buildings which remain. Bridge spans vary from 60 to 80 feet, and the building owners provide the necessary structural support and also mechanical and electrical services.

To provide for the handicapped, elevators are generally accessible throughout the system. In a few situations, changes in level on the concourse system have necessitated ramps, which generally do not exceed a pitch of 1 foot in 12 feet. Steps are avoided on the concourse itself. The Authority is presently working with public and private groups to establish a policy for extending the Capital Centre concourse system into the two adjacent renewal areas. Since the system would now occur predominantly in existing buildings and since renewal funds are limited, private enterprise will, by necessity, become much more involved in the implementation of the system. The Authority, however, will continue its planning assistance and coordination and, as a general policy, will also continue to design and construct the pedestrian bridges with public funds. Also, recently enacted state legislation authorizes the establishment of development districts and tax-increment financing. These devices can be used in future walkway extensions. The architectural firm Hammel, Green & Abrahamson was commissioned to design the bridges.

The use of the skywalk system is partially indicated in the CBD renewal project model. All the buildings named in the model photograph have been completed. Parcel 10 is being planned for a 400-room hotel which will include several retail floors. An underground, publicly financed parking garage will be built as part of the development district program.

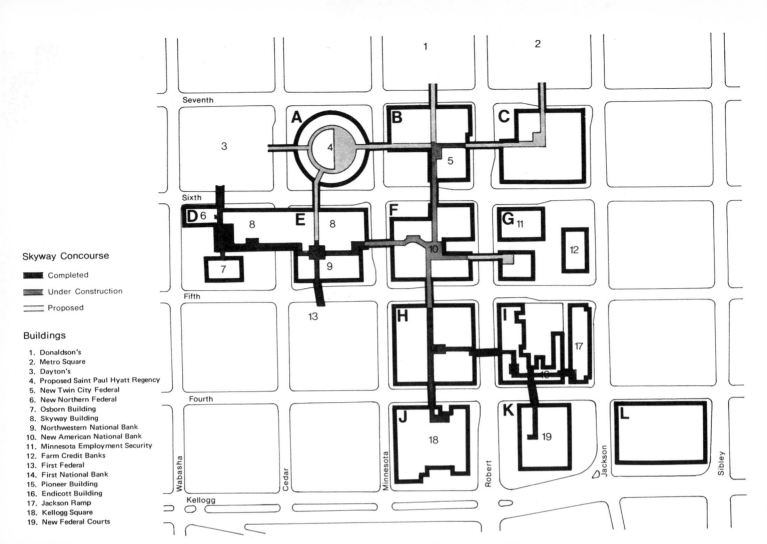

Skyway Concourse

■ Completed
▬ Under Construction
▢ Proposed

Buildings

1. Donaldson's
2. Metro Square
3. Dayton's
4. Proposed Saint Paul Hyatt Regency
5. New Twin City Federal
6. New Northern Federal
7. Osborn Building
8. Skyway Building
9. Northwestern National Bank
10. New American National Bank
11. Minnesota Employment Security
12. Farm Credit Banks
13. First Federal
14. First National Bank
15. Pioneer Building
16. Endicott Building
17. Jackson Ramp
18. Kellogg Square
19. New Federal Courts

Saint Paul, Minnesota. ABOVE: Capital Centre skyway system. (Consulting Architects: Hammel, Green & Abrahamson.) LEFT: Capital Centre downtown project model. (1) Skyway building; (2) Northwestern National Bank building; (3) Northern federal building; (4) Osborn building; (5) First National Bank building; (6) American National Bank building; (7) addition to bank building; (8) American drive-in plaza; (9) Twin City federal building and plaza; (10) Block A Urban Renewal parcel; (11) Dayton department store; (12) Minnesota State Employment Services building. (Plan for the twelve-block downtown renewal area prepared by the St. Paul Housing and Redevelopment Authority. Urban design consultants: Hammel, Green & Abrahamson.)

Saint Paul, Minnesota. LEFT, ABOVE: *Skyway building concourse. (Photographer: Paul L. Wertheimer, courtesy of Housing and Redevelopment Authority.)* LEFT, CENTER: *Skyway building second-level concourse adjacent to bank lobby. (Photographer: Paul L. Wertheimer, courtesy of Housing and Redevelopment Authority.)* LEFT, BOTTOM: *Interior of skyway building with shopping area. (Photograph courtesy of Housing and Redevelopment Authority.)* ABOVE, UPPER: *Skyway building concourse. (Photographer: Lawrence J. Kuslich. Photograph copyright Lawrence J. Kuslich.)* ABOVE, LOWER: *Bridge over Sixth Street connecting skyway building with Dayton department store. (Photograph courtesy of Housing and Redevelopment Authority.)*

An even more intensive use of the walkway system is being planned for downtown White Plains, New York, by the architects Wallace, McHarg, Roberts & Todd. Although the major objectives of the system are the same as in the cities mentioned earlier, the White Plains walkways concept is developed for more uses:

1. To establish a second-level shopping mall similar to those constructed in suburban areas, with all the additional amenities of a downtown location

2. To establish effective pedestrian linkage to the existing central business district and all parts of the renewal area from transportation nodes and nearby residential locations

3. To make use of second-level floor space for intensive commercial activity

White Plains, New York. Walkway plan. (Architects: Wallace, McHarg, Roberts & Todd.)

	Proposed Walkway System
	Potential Extension
	Access & Egress Location
	Main Entrance
	Major Space

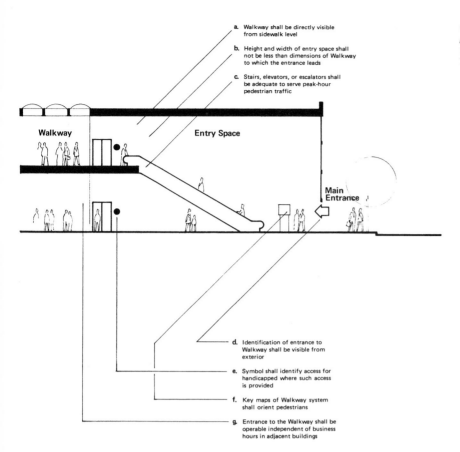

a. Walkway shall be directly visible from sidewalk level

b. Height and width of entry space shall not be less than dimensions of Walkway to which the entrance leads

c. Stairs, elevators, or escalators shall be adequate to serve peak-hour pedestrian traffic

Walkway

Entry Space

Main Entrance

d. Identification of entrance to Walkway shall be visible from exterior

e. Symbol shall identify access for handicapped where such access is provided

f. Key maps of Walkway system shall orient pedestrians

g. Entrance to the Walkway shall be operable independent of business hours in adjacent buildings

White Plains, New York. Typical main entrance. (Architects: Wallace, McHarg, Roberts & Todd.)

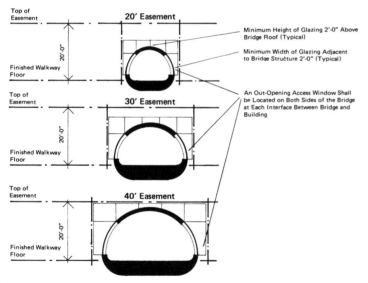

Top of Easement

20' Easement

20'-0"

Finished Walkway Floor

Minimum Height of Glazing 2'-0" Above Bridge Roof (Typical)

Minimum Width of Glazing Adjacent to Bridge Structure 2'-0" (Typical)

Top of Easement

30' Easement

20'-0"

Finished Walkway Floor

An Out-Opening Access Window Shall be Located on Both Sides of the Bridge at Each Interface Between Bridge and Building

Top of Easement

40' Easement

20'-0"

Finished Walkway Floor

Easement at Bridge Interfaces

White Plains, New York. Bridge supports beyond public right-of-way. (Architects: Wallace, McHarg, Roberts & Todd.)

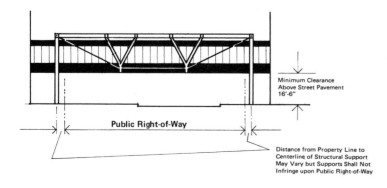

Minimum Clearance Above Street Pavement 16'-6"

Public Right-of-Way

Distance from Property Line to Centerline of Structural Support May Vary but Supports Shall Not Infringe upon Public Right-of-Way

In order to achieve proper implementation of the construction phases, standards were established by the architects to be used by the Urban Renewal Agency and other agencies concerned, as well as by the redevelopers and their professional consultants. The standards, in general, cover the following items:

1. Physical properties of the walkway system including dimensions, materials, finishes, and interfaces between buildings and pedestrian bridges

2. Performance standards for walkway elements, including environmental control, lighting, visibility, and orientation

3. Placement of furniture and accessories to be accommodated in the walkway system

4. Location and installation of signs and other graphics, as well as permanent and temporary displays, exhibits, and decoration

All parts of the walkway system except for portions over public rights-of-way are to be constructed by the redeveloper at no cost to the agency and the city, in accordance with the accepted standards and as part of the proposed improvements.

Cincinnati is also successfully utilizing the benefits of the second-level walkway. The second-level concourse connects large garage facilities to department stores, convention hall, hotels, government buildings, shops, and commercial buildings.

The main walk in the CBD runs at mid-block, serving a six-block area of office and retail space. The complete system of walkways makes it possible to walk anywhere in the ten-block heart of the city without ever coming to street level, or traffic. In some instances, however, the second-level circulation is in conflict with important retail establishments fronting on grade level. This is offset by using attractive street furniture, wider sidewalks with covered arcades or canopies, and stairs and escalators at strategic locations which will connect readily to the second-level walkway. Another important feature is a moving sidewalk that serves as a pedestrian connection to the riverfront development and the stadium.

There is no doubt that facilitating the movement of the pedestrian throughout the downtown in pleasant surroundings affords a stimulating experience.

The city of St. Louis is also favoring the building of elevated pedestrian walkways. Because new development downtown is generally given a tax abatement program by the city, the city does have the ability to require the construction of the walkway system as part of any new development in exchange for tax abatement. Small portions of the walkway system have already been implemented, including the bridge from the Famous-Barr department store to two parking garages; a bridge from the Stix, Baer & Fuller department store to a parking garage; and a bridge from the Equitable building to a parking garage. Construction is now underway for Mercantile Center, and a number of the skyways will be a part of that development. Upon completion of the convention center and the convention plaza facilities, the skyways will be extended to become a part of the total development.

As illustrated in the aforementioned examples, American cities in the process of their CBD revitalization favor the elevated system of pedestrian walkways.

Toronto is unique in the development and implementation of a pedestrian walkway system which combines elevated, grade, and subgrade walkways. D. G. Emslie, commissioner of development, points out that the pedestrian walkway system was created for the purpose of making pedestrian movement in the

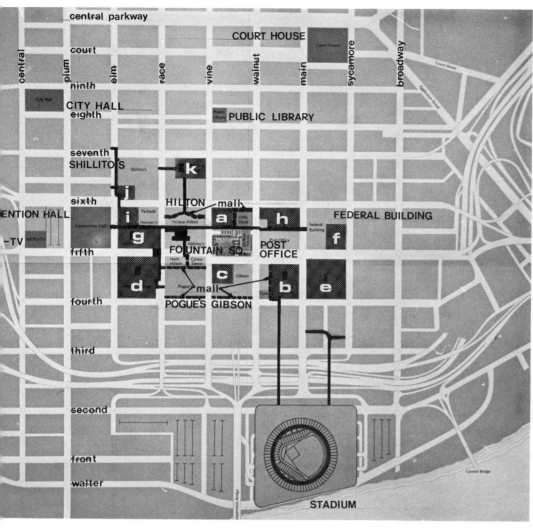

Cincinnati, Ohio. Elevated walkway system showing connections to stadium. (a) Fifth Third; (b) Federal Reserve Building; (c) proposed fifty-story office building; (d) existing parking (concept includes department store, office building, and hotel); (e) development area; (f) proposed office building; (g) Stouffer's Inn and new office building; (h) Western & Southern/Southern Ohio Bank; (i) and (j) proposed commercial areas; (k) Shillito's Garage. (Architects for Master Plan: Department of Urban Development.)

Cincinnati, Ohio. Central riverfront development. (1) Existing stadium; (2) hotel, under construction; (3) sports arena, under construction; (4) housing, first-phase construction; (5) housing, second-phase construction; (6) housing, third-phase construction. Architects for master plan: Department of Urban Development. (Photographer: Paul L. Wertheimer.)

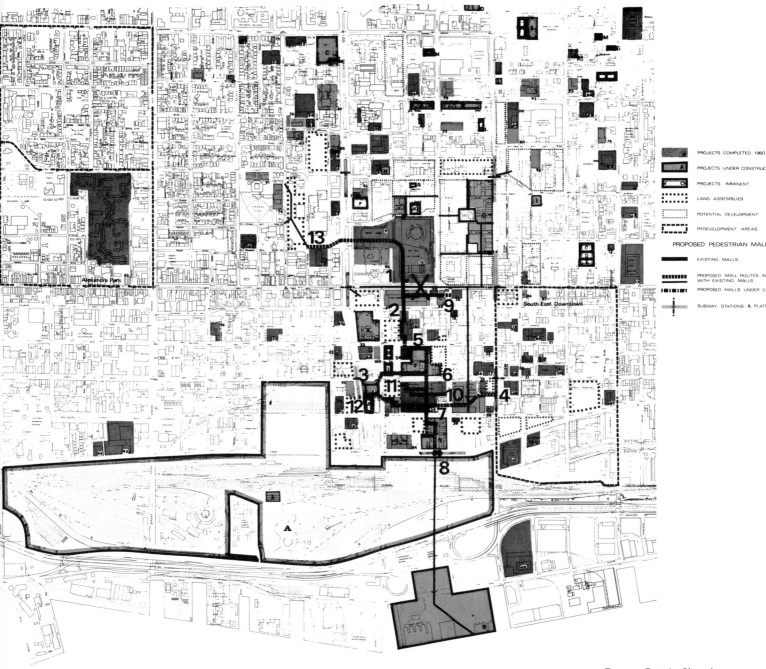

Toronto, Ontario. Plan of Pedestrian Walkway System. (Designed by City of Toronto Development Department, Research and Information Division.)

downtown core safer and more convenient, eliminating the hazards of mid-block street crossing, overcoming the problem of congested sidewalks, separating people from vehicles, creating better access to the subway transit system, and providing climate-controlled, pleasant walkway areas to protect pedestrians from the sometimes severe weather conditions. This pedestrian walkway system is being achieved by connecting developments as they are being constructed. On the accompanying plan of this pedestrian walkway system the areas numbered 1 to 13 are all designated as below-grade walkways connecting developments under the street at the concourse level. Numbers 1 to 4 are complete, and numbers 3 and 4 are direct connections to subway transit areas. The balance will be constructed under agreement with the city, primarily on a participatory basis. It is anticipated the pedestrian walkway system between numbers 1 and 10 will be completed by 1977. Number 13 in the plan is a proposed at-grade pedestrian walkway between the City Hall and the art gallery, and it may be some years before it is accomplished. The Eaton/Fairview project, comprising some 15 acres, will have below- and above-grade malls; the pedestrian routes shown on the plan are public pedestrian rights-of-way which were negotiated by the city in a land exchange between the city and the developers. The project is now under construction. The area marked "X" will be an overhead pedestrian way crossing Queen Street and connecting the Simpson's department store to the Fairview development on the north side of Queen Street.

Points 7 and 8 on the plan are being considered for overhead connections in addition to the below-grade pedestrian walkways. It is important to note that convenient access to the subway system was one of the key considerations in the total planning.

As to the cost participation for the developer and the city, it would be difficult to establish a set formula for the division of costs of the pedestrian walkway. The general basis for establishing the participatory portion for each party should be the extent of benefit accrued to the city in each individual case. In general, the city's participation should try to set its maximum at one-third the cost of construction. However, in instances where the city needs the required link for transit use and where the benefit to the developer may be minor, the city could increase its contribution to two-thirds and, in unusual cases, to 100 percent.

The city of Calgary is developing a pedestrian overhead walkway system in which the developers lease air rights over the streets from the city and bear the full cost of construction; such a system is considerably less expensive to build than a below-grade system. The leases entered into are generally very nominal. The maintenance at the present time is the responsibility of the developer, and it is understood that the city of Calgary will ultimately take over this responsibility. Calgary, with a population of 336,000, has set up its "Downtown Development Guidelines" with a view toward separating pedestrian, private, and public vehicular traffic and toward developing a traffic circulation system, increasing accessibility, and avoiding congestion. Its Plus 15 project is so laid out that pedestrians will be within easy walking distance of their destinations, parking space, and public transportation, which is at surface grade. The vehicular circulation system is based on a citywide network of limited-access, high-capacity roadways which will ultimately feed into a downtown ring system, yet to be built; this system will collect and distribute traffic to existing streets with direct connections to parking facilities, from which point the motorist will emerge as a pedestrian into the Plus 15 elevated pedestrian walkway. This elevated system leads into the downtown core and appears to have been geared to make it possible to have access from major parking areas.

In Montreal, the construction of a below-grade walkway system is a matter of negotiation between the city and the developer, with the developer absorbing the full cost and bearing the responsibility for maintenance. The city of Montreal has a bylaw which it can enforce to make it mandatory for the developer to construct pedestrian walkways. Where the city feels that a walkway is of greater benefit to the city than to the developer, the city carries out the construction at its own expense.

Plazas

The development of the plaza concept, for the purpose of providing public places of assembly for entertainment, celebrations of national and civic importance, relaxation, and leisure, has become increasingly important in the total framework of each city's image. There are several ways in which the plaza can fulfill its role. It can be included in the total concept of the master plan. It can serve as a focal point in the design of the pedestrian mall. It can be an important part of a private development project. It can also be an independent entity which fits into existing open public spaces.

One significant example is the First National Bank of Chicago Plaza, designed by C. F. Murphy Associates and Perkins & Will. According to Charles William Brubaker, president of Perkins & Will:

> The owners wished to create an urban space that would be active and interesting at all hours, contributing to the life and excitement of the city and avoiding the

FIRST NATIONAL BANK OF CHICAGO
Chicago, Illinois
ARCHITECTS: C. F. Murphy Associates and Perkins & Will

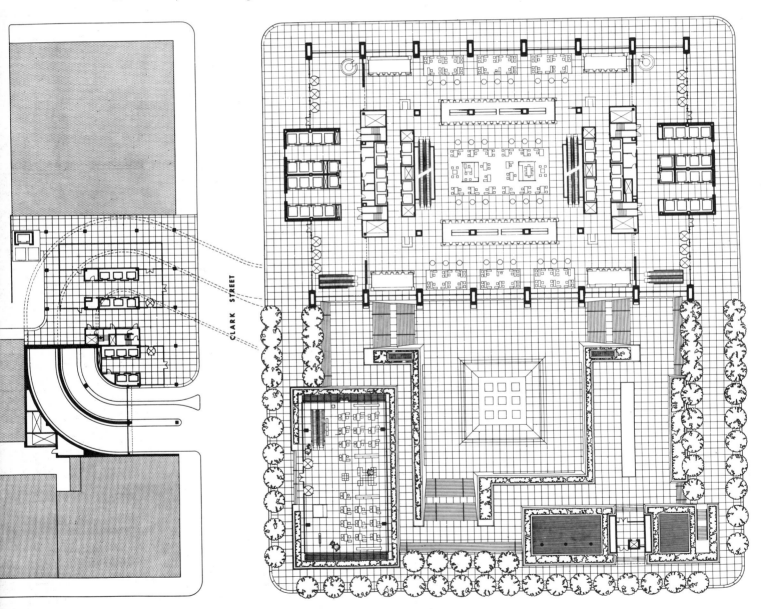

Street-level plan.

traditional financial-district streets that are dull during the day and dead after five o'clock. They recognized the importance of this most central block and their responsibility to create a lively neighborhood for the city.

The design team agreed that a lower-level plaza would be most appropriate, with banking spaces, restaurants, bars, shops, and subway entrances opening into it at this lower level. The plaza is complex, colorful, active, and accessible. At the center, in the lowest level, is a large fountain with changing volumes of water, designed by Samuel S. Hamel. Trees at street level, shrubbery, and changing flower beds are a part of the scene. A low, transparent banking pavilion is above street level at the southwest corner, and there is a restaurant entrance along Monroe Street. Broad steps provide good access from all three streets and serve as amphitheater seats for scheduled events. Flags, movable platforms, benches, and portable vending carts add to the active environment. The building and plaza materials, however, are restrained; warm gray granite is used throughout. A colorful mosaic wall by Marc Chagall was completed in September 1974. This 70-foot-long rectangle parallels Dearborn Street and is visible from streets, walks, the plaza, and surrounding buildings.

View of the plaza. (Photographer: Hedrich-Blessing.)

In Baltimore, within the framework of the master plan for Charles Center there are three plazas, each adapted to its specific setting, designed by RTKL. In all three, careful attention is paid to the patterned brick paving, the tree enclosures, the design of the lighting standards, the street furnishings, and the building of the ramps and levels.

CHARLES CENTER
Baltimore, Maryland
ARCHITECTS:
For the master plan: Planning Council
of the Greater Baltimore Commission,
David A. Wallace, Director
For Charles Plaza, Hopkins Plaza, and
Center Plaza: RTKL Associates, Inc.

Charles Plaza. Detail of lighting standards and ramp levels. (Photographer: M. E. Warren.)

Hopkins Plaza. View of completed plaza. (Photographer: M. E. Warren.)

Charles Plaza. Detail of brick patterns and street furnishings. (Photographer: M E. Warren.)

Hopkins Plaza. Night view of plaza showing its use as an open concert arena. (Photographer: M. E. Warren.)

Center Plaza featuring freestanding sculpture.

Fountain Square, in Cincinnati, won the American Institute of Architects citation for community architecture in 1974 and an honor award in 1973. The fountain, which has been a downtown landmark since 1871, had become almost blocked off from pedestrians by the congested traffic. In the words of the AIA honor award jury, "The elements in Fountain Square are well placed and effective in giving unity to the space and in relating it to the surrounding buildings. The hope is that many more such public squares can be carved out of our congested urban areas."

FOUNTAIN SQUARE PLAZA
Cincinnati, Ohio

ARCHITECTS: RTKL Associates, Inc.
CONSULTING ARCHITECTS: Belz Carey & Wright
LANDSCAPE ARCHITECT: George Patton

ABOVE: *General view. Elevated walkway in background.* LEFT. *General view showing entry to underground parking and elevated walkway. (Photographer: Joseph W. Molitor Photography.)*

In Munich, one end of the old pedestrian mall is climaxed by the Stachus Circle Plaza and fountain. The steps, which are at varied levels, serve as a gathering place where people of all ages can sit and relax. The mall won the 1974 R. S. Reynolds Award; it is described in Part 3.

Munich Mall, Munich, Germany. Plaza and fountain at the Stachus Circle at the end of the pedestrian mall. (Architect: Bernhard Winkler. Associate architect: Siegfried Meschederu of the City Planning Department. Photograph courtesy of Bernhard Winkler.)

An interesting extension of the Nicollet Mall in Minneapolis, Minnesota, is the Peavey Park Plaza, fronting the new Minnesota Orchestra Concert Hall. This plaza is another link to the continuous upgrading of urban amenities. The Loring Greenway, planned to connect East Loring Park with Nicollet Mall, gives further support to the CBD by adding a large number of residential units. Mr. Friedberg, of M. Paul Friedberg & Associates, explains his concept: "This is an urban design plan with objectives and controls for private development confirming the critical value of open space to the urban milieu. Our work, which is based on the premise that an open-space system traversing through a commercial and residential mix can be the logical matrix for an urban design plan, ties together private, public, and semipublic spaces into a lucid activity framework.

"The plan provides for 2,800 housing units in an urban renewal district of 26 acres of downtown Minneapolis and for a 1,600-foot Greenway connection from Nicollet Mall with pedestrian paths and bikeways linking the CBD to the city's major green space, Loring Park."

Peavey Park Plaza, Minneapolis, Minnesota. Perspective view from Twelfth Street and Nicollet Mall. (Landscape architecture and urban design: M. Paul Friedberg & Associates.)

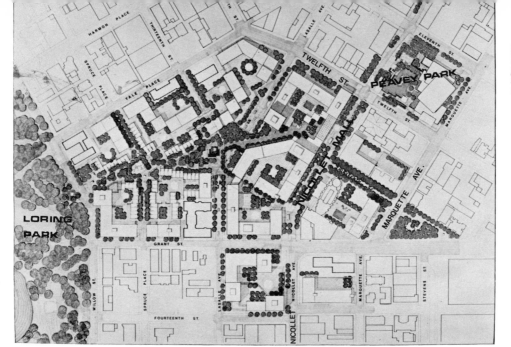

Loring Park Development, Minneapolis, Minnesota. Site plan. (Landscape architecture and urban design: M. Paul Friedberg & Associates.)

Of interest is the fact that the financing of the Loring Park development district will be by the "tax-increment" process. In this process the city of Minneapolis sells general obligation bonds, the funds from which will be used to acquire existing properties within the district, relocate the present occupants, demolish the existing structures, and administer the program. The cleared land then will be sold or leased to private developers. This city participation in the development process makes possible, by lowering the cost of land, the inclusion of features not always feasible for a developer—landscaped courts and covered parking, for example. Bond proceeds will also be used for the construction of the Loring Greenway and other public improvements within the district.

In New York City several plazas serve as attractive public spaces for relaxation and enjoyment of the outdoors. Jeanette Plaza, located in the Wall Street area of downtown New York City, combines an existing park area with newly constructed commercial and office facilities. The plaza is situated between two skyscrapers overlooking the river; there are shaded and sunny areas on split levels and a cascade of water over 200 feet long extending and wrapping around the entire design. Dining facilities are planned, as well as quick-service kiosks. Design facilities make multiuse of the space, with the lower fountain area doubling as an amphitheater.

Jeanette Plaza, New York, New York. View of the fountain area. Components were especially designed to recall the dockside atmosphere of the park's waters-edge site. [Components designed by M. Paul Friedberg in association with Exterior Systems (a division of Bajer Industries). Landscape architecture and urban design: M. Paul Friedberg & Associates.]

Police Plaza, also in New York City, is sited in a most densely populated area during working hours. This downtown plaza is a large, unique urban space reminiscent of Italian piazzas because of its size, unique location, and design. Since its dedication in September 1973, it has become the scene of a constantly changing mix of people and activities. The plaza, designed by M. Paul Friedberg & Associates, has been distinguished by awards from the Municipal Art Society and the New York chapter of the American Institute of Architects. This 3-acre civic space, which partially bridges a highway, is designed with water elements, trees, and sitting spaces, and programming is continuing for outdoor restaurants and flower stalls. Critics have praised it as New York's most successful plaza because it is primarily people-oriented.

Air Rights

In the replanning of CBDs, the use of air rights over sites owned by private interests and city, state, and federal authorities allows for greater flexibility in design and maximum utilization for building space. The procedure requires expert legal counseling, and in many cases it may become a lengthy and involved process. However, the success of many cities in utilizing the space over railroad tracks, expressways, and streets gives promise for further innovative uses in this direction.

The way in which Fall River, Massachusetts, solved the air-rights problem of construction over a federal highway is presented here as an example. Fall River, with a population of 96,000, was the first city in the nation to utilize construction air rights over a federal highway. The $6.5 million complex contains a six-story administrative building and a connecting two-story city council unit, constructed over the six-lane Interstate Route 195 between bridges at Main Street and Third Street. The original city hall, which was situated in the heart of the city for 110 years, was demolished in 1962 to accommodate Federal Highway I-195, which severed the city into two parts. With the realization of this new complex and surrounding plaza, the city has reunited the downtown business district.

The construction of the new city hall is the catalyst for additional downtown urban renewal projects, i.e., a new bank building and two nineteen-story apartment buildings, an especially essential element in the downtown revival.

The procedures involved in implementing the air-rights construction concept over a federal highway were long and complex. The concept was developed by

Fall River, Massachusetts. Perspective aerial view showing location of the new city hall over I-195 expressway. (Architects: Continental Engineering Corporation. Structural engineers: Robert Charles Associates, Inc.)

the architectural firm Strickland, Brigham and Eldridge, in cooperation with the firm Hayden, Harding and Buchanan, designers for the highway. John T. Farrell, Jr., assistant corporation counsel, has described the legal steps which culminated in the agreement entered into by the city of Fall River, the commonwealth of Massachusetts, and the federal government:

> Tom Britland, administrative assistant to the mayor, and I had discussions with officials of the Bureau of Public Roads in both Washington and Boston. At that time the law, 23 USC 111, limited the use of airspace above and below interstate highways constructed under the 90–10 federal funding program to parking. In the absence of statutory authorization their hands were tied; as 1961 approached, the city was faced with a cutoff point. Land-taking was scheduled for early 1962, with demolition to take place that fall. Unless the land-taking could provide sufficient space and the highway design could incorporate the foundations and the decking, the idea would never come to fruition. There were two other complicating factors: First, the location of the highway was still being actively opposed by many segments of the community; therefore, while the mayor could speak as the official voice of the city, he was not able, until some time later, to represent the full expression of community desires. Second, each segment of the interstate highway system was covered by a formal project agreement. The agreement for the Fall River segment was already in being.
>
> Under the auspices of Congressman Joseph W. Martin, Jr., and Senator John F. Kennedy, we were able to meet periodically with the appropriate federal officials and convince them that the proposed use of the air rights would be beneficial. The state of Massachusetts had been in general agreement from the beginning.
>
> The legal problems were the main hurdle. We are unable to trace the origin of the legislation which authorized the use of airspace above highways for other than parking. However, it appears in HR 6317, the Kennedy administration proposal for the Federal Aid Highway Act of 1961. This bill was cleared by the House committee (House Report 326) and the Senate committee (Senate Reports 293 and 367).
>
> At a meeting with Kenneth P. O'Donnell, assistant to President Kennedy, this problem was outlined by Mayor Arruda and me. It was felt that the intent of the administration and subsequently of the Congress that this type of project was envisioned by an amendment in the proposed legislation. The discussion of the amendment in the Senate on June 15, 1961, specifically referred to the Fall River City Hall project.
>
> There was also language in the amendment to the effect that prior agreements could be revised to include the utilization of air rights in accordance with the new law. The law was signed by President Kennedy on June 29, 1961. The enactment became Public Law 87–61 75 Stat. 122, et seq. The provisions we were interested in were sections 104a and 104b. The legislation and congressional history can be found in 1961 U.S. Code, *Congressional and Administrative News,* pages 141 and 1788, respectively.
>
> With the enabling legislation enacted, the rest of the steps followed in due course: (1) amendment of the highway agreement, (2) execution of the deed of the air rights by the commonwealth to Fall River, (3) adaption of the design of that portion of the highway to provide for the ultimate utilization of the air rights, and (4) the funding of Fall River's share of the highway costs.

The development of Illinois Center in Chicago provides another significant example of the utilization of air rights. It rises above the former freight yards of the Illinois Central Railroad near the city's central business district. Development of the railroad property was contemplated in the provisions of the 1929 amendment to the Chicago Lake Front Ordinance, but the Depression delayed it.

In the 1950s the Illinois Central Railroad again decided to move forward with the conversion of its downtown freight yard into a higher real estate use, and Prudential Insurance Company of America bought land and air rights for its Midwest headquarters, the Prudential building. Later, the Jupiter Corporation bought air rights east of the Outer Drive for its 900-unit apartment building, Outer Drive East, and the railroad subsequently announced plans to sell the remaining air rights to three developers: Metropolitan Structures, the Jupiter Corporation, and Illinois Center Corporation. Early in 1961, a taxpayer's suit was filed against the railroad. After several years of litigation, the Illinois Supreme Court finally decided that the railroad had full title to the property, permitting it to sell the land and air rights for development.

Early in 1967, the city of Chicago requested a master plan for the development of the property, which was adopted by the city on September 17, 1969. After the ordinance was passed, the three developers formed the joint venture (Illinois Center Plaza Venture) to develop the entire area, with the exception of the parcel bounded by Lake Street, Michigan Avenue, Wacker Drive, and Stetson Avenue, which was developed independently, but as an integral part of Illinois Center, by Metropolitan Structures. The first stage in the development of Illinois Center, well under way, includes Metropolitan Structures' separate buildings, One and Two Illinois Center, Standard Oil of Indiana's international headquarters building, and a thirty-five-story 1,000-room Hyatt House hotel. These will be connected by a landscaped plaza and newly constructed streets, including extended Wacker Drive and a 3.5-acre 80-foot-wide river's-edge esplanade park.

Art in the CBD Environment

In planning a central business district environment, art, in its various forms, must become an element that will bring spiritual and aesthetic satisfaction—as important a part of man's existence as the satisfaction of purely material needs.

The last decade has seen an ever-increasing interest on the part of the American public in all forms of artistic expression. The great proliferation of galleries throughout the country, new policies on the part of art museums aimed at interesting the younger generation in art studies, and the tendency of many large corporations to assemble works of art and to commission artists to create monumental pieces as part of their building projects all attest to the fact that a radical change is taking place in the general attitude toward art.

The urgent need to make art a vital part of our daily environment was recognized by President Kennedy in his directive of May 23, 1962, to the General Services Administration, which is responsible for a large part of the federal government building program. This order urged that funds up to 1 percent of the construction cost of new building projects be reserved for the fine arts. The same policy was followed by a number of states and large cities when they allotted a percentage of their building budgets for art. An added impetus for the integration of the arts was provided by Congress in September 1965, when it established the National Endowment for the Arts. The first allocation, in the amount of $140,000, was to be used as matching funds for outdoor art placed in public spaces in three geographic sections of the country. Grand Rapids made the first request for $45,000 to commission Alexander Calder for a large steel sculpture, *La Grande Vitesse,* in a new plaza in the downtown renewal area. (See the photograph of Civic Center Plaza.) Since that time, with the increase in federal support for the broadened program of the National Endowment for the Arts, nearly eighty art projects have been funded in twenty-seven states, with more than fifteen cities having completed their projects. (See Table 1.)

Grand Rapids, Michigan. Civic Center Plaza. Painted steel sculpture, La Grande Vitesse. (Sculptor: Alexander Calder. Photographer: Louis G. Redstone.)

TABLE 1

City	Artist	Matching Funds	Date of Grant
Grand Rapids, Michigan	Alexander Calder	$45,000	1967
Seattle, Washington	Isamu Noguchi	45,000	1968
Wichita, Kansas	James Rosati	45,000	1970
Red Wing, Minnesota	Charles Biederman	10,000	1970
Minneapolis, Minnesota	Nine artists: including Barry LeVa, William Wegman	10,000	1970
Scottsdale, Arizona	Louise Nevelson	20,000	1970
Highland Park, Illinois	Peter Voulkos	20,000	1971
Joplin, Missouri	Thomas Hart Benton	10,000	1972
Lansing, Michigan	Jose de Rivera	45,000	1972
Berkeley, California	Romare Bearden	8,000	1972
Fort Worth, Texas	George Rickey	35,000	1972
New York, New York (City Walls)	Seven artists: including Allan D'Arcangelo, Mel Pekarsky, Nassos Daphnis	10,000	1972
Las Vegas, Nevada	Mark di Suvero	45,000	1973
Minneapolis, Minnesota	Ronald Bladen	45,000	1974
Grand Rapids, Michigan	Robert Morris	30,000	1974

When Nancy Hanks was appointed chairperson of the National Endowment for the Arts in 1969, she gave new impetus and direction to government support of public art. One of her main concerns was the recovery of the CBD areas and the improvement of the environment. Art was to be used in public places such as plazas, playgrounds, airports, lobbies of government buildings, and parks —wherever people congregate. It was to include murals on exterior walls of downtown and inner-city buildings, photomurals, tapestries, prints, and other mediums. Projects supported by the endowment fall into four fairly clear divisions: projects involving artists of national reputation, projects involving artists of regional reputation, temporary experimental exhibitions testing the viability of public art in various situations (Nine Artists/Nine Spaces in Minneapolis and the Vermont Sculpture Symposium), and outdoor murals. As beneficial and stimulating as this federal art endowment program is, it can satisfy only a very limited demand, even though many opportunities to benefit from this program remain unexplored and unused by both large and small cities.

In the overall planning of the CBD renewal, the most realistic solution for the inclusion of art is for the developer to budget it as part of the total construction cost in the conceptual stages of the planning.

There are several methods of commissioning an artist. One method is to engage the artist for a particular work of art, on the basis of his or her ability and special expertise. Another method is to hold a limited invitational competition, judged by experts in the art field. In all cases, local talented artists should be considered, in addition to nationally recognized artists. An invitational competition, in which six artists participated, took place in Houston, Texas. The commission for the monumental sculpture (16 feet high by 20 feet wide by 25 feet long), located in Buck Walton Plaza, in Allen Center, a redevelopment CBD area, was awarded to Peter Reginato for a sculpture called *High Plain Drifter*.

The CBD is an important area where art in all forms—sculpture, fountains, special landscaping, well-designed lighting, good graphics, outdoor furniture, and interesting sidewalk patterns—can create an exciting atmosphere.

There are a number of ways in which art can become a part of the urban scene. In Embarcadero Center, in San Francisco, the eight-story freestanding sculpture in an interior fountain plaza entitled *Two Columns with Wedge*, by the Swiss sculptor Willi Gutmann, adds dramatic impact to the surrounding high-rise structures.

San Francisco, California. ABOVE, LEFT: Embarcadero Center. Free-form concrete sculpture fountain. (Sculptor: Armand Vaillancourt. Photographer: Eliel G. Redstone.) ABOVE: Base of sculpture as viewed from garden court of the Pacific Bank building. (Sculptor: Willi Gutmann. Photographer: Eliel G. Redstone.) LEFT: Stainless-steel sculpture, eight stories high, Two Columns with Wedge. (Sculptor: Willi Gutmann. Photographer: Eliel G. Redstone. Architects for Center: John Portman & Associates.)

In the nearby Hyatt Regency Hotel, where the atrium (lobby) serves as an indoor public space, a four-story-high anodized aluminum sculpture entitled *Icosadodecahedron* was created by Charles O. Perry over a reflecting pool.

In Detroit, at the Manufacturers National Bank Operation Center, in the heart of the CBD, twenty-six precast bas-relief panels, 18 by 18 feet, are an integral part of the two-story enclosure of the parking levels. Covering the three street sides of the building, the concrete murals provide a constant feeling of interest and discovery for the passerby. The sculptor is Robert Youngman.

In contrast to the concrete exterior, the interior lobby, as seen through the glass-enclosed entrance, highlights a suspended stainless-steel 30-foot free-form sculpture by Samuel Cashwan.

Another approach in the integration of art in public places is seen in the plaza of the First National Bank of Chicago, located in the CBD. There, an 80-foot mosaic mural was created by Marc Chagall. The color and texture elicit a vibrant and warm response from the onlooker.

Another effective technique was used by Pablo Picasso on the façade of the Architects Headquarters in Barcelona, Spain. He used the *sgraffito* technique (cutting images into the surface of a hard material—in this case, concrete) to depict a folk scene.

In Los Angeles, California, at the music center in the downtown area, a 35-foot freestanding bronze sculpture, by Jacques Lipchitz, is placed in a reflecting pool.

The role that art plays in the CBD to enhance both the people's enjoyment and the image of the city can have a positive connection with the impression visitors receive upon entering the city, specifically at airports. The recognition of this influenced the design of recently completed Michael Berry International Terminal at the Wayne County Airport, serving the Detroit metropolitan area. While visitors

San Francisco, California. Hyatt Regency Hotel. The atrium. (Sculpture, anodized aluminum, four stories high, Icosadodecahedron Sculptor: Charles O. Perry. Architects: John Portman & Associates.)

Detroit, Michigan. The Manufacturers National Bank Operation Center. ABOVE: Interior of lobby; 30' suspended stainless-steel sculpture. (Sculptor: Samuel Cashwan.) LEFT: Precast concrete bas-reliefs, 18' x 18'. (Sculptor: Robert Youngman. Architects for Center: Louis G. Redstone Associates, Inc. Photographer: Balthazar Korab.)

Chicago, Illinois. First National Bank of Chicago. The plaza; 80' mosaic mural. (Sculptor: Marc Chagall. Architects: C. F. Murphy & Associates and Perkins & Will.)

RIGHT: *Barcelona, Spain. Headquarters, Architect's Society of Catalonia, Barcelona, Spain. (Architect: Xavier Busquets. Sculptor: Pablo Picasso.)* FAR RIGHT: *Los Angeles, California. The music center; 35′ freestanding bronze sculpture. (Sculptor: Jacques Lipchitz. Photographer: Louis G. Redstone.)*

The Michael Berry International Terminal, Detroit Metropolitan Wayne County Airport. LEFT, ABOVE: *Entrance portico showing twenty-six bas-relief sculptured concrete columns. (Sculptor: Robert Youngman. Photographer: Balthazar Korab.)* ABOVE: *Interior showing the focal location of the concrete sculptured column, harmonizing with the exterior design. (Sculptor: Robert Youngman. Photographer: Louis G. Redstone.)* LEFT, BELOW: *Screen, copper mural at the departure exit. The three-sided mural, 40′ long, is of multicolored copper forms, achieved with application of the torch. (Sculptor: Narendra Patel. Architects for airport: Louis G. Redstone Associates Inc. Photographer: Balthazar Korab.)*

ATLANTIC RICHFIELD PLAZA
Los Angeles, California
ARCHITECTS: Albert C. Martin & Associates
GRAPHIC DESIGNERS: John Follis & Associates

Floor striping as part of graphic design.

Freestanding sign.

Cast bronze letters over the entry doors of the two towers, each with its separate identity.

Via Veneto atmosphere of European shopping.

may have the general preconceived notion that Detroit is an industrial center only, this first contact with the use of art in the terminal may well make them aware of the cultural amenities which the city offers. Here, twenty-four columns with sculptured bas-relief support a portico for the entire length of the building. The bas-relief concrete also forms the frieze of the canopy. The concrete sculptured element is carried inside in the form of a column, the focal point between the up and down escalators. The impression that departing passengers retain as they leave the airport is centered on a screen wall in the form of a 40- by 6-foot copper mural depicting landmarks around the world.

The several examples presented here give only an indication of the important role that art is playing in meeting people's cultural and spiritual needs. (In an earlier book, *Art in Architecture,* I explored this subject as it applies not only to the CBD but also to other aspects of the total environment.)

Graphics and Street Furnishings

As important as the integration of art is in the improvement of the city environment, well-designed graphics and city furnishings play a decisive role in linking architecture, art, and all other elements, making the "cityscape" a unified and satisfying totality.

One can witness the visual pollution of uncontrolled signage and incompatible street furnishings in nearly every city, large or small. This, coupled with sound and air pollution, calls for a new and radical approach in design concepts to our central business districts.

According to John Follis, president of a nationally known design firm, John Follis & Associates, "For a city to be effective in overcoming the visual clutter of commercial signs which usually exist in the heart of the city, it is necessary that it examine its own street signing and street furniture in public spaces and establish a design program of its own which sets an example to the private sector. Good graphic design should consider all the elements as interrelated parts of a single system, with one or two styles of lettering for all sign copy. All sign panels and supports should be related in form and materials. Color should be used to enhance readability and as an organizing device, as well as used decoratively to enliven the relatively neutral backdrop of buildings."

Entrance sign with illuminated copy—a system of colors developed for identifying various floors to help orient the user.

It is important that the graphic consultant be a part of the team with the city planners and architects and that they all work together right from the initial concept of the project. The diversified elements with which the graphic designer is concerned include (1) signs (auto, pedestrian, bus stops, buildings); (2) landscape items (flower boxes, benches, drinking fountains, bus shelters); and (3) other items such as mailboxes, trash containers, street lighting, and kiosks.

The urgent need to evolve a unified approach to the graphics and street furnishings for CBD renewal was recognized by HUD when it granted funds for research in street hardware and site improvements. The study *Operation Streetscape* was prepared in 1973 by Harold Lewis Malt Associates, Inc., for the Cincinnati CBD and excerpts therefrom follow:*

> Operation Streetscape sought to demonstrate community revitalization through the systematic design, production and utilization of street furniture, equipment used for traffic control and direction, lighting, refuse collection and communication.
>
> The designers developed and tested an integrated street furniture system within an on-going urban renewal project in downtown Cincinnati.
>
> The street and other public areas constituted forty percent of the total project area. This urban space required many lights, signs and signals and other necessities to make it safe, useful and pleasurable as well as habitable.
>
> For the most part this equipment, often obsolete in design, and uncoordinated in placement, added to the already visually polluted urban environment, with corresponding frustration and hazard to motorist and pedestrian alike.
>
> The Project goal was to demonstrate the benefits of a unified street furniture system of clearly defined function and coordinated visual impact. The process or program for development could be transferred to other municipalities.
>
> Work began with development of a work plan and program network for coordination of research and design. Process management techniques were applied to each stage of development, from initial design to production and installation. The consultant also acted as a liaison between the fragmented interests of various agencies, industry and the public.
>
> Next, an inventory and analysis of existing equipment within the 12 block, 56.14 acre CBD project area was made. Performance criteria were established for each element, including regulation codes, user needs, cost parameters, and the requirements that each component be compatible with every other.
>
> Then, numerous conceptual schemes for consolidation of street furniture elements were conceived and evaluated. The "cluster" approach offered the most economic, technical and visual benefits. It featured a major structural solution called the "multi-purpose pole" (M/P pole). This proved effective as a matrix to support, organize and energize other interrelated units. Any combination of components could be assembled within the M/P pole to serve user needs at any location as determined by the city agencies. A lighting plan for the downtown was developed and a spacing grid established for the location of multi-purpose poles with luminaires on the sidewalks.
>
> The M/P pole and other prototypical equipment were installed within the project area and evaluated. Product acceptance at all levels of the community was found very favorable. The Cincinnati Department of Urban Development (UD) initiated volume procurement through qualified low bid manufacturers. Installation of equipment and site improvements have been completed throughout much of the project area. The project has received national recognition and two design awards. In 1971, the Multi-Purpose pole was cited by the American Iron and Steel Institute for

*Excerpted from *Operation Streetscape,* brochure prepared by Harold Lewis Malt Associates, Inc., for the Cincinnati Department of Urban Development, 1973.

Midtown Plaza, Saskatoon, Saskatchewan, Canada. TOP: *Pedestrian sign. Red, white, and blue were chosen as basic Midtown Plaza colors, and this scheme is applied throughout the complex. The three parking areas are color-coded red, white, and blue: south parking surface—red; underground parking surface—white; and north parking surface—blue. The same red color is incorporated in the shopping malls as an architectural element, while white (along with black) is used for graphics in the office tower.* DIRECTLY ABOVE: *Explanatory sign—fits well into the surroundings. (Architects: Gordon R. Arnott & Associates, successor to Izumi, Arnott & Sugiyama. Graphics consultant: Paul Arthur & Associates. Photographer: Bob Howard.)*

Evanston, Illinois. Sign solutions for a special parking problem. In Evanston there has been a special problem with parking signs. This suburb, located north of Chicago, has an alternate parking program which switches from one side of the street to the other on alternate days. Varied times are also involved, as are signs denoting snow routes and their special applications. The result has been a complicated assortment of unreadable signs. The graphic designers were able to evoke a sign program which can be read and understood and is pleasant to look at. [Graphic designers: The Design Partnership, Inc. (Hayward R. Blake, project designer).]

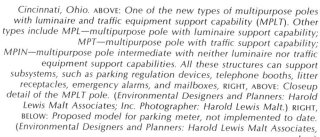

Cincinnati, Ohio. ABOVE: *One of the new types of multipurpose poles with luminaire and traffic equipment support capability (MPLT). Other types include MPL—multipurpose pole with luminaire support capability; MPT—multipurpose pole with traffic support capability; MPIN—multipurpose pole intermediate with neither luminaire nor traffic equipment support capabilities. All these structures can support subsystems, such as parking regulation devices, telephone booths, litter receptacles, emergency alarms, and mailboxes,* RIGHT, ABOVE: *Closeup detail of the MPLT pole. (Environmental Designers and Planners: Harold Lewis Malt Associates; Inc. Photographer: Harold Lewis Malt.)* RIGHT, BELOW: *Proposed model for parking meter, not implemented to date. (Environmental Designers and Planners: Harold Lewis Malt Associates, Inc.)*

Excellence in Design, Environmental Enhancement and Control Equipment. In 1972, Operation Streetscape received a Biennial HUD Award for Design Excellence.

Operation Streetscape has proved that streets can be more habitable and safe through a unified street furniture system which also gives greater visual satisfaction and contributes to a sense of community identity.

The process may be used to achieve similar benefits in any community, new or old. The report is intended to be useful to both the professional and the interested observer.

Graphics can also serve an important function during long construction periods in renewal areas in the design of colorful construction barriers. Susan Keig, graphic designer for Goldsholl & Associates, stresses the necessity of well-designed barriers geared to the total design identity of the project from construction to completion. "Here, graphics provide an interim solution and promise of fulfillment of an architectural statement, especially necessary where many city blocks, while under demolition, produce a dismal atmosphere . . . graphics then provide a positive morale booster for the public."

Traffic and People-Mover Systems

The redevelopment of any CBD area is closely interconnected with, and dependent on, a well-conceived transit system that includes a balanced mix of transportation—buses, rapid transit (underground, surface, overhead), people movers (automated car-cabs and overhead rail capsules), and in some instances moving sidewalks.

There are many examples of new transportation systems that are revitalizing cities and stimulating great economic activity. They can be a dynamic force enhancing the physical and sociological structure of the city. In Toronto, for example, this type of activity sprang up around the transit right-of-way. Toronto's old central business district came to life and spread northward along the 4½-mile Yonge Street subway in a spirit of unprecedented growth. In a five-year period 5 million square feet of office buildings and 8 million square feet of high-rise apartments were built in an area that had been on a decline.

Unlike Toronto, Stockholm, which was founded in the thirteenth century, did not choose to alter the character of the old city, but instead designed a transit system to open up new land on the periphery in the form of eighteen satellite cities centered around transit terminals. Stockholm's satellite cities have from 10,000 to 50,000 inhabitants. They are not remote and disjointed from the mother city, but are intimately connected by a fifteen-minute ride. They do, however, have their own shopping, industrial, and educational facilities. Ninety-five percent of Stockholm's inhabitants ride the subway, even though Sweden's per capita car ownership is second only to that of the United States.

According to Montgomery Ferar, vice president of Sundberg-Ferar, Inc., an industrial design firm:

> There are many types of hardware available to the transit planner. Based on traffic density, a system must be selected that will have adequate capacity. In most cities density is high enough to make automobiles alone impractical. Buses, particularly if they have a segregated right-of-way, can fill part of the gap. They are the most flexible means of transporting people and the least expensive from the capital outlay standpoint. However, unless they have an exclusive right-of-way, they are subject to the same restraints as a private automobile. A bus system is limited in capacity by the long spaces or headways that must be maintained between buses traveling at a high rate of speed for safety in braking. There are noise, vibration, comfort, and pollution

problems that could be solved by proper engineering design. A bus has difficulty of access for older and handicapped people, and it must be controlled by a driver rather than a computer, which results in high operating costs. The exclusive right-of-way, plus a dial-a-bus feeder system at the end of an express system, would be the fastest and least expensive way a city could improve its transit system.

People movers have some definite advantages over buses in that they can move more people per hour through a given corridor—anywhere from 3,000 to 15,000 passengers per hour, it is estimated. They can afford directness of route, accessibility, comfort, and convenience comparable to what private cars can provide. They have the ability to penetrate urban centers without disrupting the environment and without the high cost of tunneling. Their design should be adaptable to mass production and shop fabrication. Because of driverless automation, they should have reduced operating cost. The figures are $1.50 per mile for a bus, as compared with 9 to 13 cents per mile for a people-mover car. The land area and visual space can be kept as small as possible, and there will be low air pollution, noise, and vibration and minimum visual obstruction. The rights-of-way will be narrow because of the small vehicles and slender guideways. The estimate cost for a guideway is between $3 million and $6 million per mile (based on 1973 costs).

The system with the greatest capacity and speed is the rapid-transit train. These trains are capable of moving large numbers of people at high speeds without interfering with surface traffic. While the cost of tunneling and of aerial structures is high and while the average system takes ten years to plan and build, many cities, such as Detroit, have existing railroad rights-of-way that could be utilized, saving a great deal of capital outlay and time to satisfy an urgent need for low-energy, low-pollution transportation now. The modern transit car can hold about 200 passengers, weighs from 55,000 to 200,000 pounds, and is propelled by direct current. Traction motors feed by either a third rail or overhead catenary and usually cost between $400,000 and $750,000 per car. They achieve speeds up to 80 miles per hour and can be computer-controlled, which reduces operating costs. Made of stainless steel or aluminum, they need minimum maintenance and generally last at least thirty years. Cost per mile, depending on individual conditions, runs between $20 million and $30 million.

Another solution is being studied in Detroit by the SEMTA (Southeast Michigan Transportation Authority). Their consultants—Gannett Fleming Corddry and Carpenter—propose a combination of high- and intermediate-level transit networks which would interface to the projected people-mover system for the CBD.

An interesting feasibility study of the use of the moving sidewalk in the CBD area was prepared by The Architects Collaborative for the Boston Redevelopment Authority in 1971. Working with a team of specialists, they proposed a 4,000-foot system for the South Station–Summer Street area. It was intended to increase accessibility and integrate new systems within the present transit and automobile networks. An elevated pedestrian corridor will bring people from the new transportation center near the Southeast Expressway (a complex including a planned 5,000-car parking garage as well as bus and rail terminals) to the downtown area, and will connect with transit stations at either end.

The system is designed so that at one level above the street, pedestrians will be able to move freely from block to block within a weather-protected, comfort-heated environment without crossing traffic lines or waiting at crowded intersections. The corridor will be closely integrated with new development along its route, utilizing the protective cover and support afforded by the buildings through which it will pass. Plexiglas barrel vaults at the bridges crossing Summer Street ensure continuous weather protection.

The system will be in two segments: one portion integrated within the transportation center along Atlantic Avenue, and the other fronting on Summer Street

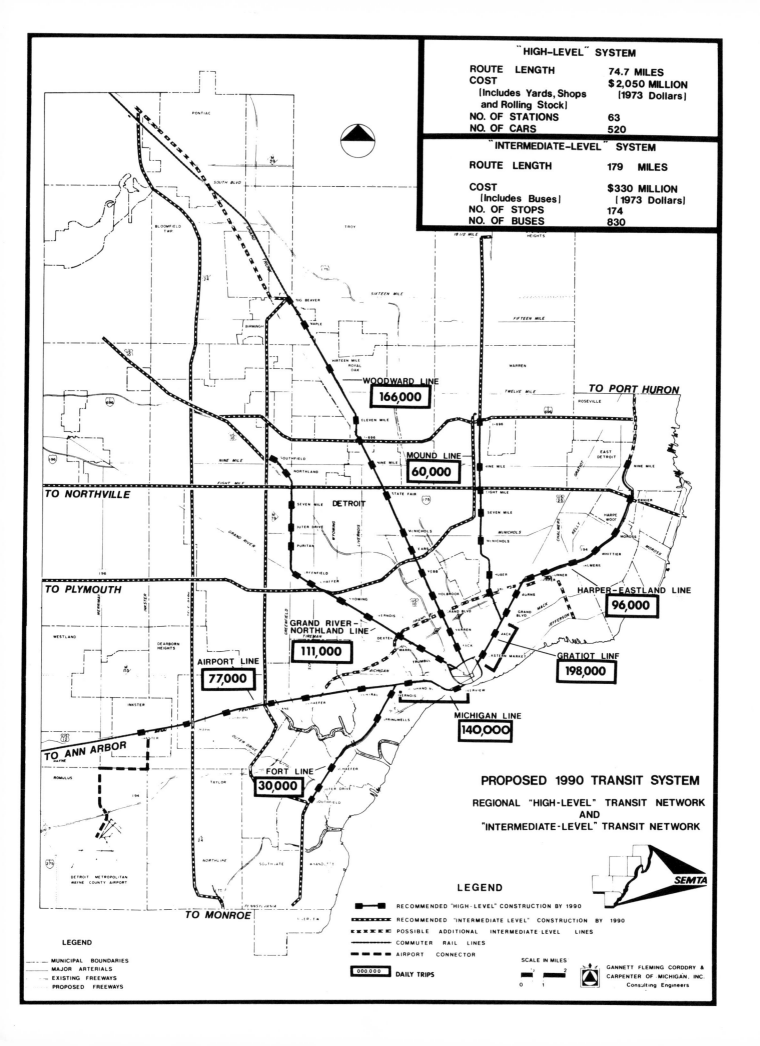

"HIGH-LEVEL" SYSTEM

ROUTE LENGTH	74.7 MILES
COST	$2,050 MILLION
(Includes Yards, Shops and Rolling Stock)	(1973 Dollars)
NO. OF STATIONS	63
NO. OF CARS	520

"INTERMEDIATE-LEVEL" SYSTEM

ROUTE LENGTH	179 MILES
COST	$330 MILLION
(Includes Buses)	(1973 Dollars)
NO. OF STOPS	174
NO. OF BUSES	830

WOODWARD LINE
166,000

TO PORT HURON

MOUND LINE
60,000

TO NORTHVILLE

DETROIT

TO PLYMOUTH

HARPER-EASTLAND LINE
96,000

GRAND RIVER–
NORTHLAND LINE
111,000

GRATIOT LINE
198,000

AIRPORT LINE
77,000

MICHIGAN LINE
140,000

TO ANN ARBOR

FORT LINE
30,000

PROPOSED 1990 TRANSIT SYSTEM

REGIONAL "HIGH-LEVEL" TRANSIT NETWORK
AND
"INTERMEDIATE-LEVEL" TRANSIT NETWORK

TO MONROE

LEGEND

RECOMMENDED "HIGH-LEVEL" CONSTRUCTION BY 1990

RECOMMENDED "INTERMEDIATE LEVEL" CONSTRUCTION BY 1990

POSSIBLE ADDITIONAL INTERMEDIATE LEVEL LINES

COMMUTER RAIL LINES

AIRPORT CONNECTOR

000.000 DAILY TRIPS

SCALE IN MILES

SEMTA

GANNETT FLEMING CORDDRY &
CARPENTER OF MICHIGAN, INC.
Consulting Engineers

DETROIT METROPOLITAN
WAYNE COUNTY AIRPORT

LEGEND

MUNICIPAL BOUNDARIES
MAJOR ARTERIALS
EXISTING FREEWAYS
PROPOSED FREEWAYS

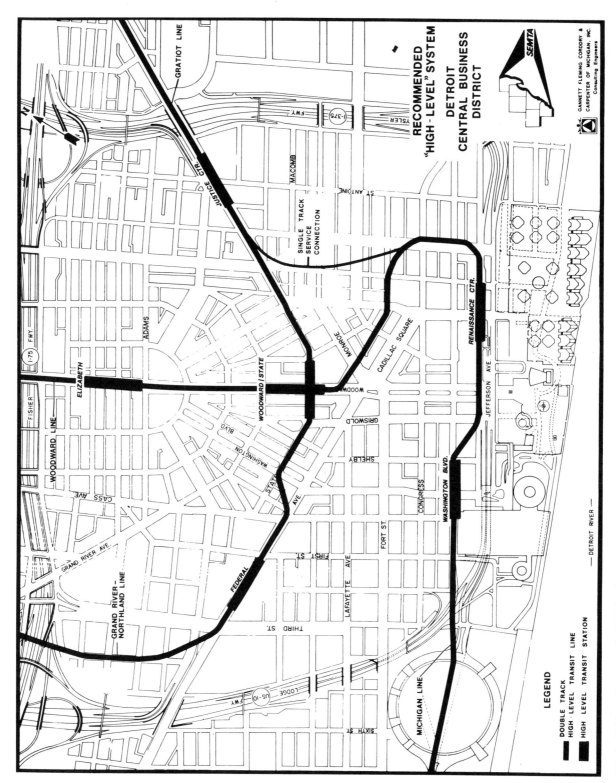

Detroit, Michigan. Recommended high-level system. (Consulting engineers: Gannett Fleming Corddry & Carpenter of Michigan, Inc.)

between the transportation center and the Winter Street connector to the proposed Washington Street Mall. The Summer Street portion will create new second-level retail spaces with increased property and rental value.

The moving walk will be able to receive pedestrians at conventional speeds (90 to 120 feet per minute) and accelerate to 210 feet per minute (normal walking clocks at 200 to 300 feet per minute). The walk will be sufficiently wide to allow hurriers to walk along with it, achieving even greater speed.

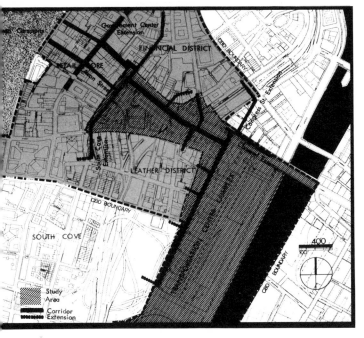

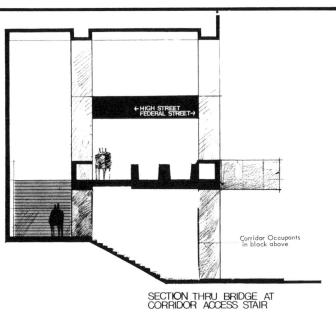

SECTION THRU BRIDGE AT
CORRIDOR ACCESS STAIR

SECTION THRU BRIDGE AT STREET
LOOKING TOWARD CORRIDOR ACCESS

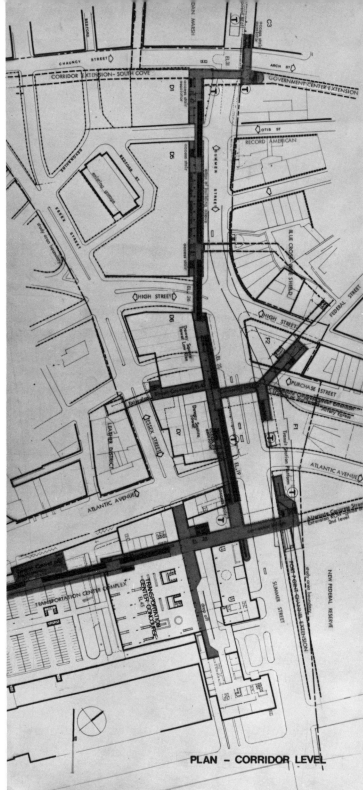

PLAN – CORRIDOR LEVEL

Boston, Massachusetts. LEFT, TOP:
Proposed pedestrian corridor. ABOVE:
*Proposed pedestrian walkway
showing the lower level.* LEFT,
CENTER: *Section through bridge at
street looking toward corridor
access.* LEFT, BELOW: *Section through
bridge at corridor access stair.*
(*Architects: The Architects
Collaborative.*)

Project Scheduling and Implementation

Project scheduling in the building industry has always been an important element in achieving both timing and control of operations. The simplest form of scheduling was the bar chart. It attempted to show the total duration of all activities in simplified form, but it generally did not provide sufficient detail to be useful except in a general way. Other more sophisticated techniques of planning have become available, involving mainly the use of network planning.

According to Ralph J. Stephenson, consulting engineer, network planning is useful from the very beginning of any project. It is a powerful control tool during early conceptual thinking, when the process of visualizing, interpreting, and articulating concepts may be the responsibility of many parties.

The two methods of network planning most often encountered are PERT and CPM. PERT, program evaluation and review technique, was established as a tool that would allow the manager to determine whether, at a certain date, all activities scheduled for completion prior to that date had in fact been completed. CPM, critical path method, approaches the problem from the opposite standpoint, attempting to define all sequential activities progressing toward the completion of the various phases of a project. By assigning durations to each activity and combining phases, the manager is able to arrive at a final listing of activities which are critical to the completion of the total project. This sequence of activities is known as the *critical path*, since all activities on that path are without excess discretionary time and must be commenced and completed on the critical dates.

In terms of construction activities, CPM has survived as the most useful tool available when expertly applied. In practice, CPM becomes simply a method of preplanning which results in an accurate, two-dimensional graphic model depicting actual work to be done. In a sense, the manager, through a network plan, creates the project procedure on paper and simulates all major decision steps taken in the actual work.

In the planning of urban development programs, CPM is now being recognized as an important tool in guiding the development of the very complex states which urban planning has to undergo. It is especially valuable in tracing the paths to be followed through the bureaucratic administrative maze common to practically every planning program today, and it can be valuable in outlining real estate acquisition, financing procedures, and preparation of design documents, as well as in the actual implementation of planning programs.

The first step in the network planning procedure is to prepare a logic plan showing all relationships that exist between the various actions in the program. Once this logic plan has been reviewed and approved by the parties involved, task durations, usually in working days, are estimated and assigned to each task. (See Figure 1.)

When times have been assigned to each task, simple computations will show the earliest time in working days at which any given task can start and finish if it is meeting all its early dates. (See Figure 2.)

With the project end date established and approved, the latest times that a task can start and finish in working days are easily determined by simply computing the network in reverse. (See Figure 3.)

Thus every task in the network diagram has an early start, a late start, an early finish, and a late finish. At this point, a choice can be made as to how resources are to be assigned to the various tasks.

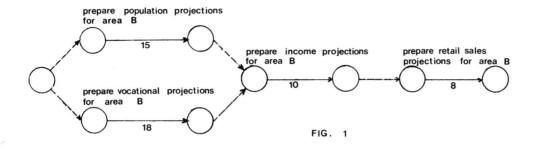

FIG. 1

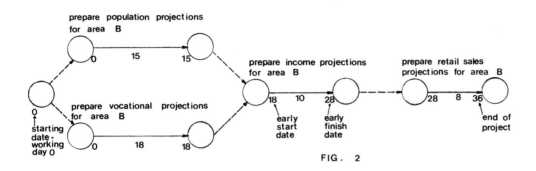

FIG. 2

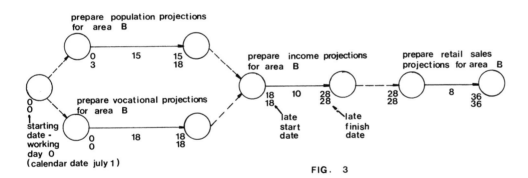

FIG. 3

If, for instance, a task has an early start of July 1 (working day 0) and an early finish of July 28 (working day 15)—a span of eighteen working days—but has a late start of July 8 (working day 3) and a late finish of July 30 (working day 18), as in the task of preparing population projections for an area, the planner has available three working days of discretionary time (float).

Does the planner start on the early start, on the late start, or at an intermediate point? The decision may be influenced by whether a draftsman is available or whether a banker can make a meeting on that day. The network assists the planner in making this decision.

Today, networks are used in all sizes and types of organizations to improve and extend the capabilities of all levels of management. The system is used to assist in a broad range of problem identification, analysis, and solution. It is a simulating tool that allows evaluation of alterations to the plan to be made by managers. For the urban planner and for every responsible individual involved in development work, network planning and the critical path method offer an excellent tool for sharpening, improving, and extending their project control techniques.

Part Three

Significant
Case
Studies

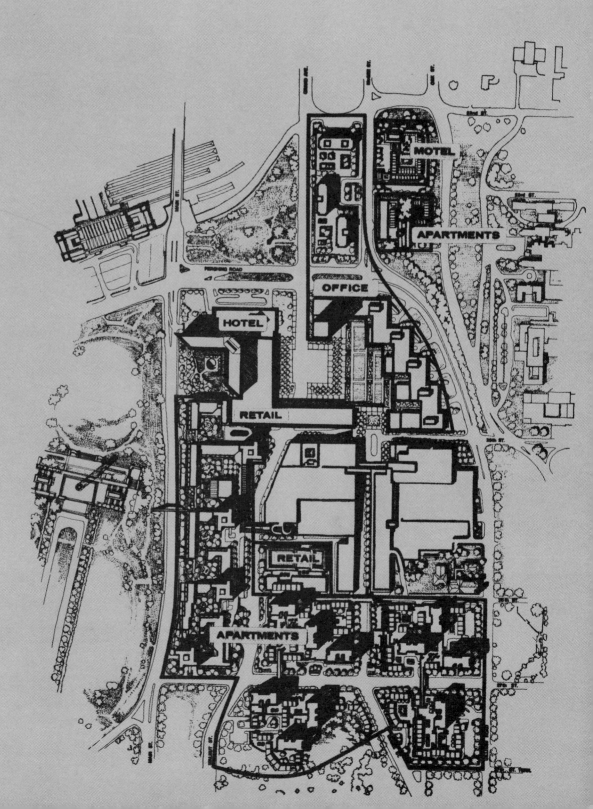

COLONY SQUARE
Atlanta, Georgia

ARCHITECTS: Jova/Daniels/Busby
LANDSCAPE ARCHITECTS FOR PHASE ONE
M. Paul Friedberg & Associates

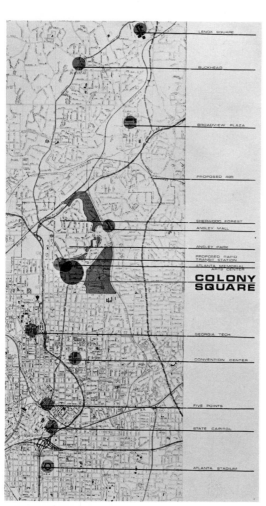

Location plan.

The architect for the project comments:

Colony Square is a privately financed 11½-acre urban redevelopment 2 miles from Atlanta's center. Facing a busy intersection and bordering on the city's upper-middle-class residential neighborhood, the project provides many of the services and amenities of urban life. Included are two office towers, two apartment towers, a luxury hotel, a skating rink with landscaped courts and plazas, and a variety of shops, stores, and restaurants—all atop a 1,750-car underground garage.

The irregular shape of the site and its relationship to other major structures in the area suggest the diagonal disposition of the major buildings to the street. The placement opens up the plaza area to the passerby and complements other irregularly sited buildings nearby.

In order to relate a variety of building types to one another to create a relationship of all the parts, a limited vocabulary of materials was established. Board formed concrete contrasts with smooth white precast; dark brown brick-bronze aluminum and bronze-tinted glass provide accents. The materials are softened by areas of heavy planting. The buildings are juxtaposed to create two major interior spaces—one active and lively, and the other more reposed. Fountains, pools, and sculpture are the focal points of these areas.

Underground elements are constructed of precast concrete. The high-rise office building is a steel frame structure, and the apartment tower is poured-in-place concrete.

The various steps taken with the government agencies and procedures of land acquisition played an important part in the realization of this project. Existing zoning ordinances and building codes did not anticipate a multiuse urban complex, and therefore much consultation was necessary with enforcement agencies to provide interpretations of intent and to seek variances where necessary.

A case in point is parking: The zoning ordinance treats each building type as a self-sustaining entity. By the letter of the ordinance, the various elements of Colony Square would have a cumulative parking requirement of about 2,200 spaces. By demonstrating the overlap effect of various uses—offices require peak parking during business hours, while apartment parking peaks at night—we were able to gain approval for 1,750 spaces minimum.

Colony Square is contiguous on one side with Ansley Park, a prestigious neighborhood with a considerable reputation for opposing commercial encroachment of its residential character. Once the land was assembled for Colony Square, it was necessary to seek rezoning to the highest commercial density permissible. Close liaison with Ansley Park residents resulted in a development plan and covenants that led to the desired rezoning "conditional" on the implementation of the approved development plan. In addition, a buffer strip of several acres along Fifteenth Street—the side of Colony Square closest to Ansley Park—was rezoned for townhouse development.

The mutual desire to respect the residential character of Ansley Park is clearly reflected in the development plan as density and use intensify from the single-family scale of the townhouses to the high-rise offices on busy Peachtree Street.

Goodwill was demonstrated by the deeding of frontage to the city along Fourteenth and Peachtree Streets, which allowed widening of these busy corridors. In addition, land at the intersection of these two streets was deeded to improve the alignment of Fourteenth Street.

The need to allow automobiles to enter the project from Peachtree Street without disrupting two-way traffic flow led to the design of parallel ramps to and from the underground parking, rather than the more traditional perpendicular curb-cut. This concept is new to Atlanta and involved a "cross-easement" agreement whereby the city retains its right-of-way (sidewalk) around the ramps and Colony Square has the right to construct ramps in the area previously occupied by the sidewalk.

Since Fourteenth Street is one-way (west), the traditional entrance to the garage is more satisfactory as it permits exit to southbound Juniper Street as well as Fourteenth.

Traffic disruption was held to a minimum during construction. It was necessary to occupy one lane northbound on Peachtree to construct the parallel ramps; permission was granted after it was demonstrated that Peachtree accommodates more traffic in its two southbound lanes than in its three northbound lanes. An agreement with the city prohibits the hoisting of any materials from the streets.

Acquisition of land was a relatively slow accomplishment that proceeded through a combination of outright purchases and some options. The procedure was to keep the parcels optioned until enough commitments could be obtained to assure a viable project whether or not the entire site could be assembled. Since there was a total of seventeen owners within the 11½ acres under consideration, timing was crucial. When eleven parcels were optioned, the key corner site was purchased, and final planning began.

Moving occupants was no great problem since most had selected new quarters prior to closing their sales. However, two or three residential owners insisted that the developer find them suitable housing in acceptable locations before they would sell.

Exterior view (model).

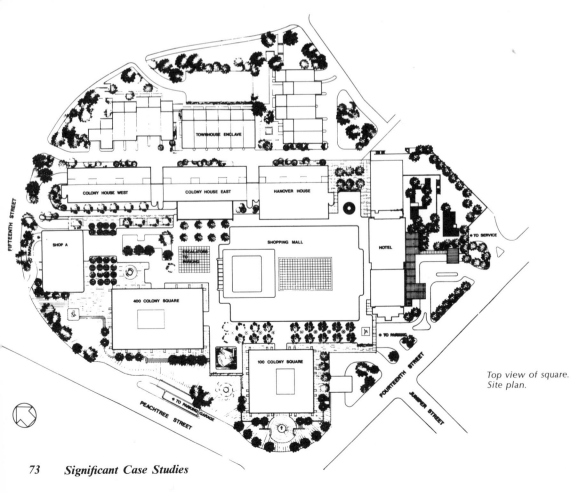

Top view of square.
Site plan.

Entrance, exterior view. (Sculptor: Dorothy Berge; sculpture of Cor-Ten steel. Photographer: Robin Johnstone.)

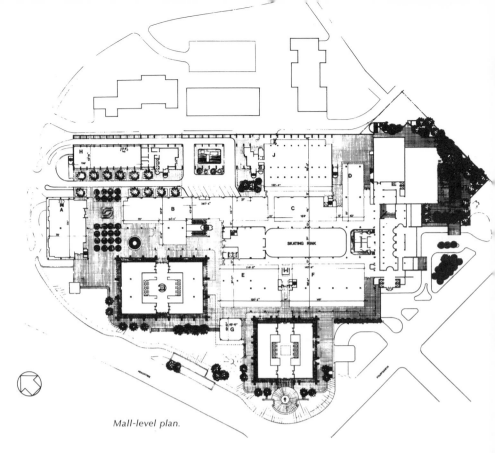

Mall-level plan.

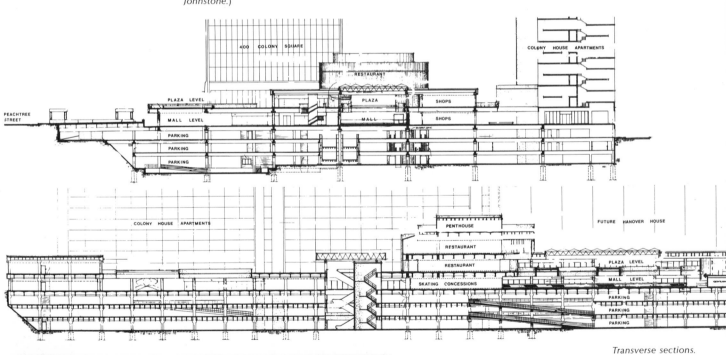

Transverse sections.

Aerial view (perspective).

Located in the center of one of the fastest-growing metropolitan areas in the United States, this projected plan encompasses some 1,000 acres with more than $994 million in new investments. This area has a variety of unique assets—an inland port, diversity of business and industry, and proximity to Washington and Philadelphia.

One of the many goals of Metro Center that were set up early in its development was to provide additional center-city services, including economic, social, and cultural establishments in the downtown, and to expand existing ones. Another goal was to improve accessibility to the center by such means as direct links between transit stops and the major employment center, peripheral parking, and better internal circulation, the latter to be accomplished by separating through traffic from local traffic and pedestrians from vehicles.

The Inner Harbor area is viewed as a combination of institutional and commercial uses. Of concern is the preservation of the heritage of Baltimore by retaining the productive use of buildings of historic and architectural value and by redesigning their surroundings to provide appropriate settings. Included in the development of the center city is a distinctive, high-quality environment with vistas, design competition for major buildings, effective sign controls, malls, plazas, and attractive street furniture.

The first stages of Metro Center include two major projects in Baltimore—Charles Center and the Inner Harbor program. The Charles Center concept was presented in 1958 to the city of Baltimore in the form of a proposal by the Committee for Downtown and the Greater Baltimore Committee. The city agreed to undertake the project, and in 1959, after the approval of an urban renewal bond issue, the Charles Center management office was established to supervise execution of the project.

The major part of Charles Center, which encompasses 33 acres, is completed. This represents some $145 million in new public and private investment. The area is centered between the city's financial district on the east and retail district on the west, and it serves as an economic focal point for the expanding region beyond.

The center provides office buildings, apartments, a hotel, a theater, commercial and specialty retail space, transit depots, public parks, overhead walkways, and underground parking garages. There are 430,000 square feet of net rentable area provided in facilities for retailing, retail services, and related commercial activities. Parking includes 1,500 tenant spaces and 2,500 public spaces.

Charles Center lies at the hub of a network of other major projects—the Civic Center, which combines a 10,000-seat sports arena, and a coliseum with 100,000 square feet of exhibition spaces. Directly north, the Mount Vernon area is being rehabilitated and restored under the urban renewal program. In addition, the city undertook to construct the Lexington Street Mall, linking Charles Center to the retail shopping area two blocks away.

Southeast of Charles Center lies the Inner Harbor area. This is the second step in the Metro Center development. It contains approximately 95 acres along three sides of the harbor basin. This area serves as a major gateway connecting the seaport with the modern business district. The city is planning a municipal center to connect with the City Hall. This plan also calls for residential and commercial complexes facing a waterfront park. The waterfront will be lined with major office buildings, apartments, and a luxury hotel. Between the boulevard, Pratt Street and Light Street, and the water will be parks, promenades, and low pavilion structures housing restaurants, theaters, and other attractions. The bulkhead around the basin will be rebuilt as a public wharf for excursion boats, tourist barges, ferries, and visiting ships. Provision will be made for hovercraft, hydrofoils, and STOL (short takeoff and landing) seaplanes.

A second stage of the Inner Harbor project includes a 68-acre section to the south of Charles Center and west of Inner Harbor Project One. It will feature a model urban neighborhood, with apartments for 1,200 to 1,500 moderate- and middle-income families. Here also will be major office buildings and commercial facilities lining Pratt Street. Planning is under way for a third Inner Harbor project, which will provide high-rise apartments on the remaining Inner Harbor piers. In the Inner Harbor project is a municipal mall extending from City Hall south to the water's edge. It is proposed to develop both sides of the mall with government buildings, while retaining the turn-of-the-century Customs House as a museum and library.

INNER HARBOR
Baltimore, Maryland
ARCHITECTS, LANDSCAPE ARCHITECTS, CITY AND REGIONAL PLANNERS: Wallace, McHarg, Roberts & Todd

Location plan.

Like that of Charles Center, the development of the Inner Harbor projects is an enterprise of the city of Baltimore. Although many municipal agencies are involved, primary responsibility rests with the Baltimore City Department of Housing and Community Development, working through Charles Center–Inner Harbor Management, Inc. This office conducts all negotiations and competitive offerings for the disposal of the project land. In addition, it supervises the design and construction of public facilities and coordinates the activities of the various city agencies and private developers.

Developers are selected in accordance with their ability to fulfill the city's basic objectives for the Inner Harbor projects. Consequently, the selection process used by the city involves detailed consideration of developers and their qualifications and of the character of proposed developments. Developers are normally selected by competitive means, unless one developer offers some benefit to the city which no other developer can provide. Developers acquire fee simple title or long-term leases to project land. They have no responsibility for acquisition, relocation, land clearance, or major public facilities, other than easements or development rights which may be retained by the city.

Inner Harbor—shoreline plan.

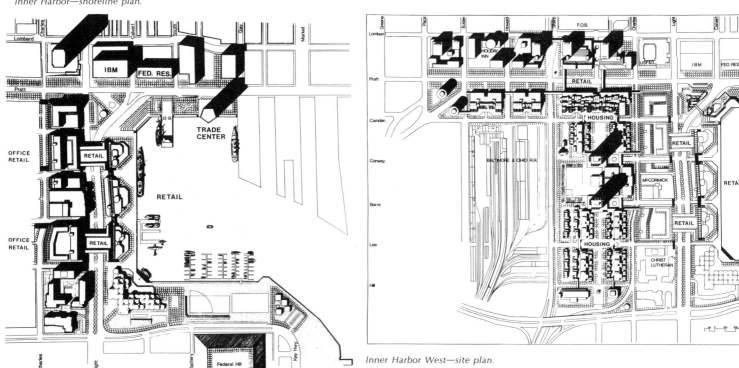

Inner Harbor West—site plan.

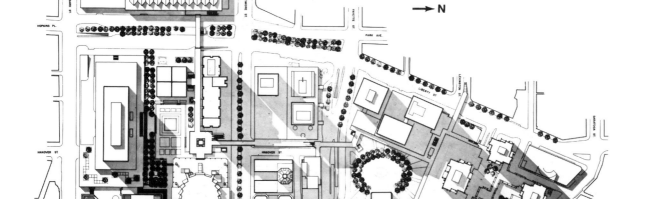

Charles Center site plan.

Aerial view of Baltimore showing Inner Harbor. (Photographer: M. E. Warren.)

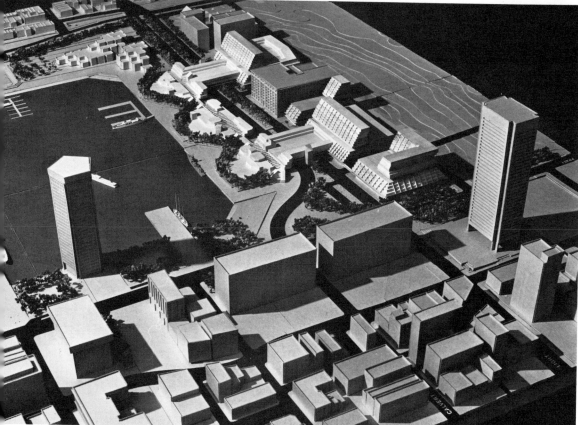

Aerial view of Inner Harbor (model). (Photographer: Harris Davis Photography.)

OAKLAND CITY CENTER
Oakland, California

ARCHITECTS:
For the master plan, Wells Fargo Bank building,
and the Clorox building: Gruen Associates
For the shopping mall: Avner Nagger
LANDSCAPE ARCHITECTS FOR PUBLIC PLAZAS:
Sasaki-Walker Associates

Oakland City Center, in Oakland, California, is a multifunctional revitalization project containing shopping, financial, office, entertainment, hotel, and restaurant facilities.

The fifteen-block project was made possible through a combination of community and federal government support.

The elements of the complex include the Wells Fargo ten-story bank building (completed in 1973). The Clorox building (under construction in 1974), two office buildings, and a hotel all interconnect with a plaza leading to a regional-type four-department store enclosed shopping mall.

The City Center, in the heart of the CBD, is bounded by Eleventh Street, Fourteenth Street, Grove Street, and Broadway.

The center marks the hub of the Bay Area Rapid Transit district's network of stations; the nearby Twelfth Street BART station, a central transfer point for two BART lines, will serve the approximately 11,000 persons who will be employed at the City Center upon its completion.

The Wells Fargo building, the first completed, is set back from Broadway to create a landscaped plaza, which is designed to harmonize in plant materials and textures with the existing City Hall Park to the north.

On the south side of the building is a large sunken court lined with restaurants that look out on its fountains, pools, and trees. The court leads directly into the BART station. Later, when other commercial buildings, department stores, and a shopping mall are added to the project, the court will continue as an underground concourse, connecting with the lower levels of the shopping mall and principal buildings.

The codevelopers of the project are Grubb & Ellis Development Co., the Wells Fargo Bank, and the Oakland Redevelopment Agency. The developer of the regional shopping center is Bay Shore Properties, Inc.

Wells Fargo Bank building. (Photographer: Balthazar Korab.)

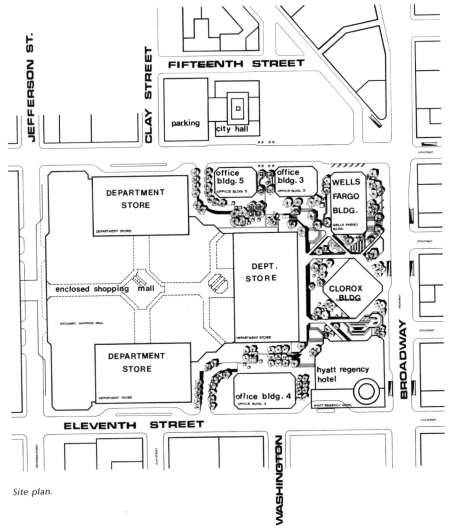

Site plan.

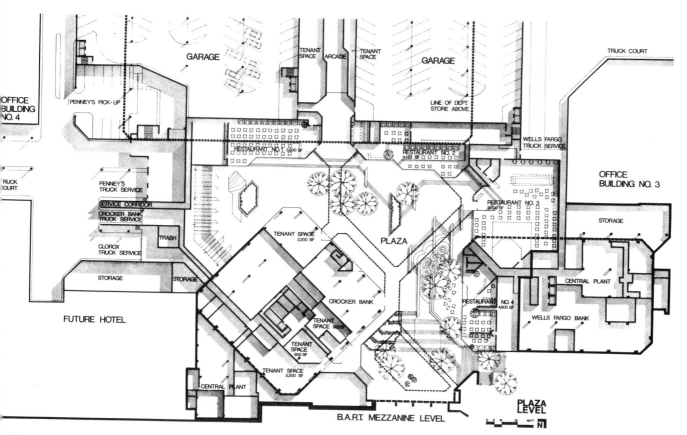

OFFICE BUILDING NO. 4

GARAGE

TENANT SPACE ARCADE

TENANT SPACE

GARAGE

TRUCK COURT

PENNEY'S PICK-UP

LINE OF DEPT STORE ABOVE

WELLS FARGO TRUCK SERVICE

TRUCK COURT

RESTAURANT NO. 1 5,600 SF

RESTAURANT NO. 2 6,100 SF

OFFICE BUILDING NO. 3

PENNEY'S TRUCK SERVICE

SERVICE CORRIDOR

CROCKER BANK TRUCK SERVICE

RESTAURANT NO. 3 9,000 SF

STORAGE

CLOROX TRUCK SERVICE

TRASH

PLAZA

TENANT SPACE 2,200 SF

STORAGE

STORAGE

CENTRAL PLANT

CROCKER BANK

TENANT SPACE 900 SF

RESTAURANT NO. 4 4,600 SF

WELLS FARGO BANK

FUTURE HOTEL

TENANT SPACE 900 SF

CENTRAL PLANT

TENANT SPACE 5,200 SF

PLAZA LEVEL

B.A.R.T. MEZZANINE LEVEL

N

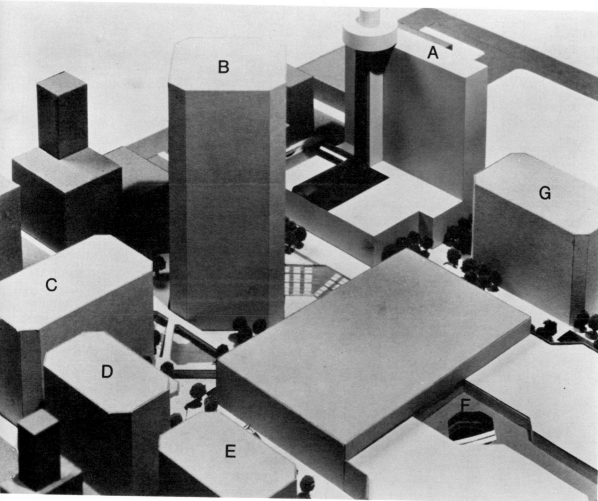

Model of complex. (A) Hyatt Regency Hotel; (B) Clorox building (under construction); (C) Wells Fargo Bank building (completed 1973); (D) office building #3; (E) office building #5; (F) east portion of regional shopping center anchored by three department stores.

HARTFORD CIVIC CENTER
Hartford, Connecticut

ARCHITECTS: The Kling Partnership
ASSOCIATE ARCHITECTS: Danos & Associates

ABOVE: *North-south section showing bridge over Church Street adjoining hotel. Standing on Trumbull Street, to left of bridge, is the shopping-center and office level. (Photographer: Harris Davis Photography.)* BELOW: *Landscaped central court showing shopping mall. (Photographer: Harris Davis Photography.)*

The entire site for the Hartford Civic Center was acquired by the city of Hartford through its urban renewal program, and the project was jointly financed by the city through its urban renewal program and by Aetna Life & Casualty Company. The city owns the coliseum, exhibition hall, public plaza, and underground garage, over which Aetna leases air rights for shops, restaurants, and commercial offices. In addition, Aetna and Sheraton are jointly financing a hotel which will be connected to the Civic Center by an overhead pedestrian bridge.

The project is unusual in that there are two clients—one a municipal body and the other a private firm—which function quite differently. However, because of the private firm's deep interest in the revitalization of downtown Hartford, the design problems were solved satisfactorily.

The Hartford Civic Center is an L-shaped three-level commercial and retail complex featuring an assembly and banquet hall seating 1,700; an exhibition hall for auto shows, boat shows, and other events; 140,000 square feet of office space; 280,000 square feet of retail space; and an enclosed pedestrian mall.

Integrated with the center are the twenty-one-story, approximately 420-room Sheraton Hartford Hotel, joined to it by an 80-foot-wide enclosed bridge over Church Street, and the 12,000-seat coliseum. The assembly and banquet hall is located in the bridge over Church Street. A 500-car parking garage under the center is also part of the complex and supplements an existing 1,000-car garage across Church Street.

The development of the Civic Center complex is another phase in the progress of revitalization of the downtown area and is intended to link to the existing Constitution Plaza, built in the early 1960s. (See photos on page 83.) According to David M. Mann, chief staff planner for the Hartford Redevelopment Agency, "Prior to the construction of Constitution Plaza, Hartford's downtown was experiencing a worsening paralysis occasioned by deterioration and migration of major retail and office functions. Constitution Plaza effectively restored the faith of commercial and office users in the city, as exemplified by the new home office of Phoenix Mutual Life Insurance and Connecticut Bank and Trust buildings. But the plaza did not provide all things for all people. It became eminently clear that physical connection to the Main Street retail area was a key ingredient to injecting diversity into life on the plaza."

The Commission on the City Plan initiated the idea of the Civic Center development to make Hartford a day/night "people place." Again, according to Mr. Mann, "Success in gaining approval of this project was directly related to community and investor concern that Constitution Plaza, essentially an 'island,' would be unable to overcome the declining forces in the downtown."

It is evident from the above that successful redevelopment has to be planned on a comprehensive scale and that the individual developments must be well integrated with one another through malls and pedestrian pathways, both at ground and overhead levels. Also, as in any downtown revival, the residential and recreational facilities play decisive roles.

The owners of the center are the city of Hartford (coliseum, public assembly rooms, and garages) and Aetna Life & Casualty (commercial portion of the complex—retail mall and offices). A partnership composed of Aetna Life & Casualty and ITT-Sheraton owns the Sheraton Hartford Hotel.

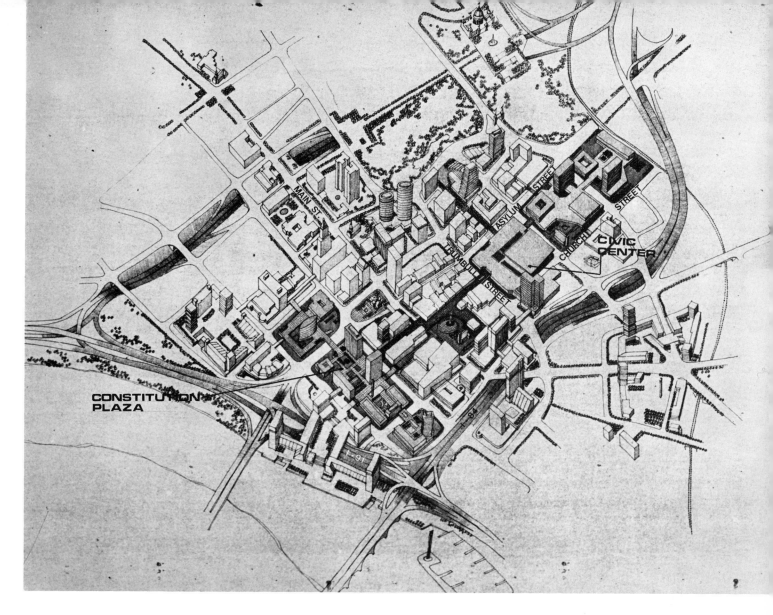

CONSTITUTION
PLAZA

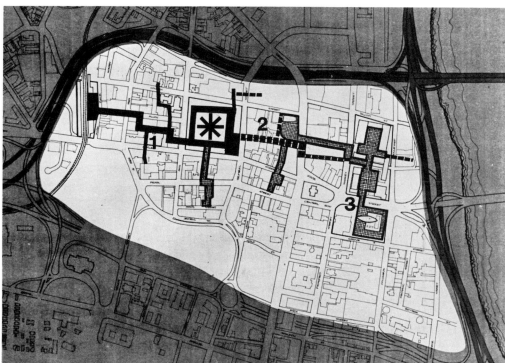

ABOVE: *Perspective view showing
location of the civic center in
relation to Constitution Plaza.
(Photographer: Harris Davis
Photography.)* LEFT: *Proposed
pedestrian circulation showing
the linkage between the civic
center and Constitution Plaza.
(Photographer: Harris Davis
Photography.)*

* civic center
1 interior
2 galleria
3 open

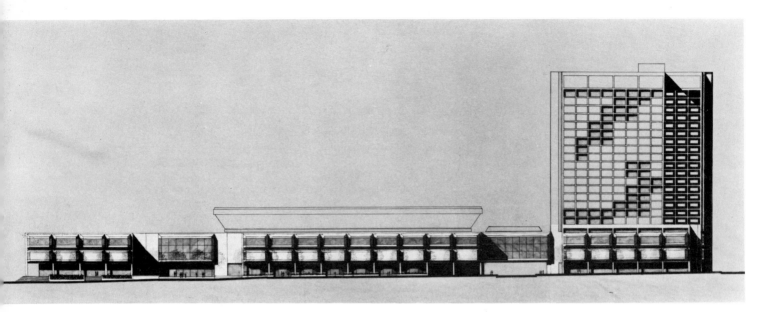

Elevation at Trumbull Street shows shopping center and office level at left, coliseum in center, bridge over Church Street to right of coliseum, and hotel at extreme right. (*Photographer: Harris Davis Photography.*)

Perspective at Church Street and Ann Street looking southeast. Coliseum and hotel are at left. (*Photographer: Harris Davis Photography.*)

CONSTITUTION PLAZA
Hartford, Connecticut

SITE PLANNING AND BASIC DESIGN OF OVERALL
PROJECT AND COMPONENTS; GENERAL DESIGN
COORDINATION: Charles DuBose, AIA Architect
LANDSCAPE ARCHITECTS: Sasaki-Walker Associates

Site location.
(*Photographer: Harris Davis Photography.*)

Aerial view of Constitution Plaza before redevelopment.

Main view of plaza.

CHAPEL SQUARE
New Haven, Connecticut
ARCHITECTS: Lathrop Douglass, FAIA

Exterior view.

Overall view (model superimposed). (1) Malley's; (2) Macy's; (3) two-level mall; (4) bridges; (5) municipal garage; (6) hotel; (7) office building.

The architect for the project comments:

The central business district urban renewal program for New Haven included a connector route from the Connecticut Thruway and eventually from the Merritt Parkway, a seven-level municipal garage, two major department stores, a hotel, an office building, underground parking and service, and two levels of shopping.

Land-ownership and legal problems were very complex, and the land cost was very high. The land stretches from the connector to the New Haven Green, whose corner is customarily referred to as the "100 percent location" in New Haven. Although the site was completely cleared at an early stage, the development was piecemeal; first to be built were the Malley department store and the municipal garage at the connector end of the project. In order to obtain the second department store, the city found it necessary to accept Macy's condition that they be located next to Malley's and the municipal garage, thus preventing the classic arrangement of department stores at either end. Because of financial and other problems, the project changed hands, and this office undertook the planning and design of the two blocks of retail stores, offices, hotel, etc., for the new developer. The two levels of basement garage and servicing connect by truck tunnel to the balance of the development. The second level of the mall connects by bridges over an intervening street to Macy's and the municipal garage, and the hotel and office building are tied into the mall. Having overcome its initial problems, the project is now successful and fully rented.

Of special interest are some ideas which the architect feels are important and may apply to other CBD projects:

The ability to change tenant mix in reasonably short periods is advantageous; tenant mix should be oriented to the needs of office employees, etc., rather than to typical suburban residents (or even downtown residents); major stores are not as important as they are in the suburbs, although any existing downtown stores should be incorporated if possible; street entrances to stores are of minor importance when malls are properly planned; lateral parking decks greatly strengthen upper levels; and the question of whether the project should be on the 100 percent site or adjacent thereto is debatable because of the economics, the high cost of 100 percent land, and the hiatus in retailing while existing stores are torn down and rebuilt, although, on the other hand, a location away from the 100 percent site creates a competitive situation with a gradual decay of the existing downtown in favor of the new project, assuming of course that the latter is properly planned.

In analyzing the impact and economic improvements of the redevelopment project, William T. Donahue, executive director of the New Haven Redevelopment Agency, has these comments:

CENTER OF NEW HAVEN

The overall central-city layout illustrates how interrelated the developments wrought by urban redevelopment are and how difficult it is to cull out one phase (such as the mall) and assess its singular impact. One solid index of our retail growth and stability, however, is the increased retail sales statistics covering the last 1½ decades.

The city also derived ancillary assets from the mall development. Its promise and eventual realization certainly helped to make New Haven more attractive to business and industry, increased local employment opportunities, and drew more people downtown during evening shopping hours. Prior to the opening of the new Malley's, Macy's, and the mall, evening store hours were in effect only on Thursdays. In 1963, Malley's added Monday evenings, and Macy's and the mall followed suit. In 1973 Macy's instituted an expanded evening-hour policy including every weeknight. It is felt, also, that the activities of the coliseum have increased evening trips to downtown.

The new image that the mall development, etc., gave to the core city was so highly visible in the last decade as to negate the need for any large-scale public relations effort. The renewal program was comprehensive and bold enough by itself to mark the city's achievements both locally and nationally. However, the official openings of each phase of downtown revitalization were marked by special dedication ceremonies. Other than these, no special events per se were planned to foster a new image. Today, however, special exhibits sponsored by various cultural, business, private, and public agencies are scheduled for display in the mall's lower level through the Chapel Square Merchant's Association.

My projections for downtown development in the near future are highly optimistic. Barring any major economic recession, I foresee continued prosperity and growth for central New Haven. An indication of our continuing ability to generate downtown investment was again evident this fall (1973) as the city received a commitment from a group of local doctors to develop one of our two large remaining vacant downtown parcels (a $12 million medical arts complex). I find our past growth rate steady and see no reason to anticipate a sudden change. Let me just say that in my opinion, the economic benefits derived from downtown revitalization are as dramatic as the aesthetic ones.

Overpass. (Photographer: George Szeberenyi.)

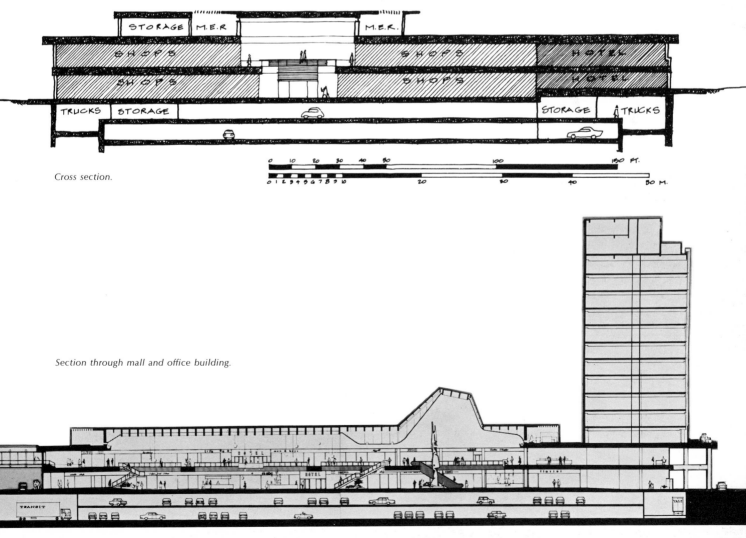

Cross section.

Section through mall and office building.

WORCESTER CENTER
Worcester, Massachusetts

ARCHITECTS: Welton Becket & Associates
LANDSCAPE ARCHITECTS: M. Paul Friedberg & Associates

Worcester, Massachusetts, with a population of approximately 187,000, provides a good example of how urban renewal can be accomplished successfully by the drastic removal of blighted structures by their replacement not only with new buildings but also with a new concept in urban living, designed to bring new life to the city. The 34-acre project site is bounded by Commercial Street, Foster Street, the New Haven Railroad tracks, Franklin Street, Salem Square, and Front Street. the center itself, however, will occupy approximately 20 acres, while a loop highway with connecting roads to the center is located on the remainder of the parcel.

The first phase includes two office buildings, two major department stores (Jordan Marsh and Filene's), two five-story parking structures, and more than 100 shops and restaurants in four buildings, all arranged around a two-level vaulted galleria, 475 feet long and 60 feet high. The second phase calls for a future office building, a convention hotel, a civic theater, and additional parking. Along the length of the galleria, landscape, artwork, fountains, and graphics are well integrated in the overall design.

The lighting is by Seymour Evans & Associates; graphics, by Chermayeff & Geismar Associates. Worcester Redevelopment Authority is the client. The developer is Worcester Center Associates. The center is a joint venture of The Berenson Corporation, Beacon Construction Company, and Arthur Shactman.

Aerial view of redeveloped area.
(Photographer: Daniel P. Duffy.)

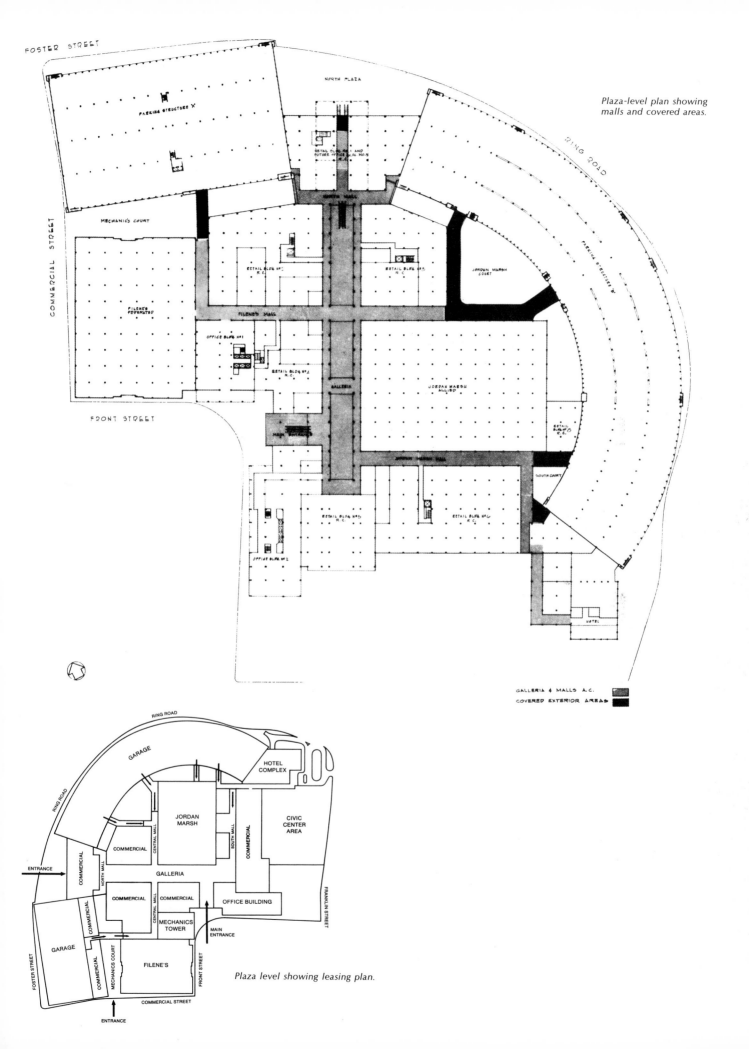

Plaza-level plan showing malls and covered areas.

FOSTER STREET

NORTH PLAZA

RING ROAD

PARKING STRUCTURE "A"

MECHANICS COURT

COMMERCIAL STREET

RETAIL BLDG. NO.1 AND FUTURE OFFICE BLDG. NO.5 R.C.

NORTH MALL

PARKING STRUCTURE "B"

RETAIL BLDG. NO.2 R.C.

RETAIL BLDG. NO.3 R.C.

JORDAN MARSH COURT

FILENE'S FEDERATED

FILENE'S MALL

OFFICE BLDG. NO.1

RETAIL BLDG. NO.7 R.C.

GALLERIA

JORDAN MARSH ALLIED

RETAIL BLDG. NO.8 R.C.

FRONT STREET

MAIN ENTRANCE

JORDAN MARSH MALL

SOUTH COURT

RETAIL BLDG. NO.5 R.C.

RETAIL BLDG. NO.6 R.C.

OFFICE BLDG. NO.2

HOTEL

GALLERIA & MALLS A.C.

COVERED EXTERIOR AREAS

RING ROAD

GARAGE

HOTEL COMPLEX

RING ROAD

JORDAN MARSH

NORTH MALL

CENTRAL MALL

SOUTH MALL

COMMERCIAL

CIVIC CENTER AREA

ENTRANCE

COMMERCIAL

GALLERIA

COMMERCIAL

COMMERCIAL

CENTRAL MALL

COMMERCIAL

OFFICE BUILDING

FRANKLIN STREET

FOSTER STREET

GARAGE

COMMERCIAL

MECHANICS COURT

MECHANICS TOWER

FILENE'S

FRONT STREET

MAIN ENTRANCE

COMMERCIAL STREET

ENTRANCE

Plaza level showing leasing plan.

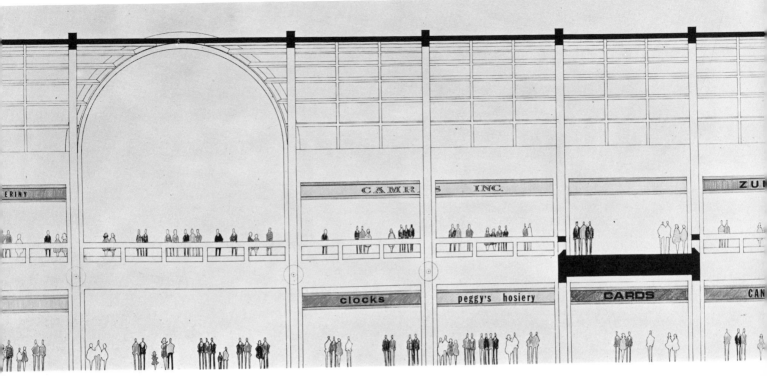

Section through the galleria.

RIGHT: *Interior of the garage south court showing interconnected bridges to retail and department stores.* [*Photographer: Ezra Stoller (ESTO).*] BELOW: *Interior of the galleria.*

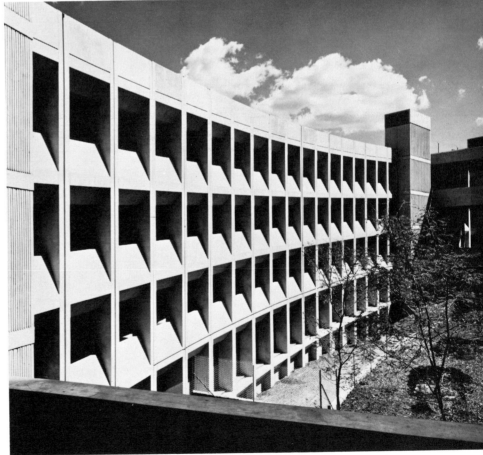

Oshkosh, Wisconsin, is one of the smaller cities (population 52,000) to have realized the importance of revitalization as a preventive measure against continued deterioration. Park Plaza provides an example of how a neglected riverfront can become a prime attraction not only for a city but also for an entire region. Park Plaza has become a regional downtown center. This redevelopment was accomplished by private enterprise without benefit of tax moneys or government aid. As with any central business district redevelopment project, whether private or government, the cooperation of civic and business leaders was a vital factor.

The project encompasses 18 acres, including 447,000 square-foot integrated structures along 1,100 feet of riverfront. Retail, commercial, cultural, social, and recreational facilities are provided. The second phase includes a high-rise bank–office building, a motor hotel, and a motion picture theater.

Bounded by the Fox River, Pearl Avenue, Division Street, Commerce Street, and Jackson Street, Park Plaza draws almost 50 percent of its shoppers from within a 40- to 50-mile radius of Oshkosh—the heart of central Wisconsin. While oriented toward the river, the complex has become totally integrated with the downtown business district since its opening in 1970.

An enclosed L-shaped mall, more than 800 feet long and topped with a two-level 1,200-car parking structure, links Park Plaza's two major department stores—H. C. Prange and Co. and Sears, Roebuck and Co.—and Kohl's Food Store, the city's largest. To create a feeling of continuity for the complex, Park Plaza buildings, including the two department stores, are built of precast concrete wall panels and incorporate cast-in-place columns, floors, and roofs. The joists and girders of the roof and floors above grade are precast, prestressed concrete. Architectural concrete, formed in variations of woodlike patterns by polyvinylchloride form liners, is sandblasted to expose the aggregate and color and to improve the texture.

A 500-seat restaurant, with space for public meetings and social functions, overlooks the river and adjoins a contoured, terraced promenade, landscaped with several hundred trees, including red maples, honey locusts, flowering crabapples, Austrian black pines, weeping willows, Redmond lindens, and nearly 800 Japanese dwarf yews.

The center court, 80 feet high, is a focal point of many local activities; with choirs at Christmastime, boat shows, banquets, dances, auto shows, art shows and many other attractions not previously available to the citizens. Sculptures and other art forms in metal, stone, and glass produce varying moods and provide visitors with varied aesthetic experiences as they walk along the mall. Suspended from the ceiling of the court is an exceptional piece of polished-aluminum sculpture,

PARK PLAZA
Oshkosh, Wisconsin

ARCHITECTS: Welton Becket & Associates
LANDSCAPE ARCHITECTS: Sasaki, Walker & Associates

BELOW: *Plaza entrance.* (*Photographer: Orlando Cabanban.*) BOTTOM: *General view of the redevelopment area.* (*Photographer: Munroe Studios, Inc.*)

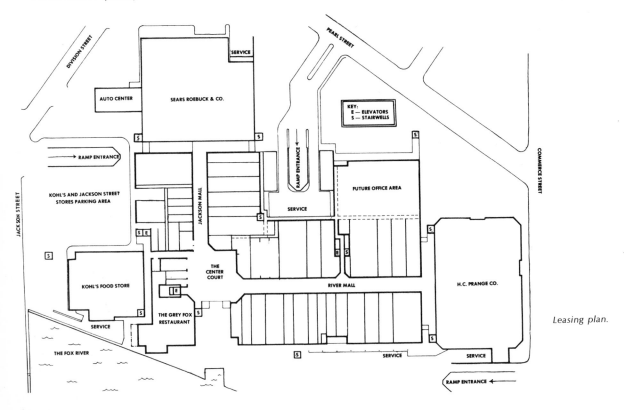

Leasing plan.

Court and sculpture entitled Triad. (Sculptor: Astides Demetrious; sculpture of polished aluminum, 3' x 30'. Photographer: Orlando Cabanban.)

30 feet high and containing three motorized, rotating elements. The sculptor is Astides Demetrious. To avoid a staid appearance, Park Plaza changes the 18-foot squares of carpeting in the malls to correspond with the changes of season; tans, oranges, and browns are used in the fall, and soft, warm pastels in the spring.

A ground-level mall was required to integrate with downtown pedestrian traffic, but soil conditions near the river prevented the building of underground parking structures. As a result, the architects planned two parking levels above the mall, a concept which solved the parking problems while giving the structure added interest. Three main parking ramps from Jackson, Pearl, and Main-Commerce carry cars to more than 1,200 parking spaces on the two deck levels. For the convenience and comfort of customers during cold weather, the major portion of the first parking level, located between the second floors of the department stores, is covered by a roof formed by the second parking level. The parking fee is kept at a minimum of 10 cents per hour. Other parking for approximately 100 cars is available near the food store. Visitors to Park Plaza can also dock their boats at piers opposite the esplanade. The privately owned busline is being subsidized by an assistance grant whereby the state pays two-thirds of the operating loss and the city pays one-third.

This redevelopment required much time and effort on the part of the developer, the architect, and city and state officials. To implement the project, the developer assembled twenty-six parcels of land on a deteriorating 18-acre site and razed more than twenty aged industrial buildings which once obscured the scenic beauty of the Fox River shoreline. The site was rezoned from light and heavy industry to the commercial category; this resulted in a better use value and a higher tax yield by enlarging the tax base through the improvement of downtown real estate and the stimulation of retail sales in the area.

To accommodate the project, tracks of three railroad companies were relocated to ease congestion on two of the city's main thoroughfares, Main and Jackson. The developers financed the relocation of one set of tracks. The city has spent most of its street funds for improving access to the downtown area (bridge, improved traffic intersections, and paving of main arterials). In addition, the State Highway Commission gave top priority to replacing a decaying drawbridge which spans the Fox River on Main (Highway 175), the principal feeder route of the Park Plaza project.

The developers are The Miles Kimball Company.

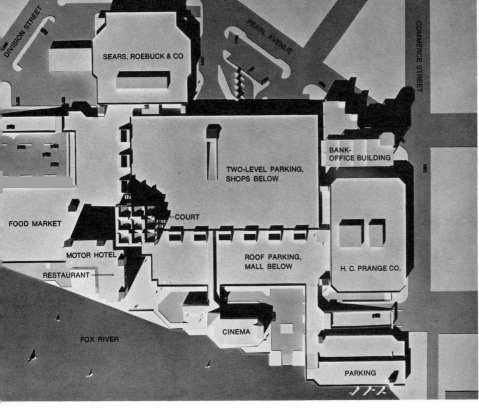

SEARS, ROEBUCK & CO

DIVISION STREET

PEARL AVENUE

COMMERCE STREET

BANK-
OFFICE BUILDING

TWO-LEVEL PARKING,
SHOPS BELOW

FOOD MARKET

COURT

MOTOR HOTEL

RESTAURANT

ROOF PARKING,
MALL BELOW

H. C. PRANGE CO.

FOX RIVER

CINEMA

PARKING

Roof plan.

ABOVE: *View of court from decked parking area.* (*Photographer: Orlando Cabanban.*) LEFT: *Detail of riverfront plaza.*

Riverfront view. (*Photograph courtesy of Welton Becket & Associates.*)

IDS CENTER

Minneapolis, Minnesota

ARCHITECTS: Philip Johnson and John Burgee
ASSOCIATE ARCHITECT: Edward F. Baker

In recent years, two significant features of downtown Minneapolis have brought it considerable national attention. One is the mall, a tree-lined, pedestrian-oriented, ten-block extension of Nicollet Avenue which extends through the heart of the city's shopping district. The other is the skyway system, a series of enclosed walkways that bridge streets at the second-story level, connecting buildings of various commerce over a twelve-block downtown area with bridges to protect pedestrians during inclement weather.

The problems involved in connecting the skyway bridges into the existing buildings were many. The only way this could have been accomplished was through the complete cooperation of building owners, since this is a 100 percent private enterprise. It was made possible in downtown Minneapolis because several buildings and blocks are owned by one corporation or individual; for instance, IDS Properties, Inc., owns three blocks of office buildings in downtown Minneapolis. These skyways go through the office buildings, which also have retail selling on the second floors. According to IDS Properties officials, the biggest problem in putting in the skyways involved tying them in with two major department stores; both these buildings are older, and one is of wooden brick, six stories high and with a cast-iron front. The level variations of the stores caused other problems. (For a detailed discussion of skyway systems, see pages 35–36.) A dominant downtown feature is the IDS Center, a multistructure complex on a full block in the center of the city; it brings the mall indoors to a courtyard and adds new dimensions to skyway-level activities.

The main feature of the center's IDS tower is the Crystal Court, which links the tower to the other structures of the center and the skyway system of pedestrian bridges. Enclosed by a grid of steel and glass topped by plastic pyramids, the triangular canopy of the court rises to 120 feet from the second-story roof of Woolworth's to the eighth story of the tower. The day-lighted 20,000 square-foot Crystal Court encloses numerous retail and public service facilities on three levels. The second floor serves as a balcony and establishes connections with four skyways to surrounding buildings, making the court the heart of the city's unique skyway system. The court is accessible at street level by entrances on each side of the center, as well as through the lobby of the tower. Strollers on Nicollet Mall cut through a 40-foot-wide entrance.

LEFT, ABOVE: *Interior view of Crystal Court.* (Photographer: *Earl Chambers.*) LEFT: *Main view.* (Photographer: Nathaniel Lieberman.)

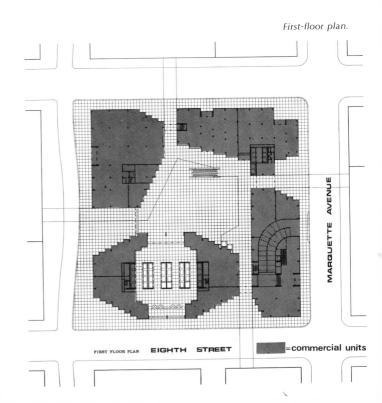

First-floor plan.

FIRST FLOOR PLAN   **EIGHTH   STREET**   ▮=commercial units

MARQUETTE AVENUE

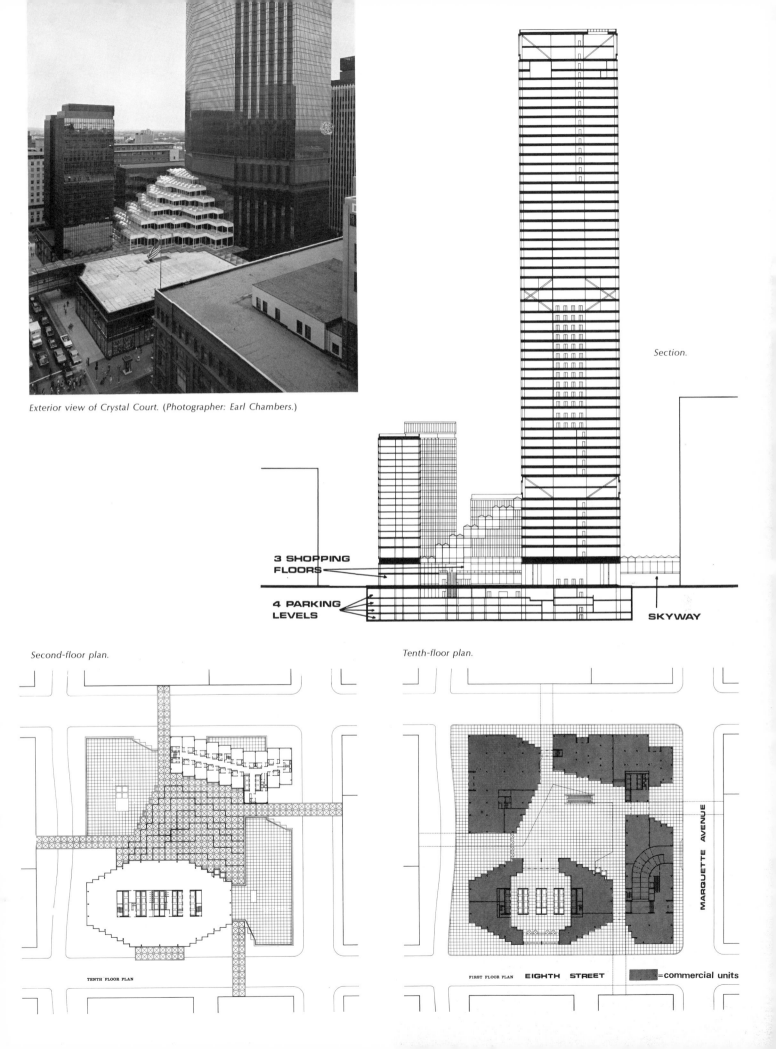

Exterior view of Crystal Court. (Photographer: Earl Chambers.)

Section.

3 SHOPPING FLOORS

4 PARKING LEVELS

SKYWAY

Second-floor plan.

Tenth-floor plan.

TENTH FLOOR PLAN

FIRST FLOOR PLAN **EIGHTH STREET**

MARQUETTE AVENUE

■ =commercial units

SAN BERNARDINO
CENTRAL CITY PROJECT

San Bernardino, California

ARCHITECTS: Gruen Associates
ASSOCIATE ARCHITECTS FOR ALL PUBLIC ELEMENTS:
  Armstrong/Ulmer

The central area of San Bernardino, California, a city of 100,000 people, was experiencing rapid physical, social, and economic decline. In 1963, an inventory of downtown structures revealed that half were well beyond the reach of rehabilitation or were too marginal to warrant renovation. Although San Bernardino serves a market area containing several hundreds of thousands of people, the obsolescent buildings, the dreary environment, and the awkward and inconvenient parking system, in combination with the availability of attractive suburban retail locations, had seriously affected Central City's economic vitality and had substantially impaired its ability to attract new investment.

The fact that every city is comprised of a unique combination of physical, social, economic, and political resources and conditions is one of the inescapable realities affecting the formulation and, more importantly, the implementation of an urban design program. This fact must be understood if any revitalization plan is to be successfully realized.

The worst of the downtown decline in San Bernardino was occurring in a 93-acre portion of Central City. Because of the critical level of social, economic, and physical deterioration, this area was cleared, and only three structures were left standing. A development program responding to San Bernardino's objectives and capabilities was prepared calling for construction on the cleared land of retail, office, financial, entertainment, restaurant, residential, civic, and cultural facilities, with all elements tied to a 1,400-foot-long pedestrian spine containing a wide variety of activities and settings; these range from an enclosed, air-conditioned shopping mall linked by a pedestrian bridge across the city's principal street to a Civic-Cultural Center set in a network of open-air plazas, courts, gardens, and arbors. The Civic-Cultural Center was designed to contain not only public buildings—the new City Hall, a theater, and an exhibit and conference hall—but private development of various kinds as well.

Basic to the renewal strategy was the understanding that the city's revitalization objectives could be achieved only through attraction of major private capital investment from outside. Clearly, inducements were needed, and there was no hesitation on the city's part to provide them. The anticipation of 35,000 daily visitors to the central-area retail center did in fact stimulate interest among developers of other than retail facilities, but the task of bringing private capital into a declining downtown area was difficult. As an additional inducement, San Bernardino has created a $12.5 million Civic-Cultural Center on a 12-acre parcel adjoining the new retail element immediately to the west. The development includes the new six-story City Hall, a 2,400-seat theater for the performing arts,

BELOW: *Bridge between cultural and shopping centers (model), area C.* BELOW, RIGHT: *San Bernardino City Hall.*

an exhibit hall and conference center complex, a network of public plazas, courts, gardens, and a five-level 1,600-car parking structure. All these were completed in 1972, except for the theater building. These civic buildings are sited so that the interior, which is less commercially desirable land, was used for public buildings and spaces, leaving the important outside and corner locations available to private investors. Currently open are four- and ten-story office buildings with financial institutions on the ground floor and office space above. Under construction is a three-story office building with adjoining commercial space on the street level. Plans also call for a four-story office building and 208-room hotel.

Because the buildings in the development are connected and thus form a unified complex, they all share in the plaza system—an urban park with shade trees, lawns, fountains, pathways, and garden courts. Terracing provides a smooth transition from D Street to the pedestrian bridge across E Street, which will link the Civic-Cultural Center to the central retail core.

Revitalization of the retail area was considered absolutely necessary if it was to compete successfully with outlying centers and achieve the stated objective of an economically alive and healthy downtown. More important, perhaps, the impact of the 35,000 visitors a day, which is projected for the planned 1 million square-foot retail complex, would assure the development of other Central City uses and facilities and the achievement of various social as well as economic goals.

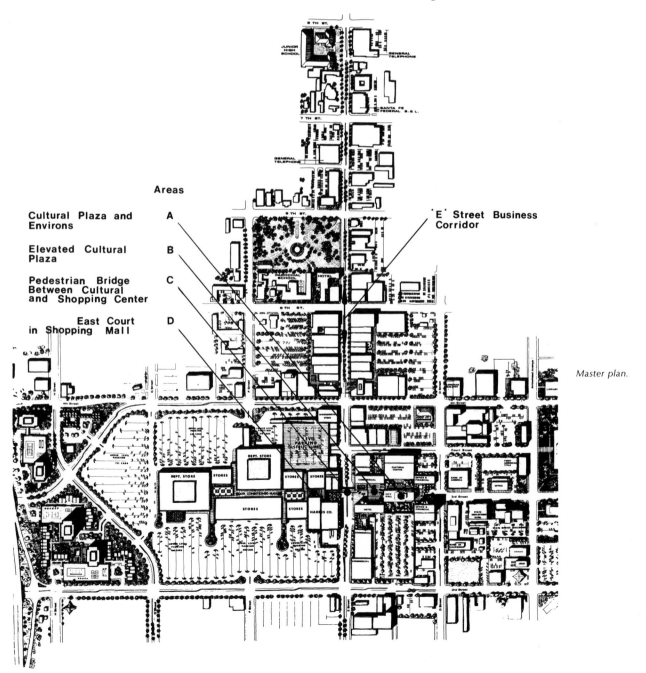

Areas

Cultural Plaza and Environs   A

Elevated Cultural Plaza   B

Pedestrian Bridge Between Cultural and Shopping Center   C

East Court in Shopping Mall   D

'E' Street Business Corridor

Master plan.

Aerial view of model showing completed and proposed structures. (1) Completed City Hall; (2) completed four-story office building; (3) completed ten-story office building; (4) existing buildings; (5) completed five-level 1,500-car parking structure; (6) completed three-story office building with adjoining commercial space at street level; (7) planned 208-room hotel; (8) planned four-story office building; (9) completed two-level enclosed Central City mall; (10) completed three-level parking structure; (11, 12, 13) the three department stores that anchor the mall; (14) proposed fourth department store; (15) proposed transportation link to join the Central City mall with the existing Inland Center (not shown in model). (Photographer: Gordon Sommers.)

To provide incentives for outside retail investment, San Bernardino embarked on the following implementation program completed in 1970:

1. Construction of an enclosed two-level shopping mall with an area of approximately 155,000 square feet which is used for civic gatherings and public affairs, art exhibits, etc.

2. Provision for free parking in two structures accommodating a total of 2,700 cars as well as the same number of cars for parking at grade.

3. Furnishing all essential road and utility improvements.

This city mall became the catalyst for expansion into a large, privately developed three-department-store shopping complex with 100 tenant stores. The Urban Land Institute report of April–June 1973 points out:

> The Central City Mall has a unique set of ownership patterns. The entire parking area including all surface parking and the three level facility are publicly owned. This is also true of the two level air-conditioned mall. The department stores own the pads on which their buildings are located, and the shopping center developer owns the pads on which the mall satellite stores are located. Access to these pads is by easement assuring the right of access via the mall parking areas.
>
> The financing for the local share of the redevelopment project has been accomplished under a provision of California redevelopment law known commonly as tax increment financing.
>
> The relationships between the public and private sector are also unique. While the city considered the project sound, a developer was not enticed in the early stages of the redevelopment proposal; therefore, the redevelopment agency proceeded to design and construct the mall as evidence that the project would proceed. It was further determined that the public would also own the parking facilities with the developer retaining the right to use them at no cost. The public benefits include significant increases in revenues from rising assessed valuation, business licenses, and sales taxes. In exchange the city is responsible for the operation and the maintenance of these public areas. Individual merchants pay essentially no common area charges.

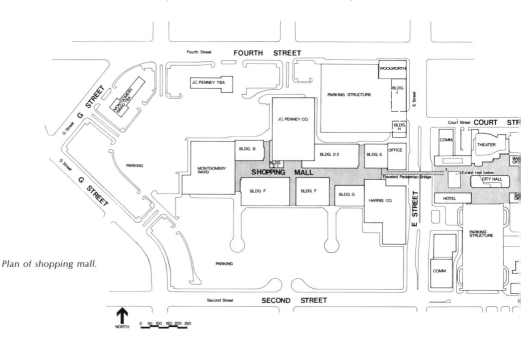

Plan of shopping mall.

The developer, John S. Griffith & Company, offers the following comments:

We would probably not enter into another arrangement where the mall was built free standing in advance of store buildings. It added additional cost to both mall and stores since HUD would not allow common structural elements. It also created design problems for store buildings.

A downtown location creates problems of non-shopper use of parking. It is probable that experience will show a parking ratio of 3.7 was insufficient, given the encroachment by non-shopper users. [Parking ratio is the proportion of the parking area to leasable area.]

Management control of the public areas should be given to the developer. Maintenance and security responsibility should have been under the shopping center management rather than the city.

A major merchandising problem has been to combat the "downtown" image which in particular implies lack of night time safety.

The developer should expect to use more personnel to provide coordination with the redevelopment agency and the city during the development and start-up time for a project of this type.

Not withstanding many problems that required creative solutions, the developer feels that the concept embodied in the Central City Mall is good and is sufficiently convinced to be participating in another similar effort in another community.

Comments from City Officials and Redevelopment Agency:

While the necessity for showing good faith required the construction of the mall and parking areas in advance of acquisition of a developer, it would have made more sense to build all elements at one time. It would have been better if the developer had maintenance responsibility but, again, this was deemed a necessary incentive to attract a developer initially.*

Debutante ball in Central City mall.

The Civic-Cultural Center complex occupies 11.5 acres of the total 93-acre urban renewal area. The Urban Land Institute report of April–June 1973 states:

Integration of public and private uses was the key to the design philosophy for the Civic Center Complex. Unlike many civic centers where public buildings stand in isolation from surrounding commercial and office activity, these uses are blended and interrelated in the San Bernardino Civic Center Cultural Complex. The plaza, running in a stepped terrace from 3rd and D streets through to the Central City Mall, is a promenade of distinction. It is designed to be alive with people. Around it are grouped uses that will generate the pedestrian traffic.

Because of the cruciform block design, public and private land uses alternate on any frontage of the superblock. City hall in the center of the block provides a civic focus for San Bernardino without isolating itself from the business and commerce of the city. The exhibit and conference facilities that are under the pedestrian plaza are designed to be serviced by the adjacent hotel site. The hotel, therefore, will not be required to create any significant meeting space within its design. The parking facility is to be used in common by all the land uses in the superblock, public and private alike.

The overall financing of the Central City project is being accomplished under a federally funded urban renewal program.

However, the financing of the local share is being accomplished under a unique provision of California redevelopment law commonly known as tax increment financing. Under this provision at the time the redevelopment plan is approved the assessment rolls for properties within the redevelopment area are frozen at the then level of assessed valuation. Subsequent to that "freeze" that portion of the taxes collected that are equal to or less than the base year are paid into the funds of the respective taxing agencies; however, that portion of the taxes levied each year in excess of the amount established by the base assessed value are paid into a special fund of the redevelopment agency to pay the principal and interest on loans, indebtedness, etc. In conjunction with issuance of bonds, the redevelopment agency may irrevocably pledge this portion of the tax income, the new tax increment, for payment of principal and interest on such indebtedness. The tax increment financing works best when the pace of redevelopment is fast since this results in the least loss of taxes to the community resultant from clearance and the earliest start of debt repayment through new tax increment. With this ability to pledge the new tax increment for repayment, redevelopment bonds are much more attractive since they in fact become a form of revenue bonds.†

The developer-owners of the private portion are: John S. Griffith and Company and Curci-Turner Company.

*Reprinted with permission from the Urban Land Institute, 1200 Eighteenth Street, N.W., Washington, D.C. 20036. Copyright 1973.
†Ibid.

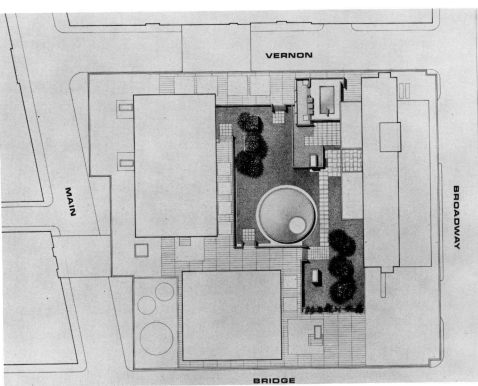

BAYSTATE WEST
Springfield, Massachusetts
ARCHITECTS: Pietro Belluschi and
Eduardo Catalano

ABOVE: *Aerial view of center.*
(*Photographer: Xenophon A. Beake.*)
ABOVE, RIGHT: *Top view of site.*

Baystate West is a $52 million redevelopment complex located on the prime block in the heart of downtown Springfield, Massachusetts. It was developed and is owned by the Massachusetts Mutual Life Insurance Company.

The complex consists of 200,000 square feet of enclosed retail space on two levels, a three-level covered parking garage for 1,250 cars, a 300,000 square-foot office tower, a landscaped plaza deck on the sixth level, and a 270-room motor hotel. It is managed by Baystate West, Inc., a wholly owned subsidiary of Massachusetts Mutual.

Baystate West was first conceived by the Springfield Central Business District, Inc., in the early 1960s, when a small group consisting of the major banks, two insurance companies, two utilities, two major downtown department stores, and other smaller businesses came together to provide the funds for the necessary surveys to determine what steps needed to be taken.

Redevelopment of the prime block, which was the biggest revenue producer for the city in terms of tax money, was the only logical choice for Springfield, and the Springfield Central Business District, Inc., launched the planning and early development. In the mid-1960s it announced the Baystate West concept at a projected cost of $25 million. Massachusetts Mutual pledged a first mortgage of $18 million at that time.

By 1967, the cost had risen to $35 million, and the project was in jeopardy; the Springfield CBD was finding it difficult to raise the additional funds, and a question of legality arose over the equity position of the banks, who, according to the state laws, were considered owners and would be exceeding the maximum amount of equity allowed at that time.

At this point, Massachusetts Mutual was approached and was asked to take over the building of the project, and in the fall of 1967 the company directors approved the idea to acquire the entire project.

Demolition of the block located between the two major department stores started the same year and was conducted in phases to make the relocation as easy as possible; the planners developed a way of constructing the unusual complex in stages so that all of it would come together at the end at the same time.

Also, because of the determination of the owners to complete the project on schedule, work went on around the clock, seven days a week, for a period of several months so that the tower, with its precast concrete slabs weighing on the average of 4 tons a section, could be enclosed. This was done so that the tower crane could be used for normal construction activities during the day and then used at night for the lifting of the slabs.

Because of the urgent need for parking space in this area, each garage floor was utilized immediately upon completion at a low rate subsidized by the owners. This policy helped attract shoppers back downtown, prior to the opening of the balance of the project.

The hotel showed great promise; it had excellent bookings even before it opened its doors, indicating the faith and confidence that people and organizations were placing in the facility.

Also significant in the history of Baystate West was the fact that Springfield's businessmen, with the cooperation of the municipal officials, had the vision to buy up the major revenue-producing block a parcel at a time, tear it down, and build a brand-new structure designed to begin the economic revival of the downtown area, restore the citizens' pride in their community, and serve as a catalyst for other redevelopment in the future.

Baystate West also serves the community well because of its location adjacent to Interstate Highway 91, running north and south, with entrance and exit ramps almost at the entrance to the parking garage. The interstate highway is connected to the Massachusetts Turnpike, running east and west, by another interstate facility, putting downtown Springfield within easy driving distance for shoppers from southern Vermont, all of western Massachusetts, eastern New York State, and northern Connecticut.

The Springfield Civic Center, located three blocks south of the complex and situated right on Main Street, has joined with Baystate West in turning the tide of economic decay. The center was constructed by the city of Springfield with a bond issue of $10 million as part of the Court Square urban renewal project.

The center, opened in 1972, had continual bookings through 1973 of major entertainment shows, sports activities, conventions, and trade shows. The facility can hold up to 10,000 for a convention and 8,000 for a sports activity, and it has an exhibition hall for trade shows attached to the arena, along with several banquet and meeting rooms.

The purpose of the center was obviously to restore Springfield as a major New England convention city, a prominence it held prior to World War II, and to assist in bringing people back to the downtown area for entertainment, which will also help to stimulate the increased sales that are being sought.

Behind the civic center, a parcel has been purchased by a Boston developer for housing to include high-rise luxury apartment buildings, medium-rise apartment buildings for the elderly, and apartments of the townhouse variety for low-income families. Adjacent to the center, a New York firm has developed a privately owned parking garage for 1,250 cars. It is designed for future expansion. Other private redevelopers have purchased existing downtown properties. They are modernizing the buildings to harmonize with the new image.

Another item of interest is the airwalk system. Baystate West is connected to the two major department stores by second-level enclosed airwalks, which are used both as passageways and as retail sales space by the stores. The ultimate plan is to connect all the downtown area with these airwalks. Baystate West was also structurally built to accommodate a third airwalk to cross another street into

Public area. (Photographer: Xenophon A. Beake.)

any new development that might be undertaken in the future on the block to its immediate north.

The complex was constructed under Massachusetts Legislation 121A, the same legislation used for the Prudential Center in Boston. The legislation, passed to encourage private redevelopment, allows the developer—subject to the approval of the State Department of Community Affairs, the Legislature, the Governor, and in this case the Insurance Commissioner—certain advantages necessary in view of the archaic building codes and the problems involved in a development of this magnitude. A developer under 121A legislation is given the power of eminent domain to acquire property, similar to the power granted to a public agency; the right to negotiate a tax contract with the city for forty years; and the right to negotiate building code variances in a package with the city. The legislation also limits the developer to a maximum of 6 percent return on the dollar, with any excess going to the city in the form of tax payments and any amount over these payments being used only for modernization and improvement. A developer is also prohibited from selling the complex at any time during the forty-year period to anyone except another 121A developer.

In the construction of Baystate West, the power of eminent domain was not used with the parcels purchased at an average cost of $43 a square foot. A tax contract was negotiated with the city which provided revenue on an escalating basis during construction. The first payment was more than the largest amount the city had ever received from the old property. Payments are based on a minimum versus a percentage of gross income after it is operational which is also based on an escalating percentage. For example, in 1967 the city received $198,000 in taxes from the old property, and in 1968 Baystate West paid $208,000. Now that the complex is open, the payments start at a $400,000 minimum versus 15 percent and then move up to $500,000 and 20 percent over a ten-year period. It is anticipated that the minimum will never be paid and that by 1981, the city will receive in excess of $1 million in tax revenue. The agreement is such that the city has a guarantee that is close to the normal amount of taxes that would be received under the ad valorem system of taxation, but it also shares in the profits as the project grows and succeeds. Thus the city is assured of its tax revenue, and developers have a guarantee and a predictability of their taxes in the years ahead.

The project architect, Eduardo Catalano, comments:

> The project began to trigger in downtown Springfield other large developments, like the civic center, the new Hall of Justice, and two new shopping-hotel-office complexes. With Baystate West we joined three city blocks with covered airwalks and plan to extend the concept to other blocks into Court Square. The airwalks linking two old department stores are used for shopping and are 60 and 90 feet wide. Shoppers on the street are protected during bad weather by large overhangs over the sidewalk. This also allowed the site to be expanded; additional shopping and parking areas are provided on the floors above. Above the parking roof covering the entire site, a new site has been created with sunken gardens, a fountain, a swimming pool, walks, a hotel, a thirty-story office tower, and a pavilion for a private club. The shopping concept is to introduce the traditional small retail stores between two large department stores. There are two floors of shopping, with a mall formed by narrow streets and plazas like those in a small city. Each plaza of two floors is different in character and contains escalators.

ABOVE: *Interior of shopping mall. (Photographer: Xenophon A. Beake.)* RIGHT: *View of shops, overhang, and shopping airwalk across Main Street linking Baystate West to a department store. The sidewalks have been partially paved with red brick and have planters and benches. (Photographer: George Zimberg Architectural Photography.)*

Model of the CBD urban renewal plan looking north.

According to acting Director of Planning Norman R. Standerfer, the Oklahoma City Urban Renewal Authority came into existence in 1961. Three project areas were established: (1) the central business district, (2) the medical-center complex, and (3) the JFK residential area.

The central business district project has four phases. Much of the redevelopment in phase 1A has been undertaken, and all the referenced projects lie within its boundaries. The following are summaries of major new shopping facilities in CBD phase 1A.

Galleria. The galleria is a four-square-block enclosed shopping mall intended to regenerate retail sales in the CBD. It will contain major department stores, small shops and stores, 3,500 parking places, and accessory facilities. The galleria will be located near hotels, the Convention Center, the Myriad Gardens Park, the financial and office district, and the governmental district of the CBD.

Sheraton Century Center. This hotel-retail complex is programmed to occupy an entire block. A fifteen-story Sheraton hotel will have over 400 rooms, with an adjoining shopping mall that will contain 175,000 square feet of retail and public-use areas. The mall will contain shops, theaters, restaurants, and clubs.

Myriad Gardens Park. When built, this park will contain a sunken lake surrounded by four levels of active and passive park areas with a botanical garden spanning the lake. Built into the embankments will be shops, cafés, museums, libraries, clubs, and other public facilities.

Tunnel System. This privately built, all-weather tunnel system is open to the public and has shopping areas located along its length. The success of the clubs, restaurants, and places of business has prompted local business people to expand the network significantly. Construction has just begun on the expanded portion.

Parking Garages. It has been the policy of the Urban Renewal Authority to design the ground level of the parking structures for office or commercial use to avoid creating dead spaces in the city. Present structures contain relocated businesses,

OKLAHOMA CITY, OKLAHOMA

ARCHITECTS:
For the model of the CBD urban renewal plan and the proposed metro concourse system: I. M. Pei
For the galleria: Frankfurt-Short-Emery-McKinley
For Sheraton Century Center: Hudgins-Thompson-Ball & Associates For Myriad Gardens: Conklin & Rossant
ASSOCIATE ARCHITECTS FOR MYRIAD GARDENS:
Hammer, Greene, Siler Associates; Victor Tabaka & Associates

new restaurants, art galleries, and the offices of the Oklahoma City Chamber of Commerce.

Of special interest is the partly implemented plan to connect all major buildings in the CBD from N.W. Third Street to the Myriad Convention Center. This underground concourse will be lined with shops, restaurants, clubs, and offices. The already-completed part of the tunnel attracts 30,000 pedestrians a day, and its success guarantees the completion of the entire system. In addition, an overhead pedestrian walkway, or "pedway," is planned between the Sheraton Century Center Hotel and the parking structure.

Regarding financing, a three-party agreement between the city of Oklahoma City, HUD, and the Oklahoma City Urban Renewal Authority was announced in June 1973, covering an amendment to the downtown project 1A in the amount of $34.7 million. This grant will enable the Oklahoma City Urban Renewal Authority to bring into development the retail galleria, as envisioned in the Pei plan, as well as the two half blocks north and south of City Hall for added municipal offices.

The allocation of these federal funds, amounting to nearly $125 million, has continued to spur private development in Oklahoma City. The Presbyterian Hospital is under construction in the medical-center area. The city's first minority-owned bank, the Medical Center State Bank, is in operation on North Lottie. A new building housing the schools of nursing and dentistry was completed in the Oklahoma Health Sciences Center. And in all three projects the Authority moved ahead with various types of public improvements—new streets, sidewalks, sewer and water lines, and public works.

The General Neighborhood Renewal Program (GNRP) study was conducted by several consultants, including I. M. Pei and Associates, and the final plan is referred to as the *Pei plan*.

Proposed metro concourse system in state of implementation.

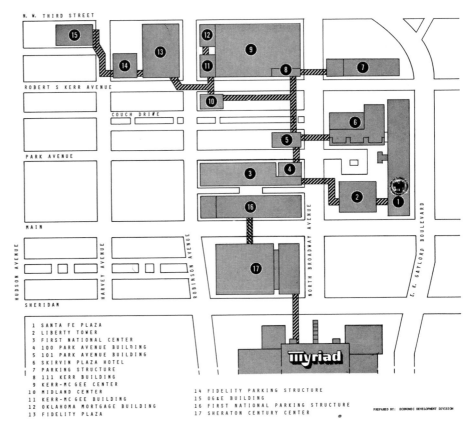

1 SANTA FE PLAZA
2 LIBERTY TOWER
3 FIRST NATIONAL CENTER
4 100 PARK AVENUE BUILDING
5 101 PARK AVENUE BUILDING
6 SKIRVIN PLAZA HOTEL
7 PARKING STRUCTURE
8 111 KERR BUILDING
9 KERR-MCGEE CENTER
10 MIDLAND CENTER
11 KERR-MCGEE BUILDING
12 OKLAHOMA MORTGAGE BUILDING
13 FIDELITY PLAZA

14 FIDELITY PARKING STRUCTURE
15 OG&E BUILDING
16 FIRST NATIONAL PARKING STRUCTURE
17 SHERATON CENTURY CENTER

PREPARED BY: ECONOMIC DEVELOPMENT DIVISION

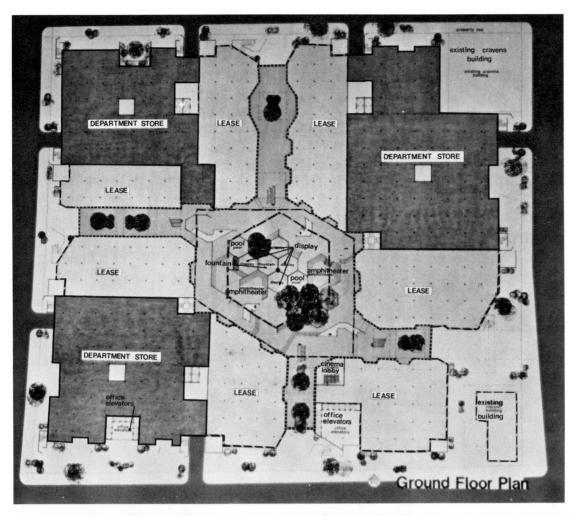

Ground Floor Plan

DEPARTMENT STORE

LEASE

LEASE

existing cravens building

existing cravens building

DEPARTMENT STORE

LEASE

LEASE

pool

display

fountain

fountain

display

amphitheater

amphitheater

pool

amphitheater

display

DEPARTMENT STORE

LEASE

LEASE

office elevators

office elevators

cinema lobby

office elevators

office elevators

existing building

existing building

property line

LEFT: *Site plan of ground floor of galleria.* BELOW: *Exterior of Sheraton Century Center (Model).*

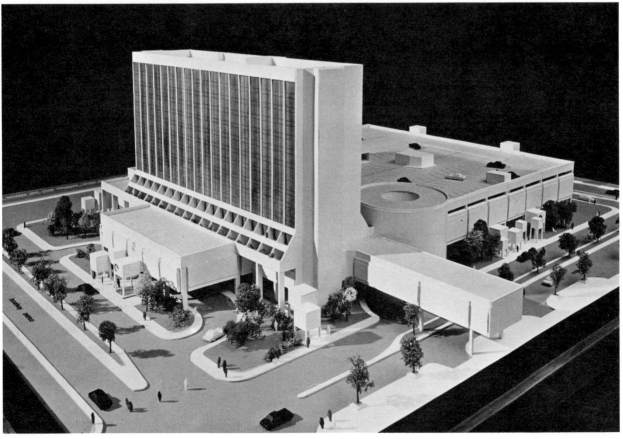

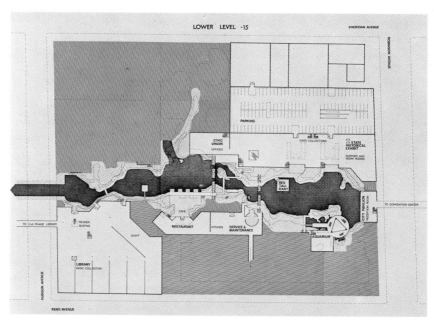

Myriad Gardens, plan of lower level (−15).

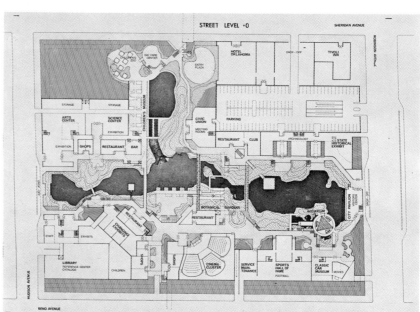

Myriad Gardens, plan of street level.

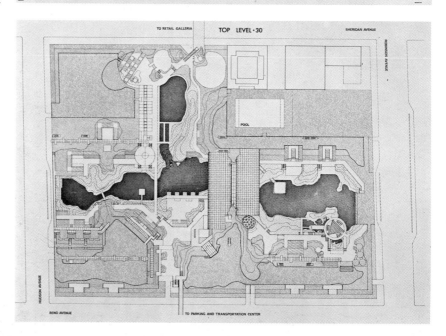

Myriad Gardens, plan of top level (+30).

The inner part of Sydney, a city with a metropolitan population of over 2½ million people, suffers from the same ills that afflict other cities in the Western world. The fact that multistory buildings now cover entire sites formerly occupied by small buildings fronting narrow streets causes inevitable congestion; the surrounding footpaths are inadequate for the pedestrian circulation, and the new buildings are robbed of light and air. Often oppressive and dark canyons are created between new buildings facing each other across a narrow street.

The Australia Square Project aimed at remedying these situations and bringing a new openness to the congested heart of the inner city. It approached the problem of rebuilding in a comprehensive rather than a fragmented way. The Australia Square Project brought under one ownership an entire city block bounded on its four sides by George Street, Bond Street, Pitt Street, and Curtin Place, an area of 60,000 square feet or approximately 1½ acres. Over a period of years the owners were able to amalgamate more than thirty different properties to create this large site in the very center of the business district and adjacent to Wynyard Station, the focal point of Sydney's electric suburban trains.

Although attempts were made to persuade the railway authorities to permit the construction of an underground tunnel to connect the project directly to the station, this concept unfortunately floundered. The Sydney City Council, however, agreed to the closing of the narrow existing internal streets and their absorption in the site. In exchange, the owners gave a strip of their site (equal in area to the closed streets) to the city. This allowed the widening of Bond Street from 30 to 50 feet.

From the outset, only two structures of minimal site cover were planned. The first one, a rectangular thirteen-story 150-foot-high building facing Pitt Street, was built prior to the amalgamation of the site. The second, a fifty-story 600-foot-high tower covering only 25 percent of the site, contained the balance of allowable floor area.

A circular form for the tower building was arrived at by a process of elimination. Any rectangular building of such height and extent placed on this site would inevitably have created objectionable canyon-type spaces in conjunction with the adjacent buildings, which follow the rectangular street pattern. This would have resulted in poor lighting and a crowded appearance. These considerations led

AUSTRALIA SQUARE
Sydney, Australia

ARCHITECTS: Harry Seidler & Associates
STRUCTURAL CONSULTANT ON THE TOWER:
  Professor Pier Luigi Nervi

Aerial view of site prior to amalgamation of all properties and closing of internal streets.

LOWER PLAZA PLAN

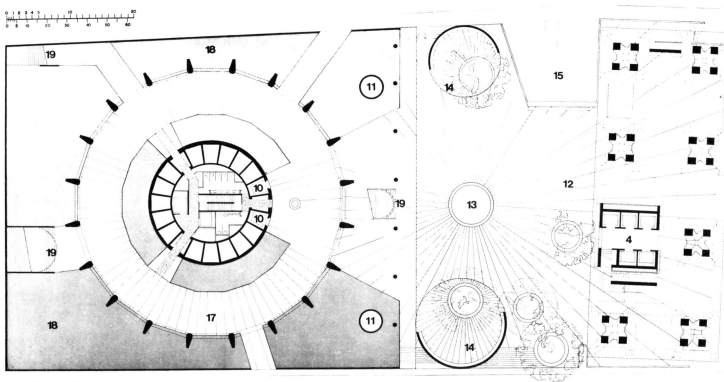

Plan of lower plaza showing the shopping.

1	UPPER PLAZA	9	HIGH RISE LIFTS
2	CALDER STABILE	10	EXPRESS LIFT TO TOP FLOOR
3	STEPS DOWN TO SHOPPING CIRCLE	11	VENT SHAFT
4	ENTRANCE LOBBY	12	LOWER PLAZA
5	TAPESTRY BY LE CORBUSIER	13	FOUNTAIN
6	TAPESTRY BY VASARELY	14	OUTDOOR RESTAURANT
7	LOW RISE LIFTS	15	RAMP DOWN TO PARKING
8	MEDIUM RISE LIFTS	16	PLAZA BUILDING

UPPER PLAZA PLAN

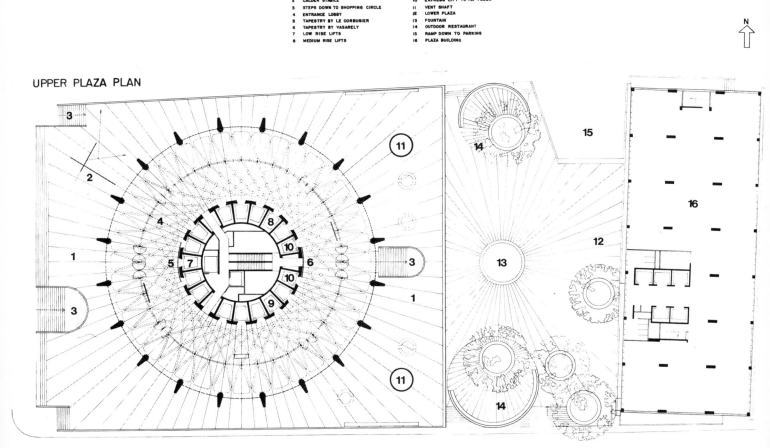

logically toward a circular building, which creates more desirable space relationships with adjacent properties and allows a maximum of light into surrounding streets. Wide, open spaces are created outside the window areas of such a building, which comes close to neighboring structures at one tangential point only. Both buildings have open ground floors, with arcades surrounding the entrance lobbies. As a consequence, virtually the entire site becomes public open space, interrupted only by entrances and stairs to the buildings. This newly gained openness in the busiest part of the city is developed as plaza areas open to the sky on two levels because of the slope of the ground. The lower plaza, level with Pitt Street, opens under the "gathered" column design of the thirteen-story "plaza" building, which becomes a kind of portico to the open space. The area extends into the circular shopping arcade under the upper plaza, which surrounds the entrance lobby of the main tower.

There is free access onto the lower plaza from all sides for easy pedestrian circulation. The design of the plaza aims at providing effective areas for recreation. By means of curved screen walls, planting beds, and benches, spaces are defined for outdoor restaurants and seating to give a sense of intimacy and enclosure. The surrounding streets are visually shut off from this outdoor space and are physically isolated by the plazas, which are raised above the footpaths. It is an area in which people can linger and relax. Judging by the large lunchtime crowds that are attracted, it fulfills an age-old need of city dwellers to find an area of retreat and intimacy. A fountain forms the focal point in this open space. It consists of vertical jets of aerated water in a programmed sequence of foamy rings in rising and falling sequences. At night, rings of colored spotlights are coupled into these sequences.

The outdoor area opens freely into the shopping arcade, which contains a full range of different retail shops selling clothing and food. The design of shop fronts has been coordinated by unifying their external framing and particularly by using standardized illuminated lettering. The diversity of the displays is thus emphasized because they gain in visual importance in relation to these neutral enclosures.

Below the bottom plaza and shopping arcade is a three-story parking station for more than 400 cars. The uppermost of these has a ceiling high enough to allow service vehicles to enter for deliveries to the shops and to the building generally. Unloading takes place adjacent to goods lift and storage areas.

An important feature is the use of art, both outside and inside. To one side of the main entrance near the corner of Bond Street stands Alexander Calder's 38-foot-high black stabile entitled *Crossed Blades,* a dynamic work to combat the visual confusion and hustle of George Street. On the inside wall are two large Aubusson tapestries. Facing George Street is Le Corbusier's *Unesco,* and on the east side hangs Vasarely's *Orion M.C.* Both are brilliantly colorful works, one embodying free form and lines, and the other a geometric pattern of bright colors, circles, squares, and ovals. The soft wool textures and folds of the tapestries impart a warmth to the public space, which is elsewhere surfaced with hard masonry materials. At night the tapestries are highlighted by the recessed "wall-wash" light fixtures, which illuminate the core wall evenly.

The owner is City Centre Development Ltd., a company owned jointly by Lend Lease Corporation Ltd. and British Financial Institutions. The lighting consultant is Edison Price (New York); graphics are by Harry Williamson.

ABOVE: *View from harbor.* RIGHT: *Detail of plaza restaurant.* (Photographer: Max Dupain, Max Dupain & Associates.)

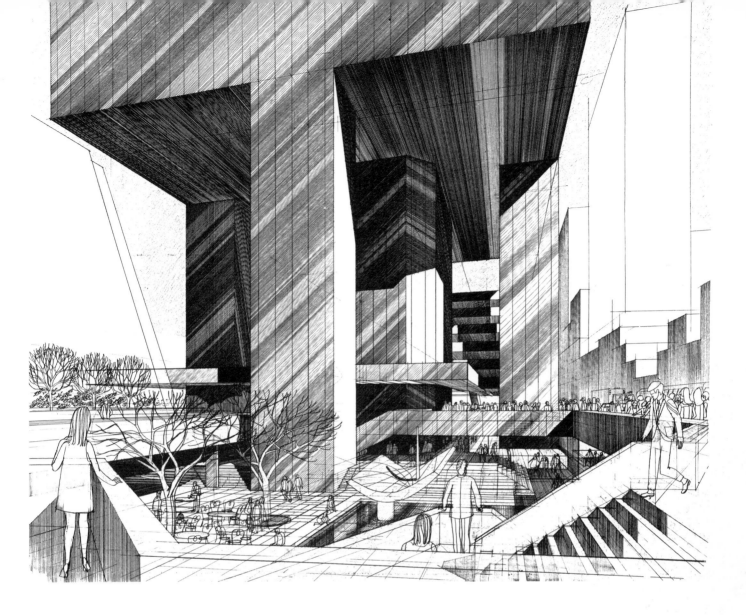

Citicorp Center, located at the intersection of two subway lines, is bounded by Lexington and Third Avenues and by Fifty-third and Fifty-fourth Streets. The center includes an office tower and retail-office mid-rise building, a church, a shopping galleria, an arcade, a concourse subway connection, and a plaza designed to provide interest and invigorating surroundings.

The architect raised the tower off the site and placed it on four 112-foot-high supercolumns, above street level. Beneath three sides of the tower base is a terraced eight-story retail-office building. An open-air plaza is positioned below street level at Lexington Avenue and Fifty-third Street. On the Lexington Avenue–Fifty-fourth Street corner a new freestanding St. Peter's Lutheran Church rises from the site of the original church. Nearly 1 million square feet of office space is included on its forty-six floors.

The design elements of the plan stress openness. Since the tower is raised above the site, sun and light reach the plaza, the street, and the terraced mid-rise office areas and filter through the church and shopping galleria. Only the columns and service core of the tower interrupt the view from Lexington Avenue.

At plaza level, water and landscaping welcome views to the church, office tower, galleria entry, and subway connection. The various activities within these areas are visible through the glass-enveloped façades surrounding the plaza.

A visually stimulating "open" space is the galleria, focal point of the mid-rise building. Rising seven stories to a skylighted roof, the galleria offers a sense of light and space removed from the heat and cold of outside Manhattan. Shoppers move from each of the three shopping levels, which form a "U" around the galleria. Escalators link over 65,000 square feet of retail space. The four office floors above

CITICORP CENTER
New York, New York

ARCHITECTS: Hugh Stubbins & Associates, Inc.
ASSOCIATE ARCHITECTS: Emery Roth & Sons

ABOVE: *Stairs (right) descend from Lexington Avenue and Fifty-third Street to Citicorp Center's sunken plaza, providing a pleasant city space. Access from Lexington Avenue to the tower is by pedestrian bridge (left).*

share the pleasant galleria view. Stepped back under the tower base, these floors enjoy additional light and views from street-side exposure, and they have their own outdoor terraces.

At Lexington Avenue street level, a pedestrian bridge leads to the glass-enclosed tower lobby and to an interior pedestrian "street" to the galleria. From the Fifty-third Street entry, through the lobby, a second inner shop-lined "street" reaches the galleria. One level below, two "streets" link the subway, church, and concourse plaza to the galleria. A through-block arcade between Fifty-third and Fifty-fourth Streets opens onto the galleria and completes Citicorp Center's continuous circulatory system.

The client is the First National City Bank.

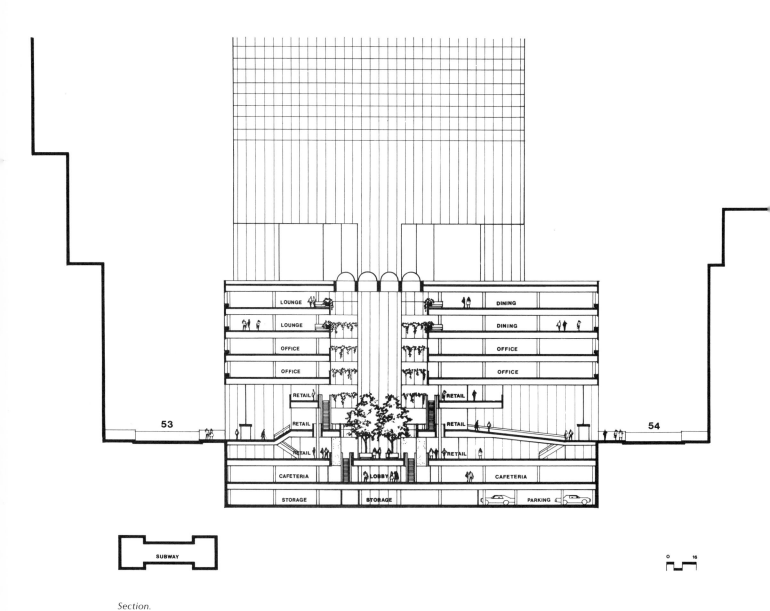

Section.

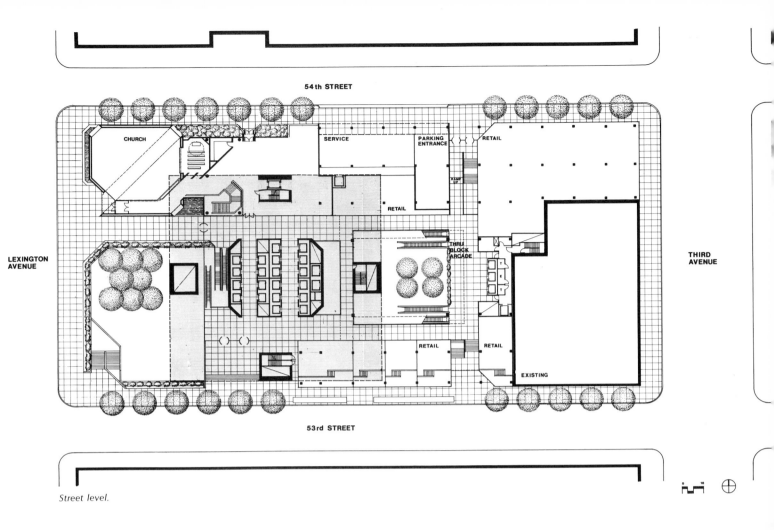

54th STREET

CHURCH

SERVICE   PARKING
          ENTRANCE   RETAIL

RETAIL

LEXINGTON
AVENUE

THRU
BLOCK
ARCADE

THIRD
AVENUE

RETAIL   RETAIL

EXISTING

53rd STREET

Street level.

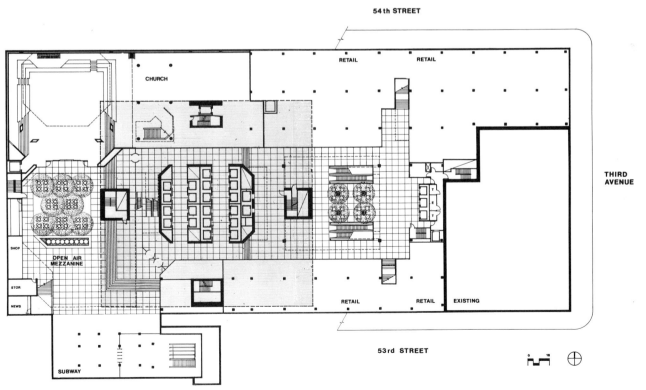

54th STREET

RETAIL   RETAIL

CHURCH

THIRD
AVENUE

SHOP

OPEN AIR
MEZZANINE

STOR

NEWS

RETAIL   RETAIL   EXISTING

53rd STREET

SUBWAY

Concourse level.

RIGHT: *The galleria, a seven-story-high skylighted space, provides three tiers of retail "streets." The 65,000 square feet of retail space is interconnected by escalators. This area is accessible from the tower, subway, and throughblock arcade.*

LEFT: *Model. General view.* [*Photographer: Ezra Stoller (ESTO).*]

According to Charles J. Urstadt, chairman and chief executive officer of the Battery Park City Authority, Governor Rockefeller in 1966 first proposed publicly that a "new town in town" be built at Battery Park on a landfill site in the Hudson River off lower Manhattan.

First, it was to turn what is now a nine-to-five, five-day-a-week financial and business area into a twenty-four-hour-a-day, seven-day-a-week community with housing, office and commercial facilities, and all the civic, recreational, and cultural facilities necessary to support the new community. Second, Battery Park City was to provide the city of New York with needed additional office-commercial and residential facilities which would be able to serve the needs of the entire city.

In order to implement the Governor's proposal to create this "new town in town," the state Legislature in 1968 created the Battery Park City Authority and gave it responsibility for demolishing existing piers in the 100-acre area in the Hudson River off lower Manhattan; dredging, bulkheading, and filling the area; putting in place all the utilities and civic facilities normally provided by the municipality; and selecting the private developers who will erect up to 6 million square feet of office space, 1 million additional square feet of commercial and shopping space and 14,100 residential housing units.

In the category of construction, landfilling was completed in the southernmost 16 acres of the site with sand dredged from the channels in the mouth of the lower harbor. This fill area is immediately adjacent to a 24-acre area which was filled with excavation from the World Trade Center, and the Authority's contractors extended this area an additional 100 feet into the Hudson to the pierhead line. The two areas together give a total land availability of more than 40 acres for construction. These 40-plus acres will serve as the site of the first 5,800 residential housing units, a 750,000 square-foot shopping center, and the office towers.

North of these 40 acres, the Authority has let a $24 million four-year contract which is now well under way to demolish the remaining piers and repeat the dredging, bulkheading, and landfill operation which was completed in the south-

BATTERY PARK CITY
New York, New York
COORDINATING ARCHITECTS: Harrison & Abramovitz
ASSOCIATE ARCHITECTS:
Jack Brown, AIA; Irving Gershon, AIA
  Horace Ginsbern & Associates
  John Graham & Company

Site location, aerial view. Adjacent to the heart of New York's financial district, Battery Park City's 91-acre site will extend from Battery Park, on the south, to Reade Street and will be bounded by the Hudson River and West Street.

Model showing public esplanade, which connects the entire development at an elevation of 7 feet above mean high water. The lower landscaped level serves as an area for relaxation and quiet activity. (Photographer: Louis Checkman.)

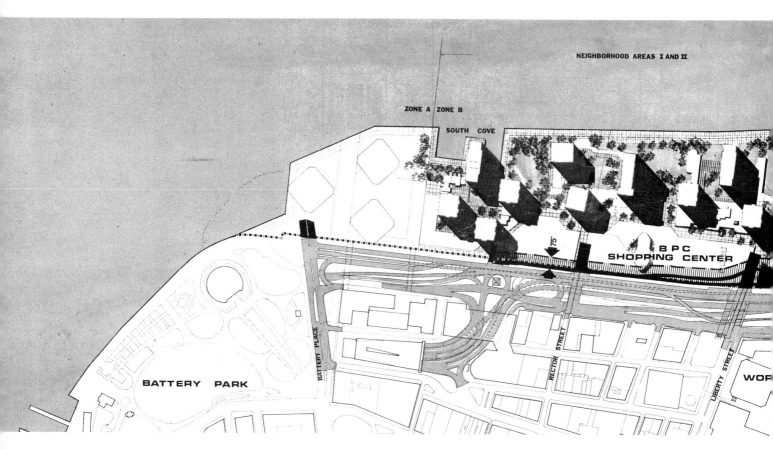

NEIGHBORHOOD AREAS I AND II.

ZONE A   ZONE B

SOUTH COVE

BPC SHOPPING CENTER

BATTERY PARK

BATTERY PLACE

RECTOR STREET

LIBERTY STREET

WO

ern 16 acres. This area, consisting of some 45 acres, will serve as the site of an additional 8,300 residential housing units, a school, and other civic and recreational facilities.

Financially, in May 1972 the Authority sold $200 million in bonds to finance the work now going forward as well as the construction of a major portion of the civic and recreational facilities which are the responsibility of the Authority. In addition, in 1973 the state Legislature transferred a $400 million authorization for Mitchell-Lama mortgages from the New York State Housing Finance Agency to the Battery Park City Authority and authorized the Authority to make up to 95 percent mortgage loans and act as the supervisory agency for more than 10,000 of the residential housing units.

The Authority entered into a letter of intent with a joint venture composed of principals of the Lefrak Organization and Fisher Brothers to erect the first 5,800 residential housing units, which will be contained in residential neighborhoods I and II, as well as the shopping center and related facilities.

The master plan for Battery Park City is the result of the teamwork of the Battery Park City Authority, the New York City Planning Commission, and the Office of Lower Manhattan Development.

Site plan.

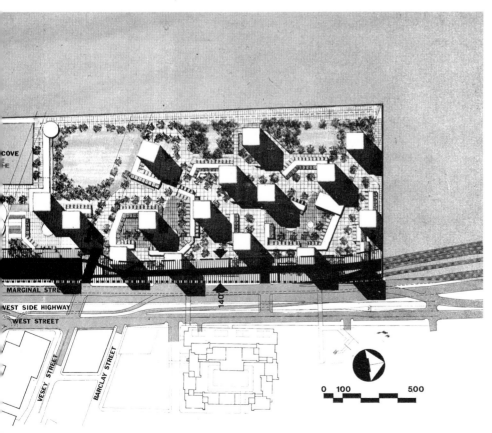

TIMES SQUARE
New York, New York

ARCHITECTS: **John Portman & Associates**

An important step in the revitalization of Times Square is the planned megastructure—a fifty-four-story hotel-retail complex to be located on the west side of Broadway between Forty-fifth and Forty-sixth streets, adjoining the theater district. The $150 million structure, designed by John Portman & Associates, will include a seven-story retail shopping center and a 2,000-room forty-eight-story hotel, opening on an inner central court.

Plans call for a new theater and glass-enclosed cafés at ground and roof levels. It is anticipated that this project will help to create a new environment in what is now a petty-crime area, with many "porno" arcades, bookstores, and "massage parlors." Times Square may again become the glamorous mecca for tourists that it once was.

Perspective view from one of the glass-enclosed restaurants.

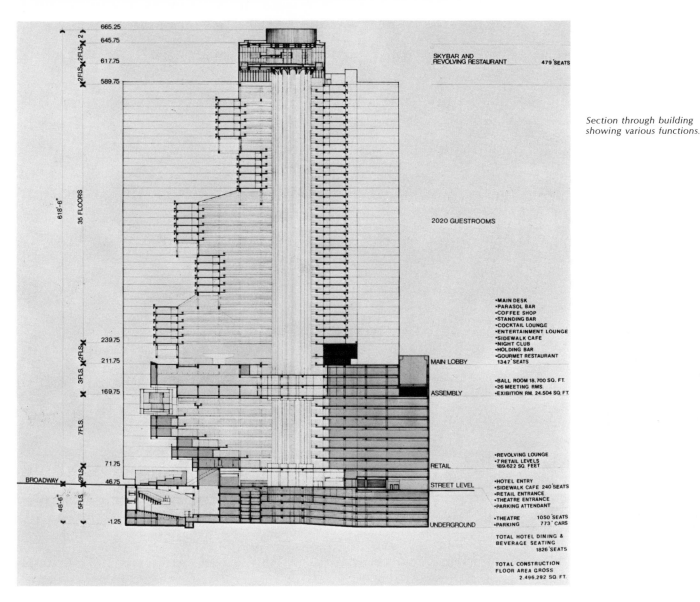

Section through building showing various functions.

665.25
645.75
617.75
589.75

SKYBAR AND
REVOLVING RESTAURANT   479 SEATS

618'-6"
35 FLOORS

2020 GUESTROOMS

•MAIN DESK
•PARASOL BAR
•COFFEE SHOP
•STANDING BAR
•COCKTAIL LOUNGE
•ENTERTAINMENT LOUNGE
•SIDEWALK CAFE
•NIGHT CLUB
•HOLDING BAR
•GOURMET RESTAURANT
  1347 SEATS

239.75
211.75   MAIN LOBBY

169.75   ASSEMBLY

•BALL ROOM 18,700 SQ. FT.
•26 MEETING RMS.
•EXIBITION RM. 24,504 SQ. FT.

71.75   RETAIL

•REVOLVING LOUNGE
•7 RETAIL LEVELS
  189,622 SQ. FEET

BROADWAY   46.75   STREET LEVEL

•HOTEL ENTRY
•SIDEWALK CAFE 240 SEATS
•RETAIL ENTRANCE
•THEATRE ENTRANCE
•PARKING ATTENDANT

-1.25   UNDERGROUND

•THEATRE   1050 SEATS
•PARKING   773 CARS

48'-6"

TOTAL HOTEL DINING &
BEVERAGE SEATING
                  1826 SEATS

TOTAL CONSTRUCTION
FLOOR AREA GROSS
             2,496,292 SQ. FT.

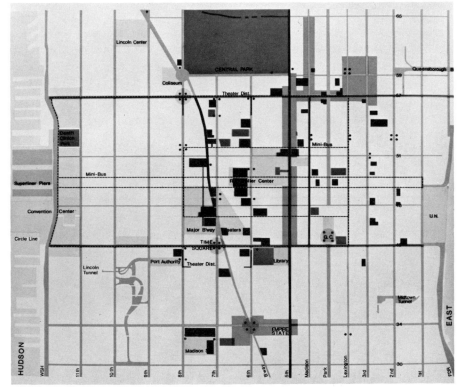

Site location of planned project.

ACTIVITY GENERATOR
MAJOR RETAIL
MAJOR OPEN SPACE
SUBJECT HOTEL
CONVENTION HOTEL
NEW OFFICE BLDGS '68+
PROPOSED HOUSING
MAJOR SUBWAY STOP

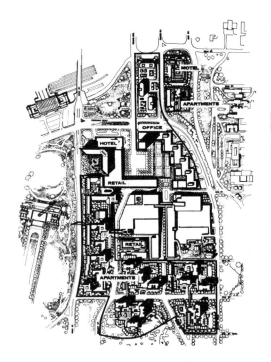

ABOVE: *Site plan.* RIGHT: *Perspective of the model showing proposed apartments in the foreground.*

CROWN CENTER

Kansas City, Missouri

ARCHITECTS:
For the master plan: Edward Larrabee Barnes, FAIA
For the Crown Center Hotel: Harry Weese
For apartments in phase one, including high-rise, terrace units, and condominiums: Architects Collaborative, Inc.
ASSOCIATE ARCHITECTS AND STRUCTURAL ENGINEERS: Marshall & Brown

Crown Center, a multimillion dollar urban development on the fringe of Kansas City's downtown business district, is a good example of how private industry can be instrumental in rebuilding deteriorated areas of the inner city.

Financed entirely by private capital, the complex is being developed by a subsidiary of Hallmark Cards, Inc., on 85 once-blighted acres surrounding the international headquarters of the Missouri-based greeting-card firm. It is located twelve blocks from the central business district, and it is expected to complement the main business area.

The groundbreaking took place in 1968, and the first structures to be completed were five seven-story interconnected office buildings, with a six-level underground garage for 2,300 cars. Also completed are a two-story bank building, a high-rise hotel, and a three-level shopping mall, which face a 10-acre square with underground parking for 4,000 cars.

Special emphasis in the planning of the complex was put on the creation of a pleasant "total environment." The hilly terrain was utilized to form the terrace leading to the central square. In addition to the landscaped planted areas, there are large fountains, pieces of sculpture by David Smith and Alexander Calder, specially designed street furniture, lighting, and graphics.

The owner is the Crown Center Redevelopment Corporation.

Aerial view of the completed part of the complex.

118

Aerial view of the city showing a superimposed model of the project in relation to the central business district.

Main entrance to Crown Center shops.

PARK CENTRE
Cleveland, Ohio

ARCHITECTS: Dalton·Dalton·Little·Newport

Stanley Cohen, editor of *Consulting Engineer* comments:

Cleveland has been refurbishing its center city since 1965, with some three quarters of a billion dollars worth of construction. The latest step in that redevelopment process is a $40 million complex of apartments and shopping facilities "Park Centre." Park Centre occupies 3½ acres on one square block of downtown Cleveland, bounded by 12th and 13th Streets and Superior and Chestnut Avenues. It was financed by a $32 million FHA loan . . . on the provision that all tenant services would be located in one square block.

Park Centre consists of twin 22-story towers with 500 apartments in each and a shopping center. The shopping center is at ground level and the floor below. It is planned for 125 retail shops, several restaurants, and a theater. The mall will be highlighted by court yards, escalators, and a glass-elevator. The four floors above the shopping center are parking levels for both tenants and shoppers, with space for 1,000 cars. The structure is of reinforced concrete, precast, post-tensioned, and prestressed. The shops and garage levels are on 62', double T, precast floors, on columns resting on spread footings. This area is topped with a plaza containing a pool, tennis courts, a recreation center, and landscaping, creating a park setting between the two towers.*

Park Centre was one of the winners of the 1974 Honor Awards for "high-quality architecture construction and superior site planning." This annual design-awards competition is sponsored by the Greater Cleveland Growth Association, the American Institute of Architects, the Garden Center of Greater Cleveland, and the American Society of Landscape Architects.

*Excerpted from an article by Stanley Cohen, editor, *Consulting Engineer*, August 1972.

Roof-terrace plane.

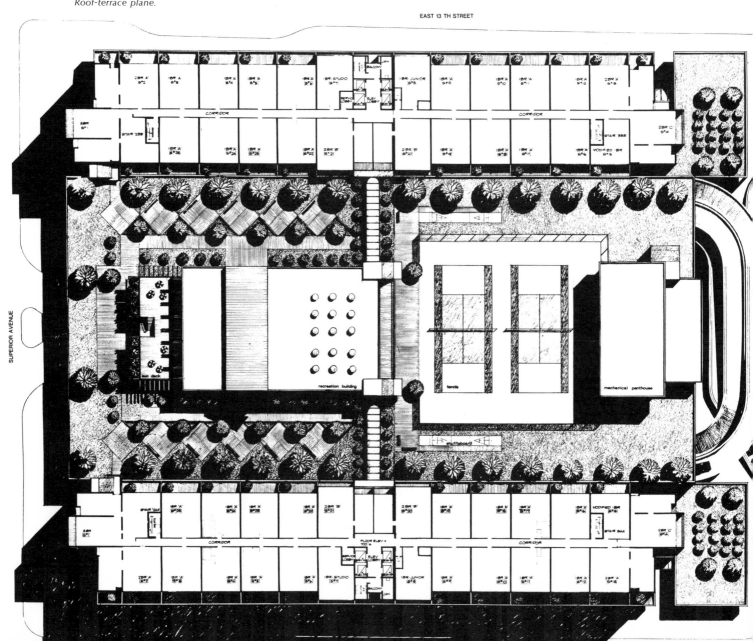

Aerial view of site.

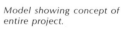

Model showing concept of entire project.

RIGHT: *Northeast exterior view.*
BELOW: *Interior of shopping mall
in completion stage.*

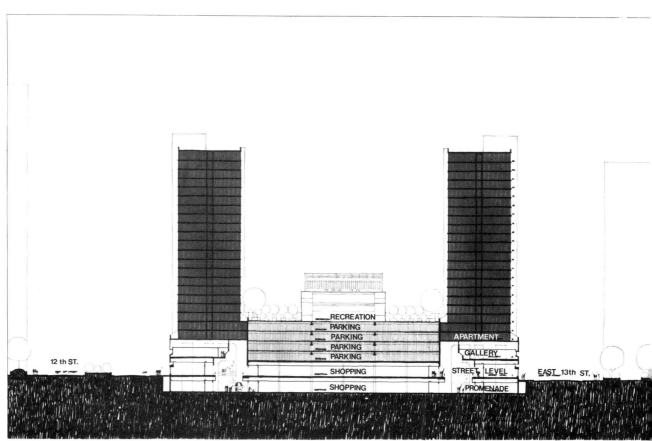

Section.

The building is built on air rights over the Canadian National railway tracks on a site of approximately 6 acres and occupies the area immediately south of Place Ville Marie and the CN block containing the Queen Elizabeth Hotel, Central Station, and the CN headquarters building.

The project was developed as a multiuse urban complex tied in with the existing weather-protected pedestrian system, which had already been developed in relation to Place Ville Marie and the CN block. The project is also directly connected to the new Montreal subway system and to the commuter tracks of the CN Central Station.

The content of the building, moving from bottom to top, is as follows:

Two levels of retail shopping directly connected to the enclosed pedestrian system, the subway, and city streets.

An exhibition hall of roughly 250,000 square feet designed to accommodate large temporary shows, such as the auto show and boat show with ancillary meeting and convention facilities.

Five floors, totaling about 1 million square feet, of merchandise-mart space designed for permanent exhibition facilities for Canadian manufacturers and wholesalers.

Office accommodation related in a flexible manner to the merchandise-mart space and providing the possibility of 100,000 square feet of office space.

An international exhibit area designed to provide permanent exhibition and office space in Montreal for all the principal trading nations of the world.

A 400-room hotel located on the roof of the building and oriented around a garden with a swimming pool, an outdoor dining area, and recreational facilities. The hotel lobby is located at roof level and is linked to the plaza hotel entry by express elevators.

Parking facilities are provided for approximately 1,000 cars in the west section of the project. A street-level landscaped plaza is developed over this parking facility and provides for an off-street entry for the hotel and a significant public open space for downtown Montreal.

The owner of the project is Place Bonaventure, Inc. The developer is Concordia Estates Development Co.

PLACE BONAVENTURE
Montreal, Quebec

ARCHITECTS: Affleck, Desbarats, Dimakopoulos, Lebensold Sise
LANDSCAPE ARCHITECTS: Sasaki, Dawson, Demay Associates, Inc.
ARCHITECT FOR PEDESTRIAN CONCOURSES: Vincent Ponte

Weather-protected pedestrian system in downtown Montreal. (Photographer: Arnott and Rogers Ltd.)

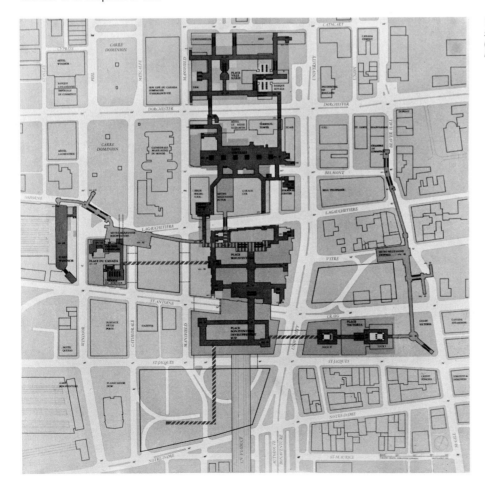

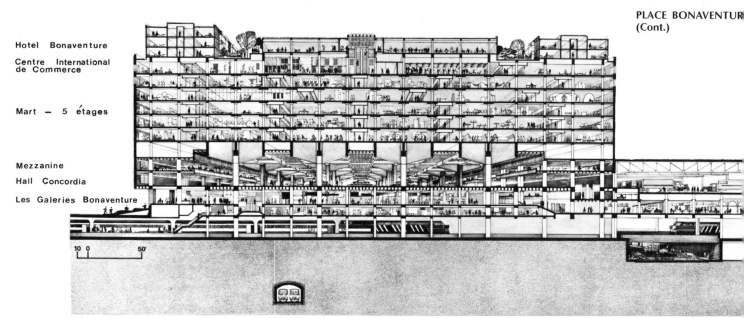

Hotel Bonaventure

Centre International
de Commerce

Mart — 5 étages

Mezzanine

Hall Concordia

Les Galeries Bonaventure

10 0   50'

Cross section looking east.
(Photographer: Arnott and
Rogers Ltd.)

Exterior view—west.
(Photographer: Chris F. Payne
Photography.)

South façade truck dock.
(Photographer: Chris F. Payne
Photography.)

The complex consists of 150,000 square feet of multilevel retail space containing seventy to eighty small, fashion-oriented shops and boutiques. It also contains underground parking for 500 cars and, above the retail space, a truck service area for both Eaton's and the proposed complex. Agreement has been reached with Metropolitan Structures, Inc., a major developer of office buildings, for the development as a separate project of a 300,000 square-foot office tower in the air rights above the shopping mall. The complex is situated in one of the very important retailing districts of downtown Montreal. It will abut and connect with the St. Catherine Street Eaton's store and will have an entrance in the McGill metro station, which serves as a link from that station south to Place Ville Marie and other major complexes in the heart of downtown. Another major entrance to the retail mall will be on St. Catherine Street, next to Eaton's and near two other major retailers, Simpson's and The Bay.

The project represents an important connective element within Montreal's famous underground network of pedestrian concourses, and it is believed that future development in this downtown sector, still one of the most viable urban areas in North America, will only enhance the competitive position of this project. The Bay already connects with the east end of the McGill metro station, and this project (along with Eaton's) will do the same at the west end.

The developers are the Rouse Quebec Ltd.

LES TERRASSES
Montreal, Quebec
ARCHITECTS: Webb, Zerafa, Menkes, Housden

Aerial view showing location of complex. (Photographer: Arnott and Rogers Ltd.)

LES TERRASSES (Cont.)

View looking north on McGill College Avenue from St. Catherine Street, showing the McGill entrance to the shopping mall.

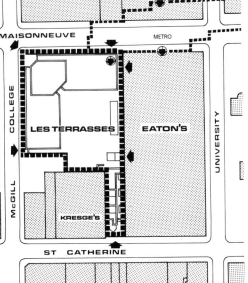

Site plan.

View showing the entrance from St. Catherine Street, with Eaton's department store on the right. A public plaza and a series of elevated landscaped terraces will replace what is presently Victoria Street.

Berkshire Common is considered a catalyst for the rejuvenation of the city's declining downtown area. Already, the impact of this new construction has been felt, not only in the interest it has generated concerning further improvements to the central business district, but also in the city's adoption of the new building code. The Common is expected to improve substantially the economic profile of Pittsfield, while establishing a direction for further development of a people-oriented city's core. This multiuse complex provides approximately 240,000 square feet of hotel-office-retail-parking facilities, organized around a landscaped plaza. Here, shade trees, benches, and an information and exhibition kiosk create an attractive meeting place and focal point for the complex.

At the perimeter of the 4½-acre site, building heights are low, maintaining the traditional retail scale of the neighborhood. This respect for surroundings, seen elsewhere in the restrained use of brick, oak, and stone, was a prime concern for the architects.

Advantage was taken of the site's 30-foot drop from South Street to Edwin Street to provide parking facilities for 320 cars unobtrusively and efficiently under the lower end and to permit two-level pedestrian access to shops at the higher end, as well as to the hotel. There is careful separation between vehicular and pedestrian traffic, and there is public and service access to all facilities. The sloping site permits two levels of shops, one fronting on the main business street and the other fronting on the interior plaza and covered arcade. Two-level shops have frontage on both areas. Two levels of office space are located directly above the shops, with the Berkshire Life Insurance Company, sponsor of Berkshire Common, the major tenant. The area covers approximately 54,000 square feet.

BERKSHIRE COMMON
Pittsfield, Massachusetts

ARCHITECTS: Hugh Stubbins & Associates, Inc.
SITE PLANNER AND LANDSCAPE ARCHITECT: John Wacker

Site plan.

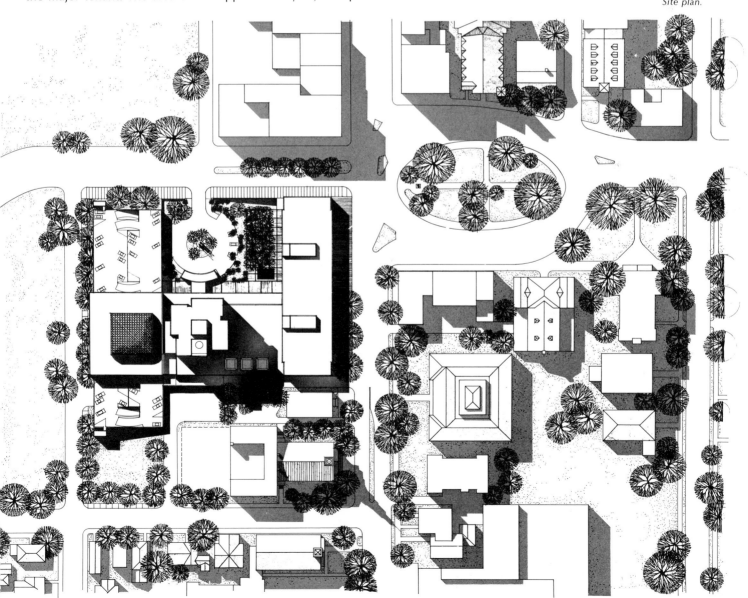

West Street

Edwin Street

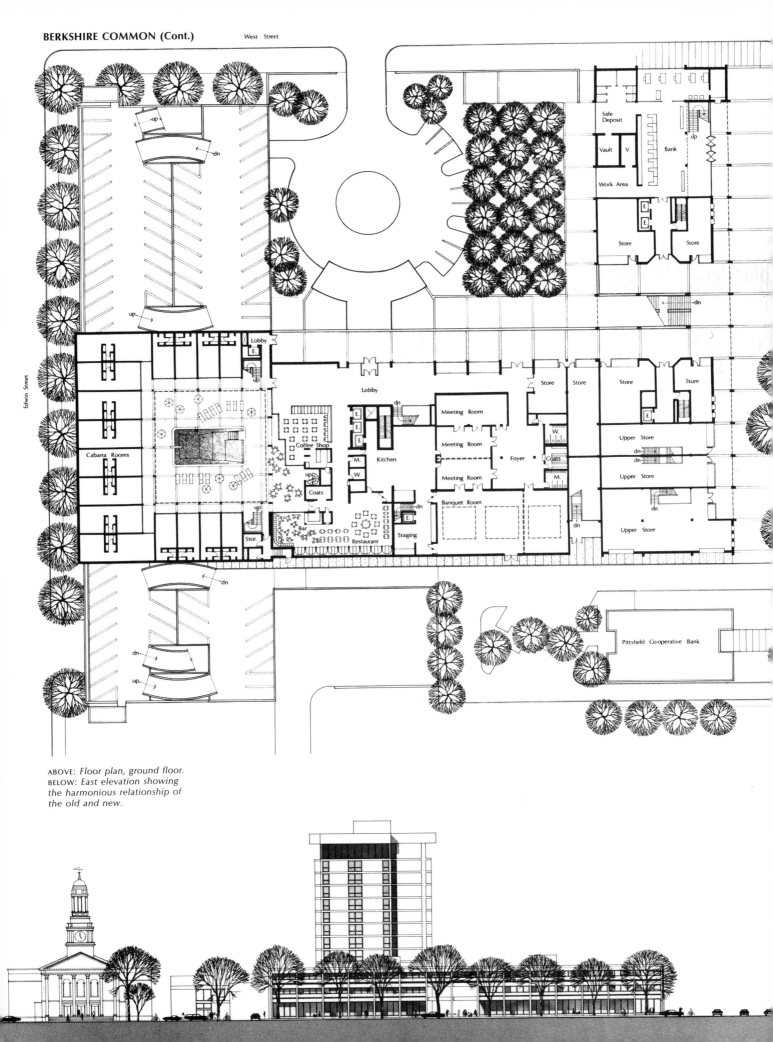

Lobby

E.

Lobby

up.

dn

Meeting Room

Store

Store

Store

Store

Store

dn

Coffee Shop

E.

E.

E.

dn

Meeting Room

W.

Upper Store

Cabana Rooms

M.

Kitchen

Foyer

Coats

dn

up.

W.

Meeting Room

M.

dn

Upper Store

Coats

Banquet Room

Bar

E.

dn

dn

Stor.

Staging

dn

Upper Store

Restaurant

dn

up.

Safe Deposit

Vault   V.

Bank

up.

Work Area

E.

E.

Store

Store

dn

Pittsfield Co-operative Bank

ABOVE: *Floor plan, ground floor.*
BELOW: *East elevation showing the harmonious relationship of the old and new.*

LEFT: *General plaza view.*
BELOW: *Shopping arcade.*
(Photographer: Jonathan Green.)

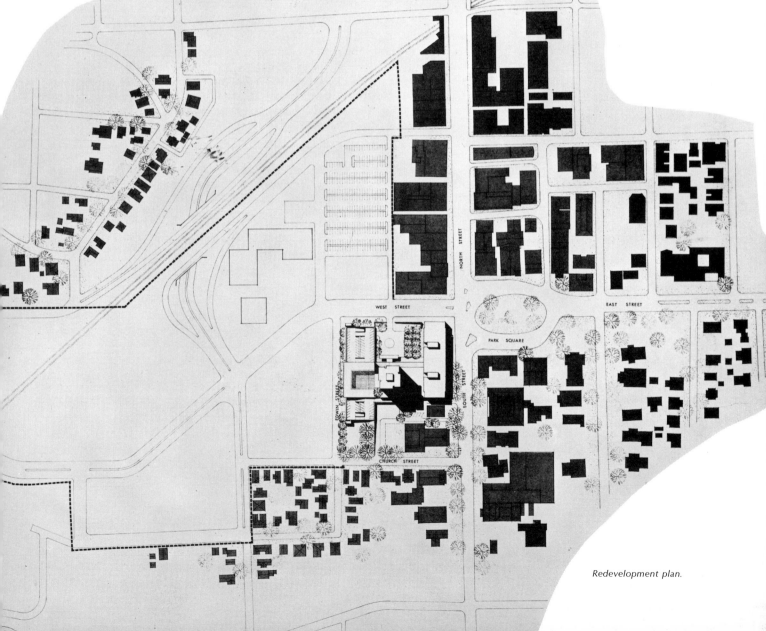

Redevelopment plan.

RENAISSANCE CENTER
Detroit, Michigan

ARCHITECTS: John Portman & Associates

CIVIC CENTER PLAZA
AND FOUNTAIN
Detroit, Michigan

DESIGNER FOR PLAZA AND FOUNTAIN:
Noguchi Fountain Plaza, Inc.
ASSOCIATE ARCHITECTS: Smith, Hinchman & Grylls
Assoc., Inc.

ABOVE: *General view of Civic Center Plaza looking from the river.*

In a number of the illustrated case studies, I have shown how important business and industrial leaders are in providing the initiative and support to keep the city vital. It is of interest to note that in the Detroit experience, in the early 1940s, a group of thirty-seven architects—The Architects Civic Design Group, under the leadership of the late Eliel Saarinen—made in-depth studies and prepared schematic concepts for the Detroit urban area. These studies, no doubt, had an impact on the preparation of the Detroit master plan, which was subsequently programmed for implementation by the City Planning Commission under the direction of Charles A. Blessing.

In 1958 the Detroit chapter of the American Institute of Architects sponsored the Architects Urban Design Collaborative, with volunteers representing various architectural firms. The working group, under the chairmanship of this author, undertook to study the Detroit central business district and to present some challenging concepts to the City Planning Commission. The illustrated report, although not intended for literal interpretation, was widely published in the press and served to alert the public to the benefits of better planning. Some of the ideas, such as elevated walkways and "people movers," are part of today's planning for central business districts in many cities!

Because of my personal knowledge of the Detroit scene and the availability of ample material, I am presenting the Detroit story in greater detail than the stories of other cities. This is not intended, however, to imply that this city is more important than any others presented in this book.

The history of planning Detroit's central business district goes back to the original governor's and judge's plan (Judge August Brevoort Woodward). The pattern of streets radiating from Grand Circus Park and Campus Martius provides downtown Detroit with an unusually exciting pattern and potential for a downtown area. The plan is based on main radial thoroughfares extending to the limits of the city—Michigan Avenue, Grand River Avenue, Woodward Avenue, Gratiot Avenue, and East Jefferson.

During the early 1940s Eliel Saarinen proposed a riverfront civic-center design, with 4,000 underground parking spaces. During the mid-1940s the Saarinens, Eliel and his son Eero, made a large number of studies, and Eero continued as adviser to the City Planning Commission on the civic center until his untimely death in 1957.

The implementation of the 100-acre civic-center development was begun in the early 1950s with the completion of the Veteran's Memorial Building, the Cobo Convention Hall and Arena, the City-County Building, and the Henry Ford and Edsel Ford Auditorium. In 1965, the city was given the first AIA National Honor Award for large-scale urban design planning (Detroit 1990). HUD and *Progressive Architecture* also honored Detroit for this concept. In the late 1960s a number of private, public, and semipublic high-rise office buildings were constructed. Many city leaders were anxious to have a covered stadium built along the riverfront on the west side of Cobo Hall. Because of legal technicalities in the Michigan state funding law, the project did not materialize. There was controversy over whether a downtown stadium is an effective daily attraction for a continuous flow of people. Also, the traffic congestion generated by the large number of cars would plague already-overloaded traffic arteries until such time as rapid transit and people movers would be in operation.

It has taken several decades for Detroit's political and business leaders to realize that unless their wholehearted commitment to a drastic and immediate rebuilding of the central business district was forthcoming, the deterioration would be irreparable. In 1970 Detroit Renaissance, Inc., was formed under the leadership of Max M. Fisher, chairman, and Henry Ford II and Robert M. Surdam, cochairmen. They engaged the services of Robert E. McCabe as president. The goal of Renaissance is to increase downtown investment by encouraging new construction and expansion opportunities in downtown Detroit and attracting developers and investors to those opportunities; by encouraging local business and major non-Detroit-based suppliers, insurers, and government agencies to locate new facilities in downtown Detroit; and by supporting and unifying the common efforts of various organizations and individuals working to stimulate Detroit's growth. Renaissance also supports many complementary activities, ranging from a comprehensive communications program for the city to cultural and educational planning.

Perspective view of Civic Center Plaza.

View of aerial structure for people mover on Cass Avenue showing proposed station near Manufacturer's National Bank building. (Engineers: Gannett Fleming Corddry & Carpenter of Michigan, Inc.)

Detroit Renaissance, Inc., and the Detroit Renaissance Foundation were organized as nonprofit, nonpartisan organizations. Program commitments and other major decisions are made by the twenty-eight members of the board of directors at bimonthly meetings. The permanent staff consists of a small number of urban specialists.

The major accomplishment of this group was the concept of a riverfront complex. According to a newspaper report, Ford said, "It all started when he got heat from Robert McCabe, president of Detroit Renaissance, Inc., the coalition of businessmen and others devoted to promoting a better Detroit, and from Lawrence Doss, president of New Detroit Inc., the group formed after the 1967 riot to help Detroit get back together again."*

On November 24, 1971, Henry Ford II submitted to the Detroit City Council his proposed plan for a large-scale, $500 million redevelopment project on 33½ acres along the riverfront. Almost fifty business firms, industries, and banks contributed to the equity ("seed money") to the extent of nearly $40 million. The approval by the council and the cooperation by all city agencies enabled the start of construction within two years. In the first stage, financing of a $200 million mortgage loan was provided by four insurance firms—Aetna Life and Casualty, Equitable Life Assurance Soc. of the U.S., John Hancock Mutual Life Insurance Co., and Travelers Insurance Co.—and by the Ford Motor Credit Company. The short-term construction loans were underwritten by twenty-eight local and national banks.

The riverfront development, named The Renaissance Center through a citywide competition for names, is planned in four stages. Stage one, which is currently under construction, includes four thirty-nine-story office buildings surrounding a seventy-story hotel. The second phase, for which no starting date is scheduled at the time of this writing, will include 1,000 apartments and several additional office buildings. The developers are the Detroit Downtown Development Corporation, a subsidiary of the Ford Motor Company. It is the general partner in the Detroit Renaissance Center partnership and is the managing partner of the group. The president of the Detroit Downtown Development Corporation is Wayne S. Doran.

Another highlight connected with this development is the Civic Center Plaza located at the foot of Woodward Avenue facing the river, just west of the Henry and Edsel Ford Auditorium. It creates a continuous link to the new Renaissance Center. The plaza will include a circular amphitheater, a fountain, and a tall pylon designed by Isamu Noguchi. The fountain, a 30-foot-high ring floating above a walled circular pool, has eighty different changes of water and light programming.

*Quoted from Al Stark, "The Challenge and the Reality," *The Sunday News Magazine,* June 24, 1973.

Renaissance Center site plan showing total riverfront development. The first phase consists of (1) the seventy-story hotel and (2) the four thirty-nine-story office towers in the central portion and are currently under construction. The second phase (3) is the riverfront housing development.

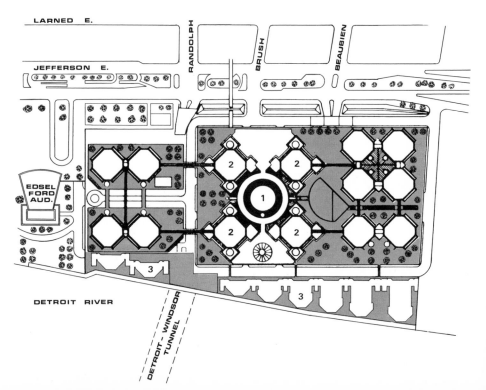

Renaissance Center under construction. (Photographer: Win Brunner.)

View from the Detroit River showing entire Renaissance Center project. The buildings in the foreground are apartment buildings.

The 8-acre plaza provides for a wide variety of uses by both large and small groups of people, many of which can occur simultaneously. The various activity areas within the plaza space allow maximum public participation. The lower level includes the tourist information center, public washrooms, security offices, dressing rooms for the amphitheater activities, a restaurant, a mechanical equipment room, and provisions for shops and boutiques. One important consideration was the need to retain Atwater Street as an east-west thoroughfare under the plaza, and the ventilation tower needed for the tunnel will be a sculptural form incorporated into the plaza design.

According to Noguchi: "The design develops a functional relationship between the fountain, the plaza, and what goes on below. The plaza, viewed as a whole will present a series of pyramidal shapes: that of the fountain, that of the stepped pyramid of the theater, the blue exhaust stack of the underground road, and the greater pyramid of the festival amphitheater as it rises to the plaza plane. The whole will be seen as a low mound with the bend in the road and the river beyond. I like to think that the effect will be American, unlike anything elsewhere. There might be something even American Indian about it, and that would be fine, I should think, for the bicentennial celebrations."

The Civic Center Plaza should serve as a catalyst for the extension of the riverfront park to the east and west of the central plaza, creating a continuous link between the Ambassador and Belle Isle bridges. Although this concept was included in the 1956 master plan, two decades elapsed before it was accepted as a realistic goal. The river-front-park plan is supported by the Community Development Commission and Mayor Coleman Young.

Much of the riverfront land east of the Belle Isle bridge has been acquired by the city for riverfront parks through tax foreclosure. With the retention of several major industrial establishments which will remain, the riverfront development for recreation, housing, and commercial and industrial uses will also become an increasing asset to the city in terms of taxes and employment.

The central business district 1956 master plan included an elevated pedestrian walkway connecting the Convention Hall, the Manufacturers National Bank operation center, and the Patrick McNamara federal building, and this concept is still valid today. This proposed skywalk, in addition to providing attractive and convenient pedestrian circulation, would also accommodate related convention amenities, e.g., restaurants, boutiques, and kiosks. It could conceivably become the beginning of an elevated walkway system serving many areas of the central business district.

Another feature included in the same master plan was the International Village complex, west of the federal building. This project, together with the existing excellent convention facilities, would have made Detroit more attractive as both a convention center and a tourist center. As I mentioned in the Overview, it was the shortsightedness of business and industrial leaders and the lack of community support which prevented the implementation of this complex (see page 137).

As has been stated previously, no one project, however important, can by itself restore the city to full vitality. By the same token, not even several projects, if they are isolated from one another will accomplish the desired results. The central

Renaissance Center section—first stage of development.

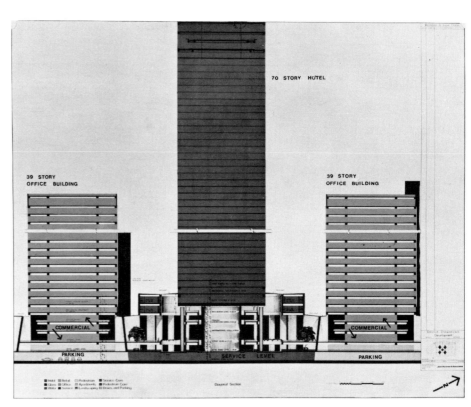

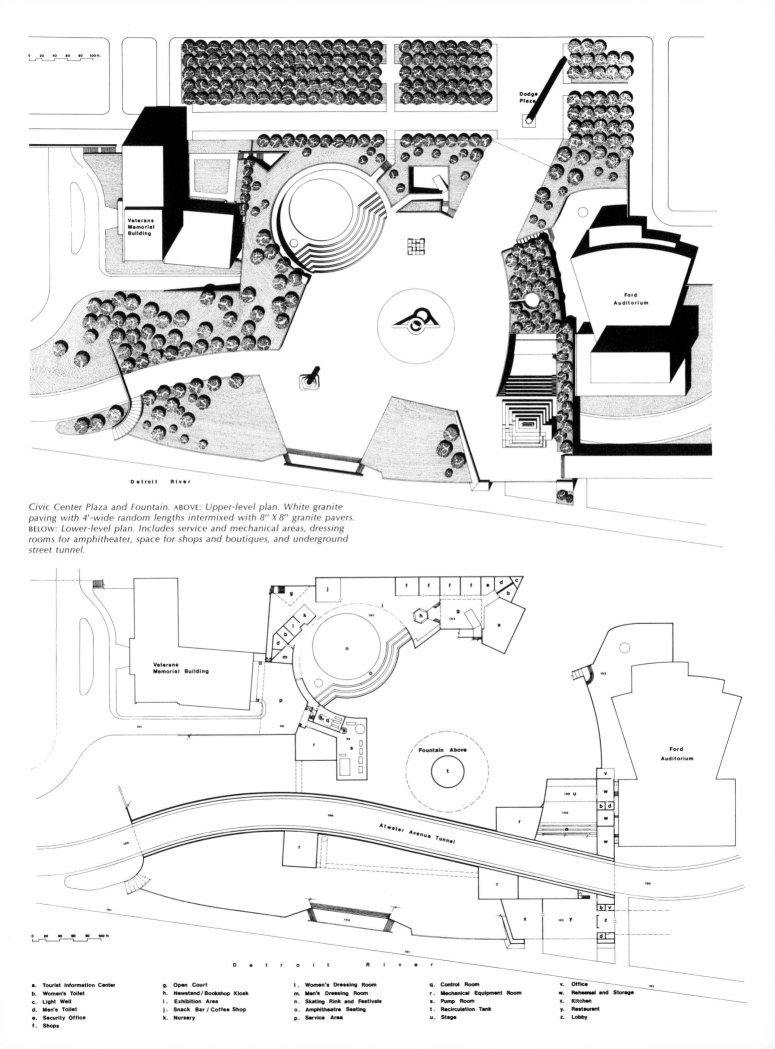

Civic Center Plaza and Fountain. ABOVE: *Upper-level plan. White granite paving with 4'-wide random lengths intermixed with 8" X 8" granite pavers.* BELOW: *Lower-level plan. Includes service and mechanical areas, dressing rooms for amphitheater, space for shops and boutiques, and underground street tunnel.*

a. Tourist Information Center
b. Women's Toilet
c. Light Well
d. Men's Toilet
e. Security Office
f. Shops

g. Open Court
h. Newsstand / Bookshop Kiosk
I. Exhibition Area
j. Snack Bar / Coffee Shop
k. Nursery

l. Women's Dressing Room
m. Men's Dressing Room
n. Skating Rink and Festivals
o. Amphitheatre Seating
p. Service Area

q. Control Room
r. Mechanical Equipment Room
s. Pump Room
t. Recirculation Tank
u. Stage

v. Office
w. Rehearsal and Storage
x. Kitchen
y. Restaurant
z. Lobby

Civic Center Plaza. View toward the Noguchi pylon. (Photographer: Louis G. Redstone.)

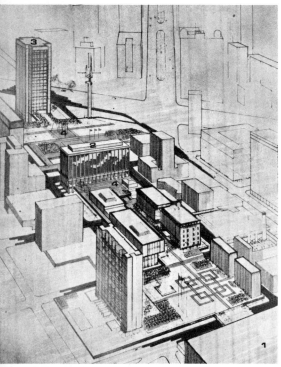

ABOVE: *Perspective view. Proposed design for elevated walkway between (1) Cobo Hall; (2) Manufacturers National Bank Operations Center; (3) Patrick McNamara federal building; (4) elevated walkway.* RIGHT: *Site plan. Proposed design for elevated walkway between Cobo Hall, Manufacturers National Bank Operations Center, and the new Patrick McNamara federal building. (Design for elevated walkway: Detroit City Planning Commission. Architects: for Cobo Hall—Giffels & Vallet; for Manufacturers National Bank Operations Center—Louis G. Redstone Associates, Inc.; for Patrick McNamara federal building—Smith, Hinchman & Grylls Assoc., Inc.)*

business district of Detroit is the focal point for the city and county governments as well as the financial and legal center for the area. Within a 2-mile radius, Detroit has developed one of the largest medical centers in the United States, a large state university complex with a student enrollment of over 35,000, and a cultural center, which includes a first-rate library, an art institute of national repute, a historical museum, an engineering building, a school for arts and crafts, and a science museum, now in the planning stages. At the time of this writing, each of these active and important areas is separated from the others and the downtown by deteriorated areas—veritable "no man's lands."

What is needed to make the city revival a reality is the provision of housing facilities for the thousands of people who work here or in the nearby downtown. The larger the number of people living and working together, the greater the feeling of security and the less fearful the atmosphere.

The need for housing units is even more pressing in the areas directly contiguous to the central business district core. There, a good beginning was made, east of the central business district, through the Federal Urban Renewal Agency. Completed to date is the Lafayette Park complex of high-rise luxury apartment buildings, low-rise middle-income units, several retirement high-rise buildings, a school, and a shopping center. Bordering east is the Elmwood low-rise housing, combining rental garden-type apartments and townhouse units. In all, plans call for a 30,000 population in this area on 187 acres of urban renewal land.

Even more critical for the success of the central business district is the implementation of plans to build luxury and middle-income apartments on the riverfront. Only by establishing a high-density downtown resident population can the varied amenities and commercial sector be economically viable.

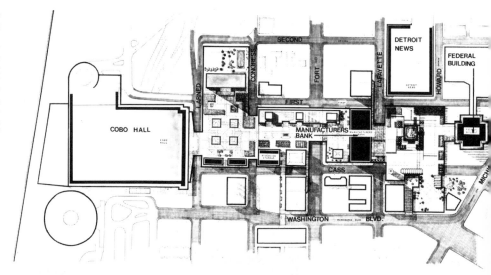

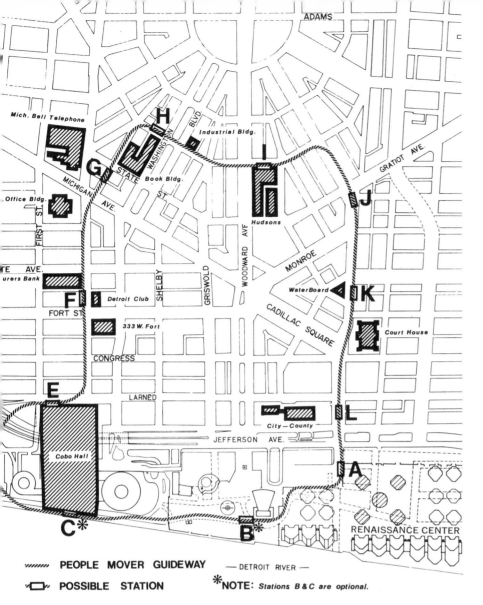

Plan for people-mover system in CBD area. (Engineers: Gannett Fleming Corddry & Carpenter of Michigan, Inc.)

BELOW: *Model of proposed International Village.* BOTTOM: *Perspective view of proposed International Village interior plaza. Project was not implemented. (Architects: Gunnar Birkerts & Associates, Inc.; Louis G. Redstone Associates, Inc.; Frederick Stickel Associates.)*

(map labels) ADAMS · Mich. Bell Telephone · WASHINGTON BLVD · Industrial Bldg. · H · I · G · STATE · Book Bldg. · MICHIGAN AVE. · Office Bldg. · FIRST ST. · J · GRATIOT AVE. · Hudsons · WOODWARD AVE. · MONROE · TE AVE. · urers Bank · SHELBY ST. · GRISWOLD · WaterBoard · K · F · Detroit Club · CADILLAC SQUARE · FORT ST. · 333 W. Fort · CONGRESS · Court House · LARNED · E · City—County · L · JEFFERSON AVE. · Cobo Hall · A · C* · B* · RENAISSANCE CENTER

/////// PEOPLE MOVER GUIDEWAY — DETROIT RIVER —

◻ POSSIBLE STATION *NOTE: Stations B & C are optional.

HOUSTON CENTER

Houston, Texas

ARCHITECTS: William L. Pereira Associates;
G. Pierce, Goodwin & Flanagan

To the nation's sixth largest city and third largest port is being added a privately sponsored expansion to the downtown area which will more than double the present central business district. In the summer of 1969, Texas Eastern Transmission Corporation and Brown & Root, Inc., of Houston, Texas, engaged William L. Pereira Associates to begin the planning of the downtown area. The area encompasses thirty-three continuous blocks adjacent to the present central business district.

The first step was for Texas Eastern to acquire all the property directly east of the downtown core, which included some 134 separate parcels of land. One of the objectives of the project is to create a "twenty-four-hour environment" that will keep the city alive night and day. The area comprises 2,000,000 square feet of land (46 acres) and 1,210,000 square feet of airspace—a total of 3,210,000 square feet. The development will support a variety of elements from office buildings, hotels, and residential units to retail, consumer, and entertainment activities.

Over the 74-acre site (air rights included) a saturation point of about 23 million square feet of building area is projected, or about 7 or 8 feet of enclosed building for each square foot of site area.

The Houston Center concept envisions a "platform city" raised approximately 50 feet above the existing street grid to separate completely vehicular and pedestrian traffic—the first 3½ levels of the structure, along with two underground levels, will be devoted to parking for over 550 cars. The roof of the garage, about 40 feet above the street level in this structure, will form the main pedestrian level and will be reached from the street by an enclosed escalator at the corner of Fannin and McKinney, as well as by elevators and stairwells within the structure.

Initial buildings will include an office tower rising forty stories above the platform level and a six-story wing which will extend along the north side of the block and across San Jacinto Street. The low-rise wing and the tower are linked at the pedestrian level by a glass-enclosed gallery, two stories high and 180 feet long.

Because the initial block of the Houston Center development will interface with the existing business district, the Fannin Street elevation will slope up gradually from the sidewalk to avoid any abrupt transition. Similarly, there will be shops along the street level to provide a smooth, functional transition between the center

Site location plan.

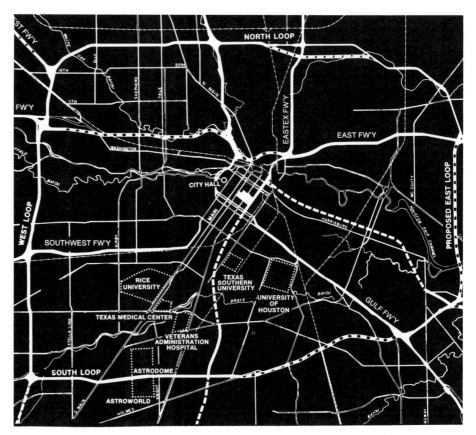

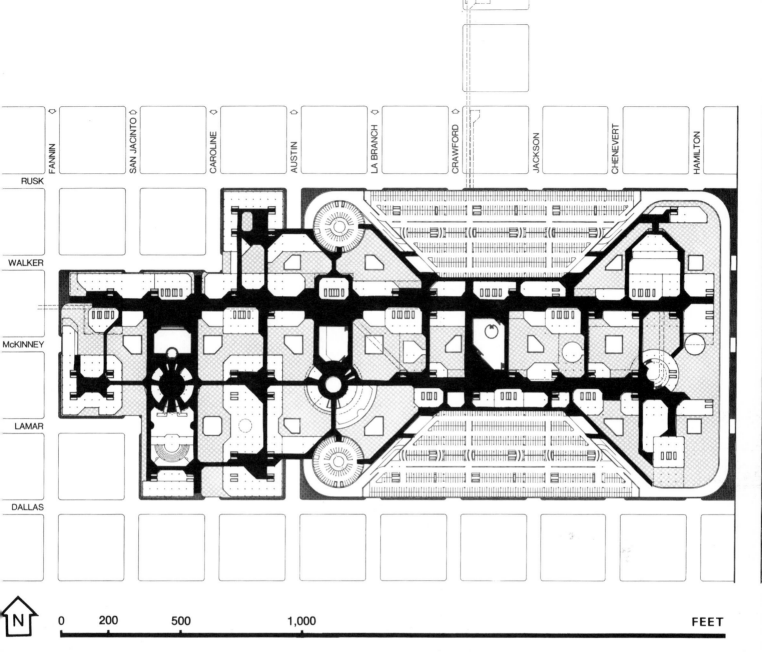

FANNIN SAN JACINTO CAROLINE AUSTIN LA BRANCH CRAWFORD JACKSON CHENEVERT HAMILTON

RUSK

WALKER

McKINNEY

LAMAR

DALLAS

N

0   200   500   1,000   FEET

Main pedestrian level plan.

■ PUBLIC ENCLOSED SPACE   ▤ VERTICAL PEDESTRIAN
                                  CIRCULATION

and the present downtown area. The first two levels of the wing structure will
also be devoted to retail facilities, and the pedestrian gallery will be lined with
shops and boutiques.

The main pedestrian mall is at the roof level of the parking structure. Here are
the entrances and lobbies for the office building and entrances to the open plaza.
An enclosed air-conditioned major axis will run east-west and north-south
throughout the complex. Moving sidewalks will connect to escalators, stairs, and
ramps. This complete three-dimensional system of pedestrian circulation permits
the user to reach any point within the project. It is at this pedestrian level that
much of the retail shopping is located, bordered by apartments, hotels, and offices.

The center provides 1.5 million square feet of retail shopping area. Included
will be four to five major department stores facing glass-enclosed plazas. Numerous specialty shops will be located along the pedestrian walkway. An important
factor is that Houston Center is almost squarely at the heart of downtown Houston.
The geographic center is Fannin Square, and the center will begin just one block
east of this point. This permits easy access and linkage to the present business

district and, at the same time, allows the new center to retain an active identity of its own.

Construction of the center has been planned in three stages. Phase one begins adjacent to the existing central business district. From there, construction will proceed in a west-to-east direction. The first stage is scheduled to be completed in 1976–1977 and will contain 5,200,000 square feet plus parking for 8,100 cars.

The visual focus on the main shopping level is the glass-walled Space Frame Plaza, which allows for visual continuity between the open spaces. It is also used for permanent and temporary displays and exhibits. The retail facilities on the perimeter would face an ice rink during part of the year or other activities, such as a sidewalk café.

In the first stage, the center will be limited to 800 residental units, with 2,100 units of housing planned for the following stages. These apartments, in part, will be in low-rise structures above the retail areas of the pedestrian mall.

Houston Center will build and operate a central thermal-energy plant and will provide chilled and hot water throughout the project. In the first stage a single plant will be constructed. As for electricity, the power will be supplied on a block-by-block basis from conduits under streets to electrical vaults in basements. Later the conduits will be built into the substructure as the physical volume increases. At this point in development, concentrated points of service will be linked to an internal distribution system, with the metering responsibility taken over by the center.

When finally completed, Houston Center's elevated pedestrian level will extend without interruption to the inner loop freeway, comprising 74 acres of office buildings, hotels, retail stores, apartments, and recreational facilities as well as extensive plazas, promenades, and landscaped open space. Altogether, 23 million square feet of floor space will be ultimately provided, along with covered parking.

The developers are the Texas Eastern Transmission Corporation.

Aerial view of downtown Houston showing how the CBD will be virtually doubled in size by the major development of Texas Eastern Transmission Corp.

LEFT, ABOVE: *Model of first-phase construction of Houston Center. Overall massing of phase one shows three major office towers (right). Circular structure in center of model is a hotel, planned to contain at least 1,000 rooms. Model also indicates the relationship of existing surface streets that will remain undisturbed, the parking levels, and the elevated loop road that will ultimately provide access to future increments of construction and reduce congestion on the surface streets.* LEFT: *Perspective showing section through parking levels.* LEFT, BELOW: *Perspective of enclosed shopping mall.* ABOVE: *Rendering of first phase.*

GREENWAY PLAZA
Houston, Texas

ARCHITECTS: Lloyd, Morgan & Jones
CONSULTING LANDSCAPE ARCHITECTS:
Mormon, Mock & Jones
ARCHITECTS FOR RETAIL MALL:
Pujdak, Bielski & Associates

Greenway Plaza, located 5 miles from downtown Houston, is being developed on a 127-acre site. It is a self-contained complex of retail, business, and residential facilities. The site acquisition required negotiations with more than 300 home-owners. Its location is central to all points of the metropolitan area via the city's extensive freeway system.

The project is being planned in three phases. The first phase of construction started in 1968 and was scheduled for completion in 1975. This phase includes an underground shopping concourse, eight major office buildings, and a three-level parking structure for 3,500 cars. Of special interest is the "sculpture garden" in the plaza area. The bronze sculptures include life-size figures of three children and an old man feeding pigeons. The sculptor is Pat G. Foley, fine arts director and artist in residence of the Kinkaid School.

Phases two and three are scheduled to be completed by 1980 and will include a luxury hotel, a sports arena, an expansion of the underground retail concourse, a landing strip for short take off and landing (STOL) aircraft atop a 2,000-foot-long multistory parking structure (see model of master plan), and an extensive complex of multifamily housing units.

The developers are the Century Development Corporation.

Model of master plan.

Sculpture garden in plaza. (Sculptor: Pat G. Foley.)

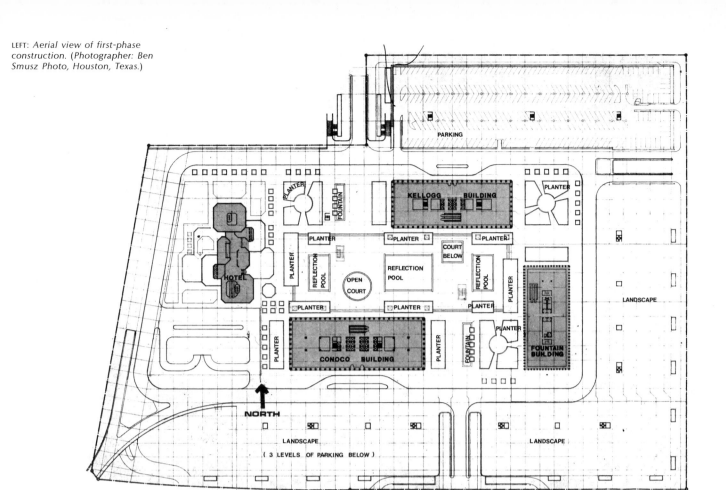

Plaza level.

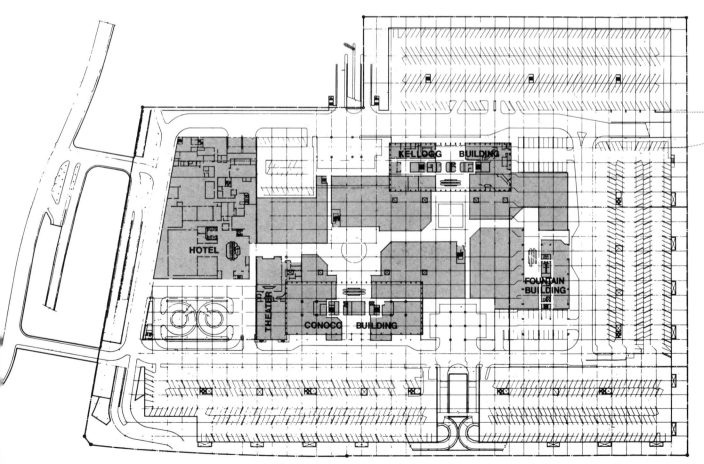

Concourse level.

ZCMI CENTER
Salt Lake City, Utah
ARCHITECTS: Gruen Associates

Zions Cooperative Mercantile Institution (ZCMI), one of America's oldest department store and located for nearly one hundred years at 15 South Main Street in downtown Salt Lake City, Utah, will be rebuilt at the same location as part of a 10-acre CBD redevelopment. In addition to the 450,000 square foot ZCMI two-level department store, there will be an additional 300,000 square feet of fifty shops (all facing the central mall space) and six levels of parking to accommodate 2,000 cars. From the parking area the pedestrian has direct access, via high-speed elevators, to the arcades and shopping area. To return to the parking levels, shoppers retrace their steps back to the elevators, which allows more exposure to shop displays. There is access from three streets to the parking levels, two of which are below the mall, and four above. There are pedestrian entrance arcades on all four sides of the development.

Access to and from the two sublevels of parking for both cars and delivery trucks is via down and up ramps from center-of-street entry lanes. Heavy-duty freight elevators and freight docks at these sublevels facilitate merchandise deliveries to the stores. Additional parking for some 1,700 cars is within one block in each direction of the center. A dominant feature of the complex is the twenty-seven-story office tower.

An interesting element is the preservation of the historic three-story cast-iron ZCMI façade, a landmark since 1876. The architectural solution was to incorporate the façade in a lighted niche on the Main Street side of the new store.

Architect Stephen T. Baird was the consultant on the restoration. Construction on ZCMI Center began in 1971 and was completed in 1975: The client is Zions Securities Corporation.

ABOVE: *Elevation at South Main Street, showing the preservation of the original façade.*

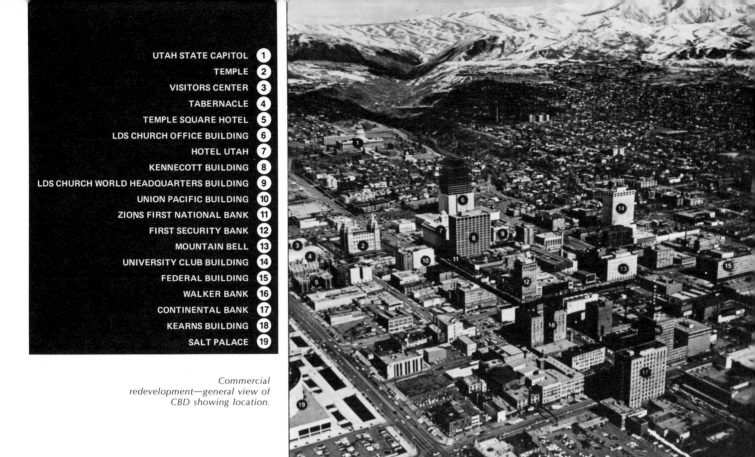

UTAH STATE CAPITOL	1
TEMPLE	2
VISITORS CENTER	3
TABERNACLE	4
TEMPLE SQUARE HOTEL	5
LDS CHURCH OFFICE BUILDING	6
HOTEL UTAH	7
KENNECOTT BUILDING	8
LDS CHURCH WORLD HEADQUARTERS BUILDING	9
UNION PACIFIC BUILDING	10
ZIONS FIRST NATIONAL BANK	11
FIRST SECURITY BANK	12
MOUNTAIN BELL	13
UNIVERSITY CLUB BUILDING	14
FEDERAL BUILDING	15
WALKER BANK	16
CONTINENTAL BANK	17
KEARNS BUILDING	18
SALT PALACE	19

Commercial redevelopment—general view of CBD showing location.

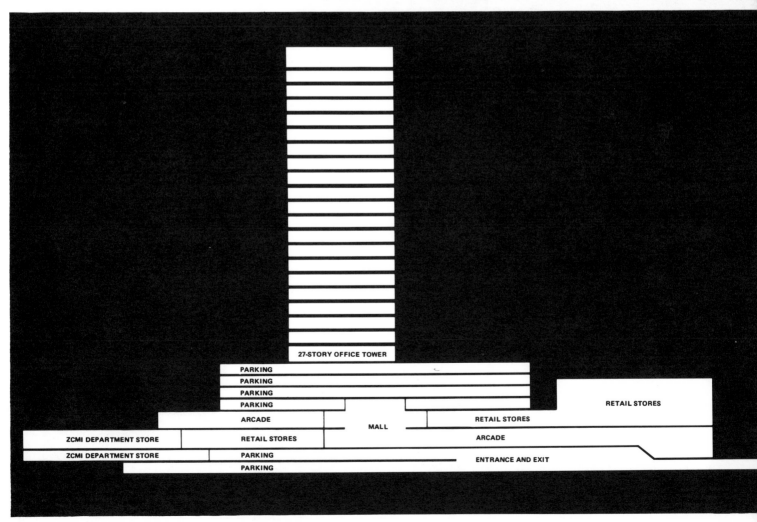

Section.

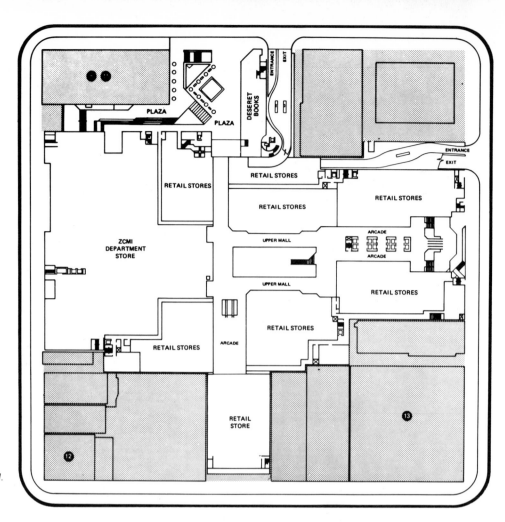

Plan of lower level.

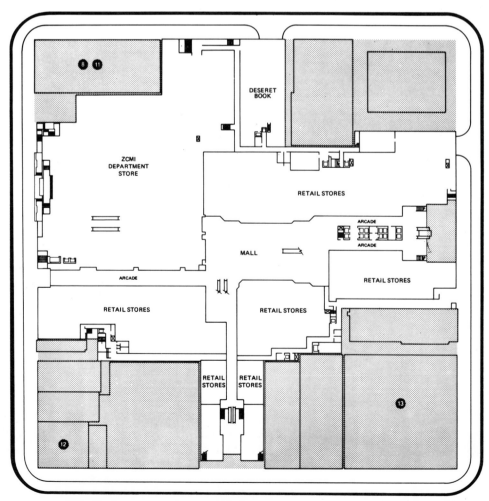

Plan of upper level.

Another addition in the CBD development is the Sheraton Salt Lake Hotel complex, which includes extensive retail facilities, all connected with an adjacent multilevel parking structure. Also, plans for the Main Street improvement call for a change in the vehicular and pedestrian traffic pattern. Because of the extra width of the existing street, the sidewalks are widened and are planned to include plantings, benches, heated and lighted bus shelters, kiosks, special streetlights, and decorative fountains.

The principal consultants for the street beautification project are Barton-Aschman Associates, Inc. The associate consultants are Caldwell, Richard & Sorenson, Inc., and Carpenter and Stringham, Architects.

SHERATON SALT LAKE COMPLEX
Salt Lake City, Utah

ARCHITECTS: C. F. Murphy Associates
PARKING CONSULTANTS: R. C. Rich & Associates

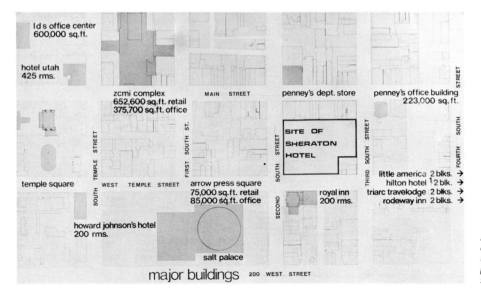

ABOVE: *Model. (1) hotel; (2) office building; (3) entrance to underground parking.* LEFT: *Site plan showing relationship to surrounding redevelopment area.*

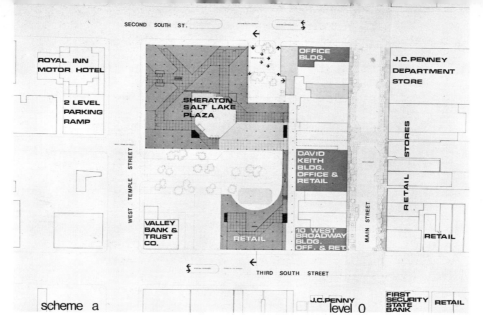

scheme a   level 0

Plan of Sheraton Salt Lake complex.

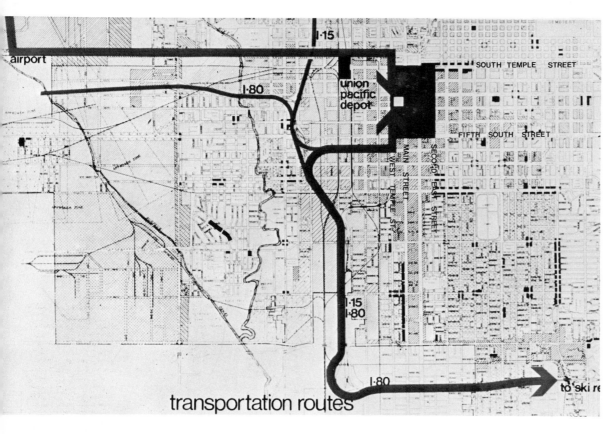

transportation routes

LEFT: *Location plan.* BELOW: *Section looking west.*

THIRD SOUTH STREET   SECOND SOUTH STREET

Like all major cities today, Vancouver has suffered from the process of obsolescence. After 1955, the flourishing activity of its traditional city center began to decline as physical deterioration took its toll of available retail and office facilities.

The remedy for Vancouver's ills was found in the concept of a renewal effort jointly mounted by public and private sectors of the community. Such cooperation permits each party to bring its particular energies and capabilities into play, and in the case of Vancouver, it resulted in a complex financed largely through private funds. To this end a private triumvirate composed of the Toronto-Dominion Bank, T. Eaton Company, and CEMP Investments, Ltd., agreed to redevelop blocks 42 and 52 as an entity.

The project was developed in two phases. Block 52 includes the multistory Toronto-Dominion Bank tower, Eaton's department store (connected to the tower), and an underground shopping concourse which connects to the block 42 shopping concourse. Block 42 has two office buildings and a Four Seasons hotel. Subterranean parking on two levels for the entire complex accommodates 2,500 cars.

This complex is anticipated to have a far-reaching effect on the surrounding areas. Beyond the aesthetic aspects, the economic effects on Vancouver are already substantial, as evidenced by increased property valuations and the subsequent increased tax revenues and by increased retail sales and sales tax revenues.

PACIFIC CENTRE
Vancouver, British Columbia

ARCHITECTS: Gruen Associates
ASSOCIATE ARCHITECTS: McCarter Nairne & Partners

ABOVE: *Exterior view (perspective).*
BELOW: *Section.*

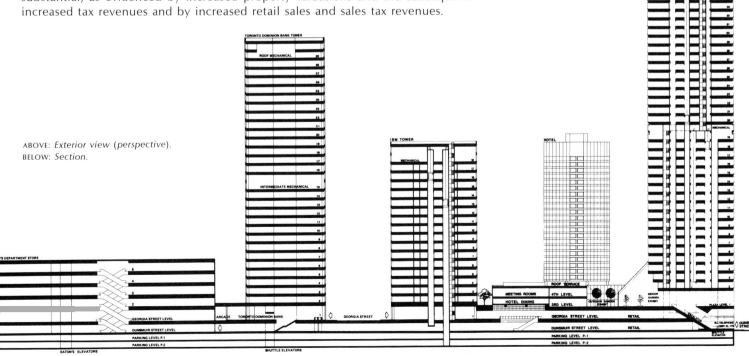

RIGHT: *Exterior view. (Photographer: Croton Studios Ltd.)* BELOW: *View showing the monumental steel sculpture located between the Toronto-Dominion Bank and Eaton's department store. (Sculptor: George Norris. Photographer: Gord L. Croucher.)* BELOW, RIGHT: *Exterior view of Eaton's department store and Toronto-Dominion Bank tower. (Photographer: Balthazar Korab.)*

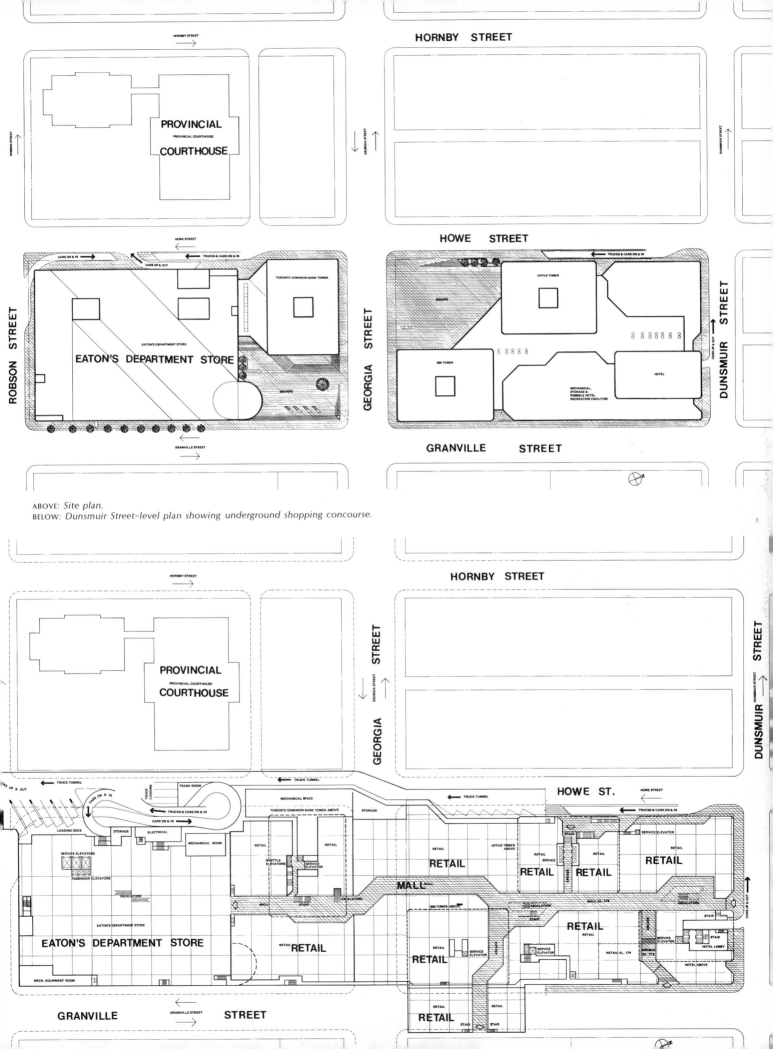

ABOVE: *Site plan.*
BELOW: *Dunsmuir Street-level plan showing underground shopping concourse.*

EMBARCADERO CENTER

San Francisco, California

ARCHITECTS:
For the master plan: John Portman
  & Associates
For the Justin Herman Plaza:
  Lawrence Halprin & Associates;
  Mario Campi & Associates;
  John S. Bolles & Associates

The Embarcadero Center, located in San Francisco, California, is part of the Golden Gateway redevelopment project. It occupies 8.5 acres of a 51-acre site on land which was formerly a wholesale produce marketplace. It is one of eight redevelopment projects in the city of San Francisco.

The entire Golden Gateway project was developed by two separate owner-developer-architect groups. Golden Gateway Center, consisting of 1,254 residential units and the twenty-five-story Alcoa building, was completed in 1967.

An important factor in the successful development of this private enterprise was the first phase, which started with the construction of the residential sector (high-rise apartment buildings and rental townhouses)—all built over two-level garages. Architects for the residential phase, including parking, are Wurster, Bernardi & Emmons, Inc., and Demars & Reay. Associated architects are Anshen & Allen. Landscape architects are Sasaki, Walker Associates, Inc.

Golden Gateway Center's Alcoa building (architects are Skidmore, Owings & Merrill; public garage—Wurster, Bernardi & Emmons, Inc.; landscape architects—Sasaki, Walker Associates, Inc.) is situated between the residential units and Embarcadero Center. The residential units, the center, and the Alcoa building are all joined by pedestrian walkways through extensive landscaped open space with fountains and artwork.

Embarcadero Center's Security Pacific Bank building (completed in 1971), the Hyatt Regency Hotel (completed in 1973), and the Levi Strauss building (completed in 1974) will be joined by two additional buildings by late 1977.

The retail commercial facilities, The Shopping Gallery, are located on three levels at all Embarcadero Center buildings.

An important feature of the entire complex is the separation of pedestrian movements from the vehicular traffic by means of elevated bridgeways and walkways. When completed, all buildings in the complex will be interconnected with elevated walkways. It is anticipated that the pedestrian will be able to walk through nearly 58 acres of downtown San Francisco without interference of auto traffic.

Another design feature of the entire complex is the generous allowance for open space over the podium levels for use as parkways, view corridors, and garden areas, planned to include artwork and fountains. Of significance to the enhancement of this urban setting is the commitment of the center's developers to allow 1

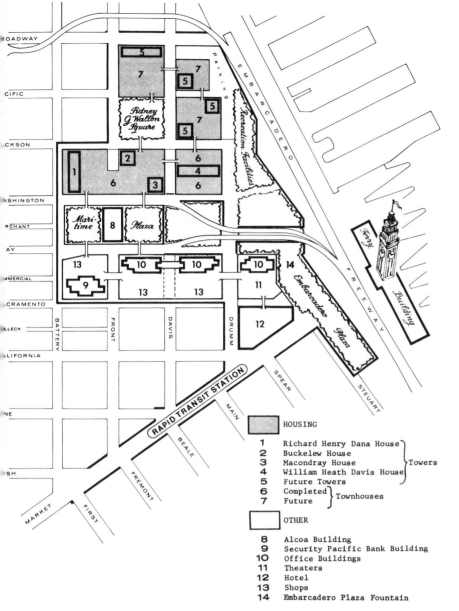

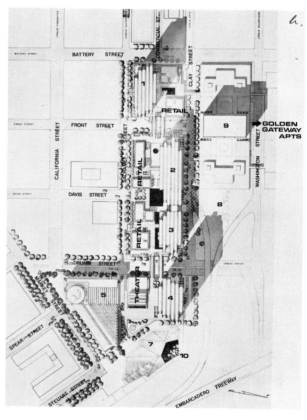

HOUSING

1   Richard Henry Dana House ⎤
2   Buckelew House |
3   Macondray House   ⎬ Towers
4   William Heath Davis House |
5   Future Towers ⎦
6   Completed ⎤ Townhouses
7   Future   ⎦

OTHER

8   Alcoa Building
9   Security Pacific Bank Building
10 Office Buildings
11 Theaters
12 Hotel
13 Shops
14 Embarcadero Plaza Fountain

ABOVE LEFT: *Site plan showing relationship of center to Golden Gateway redevelopment. (Photograph courtesy of San Francisco Redevelopment Agency.)* ABOVE: *Site plan. (1, 2) Completed office buildings; (3) office buildings under construction; (4) interim parking lot; (5) completed Hyatt Regency Hotel; (7) Justin Herman Plaza; (8) Maritime Plaza; (9) Alcoa building; (10) Vaillancourt fountain.* LEFT: *View showing the stainless-steel sculpture* Two Columns with Wedge. *(Sculptor: Willi Gutmann. Photographer: Eliel G. Redstone.)*

153

percent of the budget for art. The Justin Herman Plaza and Fountain, a 5-acre park at the foot of Market Street along the Embarcadero from the Muni Turnaround to Washington Street, highlights the magnetism of a spirited environment to which people respond. Four office buildings adjoin the hotel and entertainment facilities, all of which are connected by a brick-paved area, landscaping with trees and grass, and a pool with a free-form sculpture fountain. This phase, which contains about 3 acres, was completed in 1971. At the time of this writing, the development of the remaining park area was being implemented.

The owner-developers are Trammel Crow Co., John Portman & Associates, David Rockefeller & Associates, and PIC Realty Corporation (a subsidiary of Prudential Insurance Company of America).

ABOVE: *Model of project as viewed from waterfront. (1, 2) Office buildings; (3) under construction; (4) interim parking lot; (5) completed Hyatt Regency Hotel; (6) Golden Gateway Center Apartments; (7) Transamerica pyramid; (9) Alcoa building; (10) Ferry building. (Photographer: Karl H. Riek.)* RIGHT: *Model of project showing construction progress (fall 1974). (1, 2, 5, 8) Completed buildings; (3) buildings under construction; (4) interim parking lot; (7) Justin Herman Plaza (complete); Vaillancourt fountain (adjacent to Justin Herman Plaza—complete); (6) Golden Gateway apartments (complete); (9) Alcoa building (complete). The Golden Gateway apartments and Alcoa building are not located in the center. (Photographer: Karl H. Riek.)*

BROADWAY PLAZA
Los Angeles, California
ARCHITECTS: Charles Luckman Associates

The completed Broadway Plaza, in the heart of downtown Los Angeles, is a significant and successful example of central business district redevelopment in the United States.

A complex designated by the architect as a megastructure occupies a site of 4½ acres bounded by Seventh, Eighth, Flower, and Hope Streets. It consists of a 250,000 square-foot department store (the first major department store construction in the downtown in fifty years!); a skylighted two-level galleria, which includes special shops and restaurants; a thirty-two-story office building; a twenty-two-story Hyatt Regency hotel; and a 2,000-car multilevel parking structure with six levels of parking above the Broadway department store for the shoppers and tenants and two levels beneath the entire complex for the office building and hotel visitors.

All elements of the project flow into the galleria. The Broadway store entrance, office building lobby, Hyatt Regency entrance, and several shops open directly onto the plaza level of the galleria. Two banks of escalators and stairways lead down to the garden level, lined with boutiques and restaurants. The hotel lobby merges with the galleria at this level, which also includes a number of the hotel's special restaurants and cocktail lounges. In addition to the two galleria levels, all elements of the project share two interconnected lower levels.

Designed to provide for complete separation of automobile and truck traffic within the complex, truck ramps and service areas are located on the lowest level, below the automobile ramps. There is vehicular access from the service areas to the main ballroom of the hotel, making possible the installation of large, major exhibits. An important element in the access design is the entrance system to the department store. In addition to the main entrance from the galleria at the plaza level, there are entrances on every level from the elevator core, which runs through the heart of the store, serving as a vertical street from the six-level parking structure above.

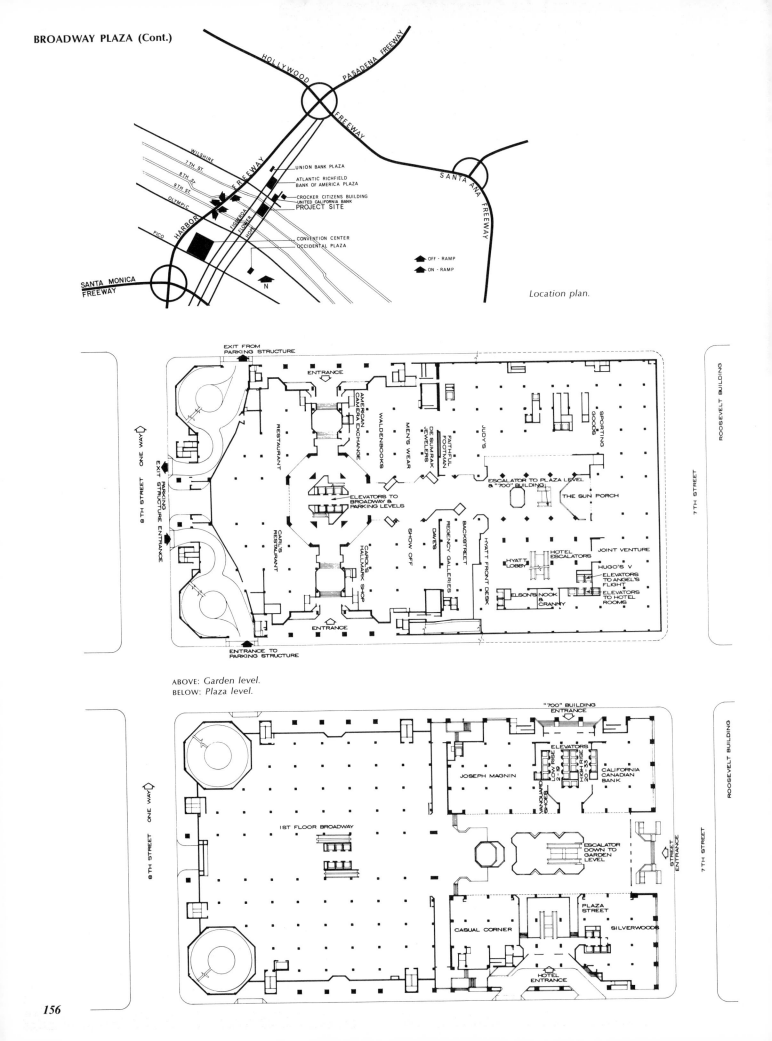

Location plan.

ABOVE: *Garden level.*
BELOW: *Plaza level.*

The two-level galleria is lined with specialty shops and a Broadway department store. Brick and wood are the dominant materials. Forty-foot-long steel banners suspended from an overhead skylight were designed to lead the eye through the large space to the reflecting pool on the lower level.

The immediate success of this development exceeded all the economic feasibility projections. The number of daily visitors is already three times as large as the original estimate of 18,000. An interesting note is that more than half of the auto traffic comes from the suburbs. A boon to the merchants is the 10-cent Sunday bus fare, which allows passengers to travel anywhere in the city.

As successful as this downtown complex is in its own right, there is a question as to whether it is sufficient to completely revitalize urban life. Unless contiguous additional developments are linked to this project in a unified plan serving the pedestrian, the project may remain an isolated "Shangri-la." Mildred F. Schmertz, AIA, senior editor of *Architectural Record,* commented in her article in the April 1974 issue:

> In the general spirit of euphoria which these centers arouse, there is a tendency to overstate their importance in revitalizing cities as places to be. Although their economic and social value is obvious, in physical terms they tend to be self-sufficient and self-serving enclaves. This is the fault of the urban context in which they are built rather than a failure on the part of their architects, or a lack of vision on the part of their developers. The downtown shopping center within a megastructure or omni-center is potentially a strong shaping force and a major urban design element. Broadway Plaza can be reached only by private motor car, taxi or bus. As its site plan indicates, apart from sidewalks, there are no nearby pedestrian networks which link up with the shopping mall, nor does Broadway Plaza reinforce or extend an existing urban design structure of pedestrian ways and civic spaces. Few would seem to walk for the pleasure of it in downtown Los Angeles and Broadway Plaza, shaped by circumstance into a self-contained entity, does not improve the world of the pedestrian until he gets inside. It is essentially an island of inward turned amenities bearing no relationship except proximity by motor car to other developments in the area.

The developers are: Ogden Development Corporation; Broadway-Hale Stores, Inc.; and Urban Center Associates.

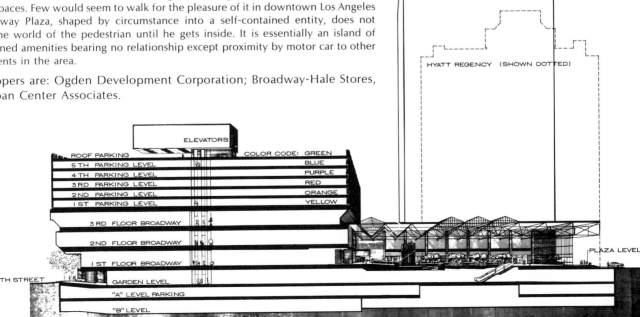

"700" BUILDING

Section.

HYATT REGENCY (SHOWN DOTTED)

ELEVATORS

ROOF PARKING | COLOR CODE: GREEN
5TH PARKING LEVEL | BLUE
4TH PARKING LEVEL | PURPLE
3RD PARKING LEVEL | RED
2ND PARKING LEVEL | ORANGE
1ST PARKING LEVEL | YELLOW

3RD FLOOR BROADWAY

2ND FLOOR BROADWAY

1ST FLOOR BROADWAY

8TH STREET

GARDEN LEVEL

"A" LEVEL PARKING

"B" LEVEL

PLAZA LEVEL

ATLANTIC RICHFIELD PLAZA
Los Angeles, California

ARCHITECTS: Albert C. Martin & Associates
LANDSCAPE ARCHITECTS: Van Herrick

Atlantic Richfield Plaza, in Los Angeles, California, is a $175 million project which includes twin fifty-two-story towers and a two-level, block-wide subterranean shopping center covering the entire block bounded by Fifth, Sixth, Figueroa, and Flower Streets. In addition, there is an eleven-level parking facility located one-half block north.

Literally a city within a city, Atlantic Richfield Plaza, with a daytime population of more than 14,000, houses a forty-store shopping center on two levels under the towers. Known as "the plaza," it draws shoppers from the total downtown work force of 250,000. The Los Angeles main office of the Bank of America opens onto one level of the plaza, as well as having entrances from the outdoor promenade at street level.

There are ten food and beverage facilities, varying from an elegant French restaurant to a take-out operation and all designed to fit the international theme of the center. They will be operated by Davre's, nationally known restaurant operators.

There is ready access to the plaza shopping center on both levels from pedestrian escalators on Flower Street at the corners of both Fifth and Sixth Streets, as well as from escalators in each of the twin towers.

Parking for a total of 2,850 cars is available at a nearby parking garage, which provides 2,350 car spaces, and also on one level under the twin towers, which accommodates 500 cars. The separate parking facility is located on 2.2 acres of Bunker Hill urban renewal land bordered by Flower, Hope, and Fourth Streets. Designed to conform to the surrounding area, the structure has been reduced by placing five levels underground. The roof of the structure, level with Hope Street, is being landscaped for viewing from neighboring high-rise structures.

Integrated into the overall master plans of the Community Redevelopment Agency for Bunker Hill, the parking facility is to be connected by an elevated pedestrian walkway extending over an adjacent urban renewal parcel and a bridge across Fifth Street. The walkway leading to an escalator and stairway will allow garage customers to bypass all traffic.

A 2½-acre outdoor promenade area, surrounding the twin towers and providing a wide expanse between them, adds an open space and a parklike setting for the central city. Facing on Flower Street, which is at a lower elevation than paralleling Figueroa Street, the open area is dominated by a brilliantly colored 14-foot-high sculpture of contemporary design by Herbert Bayer, set off by wide walkways of granite.

ABOVE: *View of the completed twin fifty-two-story towers. (Photographer: Wayne Thom, Photographer.)* RIGHT: *Plaza view. (Sculptor: Herbert Bayer. Photographer: Wayne Thom, Photographer.)*

Further creating a pleasing environment will be generous plantings of fresh seasonal flowers, jacaranda trees, a large circular reflecting pool, and pattern-creating vines on the retaining wall abutting Figueroa Street.

The Los Angeles main office of the Bank of America will be in a freestanding three-level structure between the two towers at the Figueroa Street side. Easily accessible, the main entrance will face Flower Street, but other entrances will be on Figueroa Street and in the shopping center.

The retail design consultants for the project are Pujdak, Bielski & Associates; graphics design consultants, John Follis & Associates; landscape architects, Robert Herrick Carter & Associates, Inc. The joint owners are the Bank of America and the Atlantic Richfield Company.

Perspective of the 2,350-car Bunker Hill parking facility, which serves nearby Atlantic Richfield Plaza, shown from frontage on Flower Street looking north and east. The 900,000 square-foot garage will have eleven levels—only six above the ground—and will be served by multiple access points on three sides and at three levels. It will be connected to Atlantic Richfield Plaza, one-half block south, by an elevated pedestrian walkway and bridges over Flower and Fifth Streets.

Plaza site plan.

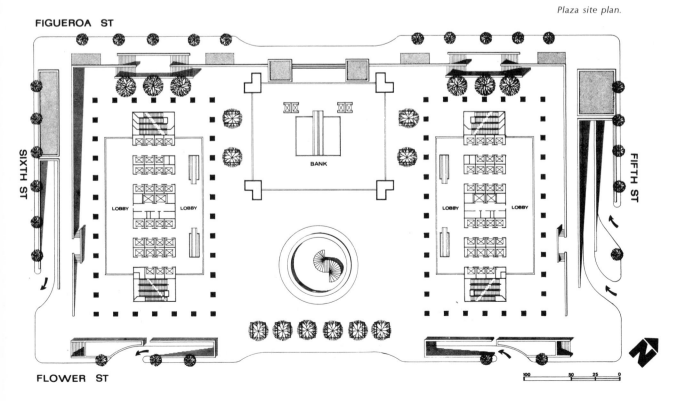

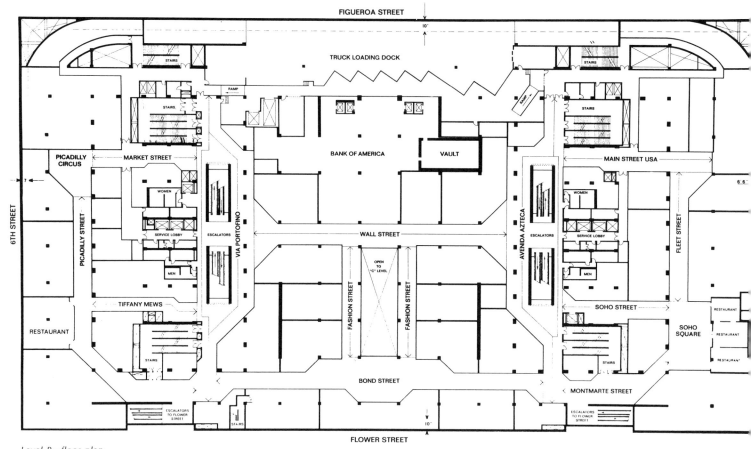

Level B—floor plan.

RIGHT: *Cross section through the center of Atlantic Richfield Plaza's twin towers showing two-level subterranean shopping center and one-level parking garage located below ground. In the center between the buildings is the freestanding main office of the Bank of America.* BELOW: *Interior of fashion plaza showing floor pattern and banners. (Photographer: Wayne Thom, Photographer.)*

Bunker Hill area is located in a block bounded on the west by Figueroa Street, on the south by Fifth Street, on the east by Flower Street, and on the north by Fourth Street. It is in an old section of downtown Los Angeles that is rapidly being revitalized to become again the center of exciting urban activities. Close by are the music center, the civic center, the Richfield Plaza, and a number of new commercial and high-rise buildings.

The thirty-five-story 1,500-room hotel provides a number of floors for retail use. Four retail floors are located above the main entrance level. All retail floors overlook the spacious atrium, and the balconies on each level are successively stepped back to allow natural light to penetrate the lower levels. The seventh, which is the uppermost floor of the podium structure, will be the fourth level devoted primarily to retail. A pedestrian bridge to the World Trade Center will be at this level. The elevator which serves the retail levels will terminate here.

The registration lobby level, at the base of the central atrium, will have a lake. Extending out over this lake will be pods around the base of the atrium which will seat 200 for cocktails. Together with these pods, the lake will cover an acre. A major work of art is contemplated for the lake. Trees and other plantings at this level will bring in the outdoor atmosphere.

BUNKER HILL HOTEL AND RETAIL COMPLEX
Los Angeles, California
ARCHITECTS: John Portman & Associates

Location map.

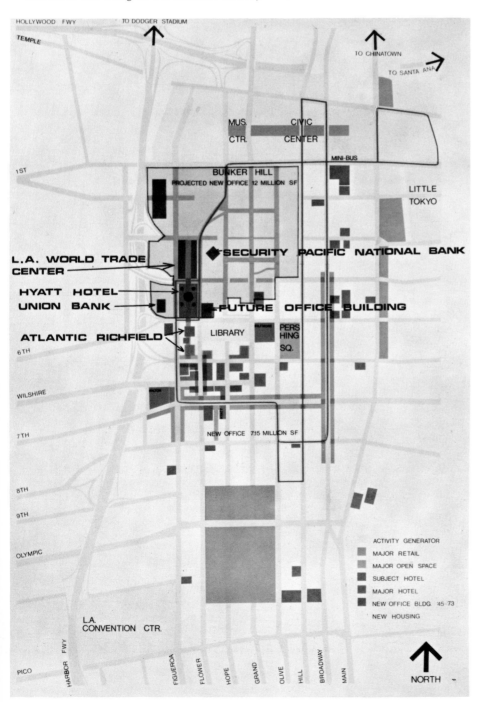

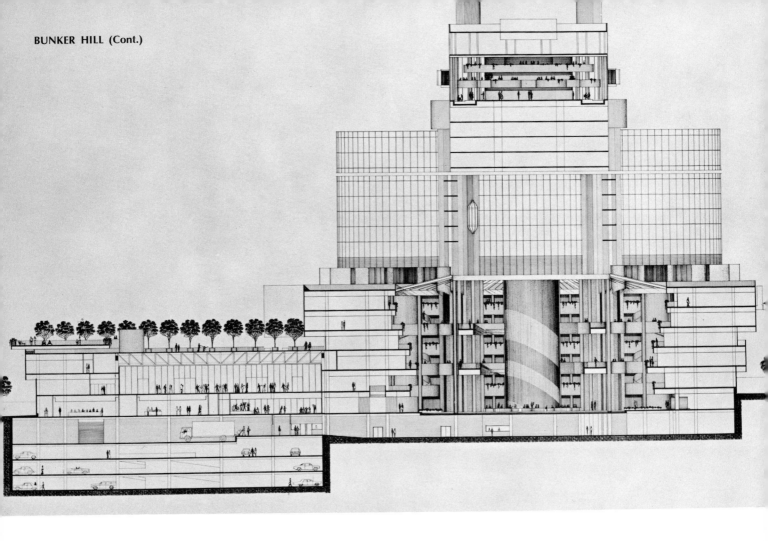

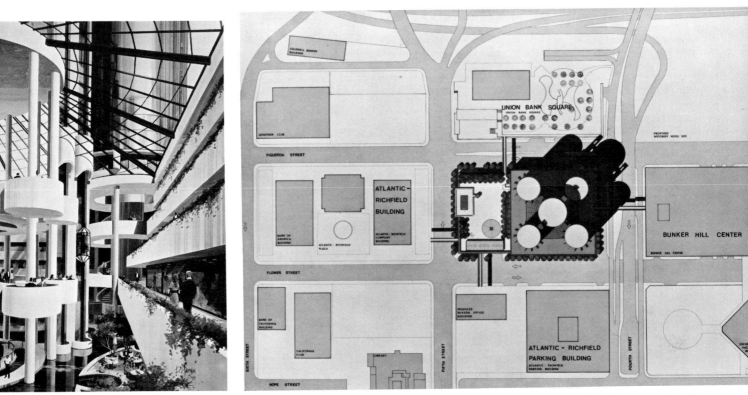

Interior perspective of the large central space, or atrium. Note the retail levels on the right and the lake on the lower left, at the registration-lobby level.

TOP: *Section of the hotel and retail area.*
ABOVE: *Site plan.*

The architect for the project comments:

The Market Street East Transportation Mall Center, located east of the City Hall, will be a unique urban "minicity" three-dimensional entity containing most of the major uses found in a city core. The goals of the project are (1) to reverse the decline in downtown retail activities, (2) to help the center city capture a major share of the anticipated office demand through 1983, (3) to create a large number of jobs in the building trades during more than a decade of intensive construction work and to create an even larger number of permanent jobs in a wide range of employment categories thereafter, (4) to complete the interface of the potentially effective transit system, (5) to provide the city with a solid economic base which will yield increased taxes, and (6) perhaps most importantly, to create a humane urban pedestrian environment for business, shopping, working, and entertainment.

Market Street East is to be built on a transportation hub which includes commuter railroads, a high-speed rail line, subways, buses, streetcars, and the automobile. It will be tied together by a three-level pedestrian walkway system through an air-conditioned skylit shopping mall. The base formed by the mall, commercial space, and parking will be surmounted with a major air-rights development of office and hotel use.

The project has experienced in the past year one more step in its evolution, a commitment by the Old Philadelphia Development Corporation and the city of Philadelphia to the realization of an idea. The charge to Bower and Fradley Architects, the coordinating architect, by the Redevelopment Authority's Market Street East staff was to design the plan to anticipate full development within the maximum allowable renewal and zoning controls. This meant an increase over the original 3 million square feet of building floor space. To accommodate this increase, the maximum building-height limit was raised from 330 to 490 feet, and the mall was redesigned to provide separated levels for the commercial activity and access to the office buildings above.

The project has already passed from the planning stage into final architectural and engineering design, with three major developers committed. On the west end of the project, Philadelphia Savings Funds Society and John Wanamaker are sponsoring a major office, garage, and commercial structure connected to the transportation mall through a major public space. On the east end, the mall center has been designed to accommodate a new downtown Gimbels department store with adjoining shop space at mall level. The third major developer, the Reading Company, is planning the first stage of its development on the 1100 block of Market Street.

MARKET STREET EAST
Philadelphia, Pennsylvania
COORDINATING ARCHITECTS:
Bower & Fradley Architects

ABOVE: *Shopping mall from street level showing escalators and stairs to the street and second level.*

Final design is under way on the public improvements to relate to these private undertakings, including the commuter-station and center-city rail link between the Penn Central and Reading Railroads, improvement and extension of the Market Street subway stations at Eighth and Thirteenth Streets to accommodate eight-car trains, a 700-car parking garage between Ninth and Tenth Streets, car and bus ramp connections to Vine Street, the rebuilding of Ninth Street, and the construction of the truck service tunnel and the shopping mall in the 900 block with extensions to Strawbridge and Clothier and Lit Brothers department stores.

A project of this magnitude, scope, and complexity must be conceived as a three-dimensional mix of public and private activities. The mall is a great, sunlit urban "people chamber" served by train and subway below and connected by escalator to the street and to the office and auto and bus access levels above. To realize such an undertaking requires innovative approaches to every facet of its design and development.

In the final analysis, the true worth of Market Street East will be the degree to which it successfully provides a series of harmonious spaces for people. Market Street East must provide that which is so lacking in our city streets today—a place where persons alone or in great numbers can find the inspiration and desire to participate once more in the full life of their city.

At the time of this writing, the commercial mall, called The Gallery, was under construction and scheduled for completion in 1977. The Gallery, containing 215,000 square feet of retail selling area, will accommodate 125 shops, restaurants and boutiques, and features a four-story glass-enclosed central court with fountains, trees, and street furniture.

The Rouse Company, which is developing The Gallery, has a ninety-nine-year lease from the Philadelphia Redevelopment Authority.

Of interest is the conclusion of a report made by the Economic Research Associates for the Philadelphia Redevelopment Authority, which follows:

A moderate increase in the dollar volume of retail sales in the central business district is anticipated. Major factors contributing to this increase will be the following:

1. Continuing substantial growth of office space, apartments and other economic activity in central Philadelphia.
2. Major improvements in the regional transportation system radiating from Center City and extension of the system to new, rapidly-growing areas.
3. Partial reorganization of downtown retail facilities to create attractive and cohesive shopping complexes which can increase the drawing power of the Center City.

Market support for new retail space in the CBD is projected at approximately 1.9 million square feet during the period 1975–1985. During the 1975–1985 period, when the new

Site plan.

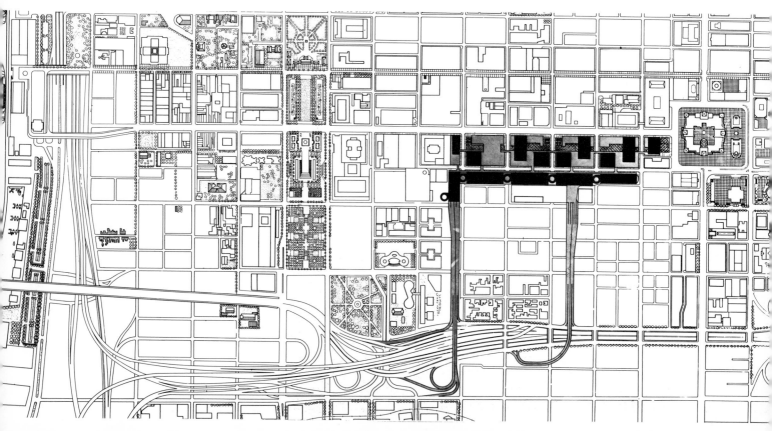

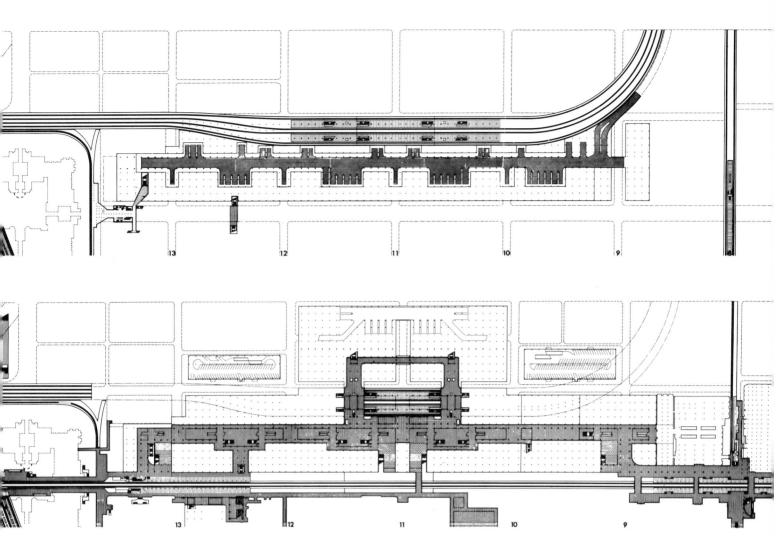

TOP: *Truck-level plan—below street level.* ABOVE: *Mall-level plan—below street level.* (Photographer: Lawrence S. Williams, Inc.)

Model of fully developed project.

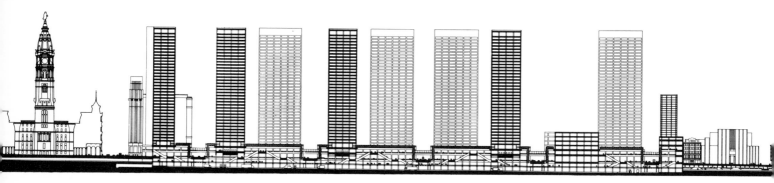

Longitudinal section through entire project. (Photographer: Lawrence S. Williams, Inc.)

retail space at the Market Street East Transportation Mall will be developed, the Central Business District is projected to support over 1.3 million square feet of new retail space.

Gimbel Brothers has been designated by the Philadelphia Redevelopment Authority as the developer of approximately 412,700 square feet of department store space at the Transportation Mall site. This will involve moving their store operations from the present Gimbel's site and will not result in an increase of department store space in Center City. Approximately 744,200 square feet of additional retail space at the Transportation Mall will have to be marketed in the future. This marketing requirement is equivalent to approximately 57 percent of the projected market for new retail space in downtown Philadelphia during 1975–1985.

While this rate will represent a substantial penetration of the total market for downtown space, ERA believes that it can be readily achieved due to the unique advantages offered by the Transportation Mall as a center for retail activity.

As noted previously, attainment of the fullest potential of the Transportation Mall Center will require the creation of an environment which can draw additional numbers of primary shoppers and the inception of an appropriate institutional framework for operations.*

The client is the Redevelopment Authority of the City of Philadelphia.

*Excerpted from a report titled *Market Support for Retail Space in the Market East Transportation Mall Complex* prepared by John K. Haeseler and Robert B. Shawn, Economic Research Associates.

Commuter train station seen from street level.

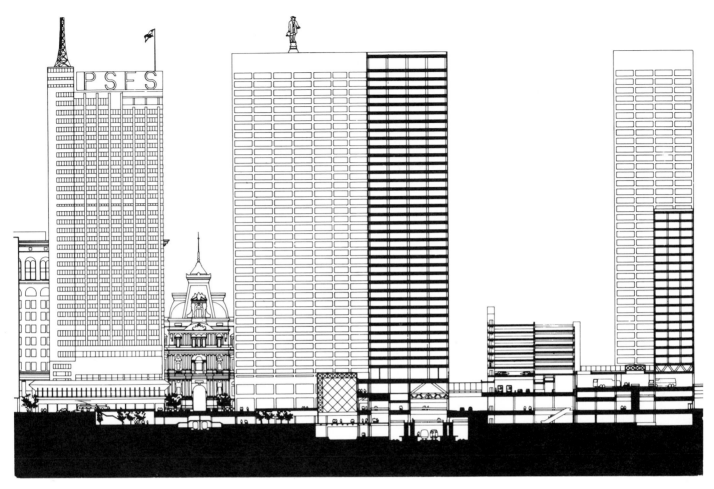

Cross section. (Photographer: Lawrence S. Williams, Inc.)

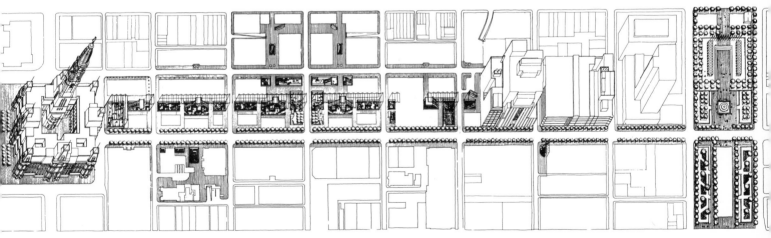

An isometric drawing showing the continuous pedestrian mall passing uninterrupted below vehicular cross streets.

FRANKLIN TOWN
Philadelphia, Pennsylvania

ARCHITECTS:
For the master plan: Philip Johnson
  and John Burgee
For Triangle Plaza: Geddes Brecher
  Qualls & Cunningham
For the residential tower: Richard Martin
  Associates

Franklin Town, a 50-acre privately financed development covering twenty-two blocks, is located in a center-city area which was grossly underpopulated and underdeveloped and was occupied primarily by obsolete factories and parking lots. To take their place, major new in-town residential facilities and a commercial center with offices, hotels, and convention and shopping facilities are planned. The entire development will be served by enclosed parking.

Franklin Town is within easy walking distance of City Hall and will cover the general area from Race Street to Spring Garden Street and from Sixteenth Street to Twenty-first Street.

Planning features include a variety of land uses, mixing residential with commercial, cultural, and recreational elements, so that the area will be used at night and on weekends as well as during the business day. Extensive green areas will be created, including a major new 2-acre "town square" connected by walkways with smaller plazas and parks; a new, tree-lined boulevard; and a "grand avenue" along which will be built theaters, shops, and restaurants.

As Jason R. Nathan, president of Franklin Town Corporation, has said, this project is nationally significant because under private sponsorship, its social commitments were equal to the benefits of the 1970 Federal Uniform Relocation Act and in some ways actually exceeded them.

The Franklin Town program calls for:

A flat guarantee to all homeowners that they will have access to a comparable replacement housing unit without financial loss.

An additional guarantee to every present owner of a single-family home that a replacement housing unit will be made available in the area within the project itself. These units are now under construction.

A guarantee to assist tenants who wish to become homeowners by providing up to $4,000 for a down payment.

A guarantee to pay tenants who wish to remain tenants up to $4,000 for rental assistance over the next four years if the rent at the new location is higher than the rent they are currently paying.

The project is sponsored by five corporations; four owned half of the land, and the fifth was an equity investor, providing the initial financing. The corporations are Smith Kline Corporation, I-T-E Imperial Corporation, Butcher & Singer, The Korman Corporation, and Philadelphia Electric Company. Participating in the loan financing are the Girard Bank and the Prudential Life Insurance Company.

The Franklin Town Corporation, which the companies have set up to carry out the development, committed itself to additional social objectives, including a housing mix to serve all income levels, supportive help for the adjoining neighborhood, and development of public parks and open spaces.

The city, through the council and the Redevelopment Authority, in turn agreed to acquire the remainder of the land needed for the approved redevelopment plan, using eminent domain if necessary. It also agreed to assist in carrying out relocation and other public responsibilities and to monitor and review the operation to see that public commitments are met. The corporation, however, is paying all costs, both public and private.

Mr. Nathan firmly believes that the Franklin Town pattern "opens a new path" for successful private initiative and investment in community redevelopment and that it can be applied, with or without write-down subsidies, in many cities where businesses have large land holdings in obsolescent areas that can provide the basic capital investment for redevelopment.

Private financing, however, Mr. Nathan makes clear, does not replace publicly initiated and subsidized renewal as an essential for the revitalization of urban areas. "It is not a substitute," he says, "but it is an important add-on."

Under the master plan of Johnson and Burgee, a 2-acre town square will be located in the heart of the residential area to the north, with a tree-lined residential, commercial, and shopping boulevard leading diagonally toward City Hall and Penn Center. Four thousand units of housing are planned, primarily in the northern sector, and will include a wide variety of types, consisting of townhouses and low- and high-rise apartments and condominiums, with rents and prices scaled to range from low-income to luxury levels. The development corporation has established a goal of up to 20 percent of the housing for low- or moderate-income

First-phase residential tower (completed).
(Photographer: Lawrence S. Williams, Inc.)

Aerial view looking
northwest from City Hall,
showing outline of projected
project.

Aerial view of the CBD
showing superimposed
model of project.

Model of project. (Photographer: Lawrence S. Williams, Inc.)

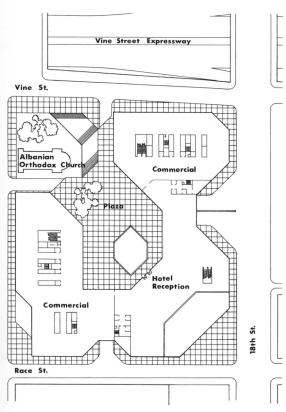

South block, plaza level.

use, depending on what forms of subsidy assistance for these units are available.

The lower part of the area, with the boulevard as its axis, will provide up to 4 million square feet of office and retail shopping space, along with hotel and convention facilities. The plan contemplates that a large proportion of ground-floor commercial space will be devoted to shops, restaurants, theaters, and hotels; this should keep the downtown more lively at night than it would be if the area were a solid phalanx of banks, brokerage houses, and other offices that go dark after business hours. Apartments will also be provided on the upper floors of some of these buildings.

One-fourth of the area will be open and public space, including parks, streets, and walkways. All the public areas will be developed by the corporation as part of the total complex.

Pedestrian ways will connect various parts of the development, but the automobile will be controlled, not banned. The automobile, Master Planner Philip Johnson believes, can be a friend as well as an enemy since it can make an area accessible to people who live some distance away and can also impart life, movement, and color to the public scene. Johnson believes that automobiles must be "a trickle, not a torrent." Feeder streets will lead to other sections, and 5,000 underground parking spaces will replace the present acres of blacktop parking.

Public transit will be by bus, but the corporation is considering the possibility of some type of "people mover" between the town square and the end of the boulevard, partly in the hope that this may reduce the number and cost of the parking spaces that will be needed.*

Of great importance in the project implementation is the staging. The first building to be built in Franklin Town was the twenty-one-story apartment building, One Buttonwood Square. As stated earlier, no downtown redevelopment can be successful without a solid base of contiguous supporting residential areas.

*Excerpted from Jack H. Bryan, "Philadelphia Is Turning Old Town into New Town," *Journal of Housing*, vol. 29, no. 5, June 1972. National Association of Housing and Redevelopment Officials.

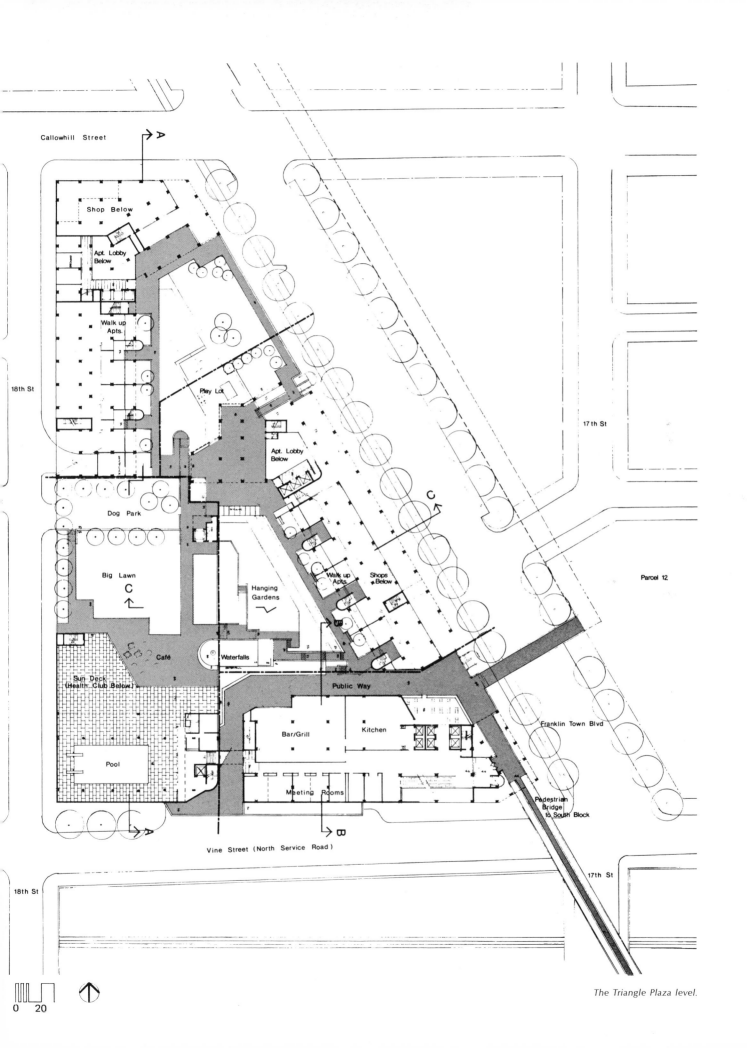

Callowhill Street

A

18th St

Shop Below

Apt. Lobby
Below

Walk up
Apts.

Play Lot

17th St

Apt. Lobby
Below

Dog Park

C

Big Lawn

C

Hanging
Gardens

Walk up
Apts.

Shops
Below

Parcel 12

Café

Waterfalls

Sun Deck
(Health Club Below)

Public Way

Franklin Town Blvd

Bar/Grill

Kitchen

Pool

Meeting Rooms

Pedestrian
Bridge
to South Block

A

B

17th St

Vine Street (North Service Road)

18th St

0 20

The Triangle Plaza level.

CUSTOMS HOUSE SQUARE
Wilmington, Delaware

ARCHITECTS:
For the master plan: Charles Luckman Associates
For the Government Center: Wallace, McHarg,
    Roberts & Todd
For the Delmarva Power building and federal
    office building: Pope, Kruse & McCune;
    Associate Architects: Vincent Kling & Associates
For the city-county building and parking
    facility: Whiteside, Moeckel & Carbonell
    and Vincent G. Kling & Associates
For the Grand Opera House restoration:
    Grieves-Armstrong-Childs
For the Customs House renovation, food-center
    building, and state office building:
    Victorine & Samuel Homsey, Inc.
LANDSCAPE ARCHITECTS FOR MARKET STREET MALL:
    David A. Crane & Partners

*Downtown Wilmington site plan. (1)
Government Center; (2) Customs House Square;
(3) Grand Opera House; (4) Du Pont Company
buildings; (5) left to right, bank buildings: Bank
of Delaware, Wilmington Trust, Farmers Bank,
Delaware Trust; (6) Hercules Company.*

The downtown redevelopment for the city of Wilmington was initiated in 1960 by the business leadership. At the request of the mayor, an organization known as the Greater Wilmington Development Council was created. The objective of this nonprofit, nonpolitical organization was to implement programs which would improve business, cultural, and sociological conditions in the city.

With the assistance of several consulting firms, the GWDC studied the economic factors pertaining to downtown retail and commercial redevelopment and prepared a report entitled *Downtown Wilmington—A Program of Development—A Plan of Action.* As a result of one of the report's recommendations, in June 1968 a nonprofit corporation called Downtown Wilmington, Inc., was formed as a nonpolitical organization composed of city, county, and state officials and community business leaders. Downtown Wilmington, Inc.'s, purpose was to interview prospective developers and to aggressively pursue the implementing of those programs recommended in the study.

The area selected for redevelopment comprised approximately 14.5 acres in the vicinity of Fourth Street to Eighth Street and King, French, and Walnut Streets directly south of the area designated for a civic center, which consisted of approximately 6 acres between Eighth, Ninth, King, French, and Walnut.

The initial concept was to have a private developer build the retail area, the office building, and a motor inn, with the understanding that the city would build parking for 5,000 cars, a truck service tunnel, a heliport, and other public facilities through bonds at an estimated cost of $20 million. However, the uncertain state of the economy (1968–1970)—high interest rates, tightness of credit, and difficulties in obtaining leases from anchor department stores—resulted in the release of the developer.

On March 17, 1970, the Wilmington Housing Authority, acting as the slum clearance and redevelopment authority, invited proposals for redevelopment of the 14.5 acres referred to above. Soon afterward, the Wilmington Housing Authority selected a new developer. For the next three years the new developer, using as a base the original conceptual plans, tried unsuccessfully to obtain commitments from two major department stores and a hotel firm. Early in 1973 the city administration, in conjunction with the Wilmington Housing Authority and the Greater Wilmington Development Council, decided to release the second developer, and this was effected on July 13, 1973.

Advertisements were placed in August 1973 for a new developer. On November 29 a specially formed committee representing the city administration, the Wilmington Housing Authority, and the Greater Wilmington Development Council announced selection of Customs House Square Associates, a company composed of three local firms and formed for the specific purpose of developing the commercial portion of the civic center. The submitted proposal labeled the project

*Delmarva Power building on the left and federal office
building on the right. Completed buildings are in the first
phase of the Government Center development.*

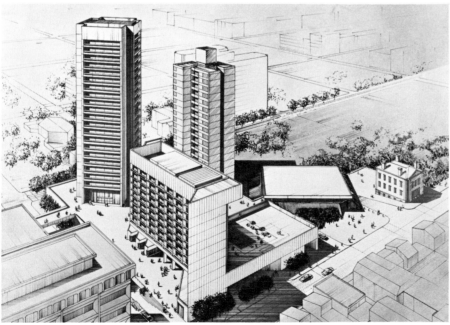

ABOVE: Aerial photograph shows the civic-center area in relation to the central business district of the city. The civic-center area is the ten square blocks in the right center of the cleared area presently being used for surface parking, except for the one completed block in the northwest corner now occupied by the recently completed Delmarva Power and federal office buildings. The old Customs House can be seen in direct center and is planned as the focal point for eight blocks of commercial development. The block directly east of the Delmarva Power and federal office buildings is being excavated for the parking garage topped with the state and city-county office buildings. LEFT: Perspective view. Center foreground is the 250-unit motor inn across the street from the recently constructed Delmarva Power building in the southwest corner of the Government Center. Tower in left rear is the condominium office building. Tower in center rear is the 192-unit residential apartment building. The food-market building can be seen in right center between the apartment tower and the old Customs House on the right. Except for the Customs House, this complex is platformed on a 1,500-car parking garage.

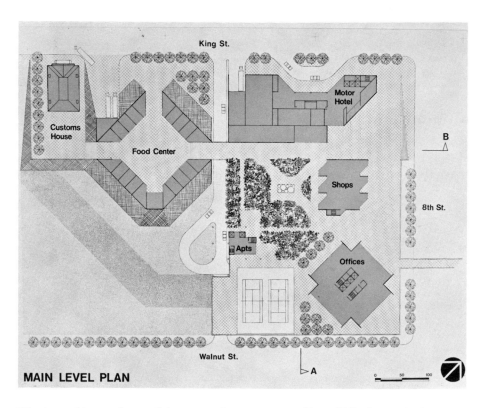

MAIN LEVEL PLAN

"Customs House Square" because the concept utilizes Wilmington's Customs House building, which is of significant historical and architectural value, as the focal point of the development.

The first phase of the new development, bounded by King, Fourth, Walnut, and Eighth Streets, includes a motor hotel, a high-rise office building, an apartment tower, a food-center building, retail facilities, landscaped plazas, and parking. In addition, the historic Customs House building, at Sixth and King Streets, has been renovated to provide office space for the developers and a large meeting room for community organizations.

The ten-story motor hotel, at the corner of Eighth and King Streets, is planned to include 250 guest rooms; banquet, ballroom, convention, and meeting facilities; a restaurant, and a cocktail lounge; and retail shopping. Pedestrians will be able to enter the complex at the corner of King and Eighth Streets through a canopy colonnade that stretches from the motor hotel to the food-center building.

The twenty-story condominium office building has available 250,000 square feet of office space. A large entrance lobby to this building opens onto the landscaped plaza and to a pedestrian bridge connecting across Eighth Street to the Government Center. The office tower rises above the top deck of the 1,500-space underground parking garage and is located near the Eighth Street and Walnut Street corner of the site. This parking facility is intended to serve also the adjacent government and commercial buildings.

The 192-unit twenty-five-story apartment tower is planned to have eight apartments per floor, arranged in a modified pinwheel layout to give the maximum visibility and cross-ventilation to each apartment with the shortest length of corridor. Planning studies have shown that there is a significant apartment market among people who are employed in the nearby Government Center and central business district and who want to live near their place of work. In a later phase, an identical apartment tower is planned to supply urban housing for future development of the Wilmington center city. The apartment dwellers will have the use of the restaurant and other public facilities in the motor hotel, as well as the open, parklike plazas and planned recreational facilities, including tennis courts.

A large food-center building is designed as a European-type market with gourmet meat, fish, and other specialty stores, opening into a large central space. Special festivals, displays, and other functions will be held in this space, which will connect with sidewalk cafés and other displays in the plaza and under the colonnade. The building will have a unique long-spanned roof with large banked earth berms surrounding it and relating its exterior shape to the adjacent Customs House building.

Adjacent to this commercial area is the Government Center complex. Already completed in 1973 were the federal office building and the Delmarva Power building. Construction is in progress for a city-county and a state office building. The land for this complex was acquired through a cooperative program of the Wilmington Housing and Parking Authorities and city, county, and state agencies. The Wilmington Parking Authority undertook to build a 670-car underground parking facility which was to serve as the platform for the two government buildings. The agreement involved the assignment of air rights and the financing, design, and construction of the facility.

Another integral element in the redevelopment of downtown Wilmington is revitalization of Market Street, which is historically the main retail stem of the business area of the city. This street, like similar streets in many United States cities, had deteriorated and become unattractive to shoppers. The idea of improving Market Street was conceived when redevelopment plans for downtown Wilmington were formulated in 1960.

Spurred by the rebuilding of the commercial area and the Government Center, the city administration approved the first phase of the Market Street Mall plan. This mall is planned in the final phase (1975) to connect to the Government Center and Customs House Square.

A key feature of the first phase is the incorporation of the balance of the restoration of the almost 103-year-old Grand Opera House, located on the east side of the block at 818 Market Street. The planned restoration was sufficiently advanced to allow a full season of musical and dance programs during the 1973–1974 season.

The city will provide $1.3 million to create the Market Street Mall, and the private sector is expected to support the project with $750,000. The retailers on Market Street will be encouraged to make façade improvements to attain a "unified concept."*

The developers are Customs House Square Associates (Gilpin, Van Trump & Montgomery, Inc.; Frederick G. Kropf and Sons, Inc.; Robino-Ladd Company).

*Material resource supplied by Peter A. Larson, executive vice president, Greater Wilmington Development Council, Inc.

Section view illustrating the three- and four-level parking facility, which also serves as a platform for phase one development.

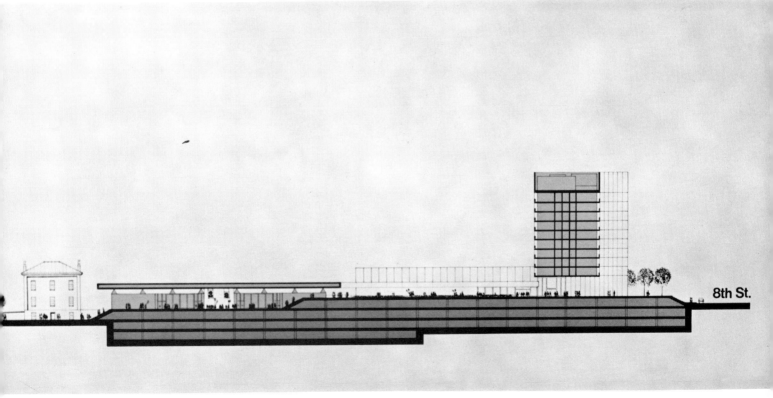

8th St.

NORTHVILLE SQUARE
Northville, Michigan
ARCHITECTS: Louis G. Redstone Associates, Inc.

Northville, Michigan, which has a population of 30,000 and is located 20 miles from downtown Detroit, provides an example of how long-range planning by city and business leaders can prevent the deterioration of a downtown area. Like many small towns near big cities, Northville was experiencing a building boom of large housing developments around its periphery. Although the usual procedure has been to provide shopping facilities near the growing suburbs, Northville's far-sighted business and community leaders forestalled this trend by deciding to build a modern shopping center in the middle of downtown.

The local merchants, headed by Charles Lapham (a member of the city council), formed the Northville Area Economic Development Committee. The committee determined that the commercial complex should be built in the central block of the city. Most of this square block was occupied by old houses which had deteriorated beyond the point where it would have been economical to save them. The Township Hall was the one historic building to be saved, and arrangements were made to move it near an old millpond on property given to the city by the Ford Motor Company.

Because of various legal problems in acquiring all the buildings, the city acquired approximately half of the block, a total of 60,000 square feet. Over a period of several years the city invited developers to buy land at half of its cost and to submit proposals for the project. None of the proposals were acceptable to the city. At this point the Common Council accepted the recommendation of a consultant, R. H. McManus, who advised that the entire half block be developed as an enclosed minimall center and that the city acquire land for 500 surface parking spaces, on both the north and south sides of the block, with the cost to be repaid by the developer over a twenty-year period and with maintenance to be provided by the city. Parking is free for shoppers.

Because the site slopes sharply from north to south, the building was designed with one level facing the main street (north) and two levels at the south side; this provided entrances not only on both levels but also in the intermediate level on the side street facing the City Hall. The bilevel structure provides an intimate enclosure for a grouping of over twenty specialty shops, continuing the personal attention to shoppers' needs that characterizes the remainder of Northville's shopping environment.

It was determined at a very early date that this project was not big enough for a major tenant. Although a major tenant does attract shoppers, makes a project easier to finance, and gives greater income security, it was felt that these advantages would be offset by the substantially reduced rental rates that such a tenant would pay.

Main Street was already an active shopping promenade with a proved capability of attracting customers. Preliminary discussions with mortgage companies led the team to believe that this center could be financed without a major tenant. This assumption did not prove to be entirely correct, since many of the tenants that were desirable for the center were too small or too financially weak to obtain mortgages. A shopping center without a major tenant, constructed in the center of town rather than in the more popular locations on the fringes of a community, requires some special effort to finance.

In this instance, the original equity capital was supplied by members of the development team in the form of cash and/or services. A few investors were brought into the picture at an early stage as limited partners, in the amount of $200,000. The original development team and these limited partners still retain the majority interest. The equity capital was sufficient to attract a finance company for a long-term mortgage.

The center, with its specialty shops and boutiques catering to all groups, has added a new vitality to the city's downtown and should continue to serve as a catalyst for further development.

The owner-developer is Northville Square Company; Thomas E. Dailey and Lawrence C. Dailey, general partners.

ABOVE: *View from South Wing Street showing the variation of street levels. (Photographer: Balthazar Korab.)* BELOW: *Section through mall.*

View from South Wing and West Cady Streets. (Photographer: Balthazar Korab.)

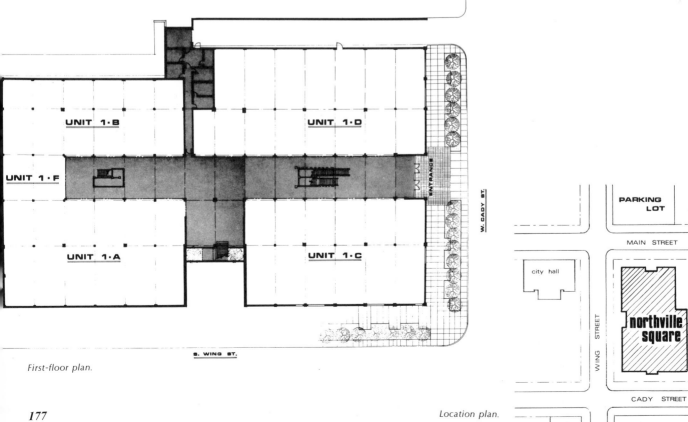

First-floor plan.

Location plan.

177

COUNCIL BLUFFS, IOWA

ARCHITECTS: Neil Astle & Associates

According to Neal R. Herst, of the Urban Renewal Department of the city of Council Bluffs, the 1970 census indicates that the population of Council Bluffs was 60,348. Despite its size and its status as the regional focal point for southwest Iowa, Council Bluffs has almost no evening activity downtown. There are no restaurants in the central area, nor are there any movie theaters catering to the general public. Of the two theaters in operation, one is a dilapidated facility that appeals to the very young crowd (tickets cost 50 cents), and the other shows X-rated movies exclusively. The stores close at 5 P.M., and there are no other popular places for entertainment downtown. With the completion of the shopping center, it is hoped that the new evening-oriented facilities will stimulate the use of the central business district. In addition to bringing people downtown, it is felt that the project will attract new businesses and residents to Council Bluffs in general. Thus not only will the tax base of the downtown area benefit from redevelopment, but also the tax base of the entire community will be strengthened.

The urban renewal project encompasses 37.7 acres of the city's central business district. Of this total, the shopping-center development occupies approximately 12.961 acres. Midlands Corporation, the private redeveloper, will acquire approximately 6.776 acres of the renewal project land, and the city of Council Bluffs will acquire 6.185 acres. The city will construct, on its land, a 1,509-car parking structure at a cost approximating $3.6 million. In addition, all public spaces such as sidewalks, plazas, and enclosed mall areas will be constructed on city-owned land. The maintenance of these public areas, including the parking garage, will be paid by the redeveloper.

Two of the major problem areas encountered by this project were the city's financing of its improvements and the resolution of maintenance and easement problems.

At the time the consolidated 12.9-acre tract was offered for sale, the city included, as an inducement to redevelopment, an offer to contribute a maximum amount of $6 million in public improvements such as a parking garage and a mall area. Midlands' proposal, which was selected as being the most beneficial to the

ABOVE: *Location plan of shopping center and garage.*
(Photographer: Kriss & McCallum.)

city, requested $4.5 million in city improvements. In order to finance these improvements without burdening the community at large with additional taxes, it became necessary to amend Iowa law to allow for so-called tax-increment or tax-allocation financing. This allows the tax base in a project area being developed to be frozen at the predevelopment level. Any increase in postdevelopment tax income is available for payment of bonds used to finance the project improvements. Robert L. Ferluga, the urban renewal director; Harold Booth, president of the First National Bank of Council Bluffs; and Kenneth Haynie, the city's bond attorney from Des Moines, were successful with the Iowa Legislature in the effort to attach this provision to the state's urban renewal law. Only four other states—Iowa, California, Minnesota, and Oregon—have this tax-increment power at the time of this writing.

Before the city could issue the $4.5 million in bonds, a referendum had to be held after petition by the opposition to the renewal project. This conflict between the renewal supporters, led by members of the downtown business community, and the antirenewal forces represented a turning point in the progress of the project. The pro-renewal forces have remained intact since the campaign and are a continual source of support for project activities.

The second major area of difficulty concerning the project involved easement and maintenance agreements between the redeveloper and the city. The agreements themselves were established in order to delineate the duties, responsibilities, and privileges of the two principal parties involved in the land disposition. The basic content of the documents was rather easily resolved between the city and Midlands Corporation. However, numerous other parties were required to review and approve various elements of the agreements. For example, the redeveloper had to have all plans and agreements approved by seven financial institutions, two title insurance companies, and Sears, Roebuck & Company and J. L. Brandeis & Sons, the two major tenants. The renewal agency had to have the same items approved by the city council and the Department of Housing and Urban Development. This large number of organizations with veto power created innumerable problems of coordination and resulted in some considerable delay. This problem was overcome through patience and diligent attempts to improve communications.

The shopping center and parking garages were scheduled for opening in mid-1975.

The owner/developers are Midlands Corporation and the city of Council Bluffs.

ABOVE: *Perspective of interior of shopping center.* LEFT: *Aerial perspective of complex.*

PRUDENTIAL PLAZA
Denver, Colorado

ARCHITECTS: Flatlow Moore Bryan & Fairburn
LANDSCAPE ARCHITECTS: Lawrence Halprin
& Associates

PARK CENTRAL PLAZA
AND SKYLINE PARK
Denver, Colorado

ARCHITECTS: Muchow Associates
LANDSCAPE ARCHITECTS: Lawrence Halprin
& Associates

FIRST OF DENVER PLAZA
Denver, Colorado

ARCHITECTS: Welton Becket and Associates
LANDSCAPE ARCHITECTS: M. Paul Friedberg
& Associates

SIXTEENTH STREET MALL
Denver, Colorado

ARCHITECTS: C. F. Murphy Associates
LANDSCAPE ARCHITECTS: Johnson Johnson & Roy, Inc.

DENVER CENTER
FOR THE PERFORMING ARTS
Denver, Colorado

ARCHITECTS:
For the master plan and theater: Kevin Roche,
John Dinkeloo and Associates
For the concert hall: Hardy, Holtzman, Pfeiffer
For the parking garage: Muchow Associates

Concern for the redevelopment of downtown Denver dates back to the early 1950s. It was at this time that the first business groups organized the Downtown Denver Improvement Association. Later, with the formation of the Denver Urban Renewal Authority (DURA), planning for the area began to proceed with the cooperation of the city council.

The Skyline project was formulated over a period of years and was finally approved by the voters in May 1967. Since that time, a number of significant commercial developments have been completed in the 113 acres of downtown renewal area and the contiguous areas, including the Prudential Plaza, First of Denver Plaza, Larimer Square, and Park Central Place. In the planning stages is the Sixteenth Street pedestrian mall, which is intended to provide access to the central business district and to create a people-oriented environment in the adjacent area.

Prudential Plaza is planned as a commercial retail- and office-space rental development to encourage pedestrian traffic in the center of the complex and to provide a landscaped area on the ground and on an upper-plaza level, which can connect with future developments on the surrounding blocks. The use and preservation of the existing historic Daniels and Fisher Tower as a focal point is recognized and, in fact, emphasized in this scheme.

The plan features a retail commercial development on two levels: a street level and an upper-plaza level, both of which are accessible to pedestrian traffic. Future connections by bridges at the upper (or plaza) level with surrounding blocks are projected. Space for 600 cars will be provided in two levels of underground parking structure, with an entrance ramp from Curtis Street and an exit ramp to Arapahoe Street.

The complex was developed by Del E. Webb Corporation, jointly with Prudential Insurance Realty Corporation.

Another completed project is Park Central Plaza. This $25 million 524,000 square-foot office-retail center is in the major commercial area of Skyline. It too provides an underground parking structure beneath the total development. Above ground are pedestrian walkways and elevated landscaped plazas. Pedestrian bridges will connect to future buildings. A unique feature of this project is the 100-foot-wide park over the underground parking structure.

Skyline Park was designed, under separate contract to the Denver Urban Renewal Authority, by Lawrence Halprin & Associates. The Park Central building was designed by Muchow Associates. The developers are Leavell-Rio Grande Central Bank Association.

The First of Denver Plaza Building, which opened for occupancy in August 1974, is part of a full-block banking-business complex (called First of Denver Plaza) in the heart of Denver's financial district. The plaza will form a main entryway to the new Plaza building and will be an open-space connector between that building, the existing twenty-eight-story First National Bank building, and a new six-story structure housing the bank's teller facilities. The developers are Urban Investment and Development Company, owner-developers of the building.

The proposed Denver Mall runs nine blocks from Broadway to Arapahoe Street. It reinforces an already strong urban framework and links together the major spaces that identify the central business district—the civic center, Zeckendorf Plaza, and Skyline Park, a part of the Skyline urban renewal internal pedestrian system.

The open-space concept is being viewed with interest by downtown Denver spokesmen who are concerned with removing auto traffic from Sixteenth Street, the city's principal retail thoroughfare, and subsequent development of a pedestrian mall.

Architecturally, as well as functionally, the Sixteenth Street Mall will be of special interest. The Daniels and Fisher Tower, with its spire, provides a historical character to the street. The scale and detail of many of the older buildings offer an appropriate setting for pedestrian-oriented activity.

Whereas as an overdevelopment of Sixteenth Street could result in canyons of tall buildings, the mall could become an organizing force for the downtown area, accommodating development while at the same time remaining at a pedestrian scale and providing vistas to the sky and mountains.

Sixteenth Street presents an interesting mix of architectural styles, materials, scale, signage, and merchandising techniques. Since there is no one predominant

Prudential Plaza location plan. (Photograph courtesy of the Urban Renewal Authority.)

Plaza-level plan, Prudential Plaza.

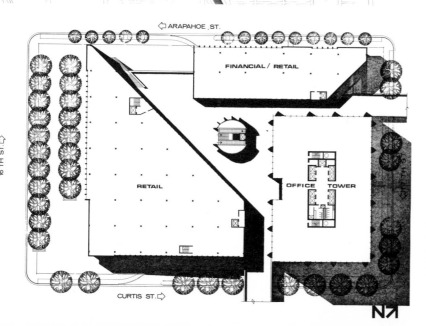

Skyline Denver showing architect's concept of the completed Prudential Plaza in relation to existing downtown Denver buildings. The plaza has 40 percent of total land area devoted to open space, with second-level mall and walkways over the street to adjoining planned new development.

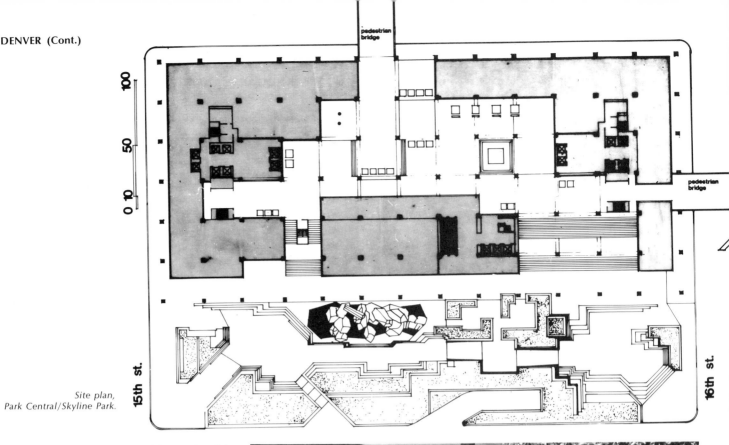

Site plan,
Park Central/Skyline Park.

15th st.

16th st.

pedestrian bridge

pedestrian bridge

100

50

0 10

Completed first section of the three-block-long linear Skyline Park in downtown Denver's Skyline urban renewal project. This park section, in front of the new Park Central Bank building, includes a fountain sculpture 75' long with waterfalls 10' high. Completed in July 1973, it was built with $613,000 of the Denver Urban Renewal Authority's funds.

Night view, Park Central/Skyline Park. (Photographer: James Maxwell.)

style distinctive enough to suggest a uniform design theme, it is necessary to develop a building materials spectrum for the mall that can unify the varied elements and at the same time be compatible with each building façade, store entrance, and marquee.

A simple and uncluttered design is used to unify the nine-block mall. Rather than compete with the architecture of the street, the mall design utilizes a series of repetitive elements—walls, paving, berms, furniture, and landscaping—to respond individually to each zone of activity, each block, and each storefront.

The basic design theme consists of a repetitive paving "matrix" that runs the entire length of the mall. This matrix forms a neutral background for special activity areas within each block. These areas are enclosed by a repetitive system of walls, landscaped berms, and modular furniture elements.

These components can be combined in a variety of ways to achieve unique spaces to serve particular functions. Within each space there are focal points for fountains, kiosks, sculpture, or play equipment to enhance pedestrian scale on the street and to provide a variety of visual interest. The individual components that make up the design concept can be categorized into paving materials, structural elements, furniture, landscaping, lighting, and graphics.

Landscaping is utilized extensively throughout the Sixteenth Street Mall to improve the basic environment of the street by providing scale, color, and texture to the pedestrian walkways, activity spaces, and passive seating areas.

To provide a contrast to the formality of brick paving, linear concrete paving, and simple architectural furnishings, the planting areas are informally designed. The basic planting units are sloping berms of various sizes, enclosed by a structural concrete retaining wall on three sides and by a concrete curb on the fourth. These planting beds are used at varying scale in approximately 40 percent of the total area to provide a contrast to the hard walkways, buildings, and streets.

Since the planted areas are intended for use as well as for appearance, ground cover, grasses, and shrubs are selected for durability and ease of maintenance. The sloping forms provide an excellent gathering place where people can eat their lunches, sit and talk, or watch the activity on the mall. The landscaped areas also create a sense of enclosure, forming activity spaces such as play lots, game pavilions, outdoor eating areas, or merely secluded resting areas, away from the mainstream of traffic.

Graphics consultants were Unit I Inc. The project was sponsored by Downtown Denver, Inc. The CBD will be further strengthened by the planned Denver Con-

First of Denver Plaza. Model of proposed project.

vention Center, the Auraria Higher Education Center (which will unify the downtown campuses of three universities), and the performing-arts center. The performing-arts center will be located in a four-block area of downtown Denver and is planned to house a theater complex, a concert hall, an outdoor amphitheater, and a parking structure, all joined by a cruciform glass-covered galleria.

The galleria, 60 feet wide and 75 feet high, is planned to tie together the many different elements of the center. The center will include two existing buildings—an auditorium theater and an arena which will be converted for theater use. Patrons coming either by rapid transit or by automobile will arrive at the block occupied by the garage. Automobile patrons will be able to go directly from their cars to balconies and terraces overlooking the galleria and then descend by means of stairs or open elevators to the galleria level. The galleria will be lined with shops, restaurants and cafés, and some spaces for street theater or community experimental theater. The concert hall will be located on one side of the crossing of the galleria, together with the amphitheater and a refurbished city building which will be used for offices. On the other side will be the theater group, which will contain a cinema in addition to the two theaters. Between these two, the galleria will widen out toward the mountain view, with a flight of steps leading down to a park. One of the city streets in the four-block area will remain open to provide access to the garage and loading docks.

Sixteenth Street Mall. BELOW: *Section of pedestrian mall showing typical requirements and design treatment for service and access.* BELOW, RIGHT: *Detailed design plan of the Curtis and Champa Street area.*

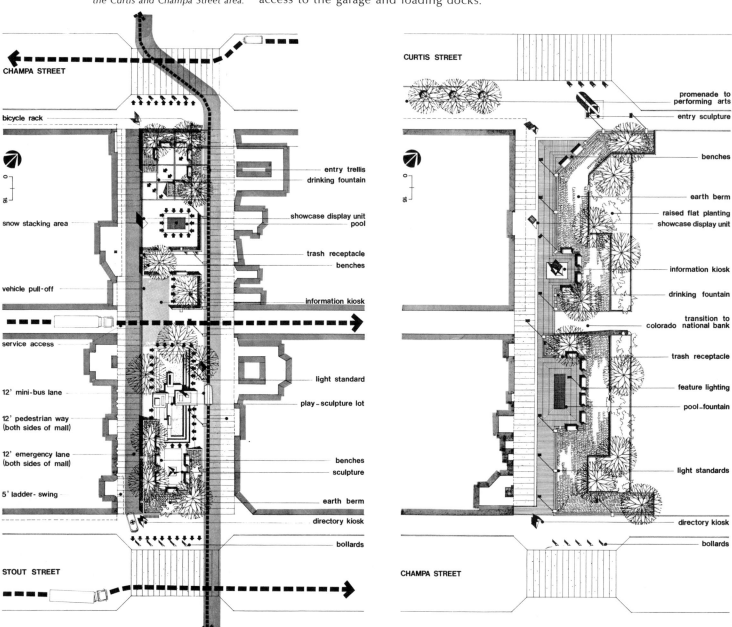

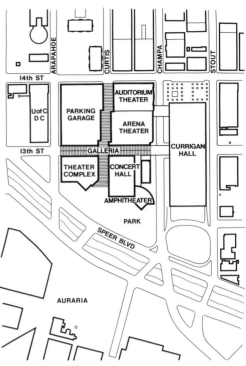

Denver Center for the Performing Arts. ABOVE: Site plan. ABOVE, LEFT: Interior view of galleria looking toward park area. LEFT: Schematic design layout.

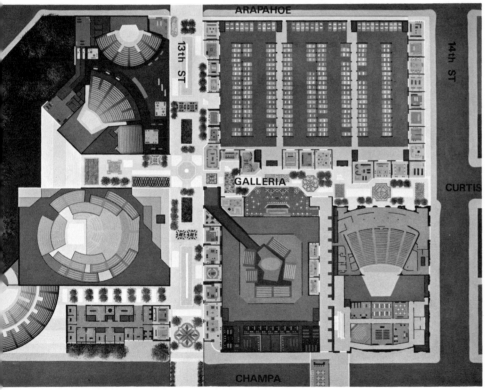

Sixteenth Street Mall. BELOW, LEFT: Proposed master plan showing handling of the traffic system. BELOW: View from mall looking northwest toward the old Daniels and Fisher Tower.

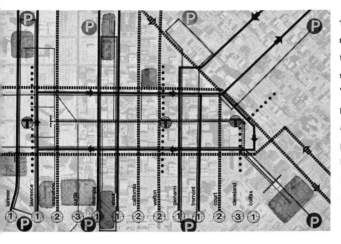

16th. street mall

mall mini-bus

traffic volume

street priority of use ③

'DART' vehicle

pedestrian access

activity center

parking lot Ⓟ

bus transit

transit stop (bus) Ⓑ

p.r.t. transit

transit stop (p.r.t.) Ⓣ

RAINBOW CENTER
Niagara Falls, New York

ARCHITECTS:
For the master plan and hotel: Gruen Associates
For the convention center: Philip Johnson and John Burgee
For the plaza: Abraham Geller, Raimund J. Abraham, and Giulino Fiorenzoli

ABOVE: Perspective view looking from the roof of the convention center toward the plaza and hotel. (Photographer: Al Le Claire.)

Rainbow Center occupies an urban renewal area of 82 acres close to the American Falls and adjacent to the Rainbow bridge, leading to Canada. The Rainbow Center master plan spells out a comprehensive redevelopment program—one of the few cases in which an entire business district has been reconstructed in a city the size of Niagara Falls. It will represent a private investment of more than $100 million, with about $60 million of public funding.

One of the major objectives of Rainbow Center is the development of downtown Niagara Falls as a multipurpose activity center for tourism, conventions and trade exhibits, and retail, entertainment, and related services; it is also intended to serve as a commercial center for the city and surrounding trade areas in terms of the traditional central business district functions.

The main feature of the center will be a plaza of unusual interest, located at the west of the completed convention center. The design of the plaza was selected by means of a competition in which 300 American and Canadian architects participated. The winning design, by the team of architects Abraham Geller, Raimund J. Abraham, and Giulino Fiorenzoli, is being closely implemented. Their technical consultant on costs was G. A. Hanscomb Partnership, and landscaping was done by Shin Obayashin.

The plaza includes a waterfall at the north end, two natural rock-garden islands resembling a gorge in the center, and a 1,200-seat amphitheater at the south end. Other attractions are an ice-skating rink which can be transformed into a dancing water display the rest of the year, and a 60-foot-diameter theater-in-the-round called Cyclorama.

An important element of the plan is a pedestrian shopping mall which connects the American Falls, in Prospect Park on the west, through a large retail complex to the new 300,000 square-foot multipurpose convention center on the east. This mall and its extensions link every element in the development: the parking garages, the convention center, hotels, stores, restaurants, apartments, offices, theaters, museums, and other activity centers.

The project is made possible through the assistance of the U.S. Department of Housing and Urban Development, the New York State Urban Development Corporation, the city of Niagara Falls, the New York State Division of Housing and Community Renewal, and the Niagara Falls Urban Renewal Agency.

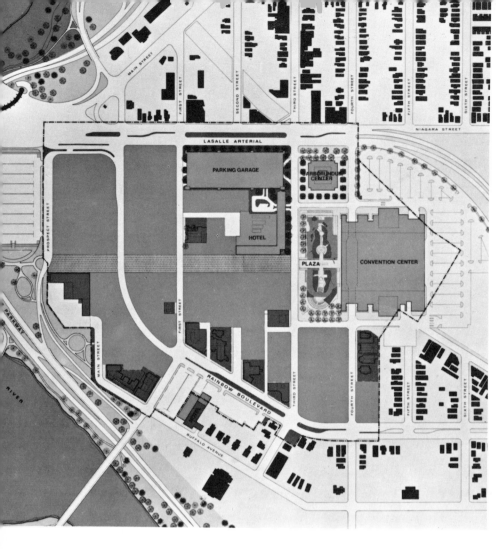

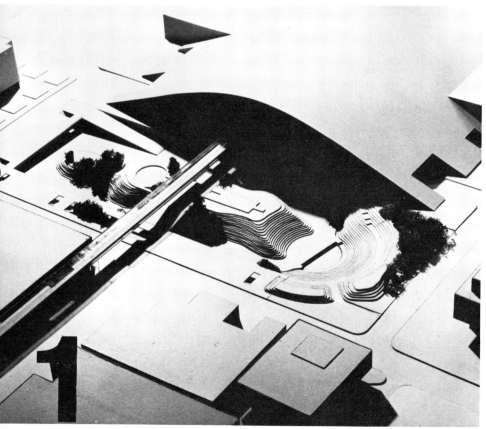

BELOW, LEFT: *Model of the plaza.* BELOW: *Aerial view of redevelopment showing the model superimposed on the site.* (Photographer: Louis Checkman.)

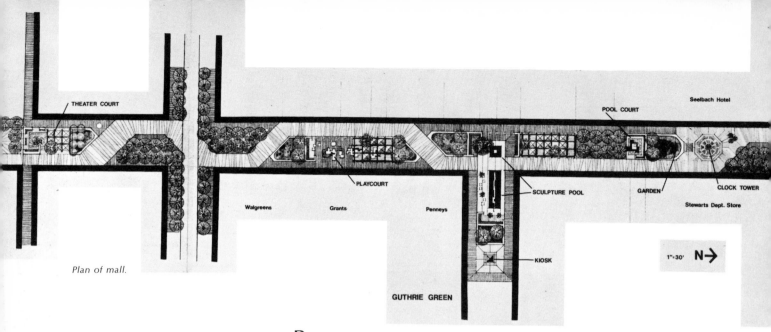

Plan of mall.

Labels on plan: THEATER COURT · POOL COURT · Seelbach Hotel · PLAYCOURT · SCULPTURE POOL · GARDEN · CLOCK TOWER · Walgreens · Grants · Penneys · Stewarts Dept. Store · KIOSK · 1"=30' N→ · GUTHRIE GREEN

RIVER CITY MALL
Louisville, Kentucky

PLANNERS AND LANDSCAPE ARCHITECTS:
Johnson Johnson & Roy, Inc.
PROJECT DIRECTOR: Richard Macias
SUPERVISING ARCHITECTS: Ryan Associated
Architects

River City Mall was dedicated in August 1973 and proved to be an important step in the development of the center city.

Fourth Street was chosen for the location of the mall, an area which once was the main commercial district before the center of activities shifted south early in the century. Yet, because of its key location between the riverfront project and the downtown core, the area became economically viable as an activity bridge between the areas to the south and the new development to be constructed along the river. Of all the private development areas in downtown Louisville, this one offered the greatest opportunity for upgrading and was assigned the highest priority.

The project area included three blocks of Louisville's Fourth Street, a strip 2,440 feet long by 60 feet wide, building front to building front. There were two cross streets which the design would have to accommodate as pedestrian conflicts within the length of the mall. A sense of the "urban canyon" prevailed, primarily because of the tall structures which formed the walls of Fourth Street. An obvious major design problem was the lack of sunlight which would be available to the pavement of this narrow, north-south-oriented street.

The concept was one of moving people alternately from one side of the street to the other and of utilizing the spaces created by this pattern for special-use areas which would relate closely to the commercial functions on that portion of the mall. Specific developments included theater-block plazas, children's play areas at various shopping zones, outdoor restaurant facilities, and locations where people could concentrate and where events or presentations could take place. The mall was intended to be totally flexible, allowing a variety of events to take place, and also to provide areas for display and for extensions of the existing commercial function. Linking the special-use zones together was a major pedestrian flow expressed in broad bands of textured concrete. The special zones were paved in contrasting brick and featured with fountains, sculpture, planting areas, and seating spaces and other facilities for pedestrians.

Ed Bennett, staff writer for the *Louisville Times,* made this evaluation of the mall in an article published at the end of the first year of its operation:

> It is undeniably a pleasant and humane place, even at times a lively and fun place; it remains something of a crystal embedded in the heart of a largely rock-drab downtown, one of the few evidences around that a civilized, yet distinctly urban, pulse beats. . . .
>
> Among almost all who want to like it, the mall provokes deeply ambivalent feelings, a constant tug-of-war between being heartened and disappointed. . . .
>
> Heartened, because it is used and shown off. Disappointed, because it is not used thoroughly and has not become a vibrant staple in the city's life. . . .
>
> There is about the mall an air of congeniality, a feeling of casual sociability, uncommon to downtowns, a diversity foreign to the suburbs and an attention to the human scale and psyche unknown to both. It brings together, sometimes in surprisingly intimate ways, all sorts of people. . . .
>
> The mall is neither a rarefied promenade, a sumptuous shopping center, an entertainment mecca nor a place for people who find their happiness in insulation and unrubbed shoulders.

ABOVE: *Children's play area.*   LEFT: *Closeup of water display.*   LEFT, BELOW: *General view of mall. (Photographs courtesy of Johnson Johnson & Roy, Inc.)*

RIGHT: *Recreation area showing informal seating arrangements.*
RIGHT, BELOW: *View of fountain area.* *(Photographs courtesy of Johnson Johnson & Roy, Inc.)*

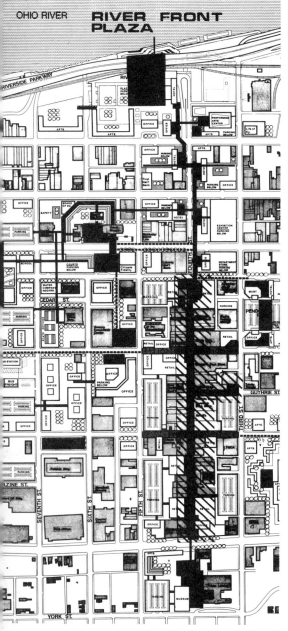

Location plan.

Sadly, the attraction is not in what there is to do, but rather, in how it allows people to go about doing what they must.

Its comfort and diversions slow people down and they pay more attention to what's around them. They stop, lean and sit, talk and watch.

For those who work or do business downtown, the mall is a refuge from routine. They can settle down into the strangely private "entry garden" near Liberty Street to read or daydream, sit near the bustle at Guthrie Green and marvel or sorrow at the human lot, or simply go for an unhurried walk. Passing friends slip out of the pedestrian flow and talk. Conversations between strangers crop up. Flirting booms. . . .

In the mornings, there is almost a neighborhood feeling to the place, because people are doing something besides coming and going. Secretaries, clerks, business men, even an occasional merchant, are scattered around, eating doughnuts, reading newspapers, chatting, simply warming in the sun. City workers are out cleaning, watering plants, worrying about the health of the groundcover. . . .

At lunchtime, the place is jammed. People go out to watch other people going out. They have their brown bags, their carry-outs, hot dogs from the hot-dog wagon, ice cream from the sidewalk machine. . . .

In the evenings, when idleness has overtaken industry and the streams of pedestrians have slowed to dribbles, all is tranquil again. Almost all the businesses close down, and there is little reason for people to be there. Yet, they are. . . .

In all, the mall is a pleasant and interesting enough place, rightfully billed by its promoters as "A Place for People."*

*Excerpted with permission from an article by Ed Bennett in *The Louisville Times,* August 3, 1974. Copyright © 1974, *The Louisville Times.*

The Riverfront area is a narrow strip extending 4,000 feet along the river from 1st to 9th Streets, between Main Street and the river. It contains approximately 85-acres of which 65 had been subject to flooding. The site is directly adjacent to the downtown, approximately $\frac{1}{4}$ mile from the center of the main shopping district running along 4th Street. The area was previously the location of industrial and warehousing activities in obsolescent and blighted buildings. A major portion of the area was devoted to parking lots, interspersed with minor commerical uses.

The site's greatest potential was in the development of water related amenities within only a few blocks of the downtown. Other favorable conditions were: land values were low and there was little relocation required. The freeway, not yet built, offered the potential for creative design concepts. Urban renewal funds were available at that time and the city had an interested developer in the Reynolds Metals Corporation, who commissioned Doxiadis Associates, Inc. to prepare development plans for the Riverfront.

There has been an interest and concern for the development of the scenic value of the riverfront from as far back as the 1830's, and plans were developed in the 1930' and 50's. What helped to refocus interest in the river and to restore some of its historic atmosphere was the introduction in 1962 of the "Belle of Louisville" sternwheeler riverboat docked at the foot of 4th Street, and serving as a tourist excursion boat.

The planner's overall objective was to tie the city to the river: to turn the city back to the river and thus eliminate the river as a backyard; to allow access to the river under different flooding conditions; to take a long-abandoned part of the city and build into it round-the-clock activity in a coordinated design, making it an area that people will want to revisit time and again, summer or winter. Implicit in this objective was integration of the design with the proposed freeway and the existing railroad, developing the riverfront itself as recreational and amenity relief for the downtown population, and creating an appropriate setting for the "Belle of Louisville."

There were many problems along the way to be resolved in working out agreements with the Corps of Engineers, Bureau of Public Roads, the railroad and the utility company. The credit for their resolution is given in the main to the project's expediter, Archibold P. Cochran. He was instrumental in getting the utility company to bury power lines; in obtaining air rights over the expressway for the city and in resolving a financial crisis by persuading the banks to sell short term notes for immediate construction financing of the parking structure.

The project has created public enthusiasm for the new image of Louisville and has stimulated downtown development. The construction activity was a catalyst for a massive downtown redevelopment program detailed in the Center City master Development plan designed by Victor Gruen Associates.*

The master plan called for the linking of the riverfront with the CBD area, with the pedestrian mall to be designed by Johnson Johnson & Roy, Inc.

*Parts taken from a study by Arthur Cotton More/Associates Architects, Planners for the Office of Water Resources Research, U.S. Department of the Interior Project No. C-2141.

RIVERFRONT
Louisville, Kentucky

ARCHITECTS: Doxiadis Associates, Inc.
ASSOCIATE ARCHITECTS: Lawrence P. Melillo, AIA,
  and Jasper D. Ward, AIA, Architects

ABOVE, LEFT: *View of riverfront from the river.* ABOVE: *Detail of fountain and pool.* BELOW: *Fourth Street dock showing the* Belle of Louisville.

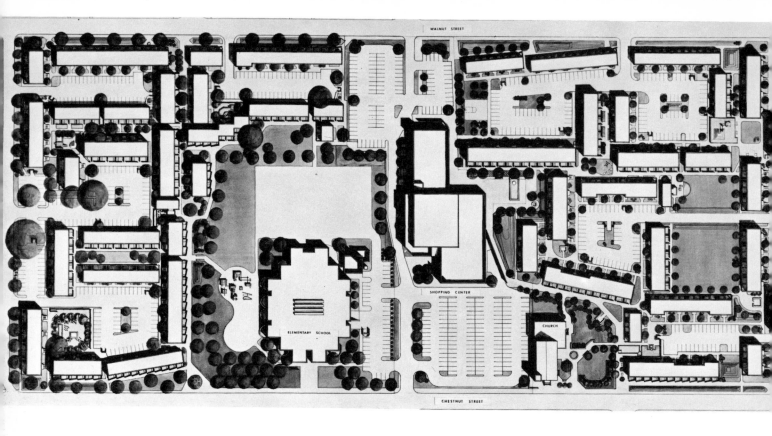

VILLAGE WEST
SHOPPING CENTER
Louisville, Kentucky

ARCHITECTS: Design Environment Group
  Architects, Inc.; John Bickel, AIA,
  Architect-Director

The renewal of Louisville also extends to the immediate neighborhood of Village West Shopping Center, which is located several miles northwest of the CBD and is part of the complete neighborhood redevelopment. This shopping center won an architectural citation for planning from the Kentucky chapter of the American Institute of Architects. The plan was chosen originally in a national competition in 1964.

The shopping center, part of a third stage of a 100-unit low- and moderate-income housing project within three blocks, was developed by and is under the management of blacks. It was financed under the HUD 236 program. The following were among the many agencies whose approvals were needed before implementing construction:

1. Louisville Urban Renewal & Community Development Agency
2. Federal Housing Administration
3. City building inspector
4. City fire marshal, including city fire department
5. Louisville & Jefferson County Planning Commission
6. City Department of Sanitation, Trash Collection
7. United States postmaster
8. Kentucky Inspection Bureau
9. Southern Bell Telephone & Telegraph Company
10. Metropolitan sewer district
11. Louisville Water Company
12. Louisville Gas & Electric Company
13. City Department of Public Works
14. Jefferson County Department of Health

The plans had to be presented for review and approval to large neighborhood groups, in addition to the government agencies. Also, considerable time was spent in negotiating construction contracts with HUD.

The center was opened in the summer of 1973 with nearly 75 percent occupancy, consisting of boutiques, small service shops, a grocery store, a drugstore, and a minitheater. Although rentals were low, ranging from $2.50 to $4 per square foot, financing was difficult because of a reluctance of Triple A tenants to come into a mall in a high-crime area. In reality, there were no problems of vandalism or security because of a tight, twenty-four-hour patrolling of guards.

The developers are Action Now, Inc.

OPPOSITE PAGE: *Master plan.*
BELOW: *South elevation.*
ABOVE: *Entrance to shopping center.*

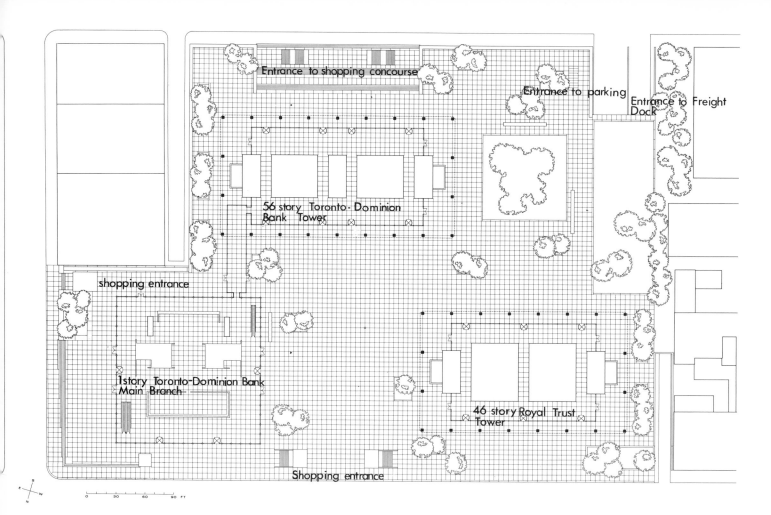

The plan labels include:

Entrance to shopping concourse

Entrance to parking

Entrance to Freight Dock

56 story Toronto-Dominion Bank Tower

shopping entrance

1 story Toronto-Dominion Bank Main Branch

46 story Royal Trust Tower

Shopping entrance

TORONTO-DOMINION CENTRE

Toronto, Ontario

ARCHITECTURAL DESIGN: Ludwig Mies van der Rohe
ASSOCIATE ARCHITECTS: John B. Parkin Associates
and Bregman & Hamann

Toronto-Dominion Centre, located in the center of the central business district of Toronto, was developed in stages. In 1969 the first stage was completed and consisted of two office towers and a single-story bank pavilion linked by a three-story substructure. The substructure contains a shopping concourse and parking for 710 cars. A third tower was completed in 1975.

The 5½-acre project includes an underground shopping concourse with an area of 150,000 square feet—fifty-six retail shops, seven restaurants, and a cinema. At the time of this writing the concourse was not connected to any other development. It is planned that ultimately the concourse will connect to the Royal Bank site to the south and the Bank of Montreal site to the north under King Street. There is also a two-level parking facility below grade for 700 cars.

The owner is Toronto-Dominion Centre Ltd.

ABOVE: Plan at plaza level. RIGHT: View showing entrance from the plaza to the shopping concourse. (Photographer: Panda Associates Photography.)

Concourse level.

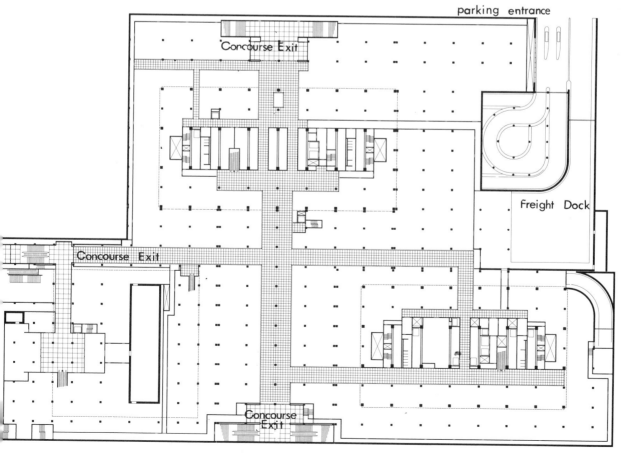

Plan at
shopping-concourse
level.

195

FOUR SEASONS SHERATON HOTEL

Toronto, Ontario

ARCHITECTS: Neish, Owen, Rowland & Roy
  (formerly Searle Wilbee Rowland)
CONSULTANT: J. E. Sievenpiper

The Four Seasons Sheraton Hotel, located south of Nathan Phillips Square, is included in the Toronto presentation because it is an integral part of the development surrounding the City Hall and the civic square.

The ground floor includes a generous motor court with vehicular entrance and egress from Richmond Street and Queen Street. Direct access to the main lobby is achieved from the motor court.

The registration lobby is immediately north of the main lobby. The remainder of the ground floor contains a retail concourse adjacent to the hotel entrances, with a separate entrance on the northeast corner of the site.

The first level below grade contains further retail space and is accessible directly by a subgrade connector from Nathan Phillips Square and the Richmond Adelaide Centre. These connectors form links in the eventual underground pedestrian connector from the City Hall to the Union Station.

An important aspect of the parking is the arrangement, between the city and the hotel owners, by which the hotel's 350-car underground garage is linked by underground tunnel to the 2,300-car city parking facility beneath the civic square.

"The reason for this was largely economic," architect Searle points out. "The peak use periods of a City Hall type of office building function are different than those of a hotel function. So it meant better 24-hour utilization of the parking facility."*

An unusual feature of the hotel design is the inclusion of an elevated landscaped area at the third-floor level; this is visible from the civic square and is reached by elevated pedestrian walkway from the City Hall through the hotel's main entrance. Included in the two levels of roof garden is the waterfall, which tumbles into the lobby year round.

*"A Special Report: Toronto's Four Seasons Sheraton Shows the New Approach to Hotel Construction," *The Canadian Building* magazine, January 1973.

View across the civic square to north elevation of the hotel. (Photographer: Panda Associates Photography.)

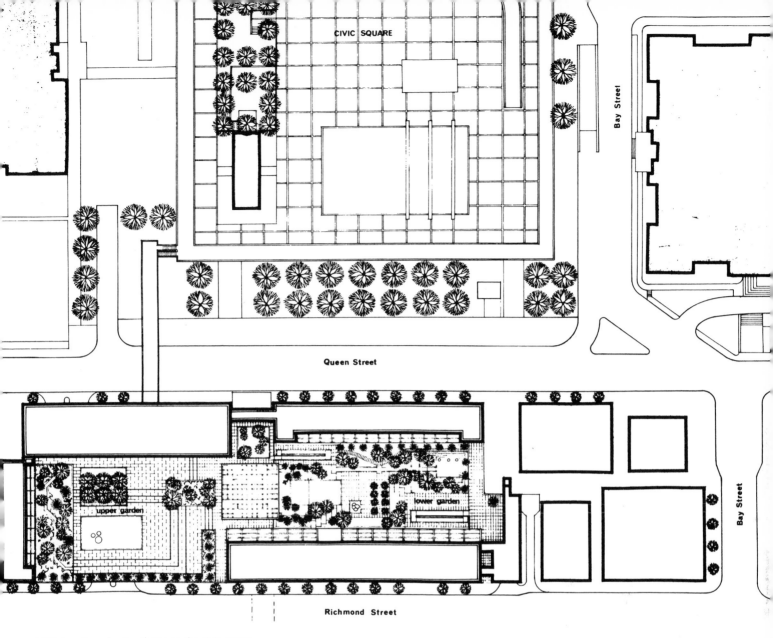

ABOVE: *Location plan in relation to the civic square.*
BELOW: *Street-floor plan.*

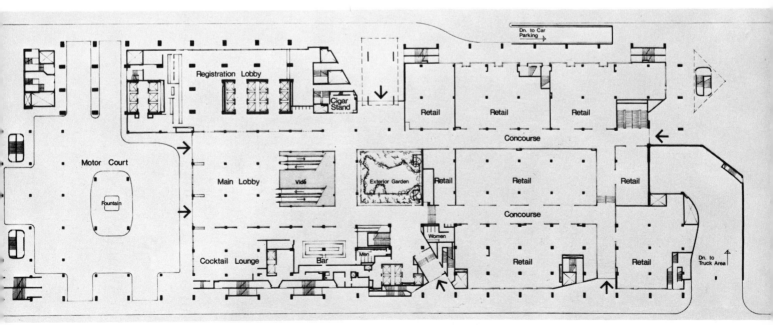

*Hotel entrance showing entrance
to the two-story shopping arcade
on Queen Street. (Photographer:
Panda Associates
Photography.)*

*Interior of two-story retail area
showing integration of lighting
fixtures with graphics.
(Photographer: Panda Associates
Photography.)*

*Landscape gardens northwest
(Toronto City Hall in
background). (Photographer:
Panda Associates Photography.)*

According to architect, Eberhard Zeidler, of the architectural firm of Craig, Zeidler & Strong,

Ontario Place started as the fulfillment of a promise by the Ontario government to replace the outdated Ontario exhibition building in the Canadian national exhibition grounds. However, the more one attempted to think through the philosophical and architectural principles of this problem, the more one became aware that the solution had to consist in more than merely the replacement of an old exhibition building with a new one. During this development three ideas seemed to crystallize and were finally molded into one solution.

First, an exhibition should not be forced into a fixed form—an architectural flexibility should be created that can adapt itself to the changing demands of exhibitions over the years. This principle of growth and change carries within it the solution to the problems of our cities in the future.

Second, such an exhibition could give new life to Toronto's waterfront. Like many other cities in the North American continent, Toronto grew within 1½ centuries into a world city. It started as a military outpost and developed as a port, but its main growth occurred toward the end of the development of the railroad and the beginning of the automobile era. This resulted in a city that cut itself off from its water by expressways and railroad tracks. Such one-sided attention to transport functions has robbed Toronto of one of its major natural identities.

Third, such an exhibition could respond to the social and psychological needs of the new metropolitan city by creating a new kind of urban park which would allow the inhabitants to participate actively with their environment and to identify themselves with their city.

The purpose of the exhibition was to show the development of Ontario from the past into the future—to show that it has not stagnated in its past, but rather can be developed and changed in the coming years. Such an exhibition required a building that would allow for great flexibility. In discussion with the exhibition designers it was established that three-story-high modules of approximately 8,000 square feet would permit the needed flexibility and growth. These modules could be joined and combined in many ways. However, the fulfillment of the requirement for flexibility could take many forms. In fact, it could have resulted in a number of warehouses of these dimensions set flatly on the ground. Obviously, more than a simple solution was required. What are the principles behind the great exhibition buildings of the past? What is it that has led us not to forget them? What makes Paxton's Crystal Palace in London, the Eiffel Tower in

ONTARIO PLACE
Toronto, Ontario

ARCHITECTS: Craig, Zeidler & Strong Architects
LANDSCAPE ARCHITECTS: Hough Stanbury & Associates

The above view of the Ontario Place model shows the total 80-acre complex, which is located offshore in Lake Ontario, south of Toronto's Exhibition Park. It was completed in 1972. Four man-made islands enclose the 350-boat marina and the five exhibition pods, which are suspended above water on columns 105' high. The east islands feature an exciting children's play area and the forum, which has a capacity of over 6,400 for special events. The west islands have the domed Cinesphere theater and the seawall, which protects the marina and the inner bays. The islands offer a variety of delightful restaurants, indoors and out, set in beautifully landscaped parklands. A scenic waterway with lagoons and an underground river wind through the islands. The view is looking north, and the shore and Lakeshore Boulevard are at the top of the photograph.

Paris, Fuller's dome at Expo, and Frei Otto's German Pavilion in Montreal still exciting to our imagination? All these buildings have one thing in common: The technological possibilities of their day were used with a clear understanding of their potential and were crystallized in a form that finally became an expression of their time.

As in an oil derrick, at Ontario Place we tried to use the minimal amount of material to float the exhibition pods above the lake by using steel in tension. The structure not only appears light, but also is light. Because of this solution, the building finally has separated itself from the ground; floating above, it gives us back the water and the land for our enjoyment.

It was also necessary to achieve the most economical solution to this problem. It was essential to break the power of the wave action of Lake Ontario. Waves at times reach a height of 18 feet. Through landfill we created islands that broke the power of the water and the wind, reducing the cost of the lake-bed foundations. These new islands also created new parkland, canals, and inland lakes on the other side of the existing highway, and yet they are connected by bridges with the Canadian National Exhibition and the city. This project has established the economic feasibility of creating a new waterfront for Toronto. It could be the catalyst for continuous development which would include the plan for Harbour City. The project would tightly knit together living, working, and recreational facilities. It would be a "water city," but with a very urban quality, similar to Venice in the middle ages.

This concept was to give, through this exhibition, form to the idea of a park that fulfills the social and anthropological needs of a megalopolis. The larger our cities grow, the more difficult it becomes to escape them, and we again have to find life within the confines of the city. This demands solutions quite different from the typical city park. Despite the immense size of Canada, the population in the urban regions is nearly as dense as that in European metropolitan areas. The parks needed for these urban centers are different from those required during the Victorian era. They must be designed with such population densities in mind. A great variety of park space is needed, and new park forms must be added to the existing ones in order to achieve variety.

On weekends, Ontario Place has had over 60,000 visitors on a land area of about 30 acres. Yet despite this density, no attempt has been made to program visitors; rather, the layout permits them to come and go as they please. It is important to create spaces that fulfill individual human desires—the wish to be alone as well as the wish to be with other people. This seeming duality is a necessity of life. Despite the large numbers of people, we have created places within this park where there is the illusion of space and solitude, even on very crowded days. West Beach is an uncrowded area where a child can play and throw stones into the water. Yet close by, just over the hill, are cafés, restaurants, boutiques, and much human activity, as well as a marina, paddle boats, a forum for symphony concerts, various forms of entertainment, and so on. The children's play area is full of spaces in which small children as well as those of school age can enjoy a variety of activities; for example, on one beach there will be 150 sailboats under the program "Sail Ontario," which will teach youngsters to sail. Interwoven are walks designed for the sheer pleasure of walking. The freedom to walk through various activity zones, with new vistas constantly opening and changing, is one of the essential ideas behind the landscaping of Ontario Place. One never comes upon the same view twice. The visitor constantly experiences new scenery, such as a different view of the framed exhibition buildings, or the various "villages" on the forum island, or, by rounding a path, of the quiet canal.

Among the main attractions in Ontario Place are the Cinesphere, a triodetic domed building which is one of the world's most advanced movie theaters; the Forum, an outdoor amphitheater with a capacity for 8,000 spectators; and Ontario Place pavilion, which is constructed of five striking modules two stories high and 90 by 90 feet square, rising on stilts out of the water. Inside the Pavilion "Pods" there is a series of mixed-media displays telling Ontario's story via images, sound, and light in innovative combinations.

The owner is the government of Ontario.

TOP: *Reflecting pool at night.* ABOVE: *Foreground: entry to tube slide. Background: exit from Soda Mountain.* RIGHT: *Main entrance bridge, exhibition pods, and Cinesphere.*

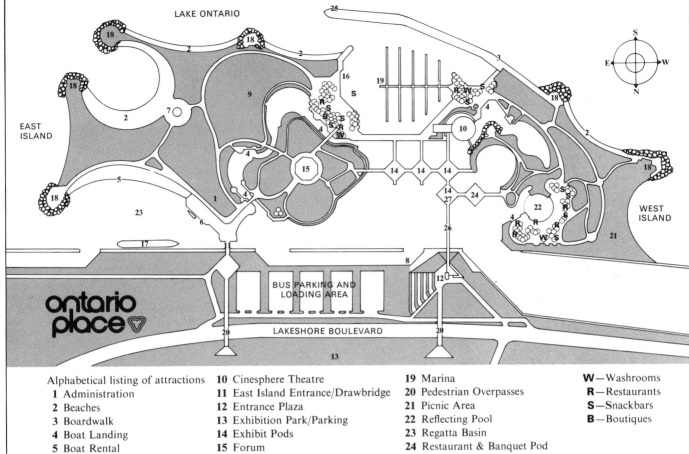

Alphabetical listing of attractions			
1 Administration	10 Cinesphere Theatre	19 Marina	**W**—Washrooms
2 Beaches	11 East Island Entrance/Drawbridge	20 Pedestrian Overpasses	**R**—Restaurants
3 Boardwalk	12 Entrance Plaza	21 Picnic Area	**S**—Snackbars
4 Boat Landing	13 Exhibition Park/Parking	22 Reflecting Pool	**B**—Boutiques
5 Boat Rental	14 Exhibit Pods	23 Regatta Basin	
6 Brigantine	15 Forum	24 Restaurant & Banquet Pod	
7 Campfire Beach	16 Harbour Boat Tours Dock	25 Sea Wall/Observation Ring	
8 Canal Boat Tours Dock	17 H.M.C.S. Haida	26 Walkway to Exhibits & Cinesphere	
9 Children's Village	18 Lookout Points	27 Welcome Wall	

71-1

Location plan.

Pedestrian bridge; West Village in background.

WATER TOWER PLACE
Chicago, Illinois

ARCHITECTS: Loebl, Schlossman, Bennett & Dart
and C. F. Murphy Associates
ARCHITECTURAL CONSULTANT: Warren Platner
& Associates

Water Tower Place combines shopping, working, and living facilities in one complex. The twelve-story base contains a shopping complex and office space. Rising from one corner is a sixty-two-story tower, with a Ritz-Carlton hotel occupying twenty-two floors and condominium residences occupying forty floors.

The unique urban shopping complex on the first seven floors is constructed around an atrium and five courts. With more than 610,000 square feet of floor space, the shopping center accommodates some one hundred stores, shops, and boutiques. Marshall Field & Company and Lord & Taylor, the major tenants, occupy nearly half the retail space.

The eighth and ninth floors include more than 200,000 square feet of office and commercial space with a separate ground-level lobby entrance. The tenth and eleventh floors include the health spa, barbershop, and other facilities of the Ritz-Carlton Hotel and the building's mechanical systems. The top (twelfth) floor of the base structure houses the public areas of the Ritz-Carlton Hotel, including restaurants, a café, a ballroom, rooftop gardens, and a greenhouse-bar. Four below-ground levels provide space for parking and receiving operations.

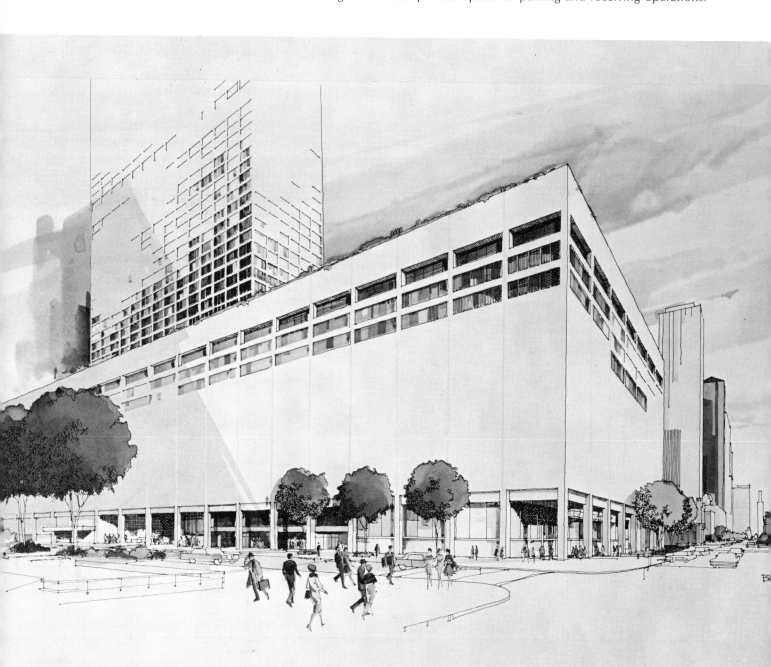

Exterior perspective featuring the twelve-story base, which includes seven stories of retail space.

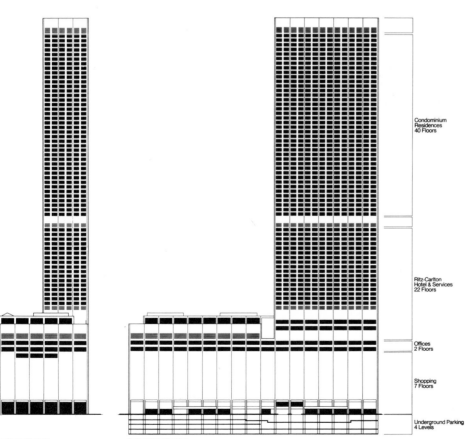

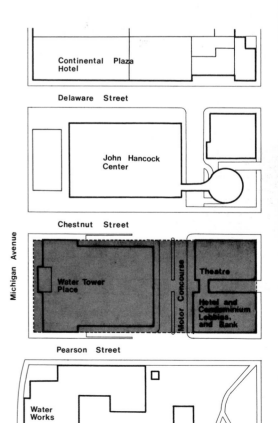

ABOVE: *Interior perspective showing the open-gallery type of circulation.* LEFT: *Pearson Street elevation showing the multifunction division.* BELOW: *Site plan.*

Condominium
Residences
40 Floors

Ritz-Carlton
Hotel & Services
22 Floors

Offices
2 Floors

Shopping
7 Floors

Underground Parking
4 Levels

Michigan Avenue Elevation

Pearson Street Elevation

Continental Plaza Hotel

Delaware Street

John Hancock Center

Chestnut Street

Michigan Avenue

Water Tower Place

Motor Concourse

Theatre

Hotel and Condominium Lobbies, and Bank

Pearson Street

Water Works

Water Works Park

ILLINOIS CENTER
Chicago, Illinois

ARCHITECTS:
For the master plan: Office of Mies van der Rohe
    and Solomon, Cordwell, Buenz & Associates
For the Prudential building: Naess & Murphy
For One Illinois Center and Two Illinois Center:
    Office of Mies van der Rohe
For the Hyatt Regency Hotel: A. Epstein & Sons, Inc.

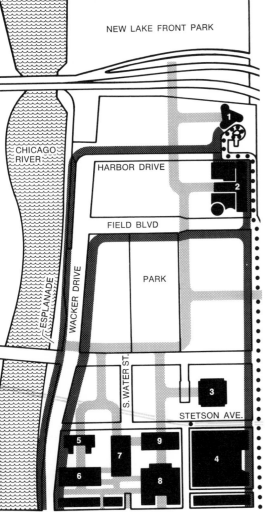

Site layout.

Key

■■■ Surface sidewalk
▒▒▒ Enclosed concourse
●●●● CTA Bus route (proposed)
● Subway and station
1 Harbor Point Condominiums
2 Outer Drive East Condominiums
3 Standard Oil Building
4 Prudential Building
5 Hyatt-Regency Chicago
6 One Illinois Center
7 Two Illinois Center
8 Three Illinois Center
9 Four Illinois Center

Illinois Center, one of the country's large downtown planned developments, is located on an 83-acre site between Michigan Avenue, the lake, Grant Park, and the Chicago River.

The Illinois Central Railroad completed a route into Chicago during the 1850s. The railroad purchased land north of Randolph Street for a depot and other terminal facilities. With the decline in importance of the Chicago harbor, the need for these facilities was no longer critical to good rail service, and the railroad sought to sell this valuable property so that it could be put to better use. Illinois Center Corporation and Metropolitan Structures have entered into a contract to purchase the land outright from the railroad.

Illinois Center is transforming obsolete rail yards and warehouses into a multi-level, coordinated mix of offices, apartments, condominiums, and hotels, all set within a framework of parks, plazas, and harbor vistas. An enclosed pedestrian concourse beneath plaza level will link the entire development and provide a wide range of shopping and entertainment opportunities. Illinois Center is a twenty-year project to be completed by 1989; the estimated cost is approximately $2 billion.

This center will link Michigan Avenue with Chicago's Loop. Illinois Center will eventually have a daytime working population of 45,000, and some 35,000 persons are expected to make their homes in the center's condominiums and rental apartments. Total office space is estimated at 9 million square feet, and 15,000 living units are to be constructed. Also included will be about $1\frac{1}{4}$ million square feet of retail space, about 4,500 hotel rooms, and 16,000 parking spaces.

Studies have estimated that the center will generate over $50 million in property tax revenue annually, as well as $1 million in city sales taxes, $1.6 million in employee taxes, and $1 million in hotel taxes.

A 6-acre park is planned for the center of the complex. Landscaped gardens, fountains, pools, and smaller landscaped areas will set off the various buildings. At the center's northern boundary along the south bank of the Chicago River, a 4-acre landscaped riverside esplanade park will be constructed along the entire length of the project, providing direct pedestrian access from Michigan Avenue to the lakefront.

Between the upper and plaza levels will be a pedestrian mall (walkway). Free of all vehicular traffic and protected from the weather, residents will be able to stroll unimpeded from Michigan Avenue to the lakeshore through a concourse of shopping boutiques, restaurants, department stores, theaters, and cultural and recreational facilities. A totally new network of streets, with three levels of traffic, will be incorporated into the project. The lower level will be used primarily by service vehicles, and there will be an intermediate level for through traffic and an upper level for local traffic. An additional north-south thoroughfare will be provided by extending Columbus Drive, which now terminates at Monroe Street, through Illinois Center and over a new bridge across the Chicago River. This will connect east-west streets on the city's near north side and ease traffic on Michigan Avenue.

Public transportation to and from the center will be provided by the city's previously announced extension of the Chicago subway system. This subway addition will link Illinois Center with the Loop to the west, North Michigan Avenue to the north, and McCormick Place to the south. In the late 1970s the new subway system is expected to serve 540,000 commuters. Commuter service will be provided by an extension of the Illinois Central Gulf commuter station into the development.

Two structures were built on the Illinois Central air rights prior to the adoption in 1969 of the Planned Development Ordinance and the Amendatory Lakefront Ordinance by the Chicago City Council, which set the guidelines for the modern development of the site. These structures are the Prudential building, completed in 1955 as the first new office building in downtown Chicago since before World War II, and the Outer Drive East Apartments, completed in 1963.

At the time of this writing, four structures have been completed under the new guidelines for development: One Illinois Center, the Standard Oil building, Two Illinois Center, and a Hyatt Regency hotel. One Illinois Center is a thirty-story office building containing 1 million square feet of office space. It was designed by the late Mies van der Rohe and was completed in 1970. The Standard Oil building, a 1,135-foot-tall structure serving as the international headquarters of

From left to right: Prudential building; Two Illinois Center; Hyatt Regency; One Illinois Center.

A free noontime play on the plaza between the Hyatt Regency and One Illinois Center. (Photographer: Photo Ideas, Inc.)

the Standard Oil Company, was designed by Edward Durell Stone and the Perkins and Will Partnership. Two Illinois Center is a twin office building to One Illinois Center and was completed in 1973. Harbor Point, a 740-unit high-rise condominium, was designed by Solomon, Cordwell, Buenz & Associates with the first phase completed. The Hyatt Regency Chicago, the first major downtown convention hotel to be constructed in forty-seven years, opened in 1974. The 1,000-room hotel was designed by A. Epstein and Sons, Inc.

In June 1974 an advisory board of nationally known authorities was organized to act as advisers and consultants to the developers in terms of the requirements and opportunities for life-style planning and amenities for the anticipated 35,000 residents and 45,000 employees. Named to the Illinois Center Advisory Board were Dr. Paul N. Ylvisaker, dean of the Harvard University Graduate School of Education; Richard Weinstein, former director of the New York Mayor's Office of Lower Manhattan Planning and Development and presently staff associate of the Rockefeller Brothers Fund; Paul Libin, managing director of New York's nonprofit Circle in the Square Theatre and president of the League of Off-Broadway Theatres and Producers; Dr. Carl Condit, professor of urban affairs at Northwestern University and architectural critic and historian; and Dr. Edmund D. Pellegrino, chancellor of the medical units and vice president of the University of Tennessee.

The joint-venture developers are Metropolitan Structures and Illinois Center Corporation, a subsidiary of IC Industries.

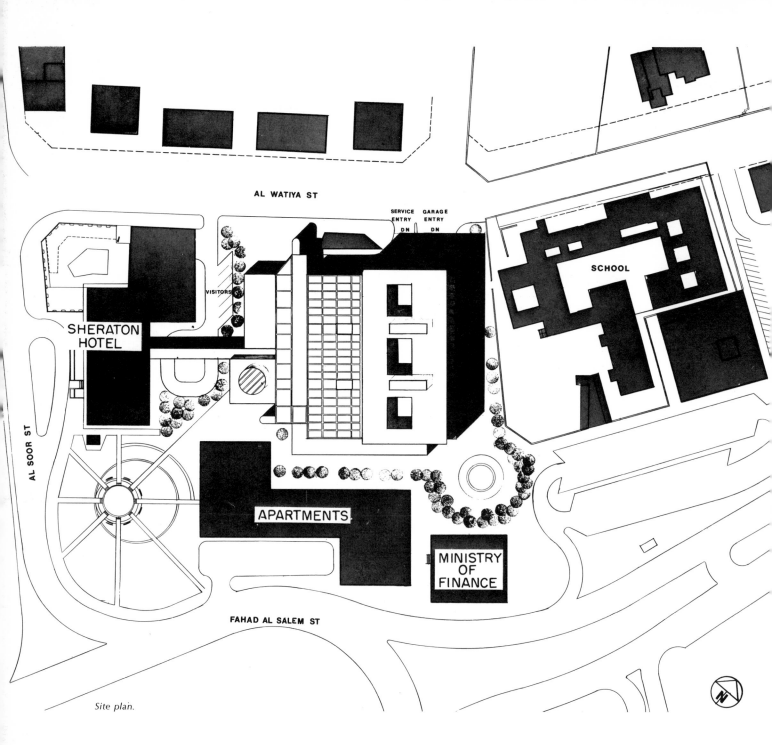

AL WATIYA ST

SERVICE GARAGE
ENTRY ENTRY
DN DN

VISITORS

AL SOOR ST

SHERATON
HOTEL

SCHOOL

APARTMENTS

MINISTRY
OF
FINANCE

FAHAD AL SALEM ST

Site plan.

KUWAIT CITY, KUWAIT

ARCHITECTS: The Architects Collaborative, Inc.

An unusual approach is used in the sheikdom of Kuwait on the Arabian peninsula. The city of Kuwait, with a population of approximately 1 million, is divided evenly between natives and foreigners. There the government designated a number of sites distributed strategically in the city core for building complexes called "car-park-commercial areas." There are about fifteen such projects being planned or currently under construction. Some of the projects combine parking, retail, and housing facilities (car-park-commercial area 10), while others have a mix of parking with retail and offices (car-park-commercial area 15). It should be noted that parking is a major element in the area coverage in these buildings. These projects are built by private developers who lease the land from the government with the condition that in addition to the parking facilities, other uses (e.g., shops, offices, or housing) must be included in the complex.

The developers for parcels 10 and 15 are National Real Estate Company.

Perspective views. ▶

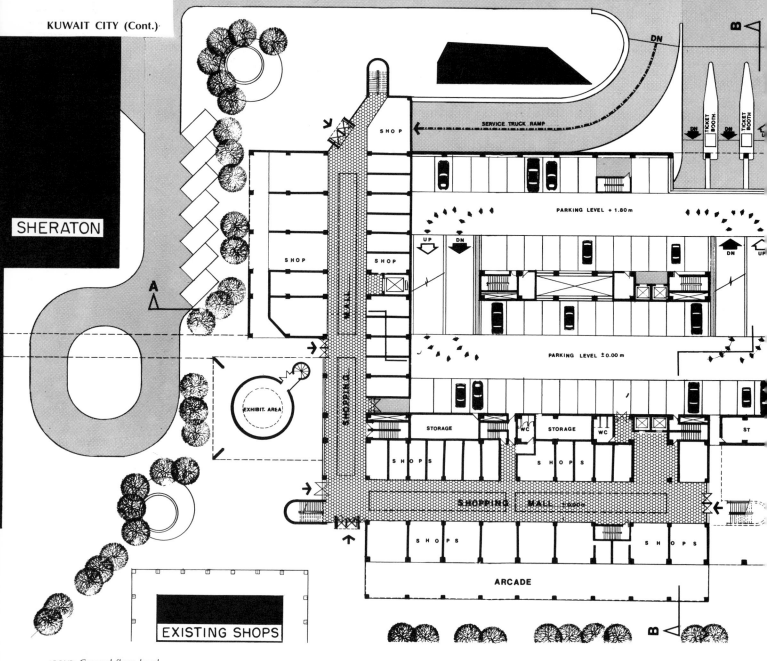

ABOVE: *Ground-floor level.*
BELOW: *Section BB.*

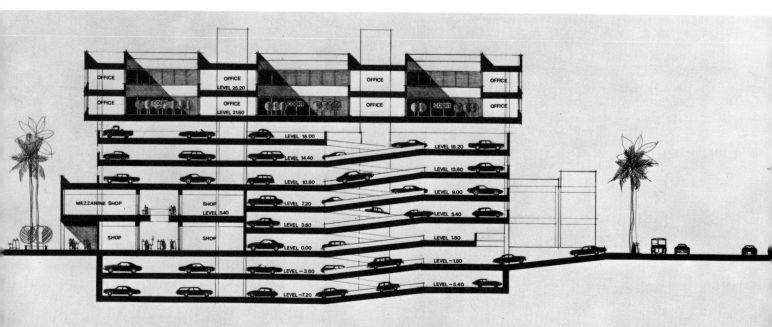

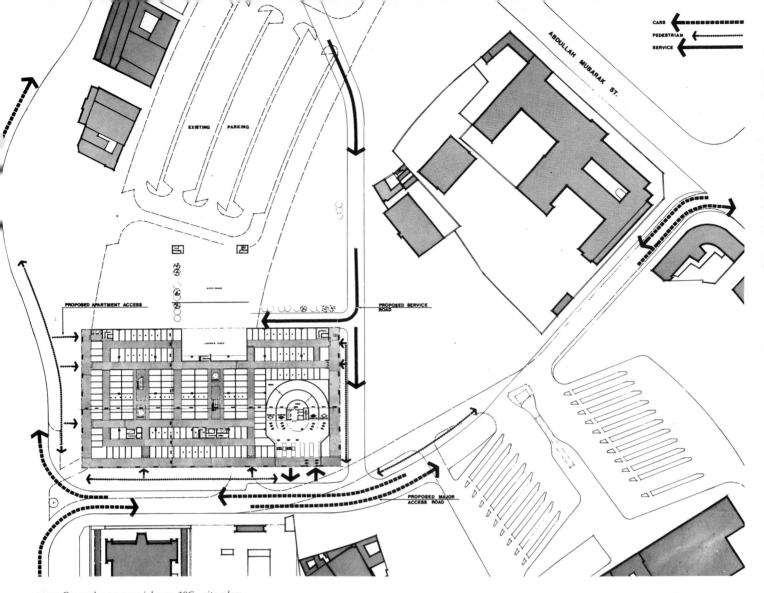

ABOVE: *Car-park–commercial area 10C—site plan.*
BELOW: *Ground-floor shopping area.*

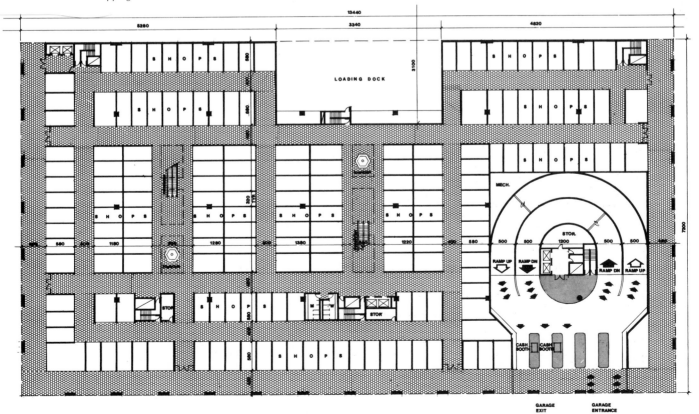

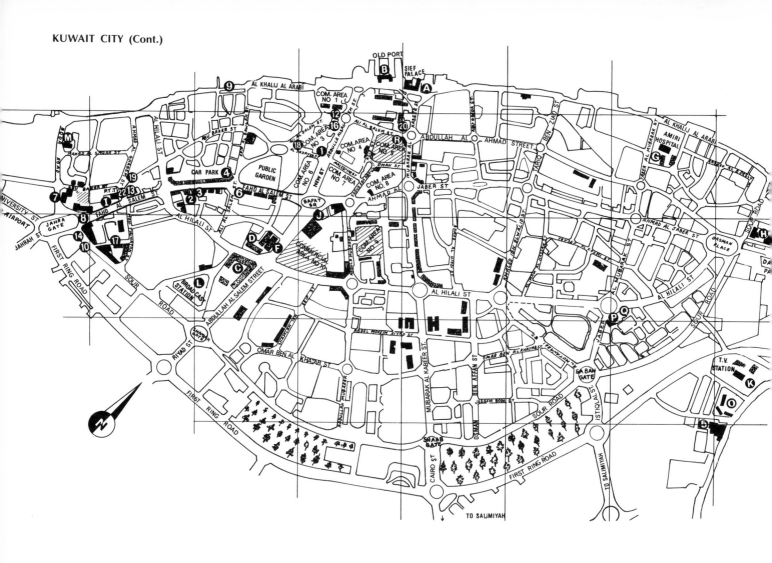

Sixth-floor level—apartments and parking.

Sections AA and BB.

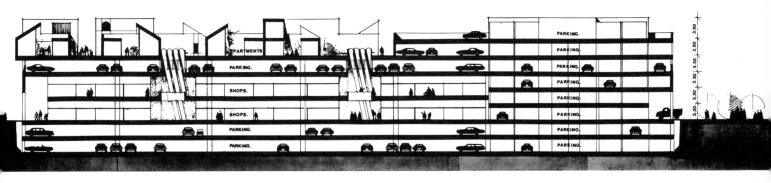

section A.A

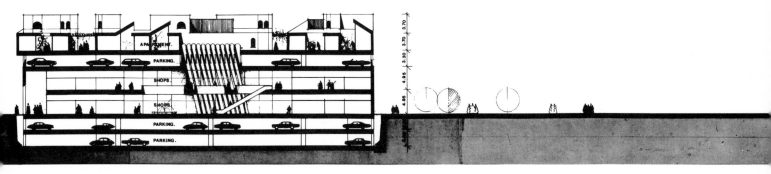

section B.B

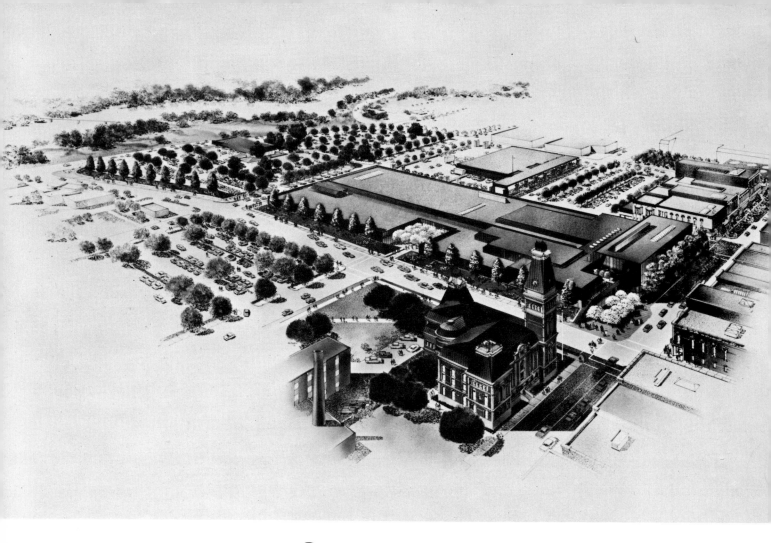

COURTHOUSE CENTER
Columbus, Indiana

ARCHITECTS: Gruen Associates;
Cesar Pelli, partner in charge

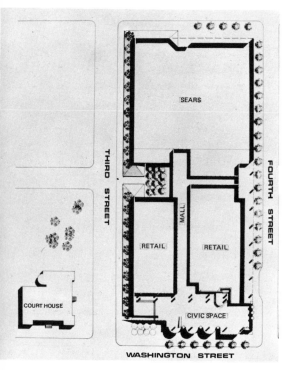

Courthouse Center, which occupies a 13-acre superblock in the central city of Columbus (population 27,000), combines a modern retail complex with The Commons, an enclosed hall specifically designed as a center of community activity. It is a part of the redevelopment plans proposed by Skidmore Owings & Merrill.

A variety of community activities take place in The Commons such as dances, benefits, exhibits, and concerts. A stage is provided for lectures, puppet shows, and small plays, while exhibit spaces in the 40,000 square-foot hall are designed for art shows, technology and science, or crafts and flowers. Other community spaces in The Commons include a playground, which is designed as a sunny, skylit space and offers a variety of imaginative playthings and activities for children's enjoyment.

The focal point of The Commons is *Chaos No. 1*, a massive kinetic sculpture by the well-known artist Jean Tinguely. It is approximately 25 feet high, 25 feet long, and 15 feet wide and is a huge machine with wheels, gears, and a large auger bit, all of which gyrate and turn at varying speeds. The entire sculpture slowly rotates on its massive base of steel.

A Sears department store anchors the retail mall, which contains over 113,000 square feet of space and twenty-five specialty shops. The mall is covered by a 15-foot-wide skylight with sloping glass on the north side and a solid wall on the south, faced with mirrors in the interior. The mirrored wall above eye level doubles the skylight into an apparent 30-foot aperture and opens the entire shopping street to the sky. Under the mirrors, a chrome tube strengthens the illusion and, with its highlights, becomes a strong linear element tying all segments of the center together. The chrome tube also contains lights, sprinklers, and air supply.

The Commons has been carefully scaled to match the predominant height of surrounding commercial buildings and the courthouse building across the street, a historic 1870 structure. Transparent glazing in The Commons makes it a part of the sidewalk life, not a space isolated from the town.

The developer is Irwin Management Company, Inc., Columbus, Indiana.

TOP: *Aerial perspective of the complex.*
ABOVE: *Floor plan-street level.*

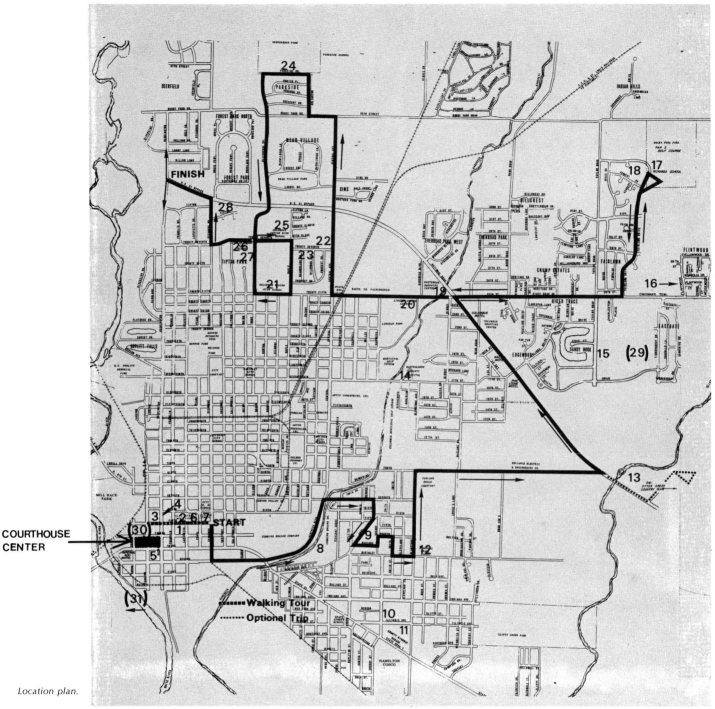

Location plan.

COURTHOUSE CENTER

FINISH

START

·········· Walking Tour
·········· Optional Trip

1. **FIRST CHRISTIAN CHURCH**
Eliel Saarinen
2. **CLEO ROGERS MEMORIAL COUNTY LIBRARY**
I. M. Pei and Partners
3. **IRWIN UNION BANK & TRUST COMPANY**
Eero Saarinen
3b.**IRWIN UNION BANK AND TRUST COMPANY (LANDSCAPE)**
Dan Kiley
4. **MODEL BLOCK**
Alexander Girard
5. **BARTHOLOMEW COUNTY COURTHOUSE**
I. Hodgson
6. **IRWIN HOME AND GARDEN**
7. **LINCOLN SCHOOL**
Gunnar Birkerts
8. **CUMMINS ENGINE COMPANY, INC. TECHNICAL CENTER**
Harry Weese
9. **FOUNDATION FOR YOUTH RECREATION CENTER**
J. Herschel Fisher & Pat Y. Spillman
10. **FRANCIS COMFORT CHILDREN'S HOME**
Joseph D. True, Jr.

11. **COUNTY HOME OF THE AGED**
Harry Weese
12. **McDOWELL ELEMENTARY SCHOOL**
John Carl Warnecke
13. **OTTER CREEK GOLF COURSE CLUB HOUSE**
Harry Weese
13a.**OTTER CREEK PUBLIC GOLF COURSE**
Robert Trent Jones
14. **HOSPITAL ANNEX**
Raymond W. Garbe
15. **FOUR SEASONS HOME**
The Architects Collaborative
16. **NUMBER 4 FIRE STATION**
Venturi and Rauch
17. **W. D. RICHARDS ELEMENTARY SCHOOL**
Edward Larrabee Barnes
18. **FIRST BAPTIST CHURCH**
Harry Weese
19. **IRWIN UNION BANK AND TRUST COMPANY BRANCH BANK**
Harry Weese
20. **LINCOLN CENTER ICE SKATING RINK**
Harry Weese
21. **HIGH SCHOOL AND PHYSICAL**

EDUCATION BUILDING
McGuire, Shook, Compton and Richey, Inc.
22. **FIRE STATION #2**
Taylor & Wood
23. **ASBURY METHODIST CHURCH**
Taylor & Wood
24. **PARKSIDE ELEMENTARY SCHOOL**
The Architects Collaborative
25. **NORTHSIDE JUNIOR HIGH SCHOOL**
Harry Weese
26. **LILLIAN SCHMITT ELEMENTARY SCHOOL**
Harry Weese
27. **SCHOOLS ADMINISTRATION BUILDING**
The Architects Collaborative
28. **NORTH CHRISTIAN CHURCH**
Eero Saarinen
(29) **FRANCIS SMITH ELEMENTARY SCHOOL**
J. M. Johansen
(30) **DOWNTOWN POSTOFFICE**
Kevin Roche
(31) **SOUTHSIDE JUNIOR HIGH SCHOOL**
Eliot Noyes

( ) denotes under construction

RIGHT: *Interior of the enclosed mall area. (Photographer: Balthazar Korab.)* BELOW: *Interior of The Commons. (Sculptor: Jean Tinguely, Photographer: Balthazar Korab.)*

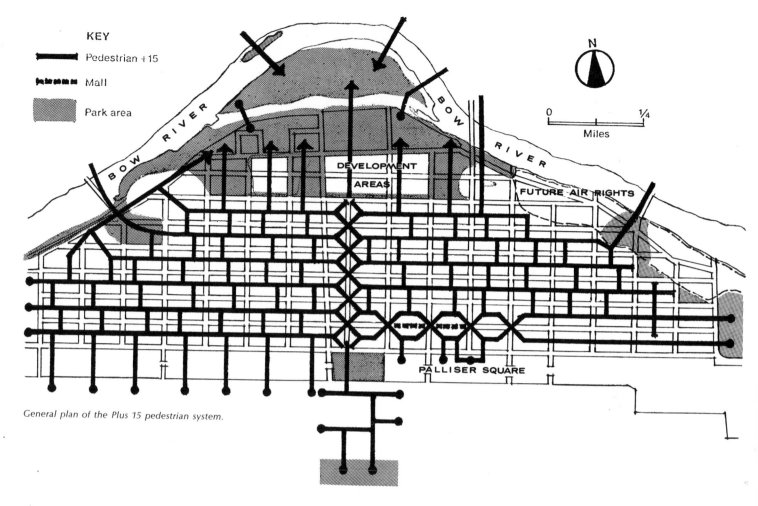

KEY

▬ Pedestrian +15

▬▬ Mall

▨ Park area

BOW RIVER

BOW RIVER

DEVELOPMENT AREAS

FUTURE AIR RIGHTS

PALLISER SQUARE

N

0   ¼
    Miles

General plan of the Plus 15 pedestrian system.

A detailed study of Calgary's downtown was made in 1966. The recommendations were approved in principle in the master plan as follows:

1. Create a good pedestrian environment
2. Improve pedestrian and vehicular circulation (including buses)
3. Provide more open space
4. Strengthen Eighth Avenue as a pedestrian shopping street
5. Connect major buildings and places of interest
6. Relieve future traffic pressures by introducing a public railway system (rapid transit)
7. Create good pedestrian access to strategically located parking facilities

It was recognized that a strong downtown for Calgary would be possible only if it continued to be attractive to business interests and was made attractive for shopping and entertainment. Residential sections located downtown would support day/night activities in an area which otherwise has little life after working hours or on Sundays and holidays.

To solve the CBD circulation problem, the Plus 15 concept was proposed by the architectural firm of Affleck, Desbarats, Dimakopoulos, Lebensold, Sise in a report done for the city of Calgary entitled *Plan for Redevelopment Action/East Calgary/Urban Renewal Areas 1a and 1b.* The Calgary Planning Department has been working closely with the architects to develop and implement this concept.

Plus 15 is a design term and is actually a measurement referring to height in feet above street level. The walkways and plazas are intended to be developed at this approximate height since the minimum height clearance for a structure over streets or lanes has been set by the city at 15 feet to allow for maintenance of utilities and the passage of vehicles. In Winnipeg, they call their proposed version Plus 16.

The Plus 15 concept is intended to improve downtown at little expense to the taxpayer. This is accomplished by offering developers the opportunity to build

CALGARY, ALBERTA

ARCHITECTS:
For Uni-City: Waisman, Ross, Blankstein, Coop, Gillmor, & Hanna
For Uni-City East: Albert Dale & Associates
PLANNERS: Calgary Planning Department

Calgary Mall, Uni-City—model of center.

over public property, e.g., plazas over lanes and walkways over streets. Since developers assume the entire expense and, furthermore, operate and maintain their structures for the benefit of the public, the city in turn permits them to increase the floor area of their buildings. The more public pedestrian areas they can provide, the more they can expand the floor area of their buildings. This is known as an "incentive" or "bonus" system, and it is a positive way of achieving public facilities through private enterprise. The creation of a number of "miniparks," which is what the elevated plazas are, will be invaluable to the public, and these, together with some miniparks provided by the city at ground level, will overcome the open-space deficiency downtown.

In 1971 the Plus 15 concept was awarded a Vincent Massey Award for Excellence in the Urban Environment.

In 1974 an improved version of the Plus 15 links was initiated. Yellow-tinted plastic was used in place of smoked glass, and its shape was curved.

An interesting stage in the urban growth of Calgary is the implementation of the town-in-town concept, Uni-City. It is being developed privately by R. C. Baxter Group, Ltd., in the northwest section of Calgary. Located within fifteen minutes of the downtown CBD, the complex includes the Calgary Market Mall, the town center, and a residential center. It is planned for a population of approximately 5,000; this will accommodate the fast-growing population of Calgary, which has an annual increase of 12,000 people. A special feature of the concept is the air rights for a pedestrian walkway over the main thoroughfares on either side of the Market Mall.

The Market Mall, which opened in 1971 as the first phase of the project, is the largest retail center in Calgary. It includes the Hudson Bay Company, Woodward's, and sixty variety stores.

The town center is designed to include community service facilities, such as a theater, a civic and youth center, a home for senior citizens, a medical complex, and a hotel.

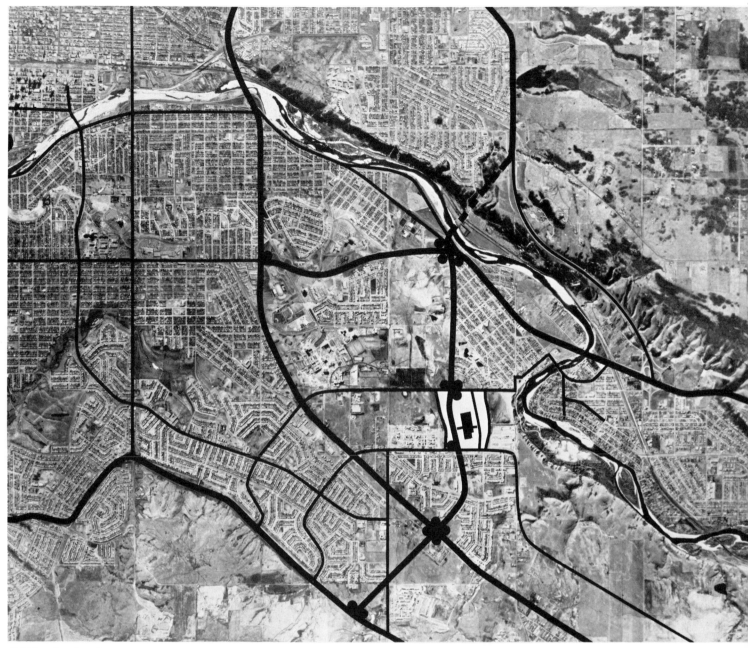

Uni-City—location plan.

New pedestrian link (1974) between Provincial Remand Centre
and Alberta Vocational Centre.

Interior of the link.

MUNICH MALL
Munich, Germany

ARCHITECT: Bernhard Winkler
ASSOCIATE ARCHITECT: Siegfried Meschederu,
of the City Planning Department

The pedestrian mall in Munich is discussed in this part because of its impact on the revitalization of the commercial area in the old city, its focusing on the preservation and restoration of historic buildings, and its direct escalator connection in several areas with underground shopping centers and subway platforms.

The city council, in 1969, awarded the design to architect Bernhard Winkler, in association with Siegfried Meschederu of the City Planning Department, as a result of a competition. The construction of the mall proceeded simultaneously with the construction of the two subway lines which cross below the Marienplatz, the city's main square for pedestrians. The city's replanning was completed for the Olympic Games in 1972.

This urban planning won, for the architects, the 1974 R. S. Reynolds Award for Community Architecture. It was judged by a jury of the American Institute of Architects (I. M. Pei, FAIA; William Brubaker, FAIA; and Henry Steinhardt, AIA). The jury, in selecting the award winner, made the following observations, among others:

> An old downtown area can be revitalized. Although some American cities are distressed by the lack of people in downtown streets at all hours, Munich shows us how to make the city attractive to many people and, therefore, busy day and night.
>
> After desire and hope, a master plan is required. With initiative by government and with support from business and citizens generally, talented design professionals can create a comprehensive and comprehensible plan to guide action.
>
> Urban vitality and spirit depend on the presence of many people working and playing. Handsome architecture alone, thoughtful planning alone or sound engineering alone won't create a lively and humanistic city. Munich demonstrates the importance of orchestrating many disciplines to create a better environment.
>
> The old city can be preserved while building the new. Preservation motives include enjoyment of the cultural heritage, historical continuity, architectural richness in form and texture and practical recognition that some older structures can enjoy new functions and new life. Generally, Munich street patterns and blocks were preserved but updated with some streets changed to pedestrian ways. Midblock passages and street arcades were cut into existing blocks. Many fine old structures were preserved and new functions were given to some buildings. Some new buildings were erected.
>
> The small shops of tradesmen and little eating places don't need to be lost. When a

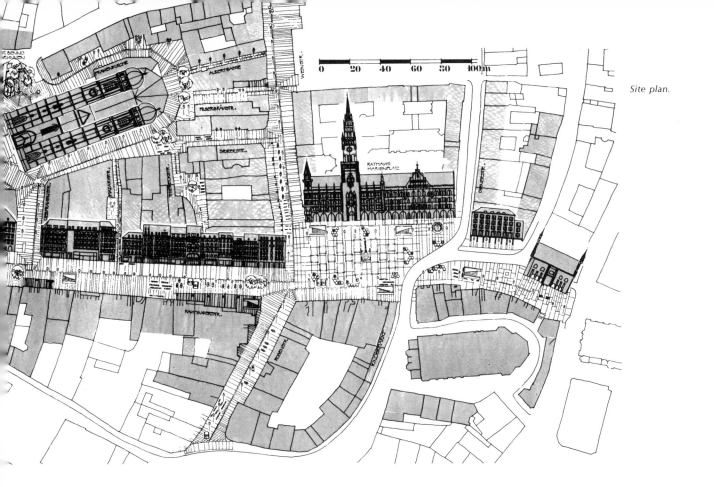

Site plan.

downtown is being revitalized, we sometimes see those small businesses which enliven a business district replaced by chain stores. . . .

The planning of infrastructure is very important. The pedestrian zone could not have been created without concurrent development of a new subway system, reducing the need for automobiles; a new highway system, eliminating through traffic from the old town; and a new parking policy that allows fewer cars inside the old town.

A special event can be a useful catalyst to get things going. Munich's 1972 Olympics created a deadline for completion of the subway—an essential coordinated action for achieving the pedestrian zone.

Proud accomplishments take time and are the product of the efforts of many individuals and organizations. The need was identified in Munich 20 years ago; the desire was generated ten years ago. Concerned citizens, politicians, businessmen, planners, engineers and architects were essential to the creation of the successful, lively and beautiful pedestrian zone.*

*Parts taken with permission from an article by Mary E. Osman, associate editor of the *Journal of the American Institute of Architects*, June 1974. Copyright © held by the *AIA Journal*.

BELOW, LEFT: *View of the fountain at the Stachus Circle.* BELOW: *General view. (Photographs courtesy of Bernhard Winkler.)*

MIGDALOR CENTER
Tel Aviv, Israel

ARCHITECTS: Arieh El-hanani–Nissan Cnaan/Architects
SENIOR ASSISTANT: Dan Tavor/Architect

Migdalor is located on one of the busiest intersections of Tel Aviv and overlooks the sea. It is a commercial 400-room hotel connected to a plaza through a five-story shopping center with underground and terraced public passages. A tunnel connects the hotel to service and loading areas in the adjacent parking building. The commercial complex forms a part of the surrounding existing commercial complex. Completion is expected in 1977.

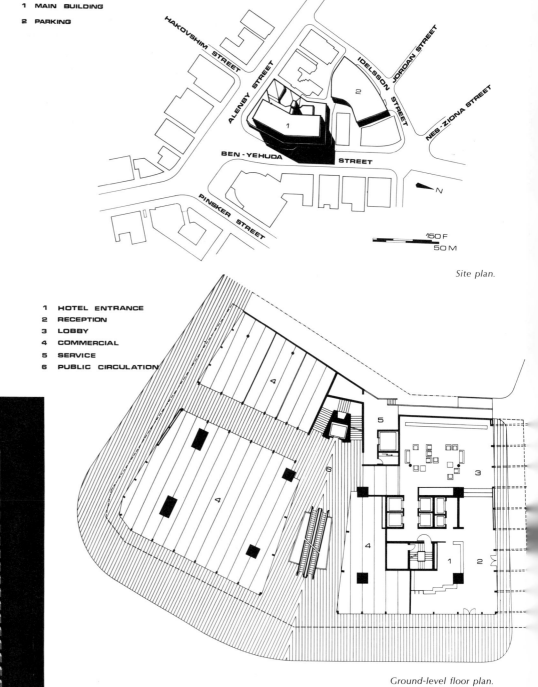

1 MAIN BUILDING

2 PARKING

Site plan.

1 HOTEL ENTRANCE
2 RECEPTION
3 LOBBY
4 COMMERCIAL
5 SERVICE
6 PUBLIC CIRCULATION

Ground-level floor plan.

Model of center.

Skopje, which was struck by an earthquake in 1963, is a new city today—modern and attractive. It is the third largest town in Yugoslavia, with about 450,000 inhabitants. At the time of the earthquake its population was 270,000; before the war it was a mere 70,000.

The size of the Macedonian capital is growing by about 12,000 inhabitants every year, as people move here from all parts of Macedonia and from other republics, attracted by the opportunities for employment and higher earnings.

The new urban design is based on the results of an international competition in which the award was won by a team of architects—Kenzo Tange, of Tokyo, and architects Radovan Miscevic and Fedor Wencler, from Zagreb, Yugoslavia. The subsequent detailed plan was done by the Skopje Institute of Town Planning and Architecture in cooperation with the award-winning architects. The principal planner of this group was Tihomir Arsovski.

To produce the impression of a medieval city, with its towers, Tange designed the "city wall," a complex of twenty high-rise blocks interspersed by lower six-story buildings, and the "city gate," a complex of commercial structures.

Another important element in the Tange design is the multifunction transportation center. The center combines a railway station, post office, and interurban bus station. The railway station has ten lines with five covered platforms raised on bridge constructions 2,000 feet in length and 30 feet high. The area below these will house ticket offices, shops, waiting rooms, cloakrooms, and other station amenities, on two levels. The next stage on the left bank of the Vardar River includes an opera house, concert hall, music and ballet academy, and movie house.

SKOPJE, YUGOSLAVIA

ARCHITECTS:
For the master plan: Kenzo Tange, Radovan Miscevic, and Fedor Wencler
For the shopping center: Tihomir Arsovski

ABOVE: *Riverside promenades on both sides of the Vardar River with connecting bridges. (Photograph courtesy of the Yugoslav Embassy.)*

RIGHT: *Model of master plan for reconstruction of the city after the 1963 earthquake. (1) City wall; (2) shopping center; (3) city gate; (4) old market; (5) cultural center; (6) university.* BELOW: *Schematic drawings for the shopping center. Nearly 1 million square feet in area includes more than a hundred shops, three department stores, two supermarkets, and a drugstore. (Photographs courtesy of Tihomir Arsovski.)*

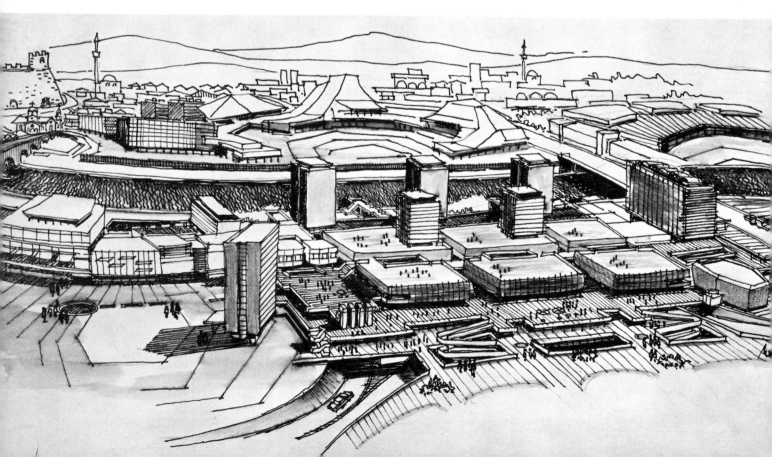

Akasaka Plaza is located in the heart of Akasaka town, a district of Tokyo. The complex encompasses an outdoor plaza and a large shopping area in the form of a two-story continuous concourse which runs the entire length of the building. The upper part of the building contains a 600-room hotel and office floors.

Parking for fifty-four cars is provided in the underground level, and for eighty cars in the parking structure.

AKASAKA PLAZA
Akasaka, Tokyo, Japan
ARCHITECTS: Design Section of Tokyo Estate Co., Ltd.

TOP: *Exterior view of upper floors used for hotel (566 rooms) and offices. The canopied part of the underground level is parking for 134 cars. The second level is for the shopping plaza.* ABOVE: *Exterior escalator leading to the shopping plaza.* LEFT: *General view.*

HAMILTON MALL
Allentown, Pennsylvania
ARCHITECTS: Cope, Linder, Walmsley

The architect makes the following comments:

Allentown, with a population of several hundred thousand, is located in the heart of the Lehigh Valley, 50 miles north of Philadelphia and 90 miles west of New York City. Although its downtown had annual sales in the late 1960s in excess of $80 million, its growth rate was threatening to flatten out with the advent of new suburban shopping and employment centers. A diminishing center-city tax base, traffic congestion, parking deficiencies, and underutilized and/or poorly maintained buildings were telltale symptoms of future decline. Accordingly, an urban renewal plan for the central business district prepared by David M. Walker Associates Inc., in 1968 advocated, as part of a comprehensive redevelopment strategy for downtown, the creation of a four-block "semimall" on Allentown's principal shopping street.

Origin and destination studies indicated that through traffic could be rerouted around the central area to serve a ring of parking garages (two of which are now built and operational), allowing five lanes of traffic on Hamilton Street to be replaced by a 22-foot-wide cartway for minibuses and emergency vehicles. (This has been now modified to allow local traffic to pick up and discharge shoppers.) On the extended sidewalk created, a whole new coordinated system of street furniture has been designed—kiosks with mailboxes, drinking fountains, telephones, and radiantly heated sitting places; planters; street trees with cast-iron gratings; benches; trash containers; fountains; light fixtures of various types; and traffic-control devices and signs. In addition, a continuous canopy system was developed along all storefronts, joined at the center of each block by a higher roof connecting both sides of the former street. The structure is of painted steel with tinted Plexiglas cladding in aluminum frames, which have offset supports clear of the building faces because of projecting basements under the sidewalk. The canopy system affords weather protection for 2,000 feet along each side of the street and acts as a strong unifying element in the street picture, bringing the two sides together and subordinating the typically uneven and disparate façades to a powerful common structure. Ironically, it replaces the nineteenth-century cast-iron arcades appearing on old photogravure prints, which were torn down "in the name of progress."

North-south streets break up the length of the mall, but each block is long enough to create its own identity and is focused on its mid-block canopy, where the major public facilities are concentrated, where the minibus stops are located, and where half streets entering from each side act as pedestrian approaches from the various parking structures and lots serving the downtown. Two small parks were included as part of the original plan. Only one remains at Seventh Street in modified form, dominated by a Civil War obelisk; here major fountains, an information and display kiosk for the whole mall, an outdoor dining area, and a covered structure for a possible farmer's market are provided.

This unique effort to revitalize the downtown of a middle-sized town is being financed by an equally unusual conjunction of local and state funds. For an estimated expenditure of approximately $5 million toward improvement of the downtown environment, it is

Site plan.

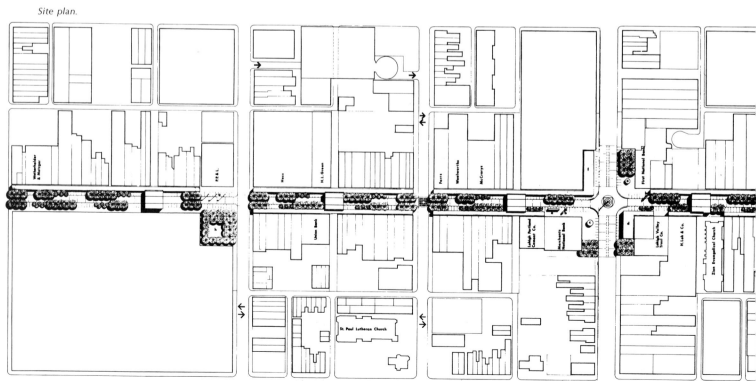

anticipated that private investment will follow in the amount of more than $40 million, and already several million dollars worth of new construction is under way. The local leadership, with a broad spectrum of community support, has made a courageous decision in proceeding with this bold step of reconstruction. The first block was completed in November 1972, and the balance in November 1973. Allentown's renewal may be a model for the state of Pennsylvania and for many intermediate-sized towns facing similar problems of urban deterioration and a changing socioeconomic role in the contemporary world.

Regarding government, legal, and financial procedures, Mr. William A. Scharf, director of the Department of Community Development for the city of Allentown, comments:

The Hamilton Mall is a project undertaken by the Redevelopment Authority of the city of Allentown. However, as with most Redevelopment Authority projects, the approval of the city council and also funding sources, in this case the Commonwealth of Pennsylvania, were needed. I, as director of the Redevelopment Authority and director of the Department of Community Development for the city of Allentown, have had coordinating charge of all facets of the Hamilton Mall from its inception in planning to the present phase of construction. Actually, we began the mall by undertaking a general study of the center city, utilizing the consultant firm of David M. Walker Associates of Philadelphia, presently called Direction Associates of Fort Washington, Pennsylvania. We completed a general plan utilizing a 50 percent grant of $30,000 from the Commonwealth of Pennsylvania, which we matched with $15,000 of city cash and $15,000 of local cash dollars raised by downtown business people.

ABOVE: *Detail of street accessories showing interesting handling of graphics.* LEFT: *Aerial view showing the canopied sidewalk.* LEFT, BELOW: *Detail of canopy lighting.*

BEERSHEBA TOWN CENTER
Beersheba, Israel

ARCHITECTS: Karmi Architects & Co., Ltd.

This building complex received the International Award from the Reynolds Metal Company in 1970 "for the design of a community in which architectural planning and design have made a most significant contribution."

As cited by the jury of the American Institute of Architects, "Beersheba was selected as an outstanding symbol of the Israeli new urbanization program since it is the oldest and largest of a series of some 25 new, reconstructed and substantially enlarged towns started little more than 20 years ago. The very existence and growth of the country depends in large measure on the placement and the social and economic success of . . . new towns."

Beersheba lies at the entrance to the Negev Desert, about 100 miles south of Tel Aviv, and is now the administrative, commercial, and social center of the Negev district, which comprises almost 40 percent of the country's land area. It has about 70,000 residents, and a population of 250,000 is projected by the year 2000.

A key element in the Beersheba master plan is this new Town Center building, a megastructure with an open-air gallery, stores, offices, and apartments on different levels. The building is of linear design and thus can be extended down its axis through the community as required.

Several types of housing are provided, from high-rise apartments with projecting room units cantilevered from a central core to low-density "patio houses" in a "carpet development."

The master plan promises to integrate older housing areas and an existing commercial and entertainment center with the new facilities, an aspect praised by the jury. The plan also is overcoming serious deficiencies in an earlier scheme, the jury noted in its report.

"The jury believes Beersheba to be of international significance in the evaluation of town planning," the report said. "It represents the full spectrum for community evolution. It is, in the totality of development of new and old, an outstanding symbol of a national urbanization policy."

ABOVE: Model showing master plan. High-rise apartments have projected living units cantilevered from a central cone. BELOW: Interior perspective section.

Interior showing shopping mall and upper office and residential floor completed. (Photographer: Paul Gross, Ltd.)

Exterior view completed. (Photographer: Paul Gross, Ltd.)

MIDTOWN PLAZA
Saskatoon, Saskatchewan

ARCHITECTS:
For the center: Arnott MacPhail Johnstone
  & Associates, Inc.
For the auditorium: Kerr, Cullingworth, Riches
  & Associates

A culmination of ten years of planning and work, Midtown Plaza is the result of complete removal of the main Canadian National Railway yards from the heart of the city, which freed some 32 acres of land for urban renewal.

For Saskatoon, with a population of 127,000, the agreement to move CN's downtown terminal and station facilities to a new location on the city's western outskirts made it possible to change its central core from a maze of railway operations into a unified scene of commercial and cultural activity.

Built around a twelve-story office tower, the plaza covers almost four square blocks and encloses under its 10-acre roof some fifty businesses, including two department stores, a supermarket, and a theater. Parking for 790 cars is provided beneath the plaza proper, with adjacent surface parking for an additional 1,000 cars. Apart from the plaza, but complementing the development, is the city's new 2,000-seat Centennial Auditorium. The new plaza generated concern about parking among retail businesses along Second Avenue and the existing retail establishments, resulting in some further improvements in parking for their area.

The plaza opened in 1970, when the entire economy of Saskatoon and the province was at a very low ebb because of the nationwide economic recession that had hit that year. The plaza had an appreciable effect in lowering the sales volumes in established businesses downtown when it first opened, but the extent of this cannot be measured because of the economic conditions existing at that time. However, economic conditions have improved significantly since 1970, and volumes generally are back up, certainly to the point where businesses in the old area no longer claim that the plaza is hurting them.

It is interesting to have the evaluation of Mr. H. E. Wellman, director of Planning and Development, after three years of the plaza's operation:

> The addition of a climate-controlled shopping center, with 1,700 parking spaces (700 of them underground), has unquestionably drawn a large number of shoppers back to the downtown area, and once they are there, they use the old central business district facilities as well. The one thing we have not been able to measure is the actual consequence of adding this much new space, with its unique characteristics, to an established central business district of traditional layout and all its attendant drawbacks. In some cities of our size, the results might have been disastrous, simply because of the inability of the economy to absorb an increase in the size of the central business district of that magnitude, but the market area seems to have been flexible enough to handle it. Since our radius for shopping covers about 80 miles around the city, we are drawing not only more city residents into the central business district but also more of the people from the rural areas.

> It is my personal opinion that when an area is as dependent on its rural trade as Saskatoon is, the greatest advantage you can give to a farmer who is unfamiliar with city traffic is plenty of parking spaces, with wide stalls and aisles for easy maneuvering. The plaza more than meets that criterion, while many of the other parking garages in the central business district do not.

> The central business district in Saskatoon had always been a strong entity because of planning policies which have limited the amount of suburban growth, particularly shopping centers. We have regional shopping centers outside the central business district, but not to excess and not to the extent that they severely hurt the central business district. Consequently, people have always been used to coming downtown. The attractions are now that much greater.

> If the tenants in the plaza had been made up largely of stores relocating from other parts of the central business district, we would have had serious consequences because it is not likely that new businesses would have moved in to fill the gaps. As it was, about

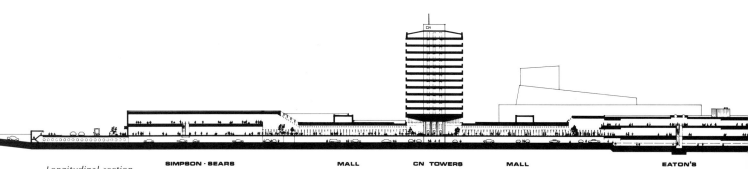

Longitudinal section.

SIMPSON·SEARS   MALL   CN TOWERS   MALL   EATON'S

50 percent of the tenants in the plaza were new to Saskatoon and offered worthwhile competition to the established businesses. As a result, the consumer benefited all around, especially since some of the old business establishments had been taking their customers pretty much for granted.

In my mind, the fact that the plaza did not destroy the old central business district economically and that it has become an addition to it rather than a replacement for it (as it might well have done in the light of all other circumstances) is due largely to the wisdom of the developer in selecting outside tenants as far as possible, rather than simply renting to established businesses.

The decision by Eatons to move into the plaza could have had serious consequences on the central business district because they had been the anchor on the east side of the area. As it was, the smaller businesses nearby, who had drawn their trade partly from activity generated by Eatons, were generally the ones who were initially hardest hit by the shift in the center of gravity. Some of them have since moved into space vacated on Second Avenue by merchants who had moved into the plaza, and they are now back on the main pedestrian routes. The ones who stayed have helped to preserve Third Avenue as a main shopping street.

Another positive factor in the stabilization of the old retail area is the conversion of the old Eaton store into a discount-type chain-store operation of the kind known as "army and navy stores" in Canada. This is considered a major shopping drawing card for high-volume pedestrian traffic. It would appear that the central business district is becoming more meaningfully compact and that there is less tendency for individual major commercial operations to move out into the other edges of the area.

The owners are Crescent Leaseholds Ltd.

Exterior entrance. (Photographer: Bob Howard.)

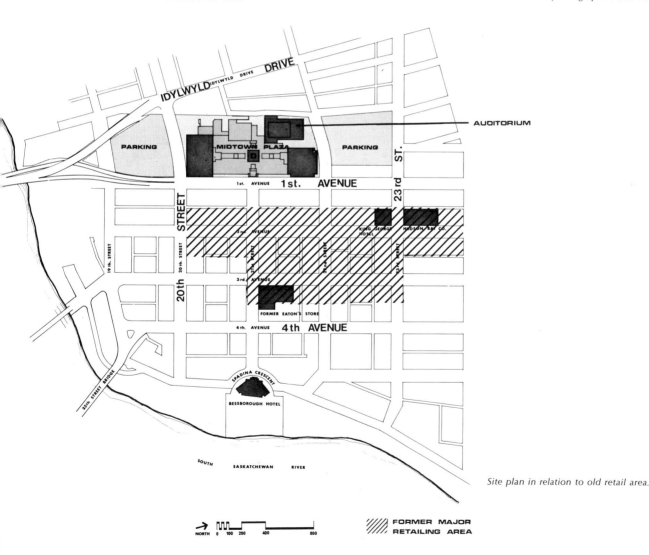

Site plan in relation to old retail area.

MIDTOWN PLAZA (Cont.)

Aerial view after construction.

*Saskatoon Centennial Auditorium.
(Photographer: Creative
Professional Photographers Ltd.)*

*Photograph taken from Eaton's
dining mezzanine overlooking
two-story forecourt and showing
sitting area for shoppers.*

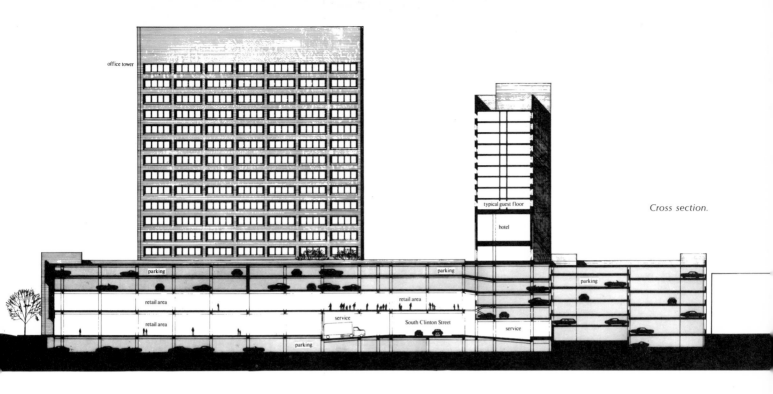

office tower

typical guest floor

hotel

parking

parking

parking

retail area

retail area

retail area

service

South Clinton Street

service

parking

Cross section.

The project is located south of historic Clinton Square on a 2½-square-block site bordered by South Salina, West Fayette, South Clinton, and West Water Streets. The concept features a shopping and pedestrian mall which is built over West Washington Street and connects to the office building. The second-floor retail area is also connected over South Clinton Street to the projected hotel and garage structure. The project was completed in 1974.

The developer is the New York State Urban Development Corporation.

CLINTON SQUARE
Syracuse, New York
ARCHITECTS: Welton Becket and Associates

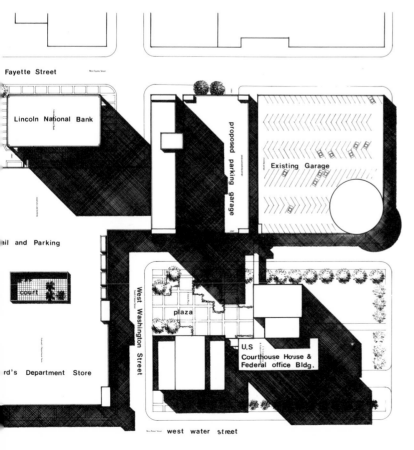

Fayette Street

Lincoln National Bank

proposed parking garage

Existing Garage

ail and Parking

court

West Washington Street

plaza

U.S Courthouse House & Federal office Bldg.

rd's Department Store

west water street

LEFT: *General site plan. (Photographer: Gil Amiaga.)*
ABOVE: *Exterior view.*

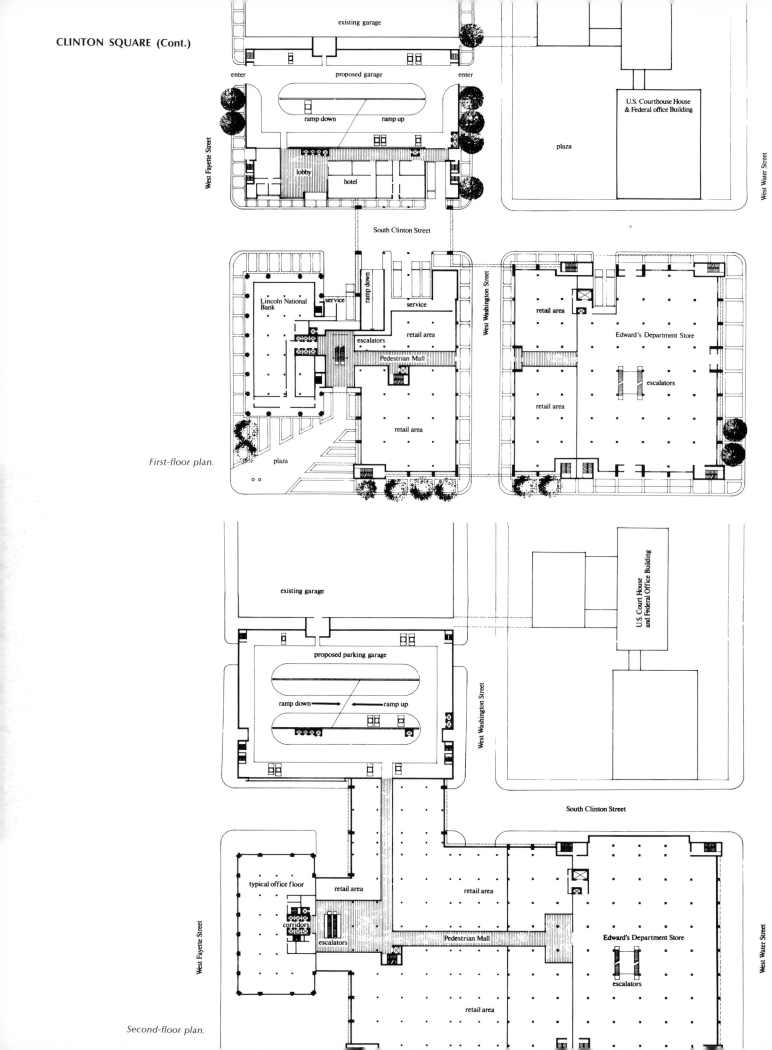

CLINTON SQUARE (Cont.)

existing garage

enter   proposed garage   enter

ramp down   ramp up

U.S. Courthouse House
& Federal office Building

plaza

West Fayette Street

West Water Street

lobby

hotel

South Clinton Street

First-floor plan.

Lincoln National
Bank

service   ramp down   service

escalators

retail area

West Washington Street

retail area

Edward's Department Store

escalators

Pedestrian Mall

retail area

retail area

plaza

existing garage

U.S. Court House
and Federal Office Building

proposed parking garage

ramp down ⟶   ⟵ ramp up

West Washington Street

South Clinton Street

typical office floor   retail area

corridors

escalators

West Fayette Street

retail area

retail area

Pedestrian Mall

Edward's Department Store

escalators

West Water Street

Second-floor plan.

This privately financed central business district project is in the prime location in Buffalo. The project consists of an office tower of 350,000 square feet, two levels of shopping, a level consisting of offices leased to the telephone company, and three levels of parking partially below grade. The project is in an area of recently constructed office towers, and there is recognition of the need to link the second retail level to existing department stores and offices by bridges over major streets.

One bridge was built to the new county office building. Architect Lathrop Douglass feels strongly that multilevel circulation in downtown areas is essential. Main Place needs to be connected to existing major department stores, other office buildings, and the municipal parking garage.

A significant development has been the closing of store entrances on Main Street. Even though Main Street is the chief shopping route of the city and even though the stores that took space fronting on Main Street as well as the mall paid much higher rents, a substantial number of the Main Street fronts have been closed off from customer access and consist only of show windows. This apparently is due to the very large percentage of shoppers utilizing the mall in lieu of Main Street and also, to a lesser extent, to the control problems of two entrances.

As a result of private negotiations, 560,000 square feet of land was acquired from sixty landlords. This includes the land the bank is built on, which is leased to the center for fifty years.

The city built a 1,000-car three-level underground ramp beneath the center. A merchants association leases the garage from the city and guarantees payment of the forty-year bonds. Rates are minimal. The center owns the land.

The center includes sixty-two stores, 203,000 square feet of retail space, 40,000 square feet of mall space and 70,000 square feet of office space at the third level.

The developer is the Central Buffalo Project Corp.

MAIN PLACE
Buffalo, New York

ARCHITECTS:
For the mall, stores, mall offices, and parking garage: Lathrop Douglass, FAIA
For the office tower and Erie County building: Harrison & Abramovitz

LEFT: *Street view.*
ABOVE: *Mall and stairway.*

233

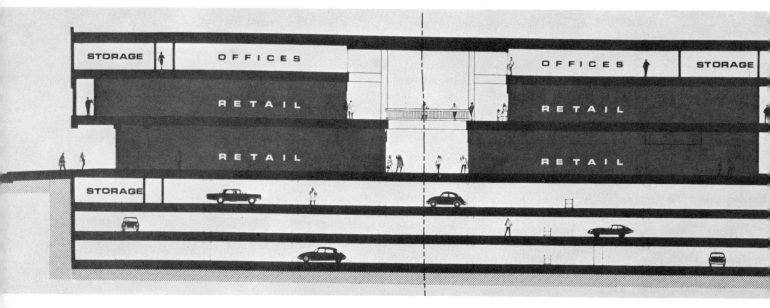

Cross section.

RIGHT: *Aerial view outlining location for mall, stores, and parking garage.* BELOW: *Section through mall showing tower location.*

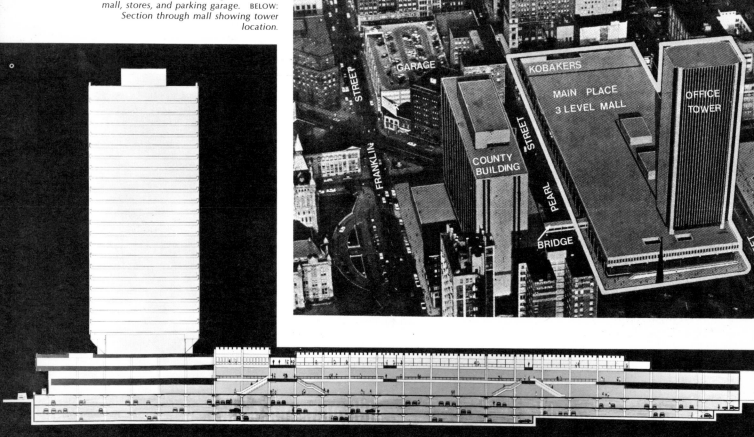

This project is located in the heart of the 130-acre White Plains central renewal project. The mall's tenants include nine whose businesses were uprooted by the replanning of the neighborhood and more than twenty-five from other parts of the city.

The mall occupies a 3.7-acre site bounded by Hamilton Avenue, Grove Street Extension, Barker Avenue, and Cottage Place, a short distance from Main Street and midway between two major department stores.

Since the site slopes downward from Cottage Place to Grove Street, the mall has the appearance of a two-story building on three sides and of a one-story building on the fourth. A split-level scheme with parking on the roof and on the grade level adjacent to the upper level allowed the architects to develop the site's maximum usable space. Parking is provided for 230 cars on the roof—accessible by ramp from Barker Avenue—and for 137 cars on the Cottage Place side.

Inside, all stores and shops open off the L-shaped mall on the lower level and a T-shaped mall on the upper. The lower level also contains storage and service areas, with a truck dock accessible from Barker Avenue. The exterior, with its bold vertical wall panels and exposed aggregate, provides a pleasant contrast to the smooth finish of the warm-toned concrete spandrel bands at the second level and rooftop. The row of ground-floor display windows is shaded by the overhanging second level on both Hamilton Avenue and Grove Street. Projecting canopies delineate the mall's street-level entrances on both of these elevations. The rectangular building has a reinforced concrete structural system.

The developers are M & D Furtsch Company & Benerofe Associates.

WHITE PLAINS MALL
White Plains, New York
ARCHITECTS: Welton Becket and Associates

ABOVE: *Exterior* (*perspective*).

Close-up view of aggregate exterior wall panels contrasted with rows of ground-floor windows.

Upper-level plan.

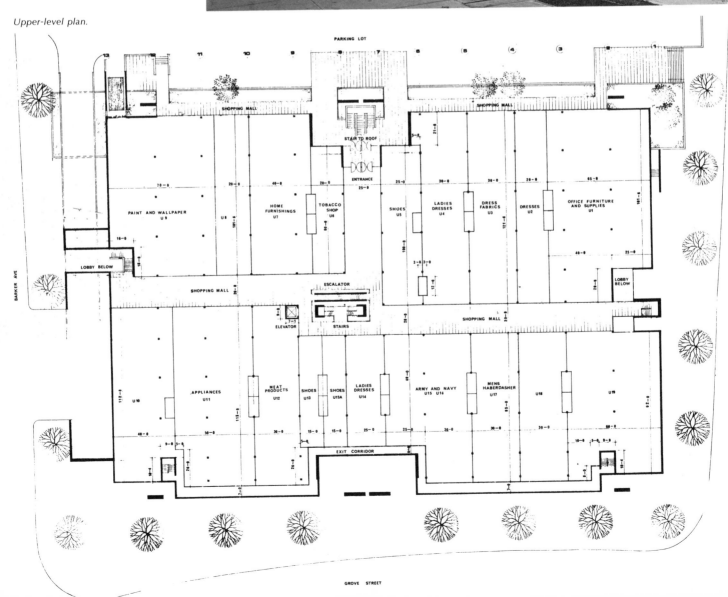

An interesting example of mall planning in a downtown area is Washington Square in Lansing, Michigan. The total project encompasses an area three blocks wide and seven blocks long, to be tied in to the state capitol complex. The completed phase one comprises three blocks along the former Washington Avenue designated as blocks 100, 200, and 300. The first block serves as the entry. Here a sunken plaza surrounds a pool in which a sculptured concrete fountain is located. As in the other blocks, wooden benches, paving patterns, trees, flowers, and kiosks add to the colorfulness of the square.

The focal point of Washington Square is the center of the 200 block. The spacious plaza is oriented to downtown business activity and provides for outdoor sales events, festivals, and special activities. At each end of the main plaza, smaller plazas are enclosed with low walls, spring-flowering trees, and plantings. The 300 block has two interesting features—a children's play plaza and an exhibit area. The exhibit area is an open plaza centered on the secondary pedestrian walkways leading to the Capitol Avenue parking structure. A reflecting pool is located in the center of the exhibit area, surrounded by large paved areas on which canvas-covered sales or display booths may be located. Permanent sleeves in the paving accommodate portable metal supports for the canvas tops. This enables the area to be used also for concerts, exhibits, and other public gatherings. Its proximity to Lansing Community College offers an opportunity for college-related programs.

Careful attention is given to signage, graphics, and lighting. The lighting is designed for overall illumination as well as for the localized areas of seating, plantings, and sculpture. The second stage of the mall is planned to continue south of Michigan Avenue and east and west on Michigan. Kiosks serve many important functions within Washington Square. They provide space for announcements, directories, and posters, and they house newsstands and public telephones. The kiosks, located in two areas of the square, are illuminated at night.

WASHINGTON SQUARE
Lansing, Michigan
LANDSCAPE ARCHITECTS:
Johnson Johnson & Roy, Inc.

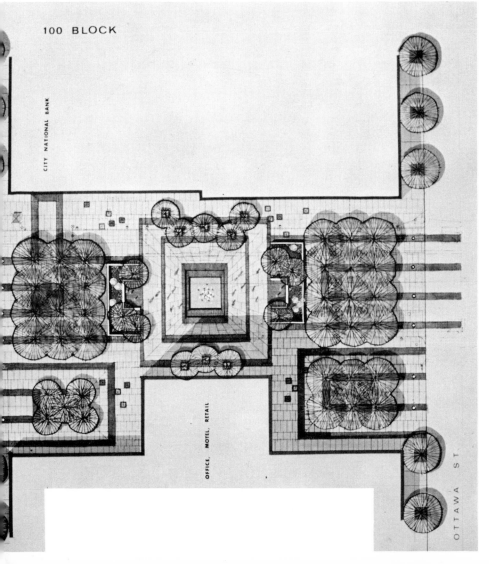

ABOVE: *Kiosk.*
LEFT: *Washington Avenue Mall plan.*

WASHINGTON SQUARE (Cont.)

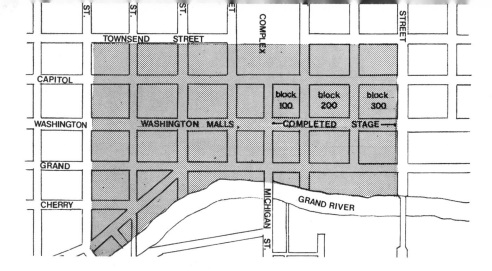

CLOCKWISE, STARTING ABOVE:
*Location plan.   Children's play plaza built of
wood in the 300 block.   View toward
sculptured fountain in the 100 block.
(Sculptor: Robert Youngman.)   General
layout.   Sculptured drinking fountain.*

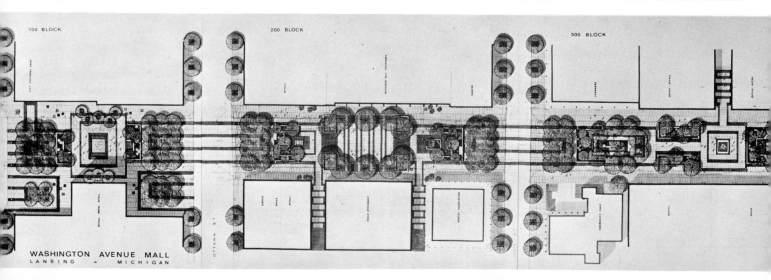

100 BLOCK   200 BLOCK   300 BLOCK

WASHINGTON AVENUE MALL
LANSING · MICHIGAN

Lafayette Plaza, which is located in Bridgeport, Connecticut (population 156,000), was developed by private enterprise. The 730,000 square feet of retail space is anchored by Gimbel's and Sears. Gimbel's, which was built at a subsequent stage, is located north of State Street and is connected to the project by a pedestrian bridge. The architects for Gimbel's are Abbott Merkt & Company. The project includes a seven-story office building. The city built a 3,000-car seven-level garage, which connects directly to both levels of the mall and to roof parking over the stores. The parking charge is nominal.

Although this project sparked a large amount of CBD redevelopment, the center itself had difficulty in securing full occupancy. The reason for this, according to the architect, Lathrop Douglass, FAIA, is that the plaza is three blocks away from the city's main retail center and is isolated. Also, because of the convenient connection between the roof level and the second level, the first level was more difficult to lease. The new master plan prepared by Gruen Associates calls for a connection between the roof level and the second level, the first level was more covered mall.

Another factor which anticipates improved economics of Lafayette Plaza is the building of the connector route between the Connecticut Thruway and the Wilbur Cross Parkway, which is located on the periphery of Bridgeport. This allows Lafayette Plaza to compete with a large suburban mall by shortening travel time to the plaza.

The developer is Hammerson, Fusco & Amatruda Corporation.

LAFAYETTE PLAZA
Bridgeport, Connecticut

CONSULTING ARCHITECT AND PLANNER:
Lathrop Douglass, FAIA

ABOVE, LEFT: *Overall view. (1) Sears, Roebuck & Co.; (2) two-level stores; (3) Gimbel's; (4) offices; (5) seven-level parking; (6) hotel; (7) T.B.A.* ABOVE: *Entrance. (Photographer: George Szeberenyi.)*

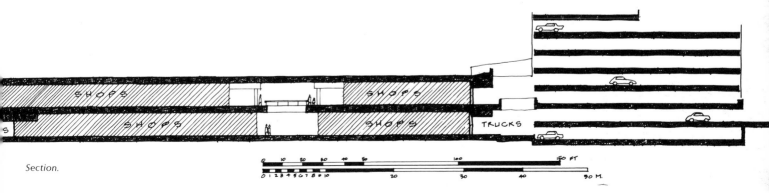

Section.

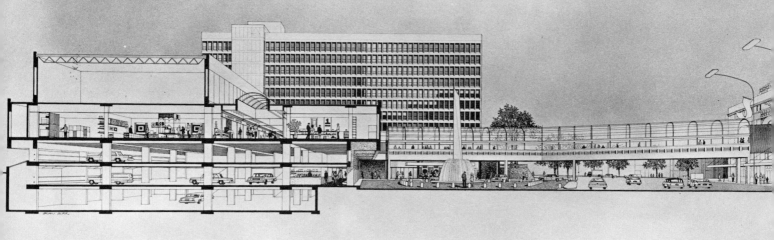

Located in a blighted area in the existing CBD area of Newark, the $50 million Gateway project involved the rebuilding of a five-block urban renewal area adjacent to Penn Central Station. Completed in 1972, it provides enclosed air-conditioned elevated walkways for shoppers and office workers that connect all buildings to the upper level of the station; this achieves separation of pedestrian and automobile traffic.

Elements of Gateway are a thirty-story office building (completed in 1970), a 260-room Downtowner hotel (completed in 1970), and 70,000 square feet of retail space, with a built-up area of 500,000 square feet. Gateway II, an eighteen-story office building containing 800,000 square feet, was completed in spring 1972.

The eighteen-story Western Electric building is the principal tenant of the complex. The main entrance lobby is a large, glass-enclosed, two-level space. The lower street entrance level is connected by escalator to the pedestrian level above, where the shopping arcade is located.

Future stages call for additional office building and apartment buildings.

The developers are Gateway Urban Renewal Corporation (a joint venture of Food Fair Properties Incorporated of Philadelphia and Gene A. Genola, Asbury Park, New Jersey).

GATEWAY
Newark, New Jersey
ARCHITECTS: Gruen Associates

ABOVE: *Section showing connecting walkway between the complex and Penn Central Station.* LEFT: *General view of the redeveloped area showing elevated enclosed walkway to Penn Central Station.*

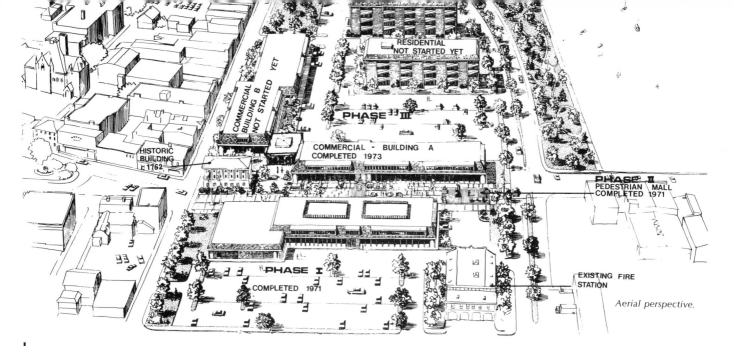

Aerial perspective.

Long Wharf Mall is situated in a redevelopment area in the center of the business district along Newport's famous waterfront. This area in the past was characterized by a series of bars and bistros, run-down housing, and other questionable establishments. The Newport Redevelopment Agency cleared this land for an extensive redevelopment project.

The implementation of the project was scheduled in three phases.

Phase one. A major Providence bank, Industrial National Bank (through its holding company, Westminster Properties), was instrumental in organizing this project. As the major stockholder, the bank organized with four local businessmen to form Long Wharf Mall Associates. This phase included retail, office, and apartment units.

The primary objective with regard to design was to preserve the long and illustrious architectural history of Newport. Immediately adjacent was the Market House (1762), and within a short distance was the first Rhode Island statehouse, now called the Colony House (1760). To preserve the heritage and at the same time make a contemporary statement was the problem. The use of traditional forms and materials indigenous to old Newport, such as the mansard roof and the brick arch, set the architectural motif. This approach met with the approval of the very active Preservation Society as well as the Newport Redevelopment Agency.

The owner of phase one is Long Wharf Mall Associates.

Phase Two. On what was originally Long Wharf, a city street, the city decided to build a pedestrian mall. Many ancient subsurface utility lines caused numerous problems, which were overcome after persistent consultation with the local utilities. A nautical theme was carried out on the mall with flags and nautical graphics on the buildings adjoining the mall.

The owner of phase two is the city of Newport.

Phase Three. The commercial development was completed in 1973. The residential portion is planned for 100 new luxury apartments.

The owner of phase three is Commercial Investment Corporation.

LONG WHARF MALL
Newport, Rhode Island

ARCHITECTS:
For phase one, phase two, and commercial building adjacent to mall: Fenton G. Keyes Associates
For commercial development on Thames Street and residential development: Samuel Glazer

ABOVE: *View from mall showing the historic preservation feature.* LEFT: *View looking northeast. (Photographer: Robert P. Foley.)*

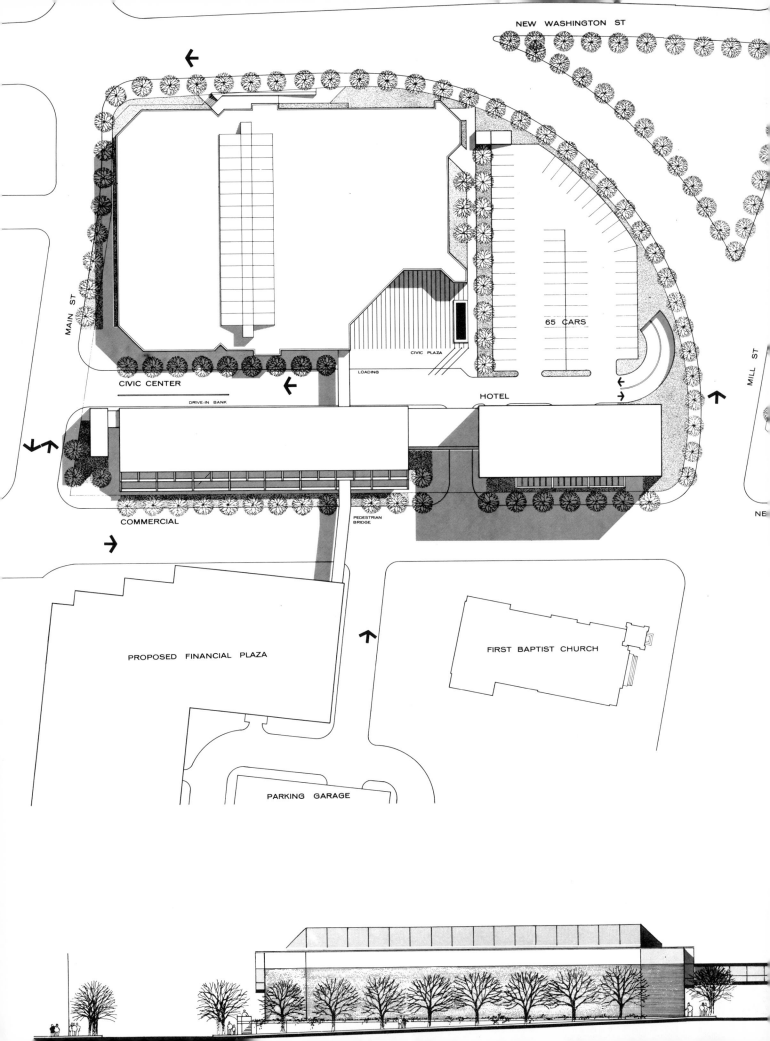

NEW WASHINGTON ST

MAIN ST

MILL ST

65 CARS

CIVIC PLAZA

LOADING

CIVIC CENTER

DRIVE-IN BANK

HOTEL

NE

COMMERCIAL

PEDESTRIAN
BRIDGE

PROPOSED FINANCIAL PLAZA

FIRST BAPTIST CHURCH

PARKING GARAGE

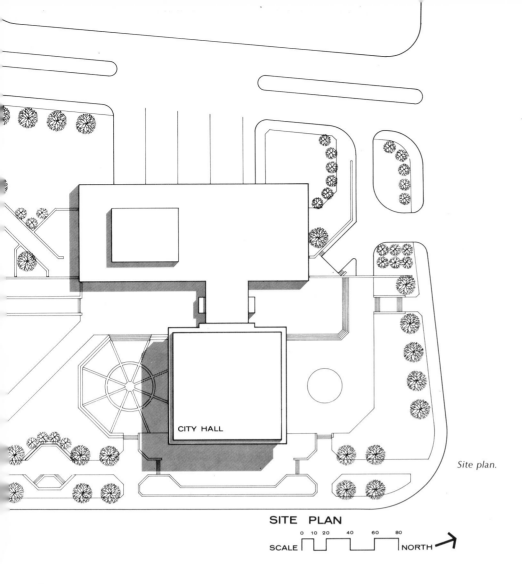

Site plan.

SITE PLAN

SCALE `0 10 20  40   60  80` NORTH →

CITY HALL

Located south of the new City Hall, the Poughkeepsie Civic Center complex includes a civic center with an ice-skating arena, a shopping mall, and a hotel. As a public service, the McCann Foundation, which is building the civic center, will present it to the city as a gift. The city then plans to lease the center to a nonprofit organization for a fifty-year period to operate it independently.

The concept of the project is a compromise from earlier, more ambitious plans, due primarily to economic factors. An obvious handicap is the lack of sufficient parking space on the site, although a 700-car parking structure is being planned two blocks away, to be connected by pedestrian bridge to the commercial structure and the civic center. An east-west state arterial access road is considered important to the progress of this development.

POUGHKEEPSIE CIVIC CENTER
Poughkeepsie, New York
ARCHITECTS: Sargent-Webster-Crenshaw & Folley

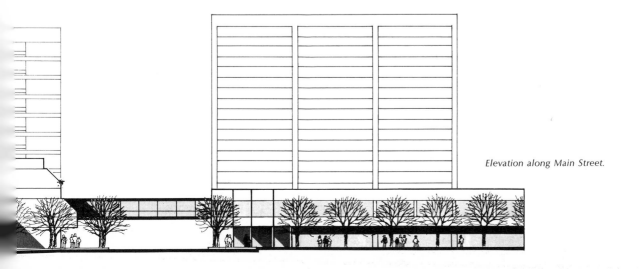

Elevation along Main Street.

BURLINGTON SQUARE
Burlington, Vermont

ARCHITECTS: Office of Mies van der Rohe
and Freeman, French, Freeman

Burlington, Vermont, is a city of 39,000 located on the east shore of Lake Champlain. Although it is small, Burlington is beset with all the central-city problems of decline faced by larger cities. Not as many people are coming downtown to shop, there is not enough parking, and the city center shows symptoms of decline. Like other cities across the country, Burlington plans to change the city center to keep it vital.

The concept of this urban renewal project is to revitalize downtown with a mix of new office buildings, apartment buildings, and hotels integrated and tied together by a spine of retail and department stores with ample parking facilities.

The site for Burlington Square is an urban renewal area of 17 acres located on three blocks between Church Street, the main shopping street, and Lake Champlain. In order to make the project a single contiguous parcel, the developer assembled an additional 3 acres of private parcels to connect and front on Church Street and worked out a comprehensive traffic pattern for the entire central business area. The two existing streets which bisected the site were vacated with the approval of the city.

Burlington Square will reinforce the existing downtown shopping area, since Church Street will be used as the base mall, with the new complex as a tee extension stretching from Church Street to a planned lakefront park.

A below-plaza pedestrian mall starting at the entrance pavilion on Church Street will interconnect all the proposed and recently completed buildings. It will be lined with shops, restaurants, and theaters. Mall entrances, light courts, and clerestory structures on the plaza will bring daylight to the mall. Future plans call for a direct pedestrian and vehicular connection across Battery Street to a park and a depressed beltline highway which will border the lake. The stepped plaza is composed of a series of terraces which conform to the profile of an 80-foot slope from Church Street to Battery Street.

Existing off-street parking will be tripled by the addition of underground parking facilities and two above-grade parking structures. Phase one will provide parking for 1,100 cars and phase two, parking for an additional 2,000. The initial phase of the project will include the entrance pavilion fronting on Church Street, a sixteen-story apartment tower of 100 units, a bank, a parking structure, a department store, a 200-room hotel, a four-story office building, and 100,000 square feet of retail space. Subsequent construction will add an apartment tower, a second department store, another parking structure, and a five-story office building.

The developer is Mondev Corporation Ltd.

Location plan.

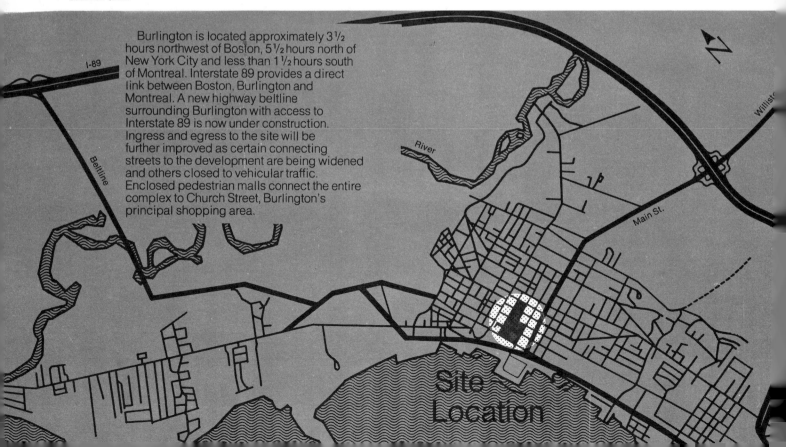

Burlington is located approximately 3 1/2 hours northwest of Boston, 5 1/2 hours north of New York City and less than 1 1/2 hours south of Montreal. Interstate 89 provides a direct link between Boston, Burlington and Montreal. A new highway beltline surrounding Burlington with access to Interstate 89 is now under construction. Ingress and egress to the site will be further improved as certain connecting streets to the development are being widened and others closed to vehicular traffic. Enclosed pedestrian malls connect the entire complex to Church Street, Burlington's principal shopping area.

Site Location

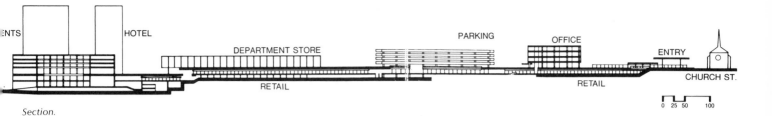

Model of the master plan. (A)
Primary entrance to project; (B)
office building; (C) office building
(completed); (D) parking structure;
(E) department store; (F) apartment
building; (G) hotel. (Photographer:
Yvan Vallée et Associés.)

CRETEIL, FRANCE

CONSULTING ARCHITECTS AND PLANNERS:
Lathrop Douglass, FAIA, and
Aaron Chelouche, AIA, SARL
ARCHITECTS FOR THE SHOPPING COMPLEX:
Dacbert & Stenzel

Creteil is an old French town that is growing very rapidly because of its proximity to Paris. Anticipating the problems of this growth, the government established a site for a new town center and is promoting the development of this area. Included in the complex are apartments, office buildings, amusement and recreational facilities, government buildings, a new commercial center, and parking decks. Creteil is linked to Paris by railroad, a subway extension, and local and express highways.

The commercial center, which is an integral part of the master plan, consists of two levels of malls with 150 satellite stores, Printemps and B.H.V. department stores, and three parking levels, including grade, one deck, and the roof level. The total gross leasable area is 1 million square feet; there are spaces for 5,600 cars.

Creteil will be both a shopping center and the central core for a new town of 100,000 people. An amusement center of 214,000 square feet will be built adjacent to the shopping center. It will include six cinemas, a bowling alley, and other recreational facilities. In addition, the center has 374,500 square feet of office space.

Of special interest are the basic factors influencing the development of the "new-old" towns and new towns around the large French metropolitan areas. In France the problem is quite different from that in the United States and Canada. In Paris, for example, in order to control the large increase in the metropolitan population, the government decided to enlarge the satellite towns on the periphery of the city. All these towns (see the map of Paris environs) are connected to the Paris subway system and to the express highways.

Lathrop Douglass, FAIA, and Aaron Chelouche, AIA, planners for the Creteil Commercial Center and several other satellite-town commercial centers, comment: "In planning the central business districts of the 'new-old' towns, public agencies prepare master plans, buy up vacant or nominally priced land, construct local prefectures and other government buildings, and provide transportation and other public necessity items. After making provisions for open space, the remaining available land is sold to developers at a figure which pays for the public improvements and, it is hoped, allows the developer to build the new town center or residential districts as basically master planned and in such a way that the venture can be a profitable investment."

Because more equity, or "front" money, is normally required for private developments in France than in the United States, it is customary for one of the major banking interests of Paris to be included in the development teams.

The developers are S.E.G.E.C.F.-Serec.

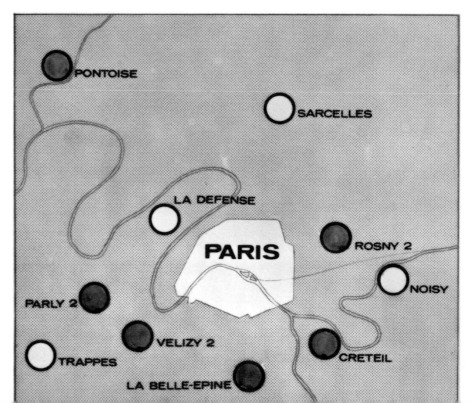

246   *Location of the satellite towns.*

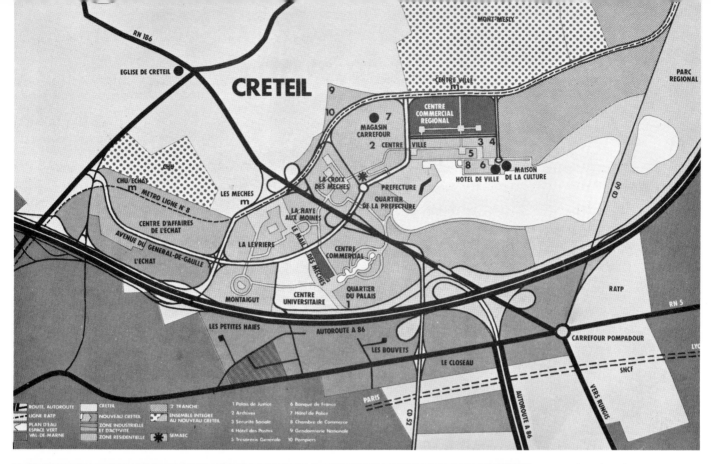

CRETEIL

Legend:

ROUTE, AUTOROUTE
LIGNE RATP
PLAN D'EAU
ESPACE VERT
VAL-DE-MARNE

CRETEIL
NOUVEAU CRETEIL
ZONE INDUSTRIELLE
ET D'ACTIVITE
ZONE RESIDENTIELLE

2 TRANCHE:
ENSEMBLE INTEGRE
AU NOUVEAU CRETEIL
SEMAEC

1 Palais de Justice
2 Archives
3 Securité Sociale
4 Hôtel des Postes
5 Trésorerie Générale

6 Banque de France
7 Hôtel de Police
8 Chambre de Commerce
9 Gendarmerie Nationale
10 Pompiers

ABOVE: *Site plan of new town center.*
LEFT: *Model of the new town center.*
BELOW: *Section through shopping complex.*

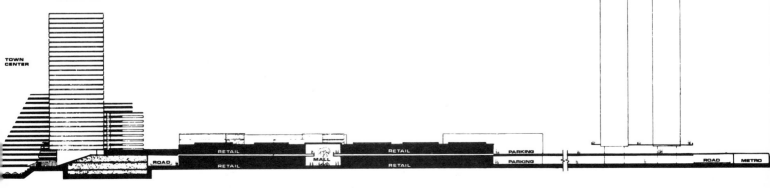

Polygone Center is a major CBD renewal in Montpellier, which has a population of 125,000. The site is at one end of the main plaza of the city near the Place de la Comédie and occupies terrain that is substantially lower than the plaza. The mall has two levels. The upper-level mall connects directly at one end with the plaza and Place de la Comédie. The lower-level mall connects with the depressed highway and railroad. Parking for 2,000 cars is on four decks beneath the project. The Galeries Lafayette department store acts as an anchor at the opposite end of the mall from the plaza. The total gross leasable area is approximately 400,000 square feet, of which 160,000 square feet is the department store. The overall project also includes a new municipal building, a hotel, office buildings, etc., all of which are contiguous to the retail area and occupy the low-lying land.

The developer is SOCRI SA.

POLYGONE CENTER
Montpellier, France

CONSULTING ARCHITECTS AND PLANNERS:
Lathrop Douglass, FAIA, and
Aaron Chelouche, SARL
ARCHITECTS FOR THE MALLS, STORES,
AND PARKING: Boyer and Borrel

Aerial view showing location of new
shopping complex.

248

Trenton Commons is a comprehensive plan aimed at revitalizing the State Street area of downtown. State Street, between City Hall and the State Capitol, is closed to traffic to create an auto-free pedestrian shopping street. Traffic is rerouted to a one-way loop system around the perimeter of the area. This improves general traffic circulation and thus accessibility to downtown. A number of new parking garages are planned at convenient locations around the loop.

Integration of the Commons with adjacent residential, commercial, and office development is a key element in the design. This is accomplished largely by means of a comprehensive pedestrian linkage system which includes overhead bridges, widened sidewalks, arcades, and new walkways. Use is made of the existing open center-block areas and spaces between buildings for new walkways, a number of small parks, and a major public square.

An improvement program assists in the reuse and redesign of existing stores, storefronts, signs, and canopies. The brick paving on State Street was extended to become an attractive walking surface. Kiosks, outdoor markets, restaurants, and special lighting are further planned improvements. State Street is a major redevelopment proposal which utilizes the center-block space behind the shops. Strategically located, the square is planned as a multilevel public space for outdoor meetings, exhibitions, entertainment, and recreation. It will be surrounded by new and existing commercial facilities, cinemas, restaurants, a parking garage, and a bus terminal, with important pedestrian links to other areas.

This plan reveals a growing potential for revitalization with a minimum of cost. Thus, an increase of regional population, new residential development within the core itself, and the expanding daytime office population are anticipated. Trenton also offers the stability of being a center for state, county, and city government. Physical characteristics and historical elements make State Street suited to the development of a vital pedestrian shopping mall.

According to John P. Clarke, director of the Department of Planning and Development:

> There were seventeen vacancies in the mall area prior to start of construction. As construction progressed, the number of vacancies decreased to a very few with no vacancies existing after the completion of the mall development. Real estate brokers

TRENTON COMMONS
Trenton, New Jersey

ARCHITECTS AND PLANNERS: Lee Harris Pomeroy
  & Associates

ABOVE: *Perspective view of mall and walkway.*

249

Model showing State Street Square in relation to the mall.

reported a 400% increase in downtown rental and property sales. Retail sales are anticipated to increase by 10 to 15%.

The majority of commercial businesses on the Commons is conducted during the working day. Approximately 30,000 people comprise the daily working population which are located within walking distance of the central business district. The vast majority, some 20,000 persons are employed by the State of New Jersey, and continued increases in this number are anticipated. With these facts considered, the attraction of daytime shoppers to the Trenton Commons is the main focus.

The establishment of the Clean and Safe Neighborhood Programs has enabled us to increase the numbers of foot patrolmen on the Trenton Commons. The problem of transportation has been eased by the establishment of a one-way loop around the Commons. For the future, plans are being considered for the establishment of a jitney bus service which will service nearby office and residential areas.*

The sponsors of the Commons are the city of Trenton, HUD, Heart of Trenton, the Trenton-Mercer Chamber of Commerce, and the Trenton Parking Authority.

*Material excerpted from *Trenton Commons*, brochure prepared for the Department of Planning and Development, city of Trenton, N.J., Jan. 25, 1972.

Plan of mall.

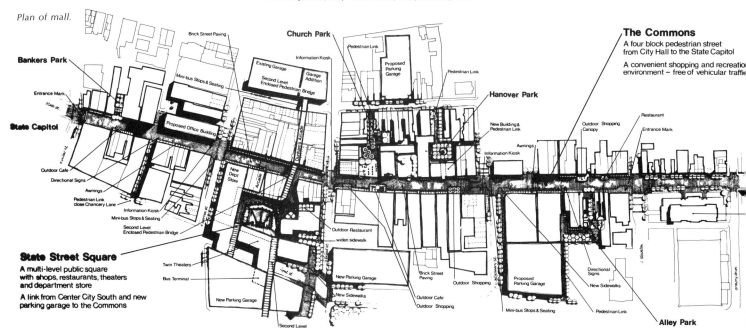

Bankers Park

Entrance Mark

State Capitol

Outdoor Cafe
Directional Signs
Awnings
Pedestrian Link
close Chancery Lane
Information Kiosk
Mini-bus Stops & Seating
Second Level
Enclosed Pedestrian Bridge

State Street Square

A multi-level public square with shops, restaurants, theaters and department store

A link from Center City South and new parking garage to the Commons

Twin Theaters
Bus Terminal
New Parking Garage
Second Level
Enclosed Pedestrian Bridge

Brick Street Paving
Mini-bus Stops & Seating
Existing Garage
Second Level
Enclosed Pedestrian Bridge
Information Kiosk
Proposed Office Building
New Dept Store
Arcade
Dudley Arcade

Church Park

Pedestrian Link
Proposed Parking Garage
Pedestrian Link

Hanover Park

New Building &
Pedestrian Link
Information Kiosk
Awnings

Outdoor Restaurant
widen sidewalk

Brick Street
Paving
New Parking Garage
New Sidewalks
Outdoor Cafe
Outdoor Shopping
Outdoor Shopping

The Commons

A four block pedestrian street from City Hall to the State Capitol

A convenient shopping and recreation environment – free of vehicular traffic

Restaurant
Outdoor Shopping
Canopy
Entrance Mark

Proposed Parking Garage
Mini-bus Stops & Seating
Directional Signs
New Sidewalks
Pedestrian Link

Alley Park

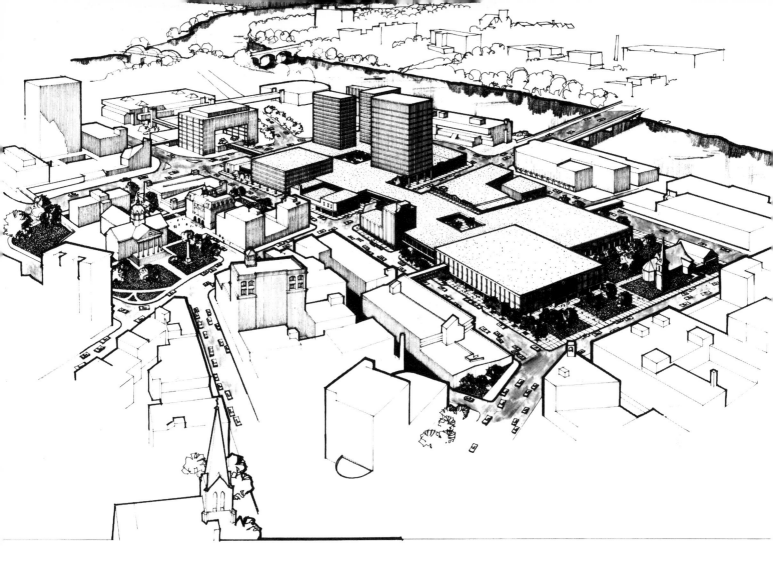

Binghamton is one of the six principal urban centers in New York State. It is located approximately 200 miles northwest of New York City and is the marketing center for a large area of south-central New York and north-central Pennsylvania. Binghamton has a population of 64,000 and is the center of the 270,000 standard metropolitan statistical area. This population has been steadily increasing during the past decade. The rapid growth of the state university at Binghamton and the aggressive recruiting policies of local industries have resulted in a better-educated, more technical work force with a younger family composition.

Downtown Binghamton is the business, financial, government, entertainment, and shopping center of the region. The most striking characteristics of the Binghamton market are the lack of quality shoppers' goods and the absence of important suburban shopping areas. Although amply supplied with discount stores, the area does not have a level of shoppers' goods commensurate with the income and sophistication of its population. It also does not have any enclosed shopping malls, and downtown Binghamton is still the most significant shopping area in the region.

Industries include a number of large industrial companies as well as smaller branch plants for other important companies.

The redevelopment program has to date made a good start with the recent completion of a large number of new buildings. These include a multimillion-dollar governmental complex, a number of bank buildings, and a county arena, which has been attracting full houses for all major events. A future performing-arts-center facility is in the process of being planned by the county government.

The commercial complex, which is being developed by Mondev-Binghamton, occupies a 7-acre site in the 100 percent core area of downtown Binghamton. Approximately half of the site is vacant land owned by the Binghamton Urban Renewal agency. The other half is to be acquired and cleared by the Binghamton

BINGHAMTON, NEW YORK

ARCHITECTS:
For the master plan: Blair Associates and
  Werner Seligmann Associates
For the Mondev project: Office of Mies van der Rohe

ABOVE: *Perspective view focusing on the commercial area.*

Parking Authority. The Parking Authority will construct below-grade parking ramps and lease the air rights to the developers. The project area is bounded by Henry Street on the north, State Street on the east, Hawley Street on the south, and Water Street on the west.

Major street realignments, widenings, and reconstruction were undertaken in the 1960s in conjunction with Binghamton's downtown renewal program. As a result, access to downtown and internal circulation within the core area are satisfactory. As to parking facilities, the 3,400 on-street and parking-lot spaces now serving the downtown area will be augmented by 1,000 new spaces in the new development project. A planned network of overhead pedestrian bridges is being implemented to separate pedestrian from automobile traffic in downtown Binghamton.

At the end of 1974 five bridges were complete. They have all been financed from public funds—partly federal renewal funds, partly city funds, and, in one instance, County Broome funds, as a share of the total cost. One of the existing bridges on State Street connects a small, 21,000 square-foot retail building with the State Street parking structure.

The important factor in the developer's concept is that the project combines shopping, housing, parking, hotel, recreation, and related commercial facilities. The plans call for integration of this complex with existing major elements by means of new pedestrian links. The sum total of this planning could very well lead to a vibrant day/night urban lifestyle!

Plan of commercial area as developed by Mondev Corporation Ltd.

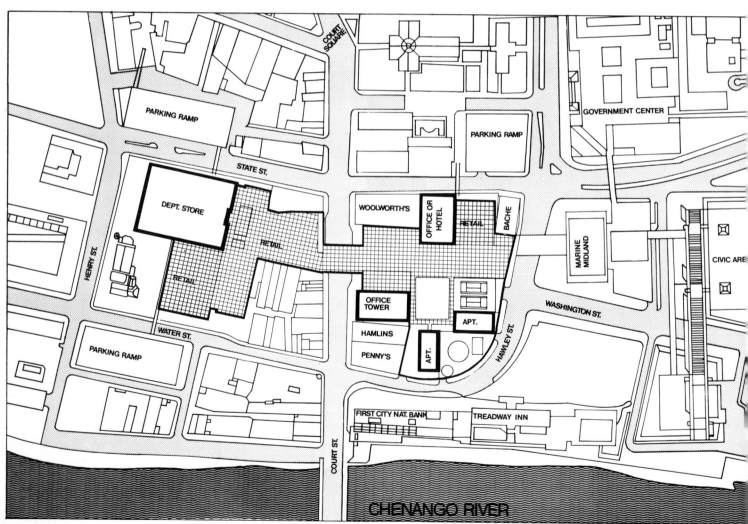

Department Store	150,000 sq. ft	Office	150,000 sq. ft.
Specialty Shops	150,000 sq. ft	Residential	200 units
Malls, Public Spaces	50,000 sq. ft	Parking	1000 Interior Spaces

The Central City District of San Antonio is over 250 years old, rich in history, tradition, and uniqueness. Until the 1950s, the downtown district had been the regional focus of government, business, services, culture, entertainment, shopping and (of a diminishing intensity) living. After World War II, downtown development declined while vast new housing projects were built on the city's edges to satisfy critical shortages accrued during the war years.

Early 1970s show the Central City District physical plant antiquated. The last major building "boom" took place during the latter 1920s and early 30s making the average age of structures and facilities downtown over 50 years old. While industrial technology made mechanization of and mass-participation in the products of society a reality, little change to accommodate this "new society" was made downtown. People left downtown obsolescence for a new contemporary suburban standard of living.

Decentralization of business, services, and shopping gained momentum in the 60's, following the population market base. This exodus left the Central City District not only physically obsolete, but under-utilized and under-developed. The vast source of cheap, useable land in large areas of Bexar County encouraged building low-density, sprawling suburbs.

In 1968, there was a renewed interest in its downtown with the development of Hemisfair, the first world's fair held in the southern United States. Hemisfair left a $100-million legacy in the center of the city, a ninety-one acre urban plaza of old, historic and new, contemporary structures. Main public structures are the $15-million Civic Center (12,500 seat Arena; 2,800 seat Theatre for the Performing Arts; and 200,000 square feet. Exhibition Hall), the $6.5-million theme tower—the 750 foot Tower of the Americas, and a $4-million new river extension into the fairgrounds.

The Hemisfair Plaza is gradually being developed into a cultural-convention center. Included are five local and professional theatre groups, the San Antonio Symphony and Opera, the Institute of Texan Cultures, the first branch of a foreign University in the United States—the National University of Mexico, and a downtown branch of the Witte Museum. The Convention Center during the first six months of 1972 generated $26-million from 370 conventions with projected increases of 30% per year. Proposed for construction in the Civic Center project are a $12-million Federal Center (using the U.S. Pavilion Site) and a $10-million State office building.

Hemisfair '68 influenced a general "paint-up and fix-up" effort throughout downtown in addition to new construction. A $10-million, 500 room "modular" luxury hotel, new restaurants, night clubs, boutiques, and a 250 room luxury motor-inn, utilizing an existing historic building and parking garage, have been developed along the river. Several additional motor hotels were constructed.

The 1970's have witnessed significant new development trends. A $12.5-million bank-office-building-parking garage complex has been constructed at historic Travis Park. A $20-million bank-office tower (the largest ever constructed downtown) has been completed (1974). Rosa Verde Urban Renewal, a multi-million dollar project is generating

SAN ANTONIO, TEXAS

ABOVE, LEFT: *View of Institute of Texan Cultures.* ABOVE: *New hotel, La Mansion, on riverfront. (Photographs courtesy of the Department of Planning and Community Development.)* BELOW: *View from river of the civic-center arena. (Photographer: Jay William Barnes III.)*

mixed-use redevelopment of the Public Market district into a unique regional shopping center, including a triple-tower medical-professional complex, a motor hotel, and a significant residential apartment complex. Additionally proposed or under construction are a high-rise telephone building, apartment towers, commercial complexes, and a new downtown "academic mall" high school, one of two to be constructed in the central city.*

With the exception of the banking industry, virtually all the above projects have been funded or stimulated by public investments. The private projects center primarily in the convention and tourist facilities.

Notwithstanding the benefits stimulated by Hemisfair, business and political leaders realized that in order to restore the city's vitality and continued attraction, they must develop plans reaching into the 1990s.

Among the many items which the River Corridor Feasibility Study, funded by HUD, is responsible for reporting and making recommendations on is the importance of, and the absolute necessity for, flood control. There is a continuous history of river flooding; the last major flood occurred in 1946, and there is some degree of high-water damage every eighteen months.

At the same time, the problem of the drying up of other water sources (artesian wells and springs) has to be met by pumping in order to keep the river flowing. Added to this is the fact that water is polluted by urban effluents by the time it reaches the Paseo. Since the mid-1950s, the Army Corps of Engineers has been working on the flood-control problem. The city's share of the costs was handled by the San Antonio River Authority through a bond issue for $12 million. Because of a lack of funds, 4 miles of flood control from Johnson Street north to Pershing Street remain to be engineered.

The San Antonio River Corridor Feasibility Study for 1990 was submitted in June 1973 by architects Skidmore, Owings & Merrill and Marshall Kaplan, Gans & Kahn. This study deals in detail with the general feasibility survey, river flood control, the corridor as the regional center, neighborhood life in the corridor, the framework for decision making, and managing corridor revitalization. What is important in this report is the challenge that it brings to the city and its recognition that accomplishing a sound revitalization will require much effort, dedication, and financing.

That the citizens of San Antonio are receptive and sympathetic to the idea of making the river corridor the city's "aesthetic spine" was evidenced by Ordinance #41441, approved October 12, 1972,

Establishing standards for the development of the San Antonio River Walk area; creating an Advisory Commission to advise on all matters pertaining to development of the River Walk area; providing a procedure for review by such commission of all applications for building permits in the River Walk area.

The purpose of this ordinance is to preserve and promote the natural beauty and distinctively quaint and romantic character, including the historical aspects, of the River Walk, which is so intimately connected with the history and life of San Antonio; maintenance of the charm and atmosphere of Old San Antonio along the River Walk, and the promotion of an integrated shopping, living, entertainment, and recreation area for visitors and the people of this City, to the end that the public welfare will be promoted and advanced through the preservation of property values and the resulting benefits to the economy of the City flowing from the promotion and maintenance of San Antonio as a leading attraction for tourists; and most importantly, to preserve and promote the quality of life for the citizens of this City.

Special provisions control the signs, graphics, visual displays, outdoor furniture, and materials used. All are expected to conform with the total character of the area, and use such materials which are in keeping with early San Antonio design. Attention is paid also to control of noise pollution. [For details, see River Walk Policy Manual.]

Over the years, a number of small and large businesses have been located along the River banks. At the time of Hemisfair, there were hotels and motor lodges, eight quality restaurants, six night clubs, a number of boutiques, gift shops and a Billboard Theater. Currently special events, i.e., plays, dances, art shows, river parades, traveling minstrels, the famous Fiesta Week, all contribute to the most important goal: to provide interesting and vibrant "happenings" for local residents as well as tourists and visitors.†

View showing Tower of the Americas. (Photographer: Jay William Barnes III.)

One of the San Antonio River flood-control channels. (Photograph courtesy of the Department of Planning and Community Development.)

*Excerpted from Development of the Central City District, report published by the San Antonio Community Renewal Program, 1972.

†Excerpted from River Walk Policy Manual, River Walk Commission, city of San Antonio, 1973.

Part Four

Projects in Planning and Initial Implementation Stages

While Part 3 deals with central business district redevelopments, either completed or in the process of implementation of the various phases, Part 4 presents a number of projects which are in the planning stages and are under active consideration by private interests, public authorities, or both. This category also includes some imaginative concepts which are being partly implemented. Several of these may seem visionary at first glance and remote from practical implementation. However, they definitely serve as an inspiration to evolve new approaches in unexplored directions.

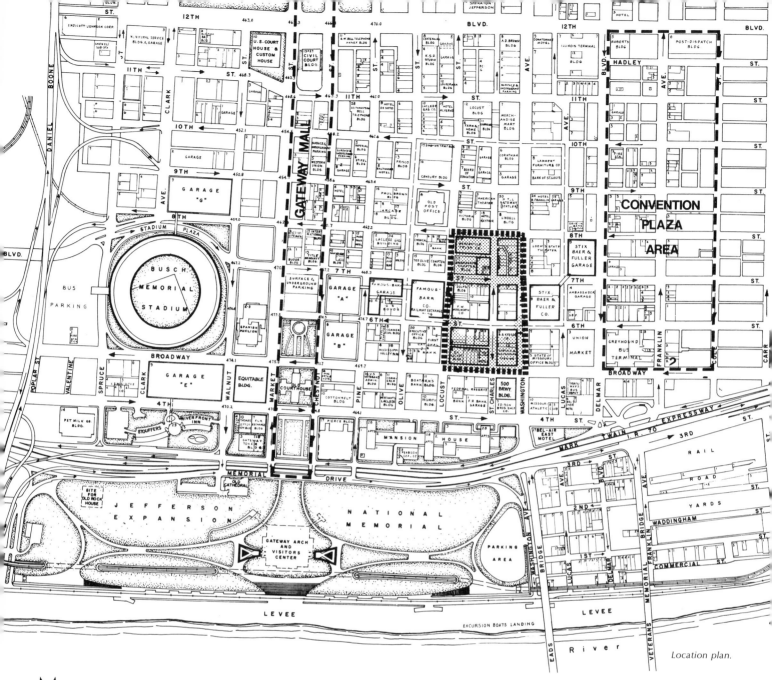

Location plan.

MERCANTILE CENTER
St. Louis, Missouri

ARCHITECTS FOR THE MASTER PLAN AND DESIGN:
Thompson, Ventulett & Stainback, Inc.
SUPERVISING AND COORDINATING ARCHITECTS:
Sverdrup & Parcel & Associates, Inc.

Mercantile Center, in downtown St. Louis, is a comprehensive urban development which should have an impact on the revival of the city's central business district.

With its first phase, started in 1973, the development offers a full spectrum of uses for the city and its visitors. Within the six-block project area, bounded by Locust Street, Broadway, Washington Avenue, and Eighth Street, one finds office space, a variety of shops, restaurants, entertainment and hotel facilities, open landscaped plazas, enclosed gardens, and pedestrian malls.

The project area is in a unique central location in the city. It is situated between two major department stores, adjacent to the state's largest banking institutions, and within easy walking distance of Busch Stadium, a major high-rise residential development, and the proposed new civic convention center.

The development plans the closing of St. Charles Street and certain alleys to create three large blocks, connected by enclosed pedestrian bridges. It further plans pedestrian connections to the Mansion House area to the east as well as to the department stores to the north and south. These pedestrian ways will provide free and easy movement throughout the complex in a safe and air-conditioned environment.

The closing of St. Charles Street was extensively researched. An analysis made of existing traffic conditions in the redevelopment area indicated that its closing would not have a detrimental effect on traffic volume or the circulation around and through the development. Utility easements in St. Charles Street will be relocated in easements provided by the Mercantile Center Redevelopment Corporation.

Mercantile Center will have four major high-rise structures totaling more than 3 million square feet, an 800-room hotel, and two levels of shops, restaurants, and entertainment facilities of approximately 150,000 square feet. All the facilities will interconnect through a system of enclosed malls and bridges focusing around a large, enclosed garden containing sculpture, fountains, flowers, and trees. Sunlight will enter into this space through large skylights, which will also provide views upward of the surrounding towers.

Large, open areas are provided around the base of each office tower and at the street corners. The spaces were designed to create open vistas into the complex at the pedestrian level, provide views around corners for vehicular traffic, and allow sunlight to enter the plaza, the landscaped areas, and the special outdoor seating and dining areas. Thirty-four percent of the property area has been devoted to outdoor open space, and an additional 9 percent has been provided in an enclosed garden at the street level.

The office towers will rise from the two superblocks to the west, while the third block will be devoted entirely to the hotel, its parking, and other amenities. Although retail space will be provided in all three blocks, the principal retail area will be located in the center block. On the first level, or "street level," retail space will be oriented primarily to pedestrian traffic along the sidewalk, with entrances into the complex in the center of the block on each of the four sides. Office workers, as well as shoppers, will move by escalator to the second-level, or "lobby-level" retail space, where all the office building lobbies are located. At this level pedestrian bridges will carry people over the streets to their desired destinations.

Service for the project is handled below street level. The west office tower has its own service with access off Washington Street. The remainder of the project is serviced from a system with ingress and egress on Sixth Street. This system provides for a tunnel under Sixth Street to service the office and retail facilities as well as the Famous-Barr department store. Phasing of the construction will allow uninterrupted, greatly improved service for the Famous-Barr operation. The total plan will provide for a workable separation between trucks and service areas and the pedestrians.

The $150 million project, organized under the name Mercantile Center Redevelopment Corporation, was certified in October 1972 in accordance with the Urban Redevelopment Law of Missouri Revised Statutes, 1969. It received the approval of the city aldermatic board in April 1973.

Construction of the first phase, a thirty-five-story Mercantile Tower office building with a 400-car low-rise garage, was initiated in August 1973. The implementation of the entire development is scheduled to be accomplished in six stages, with completion to be achieved over a ten-year period.

The developers are Crow, Pope and Land Enterprises, Inc., in joint venture with the Mercantile Trust Co. N. O. of St. Louis. Financing for phase one was arranged through Mercantile Mortgage Company. Permanent financing is being provided by New York Life Insurance Company, and interim financing by Bankers Trust Company.

Aerial view showing site location. (Photographer: Clyde May, Photography, Inc.)

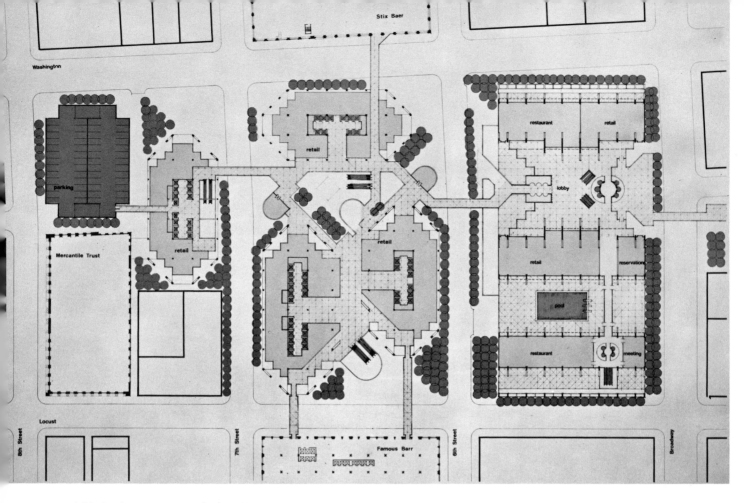

ABOVE: *Lobby level.* BELOW: *Longitudinal section.*
(*Photographer: Clyde May, Photography, Inc.*)

OMNI INTERNATIONAL
Atlanta, Georgia

ARCHITECTS: Thompson, Ventulett
& Stainback, Inc.

Omni International, in Atlanta, Georgia, is a privately developed multifunction commercial venture, to be constructed in a single phase over owned and leased (air rights) property. The 6-acre site is the beginning for future development within a 50-acre railroad yard near the urban core of Atlanta. It is unique to the city in its scope and potential for countering the move to suburbia. The major elements included are retail (shops and "bazaars"), 120,000 S.F.G.; restaurants and cinemas, 70,000 S.F.G.; office space, 600,000 S.F.G.; a trade pavilion, 70,000 S.F.G.; a hotel (500 rooms), 400,000 S.F.G.; and a "great space," approximately 11 million cubic feet. (S.F.G. refers to "square foot gross" areas.)

The architect makes the following comments about solution of design problems:

A two-level shopping arcade will be provided around an especially attractive feature: a public indoor skating rink. The recently completed arena nearby will be used as an anchor; above, there will be office space, a hotel, and a trade pavilion (on receding levels) enclosing a great space roofed with a long-span system and skylights. Large glass infilling panels will be added for seeing in and out, and circulation and individual building cores will be organized so that all citizens of this minicity can enjoy the great space and find occasions to visit one another there and feel an identity with the whole rather than the part (the cubicle, floor, or building). Dynamic elements will be added such as laser sculpture and a 200-foot-long escalator over ice to delight the tenant, shopper, or visitor. All space, including the great space, will be air-conditioned. Insulating glass will be solar bronze. The building skin is limestone.

The owner-developer is International City Corporation, Atlanta, Georgia.

Model, view from the top level showing escalator, skating rink, restaurant, and the great space. (Photographer: Architectural Photography of Atlanta.)

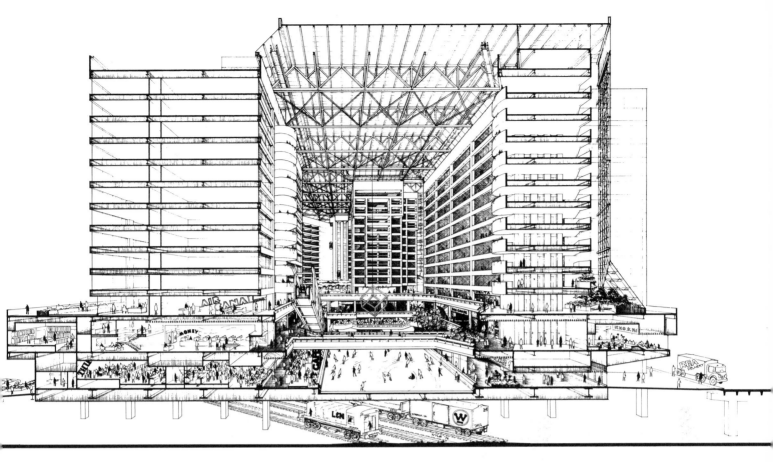

ABOVE: *Interior view showing sections through all levels.*
BELOW: *Service level showing the rail yard.*

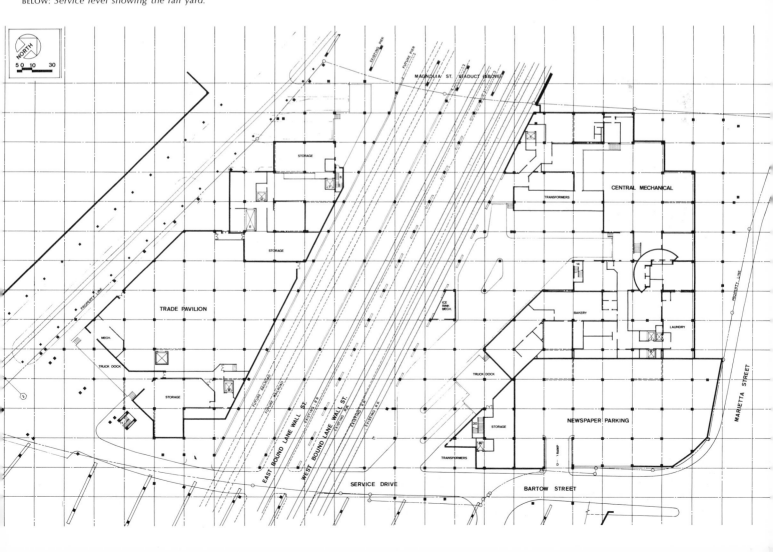

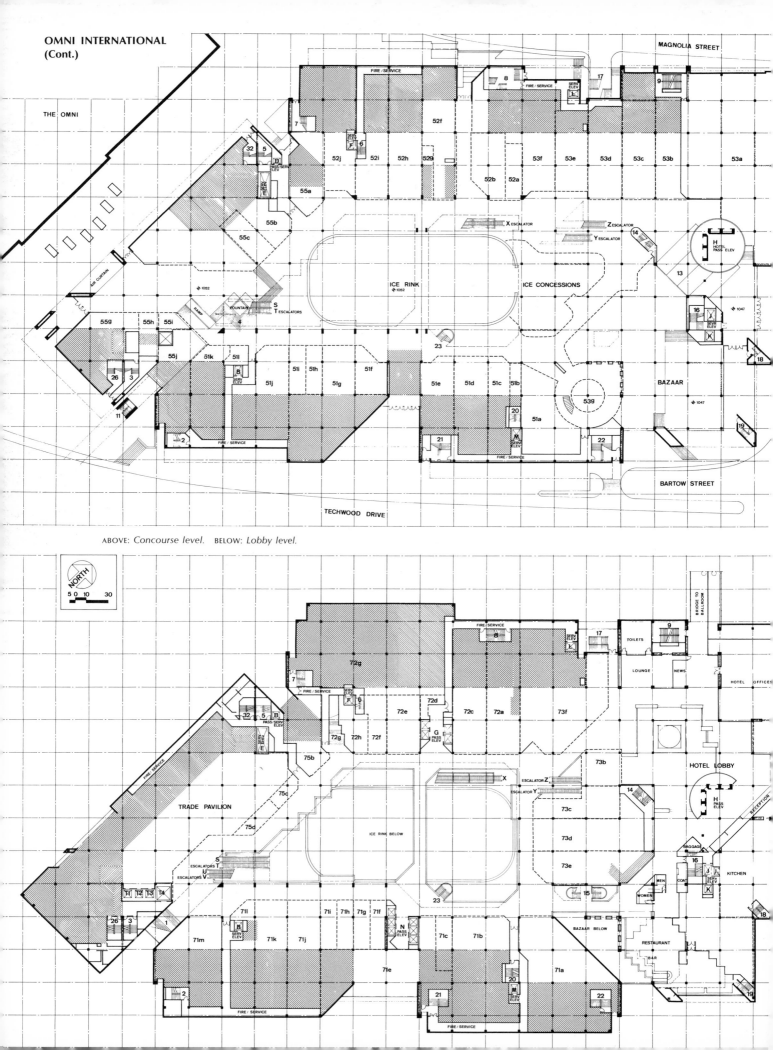

ABOVE: *Concourse level.* BELOW: *Lobby level.*

THE OMNI

MAGNOLIA STREET

FIRE / SERVICE

FIRE / SERVICE

8

SERV ELEV

17

9

7

52f

32 5

D PASS/SERV ELEV

SERV ELEV E

F 6

52j 52i 52h 52g

52b 52a

53f 53e 53d 53c 53b 53a

55a

55b

X ESCALATOR

Z ESCALATOR

Y ESCALATOR

14

55c

13

H HOTEL PASS ELEV

ICE RINK

ICE CONCESSIONS

1052

1052

1047

16

SERV ELEV

X

AIR CURTAIN

55g 55h 55i

RAMP

FOUNTAIN

S T ESCALATORS

18

BAZAAR

26 3

55j

51k 51l

B SERV ELEV

51i 5lh

51f

51e 51d 51c 51b

539

1047

11

51j

51g

19

20 SERV ELEV M

51a

2

FIRE / SERVICE

21

22

FIRE / SERVICE

BARTOW STREET

TECHWOOD DRIVE

NORTH

5 0 10 30

BRIDGE TO BALLROOM

FIRE / SERVICE

9

SERV ELEV

17

TOILETS

72g

7

FIRE / SERVICE

SERV ELEV

F 6

72e 72d

72c 72a

73f

LOUNGE

NEWS

HOTEL OFFICES

32

PASS/SERV ELEV

SERV ELEV E

72g 72h 72f

G PASS ELEV

75b

73b

HOTEL LOBBY

FIRE / SERVICE

TRADE PAVILION

75c

75d

ESCALATOR Z

ESCALATOR Y

14

73c

H PASS ELEV

RECEPTION

ICE RINK BELOW

73d

BAGGAGE

S T ESCALATORS U V

73e

16 SERV ELEV X

KITCHEN

11 12 13 T4

23

15

MEN

WOMEN

COAT

26 3

1

71i 71h 71g 71f

N PASS ELEV

BAZAAR BELOW

18

71m

B SERV ELEV

71k 71j

71c 71b

RESTAURANT

BAR

71e

20 SERV ELEV M

71a

2

21

22

19

FIRE / SERVICE

FIRE / SERVICE

Downtown Peoria, Illinois, is the center of the second largest metropolitan area in the state and serves a population of over 350,000 persons. The CBD encompasses approximately 200 gross acres devoted to central-area uses including offices, retail and service operations, government installations, hotels, and miscellaneous uses associated with a central area.

Like most cities its size, Peoria experienced a decline in central-area activities during the 1950s. Retail sales followed a downward trend, there was no appreciable permanent downtown residential population to stimulate after-dark activities, and the physical plant of the area was deteriorating into an unattractive environment. During the 1960s, however, this declining trend was reversed through the commitment of public and private efforts; more than twenty major buildings were erected during the decade.

In the early 1970s Peoria once again began to experience a gradual decline in its market position under strong competition from outlying suburban retail centers. Determined to preserve the vitality and integrity of the CBD, as well as a large investment made during the 1960s, business and government leaders decided to undertake a comprehensive planning and urban design program for the downtown. In October 1972 the city retained Angelos C. Demetriou, AIA, to prepare a comprehensive redevelopment plan for the CBD and to guide subsequent efforts, both public and private, in the rebuilding effort.

Associated with Mr. Demetriou, who acted as the prime consultant, were Hammer, Siler, George Associates, Inc. (economic consultants); Scruggs and Hammond, Inc. (landscape consultants); Barton-Aschman Associates, Inc. (trans-

PEORIA, ILLINOIS
ARCHITECT–URBAN DESIGNER:
Angelos C. Demetriou, AIA

ABOVE: *Aerial perspective of the CBD concept.*

*View of the existing riverfront
(1974).*

portation and parking consultants); and Goldsworthy & Fifield (legal consultants). The study was financed by the Peoria Downtown Development Council, a non-profit organization of civic and business leaders. The study was completed in January 1974 and was approved by both the city council and the city planning commission.

In addition to drawing up the master plan, the Demetriou firm was retained to further develop the elements of the plan, including the preliminary designs for the downtown mall (a conversion and expansion of the existing primary retail street into a glass-covered shopping gallery) and the residential complex on the Illinois River waterfront.

Because of the geographic limitations of the CBD boundaries, beyond which it cannot expand, the designers decided to develop a long-range plan to the year 2000 in order to protect the limited valuable space from undesirable development and provide for its optimum use. "The objective of the study was the rebuilding rather than the replanning of the downtown," they said.

The "forum" concept, according to architect Demetriou, aims to create a multi-use, high-capacity complex—a governmental center for city, county, state, and federal facilities; additional corporate headquarters, financial institutions, and commercial enterprises; meeting places (forums) for community activities such as conventions, sports events, entertainment, and cultural activities serving the entire metropolitan region; modernization of retail facilities and improved parking accommodations; and utilization of the waterfront for permanent residential facilities.

A major feature in the redevelopment of the retail complex is the consolidation of the three already existing department stores. These are planned to be interconnected by a glass-covered minimall. A protected skywalk system is planned to connect to other commercial facilities in the downtown.

Special attention is paid to the modernization of the transportation systems, the parking, and the rerouting of the non-CBD-bound traffic.

In order to implement these plans, the city of Peoria established a special office headed by a downtown development expediter. The Peoria Downtown Development Council established a similar office headed by a president. When the plan has been fully implemented, the Peoria downtown will again be reestablished as a diversified and enriched environment.

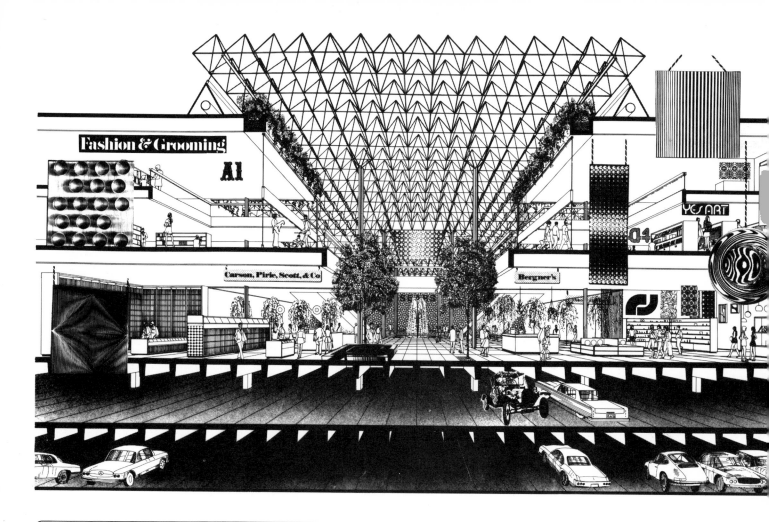

LAND USE PLAN

- Governmental
- Office-Commercial
- Primary Retail
- Civic Center
- Institutional Cultural
- Hotels Motels Transient
- Residential
- Supporting Commercial
- Public Parks
- Parking

ABOVE: *Interior of proposed minimall. The glass-enclosed mall is to connect the three existing department stores—Sears; Carson, Pirie, Scott & Co.; and Bergner's.* LEFT: *Land-use plan for the CBD.*

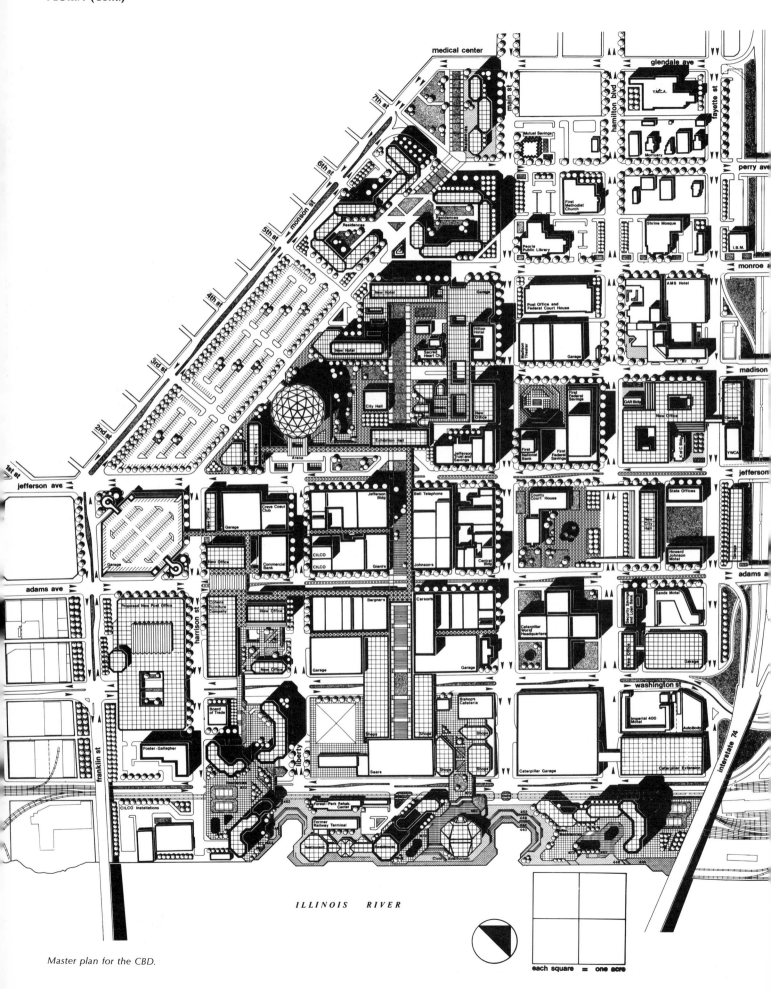

Master plan for the CBD.

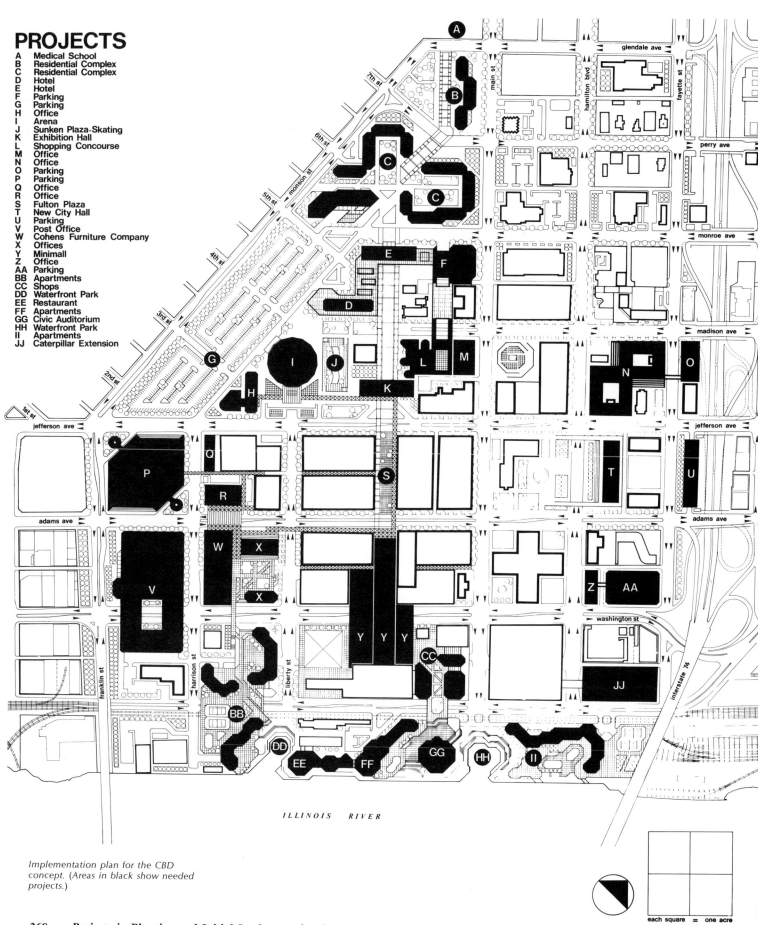

PROJECTS

A Medical School
B Residential Complex
C Residential Complex
D Hotel
E Hotel
F Parking
G Parking
H Office
I Arena
J Sunken Plaza-Skating
K Exhibition Hall
L Shopping Concourse
M Office
N Office
O Parking
P Office
Q Office
R Fulton Plaza
S New City Hall
T Parking
U Post Office
V Cohens Furniture Company
W Offices
X Minimall
Y Office
Z Parking
AA Parking
BB Apartments
CC Shops
DD Waterfront Park
EE Restaurant
FF Apartments
GG Civic Auditorium
HH Waterfront Park
II Apartments
JJ Caterpillar Extension

Implementation plan for the CBD concept. (Areas in black show needed projects.)

each square = one acre

Preliminary conceptual model of the entire development with the CN Tower in the center. (Photographer: Panda Associates, Photography.)

METRO CENTRE
Toronto, Ontario

ARCHITECTS, GROUP ONE: John Andrews and Webb Zerafa Menkes Housden

The completed 1,800' CN Tower is the first phase of the development. A transmission mast at the top will contain antenna systems for television and FM radio stations. A revolving dining room and public observation areas are located two-thirds of the way up, and a smaller observation area is located about 300' from the top of the structure. (Photographer: Panda Associates, Photography.)

One of the largest downtown redevelopment projects presently being undertaken is Metro Centre, in Toronto, Canada. This is a fifteen-year $1 billion project occupying 190 acres of railway land between the CBD and the Lake Ontario waterfront. The project is being developed by Metro Centre Developments, Ltd., a partnership between the Canadian National and Canadian Pacific Railways, through their realty subsidiaries.

The project consists of four major elements: an extensive transportation facility for local and rapid transit, a commercial-office area, a residential section, and a communications and broadcasting complex. The project will enable the downtown core to grow southward and occupy a strategic area that has separated Toronto from its lakefront for more than 100 years. Metro Centre is designed as a lively and livable place for people, with at least 36 acres of public parkland. Planning for pedestrians includes a network of enclosed shopping malls and open-air promenades which will make it possible to walk from Front Street to the new waterfront park.

The transportation center is designed to bring together mainline railway passenger services, GO commuter trains, an intercity bus depot, and Toronto's first downtown air terminal. It will be closely connected with rapid transit, including the subway and the new intermediate-capacity system. The complex will include a hotel, a large convention center, a trade mart, and offices for transportation companies.

The commercial and office area, situated mainly between Front Street and a new east-west thoroughfare called the Esplanade and located approximately 500 feet south of Front Street, will consist of a variety of office buildings with a shopping concourse extending through the lower levels. Shops, restaurants, and other amenities will serve a pedestrian walkway system which opens at several locations into sheltered courtyards and provides direct connections to the transportation facilities.

The residential sector will create several downtown neighborhoods with living space for 22,000 people in a greenbelt setting. It will feature a variety of housing for different income groups and extensive community facilities.

The communications and broadcasting center includes a transmission-observation tower; headquarters and production facilities for the CBD's national English-language TV and radio networks; the new Massey Hall (auditorium), home of the Toronto Symphony Orchestra (planned for the future); offices and studios for private radio and TV; and companies involved in film production, graphics, advertising, public relations, and other communications fields.

The CN Tower, completed in 1975, rises to 1,805 feet, making it currently the world's tallest structure. Its main purpose is to improve television and radio reception, to speed up vital business communications transmitted by microwave, and to make land-mobile radio systems more efficient.

Metro Centre will also be a "people place." The base of the tower will be in

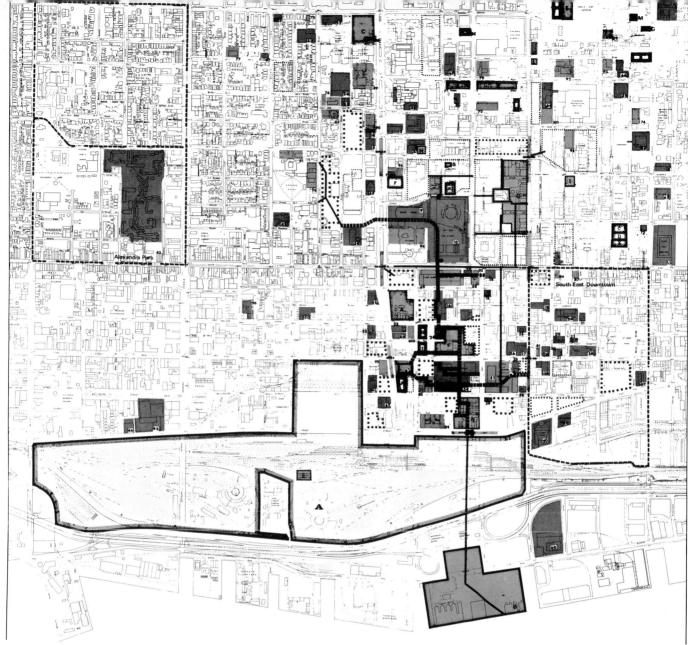

Location plan.

a parkland setting with landscaped terraces sloping to a large reflecting pool. There will be boutiques, restaurants, and space for strolling. The surrounding pool will be crossed by a glass-enclosed walkway leading to the base of the tower. Four glass-enclosed elevators running on the outside of the tower will take visitors up to the circular seven-story sky pod between the 1,100- and 1,200-foot levels. On arrival at the sky pod, visitors will be able to look at the 75-mile vista from two public observation levels. One is to be fully enclosed, and the other open to permit more of a feeling of the elements and a sense of altitude. On level four, at 1,140 feet, will be a revolving dining room and lounge accommodating approximately 400 patrons. Diners will be seated at tables on a two-tiered floor which revolves 360 degrees.

The participation of the Canadian federal government and city authorities in building the new auditorium for the Toronto Symphony and other musical groups is anticipated. The city is to contribute the land for the auditorium, and the federal government the funds. The government also took steps to acquire a large area of harbor front which is to be converted to a waterfront aquatic park by dredging and creating a new set of islands in the outer harbor.

The major significance of the Metro Centre project is the shift in the downtown area from the heavy industrial and railroad functions to "people activities," thus further extending and strengthening the heart of the CBD.

At the time of this writing, with the exception of the completed CN Tower, the overall concept was still being studied by various governmental agencies, whose approval is required for the total acceptance of the program.

BUFFALO, NEW YORK
ARCHITECTS: Wallace, McHarg, Roberts & Todd

Downtown Buffalo lies at the eastern end of Lake Erie at the entrance to the Niagara River. It was in its early history the major transshipment point to and from the West on the lakes and was the junction first with the Erie Canal and later with the railroads.

Heavy industry subsequently grew to the north and south of what is now downtown. Manufacturers used this geographic point to convert the high-bulk, low-value raw materials shipped from the West into high-value, low-bulk products to be shipped East. The steel and grain products industries are examples.

As a consequence of this history, downtown is located asymmetrically to the urbanized area of the region. This fact has both advantages and disadvantages. The proximity to the lake is an asset which should be exploited. On the other hand, its location puts it in a somewhat weak position to tap potential retail markets. This disadvantage can be overcome by improving downtown's accessibility to the region. Current and proposed transportation facilities will improve its position.

Downtown is presently characterized by a somewhat disconnected and discontinuous pattern of uses. This applies particularly to the Main Street shopping core. Lafayette Square, Genesee Street, and the Division Streets introduce wide breaks in the continuity of the shopping frontage in Main Street. Downtown frame uses, such as department-store warehouses and other service activities, preempt important and valuable sites and additionally reduce the potential for an inviting street quality, thus inhibiting development. It is anticipated, however, that when the projected transit system is built, there will be a realignment of values so that sites which at present seem undesirable for development will become highly attractive.

The future pattern of land uses will be much more compact and will tend to realign itself along more rational lines as a result of an integrated approach to public investment in elements of the movement system.

In the Buffalo master plan the key feature is the Main Street Mall. It is the main connective element between rapid transit, parking, shopping, and offices, and it also forms the major civic place for pedestrians in the city. New private building will tie into the pedestrian movement system in order to preserve continuity in the downtown pedestrian system. It will provide the setting for a variety of stores, shops, restaurants, hotels, and other facilities, such as the projected new convention center, available on a scale and in a concentration not possible anywhere else in the region.

The members of the Main Street Mall and Parking Committee unanimously accepted the premise contained in the Interim Report CBD plan that the Main

Street Mall was a key element in the Downtown Concept plan. Wallace, McHarg, Roberts & Todd designate it as one of the key features in overall development, and Larry Smith & Company, Inc., label it as the key element in the continued improving performance of the retail section.

The committee studied carefully the plans for the physical structure of the mall as prepared by the consultants. The relationship of the mall to existing buildings, to proposed new construction within and outside the mall, and, particularly, to the proposed rapid-transit system is a matter of prime importance. The preliminary plans have a flexibility that will permit attaching the roof of the mall to existing buildings and erecting new ones before, during, or after the mall construction. Most importantly, final plans for the mall will go forward together with final planning of the subway section in the same area so that construction and use may be properly tied together.

The type of facility envisioned is a covered, skylit, air-conditioned and heated structure. It will be light and airy with planting, paving, benches, small convenience shops, adequate security, and police protection from parking space to destination or from transit car to destination (a service not possible in the present physical arrangement of the downtown).

The mall will extend from north of Chippewa Street to Main Place on the south. It will have extensions east and west on Huron Street, Court Street, Lafayette Square, and Eagle Street. The extensions will connect to the convention center, major off-street parking facilities, the transportation center, building lobbies, and stores. Three subway stops will be within the mall itself, two on the Buffalo-Amherst line: theater (between Chippewa and Huron Streets) and Lafayette Square, which also will be a stop on the Kenmore-airport line.

At the time of this writing, the plan for downtown, containing the mall and subway concept, has been approved as official city policy. According to Thomas A. Todd, of Wallace, McHarg, Roberts & Todd, architects for the master plan:

> The Niagara Frontier Transit Authority with UMTA funding has proceeded with the overall engineering, with Bechtel as the contractor. They have worked on the assumption that the mall will act as the mezzanine for the subway, permitting shallower construction of the subway and thus affording substantial savings in construction costs. The city has sold a bond issue for the purpose of proceeding with detailed design of the mall in order to have the design of the mall and subway advance at the same rate.
>
> The point is that the project is about halfway through a ten-year process of becoming a reality. Every month sees it advance a little bit toward this reality.*

*Material based on information published in a brochure entitled *A Comprehensive Plan for Downtown Buffalo, New York,* April 1971, which includes the report of the mall committee.

Model of downtown Buffalo master plan.

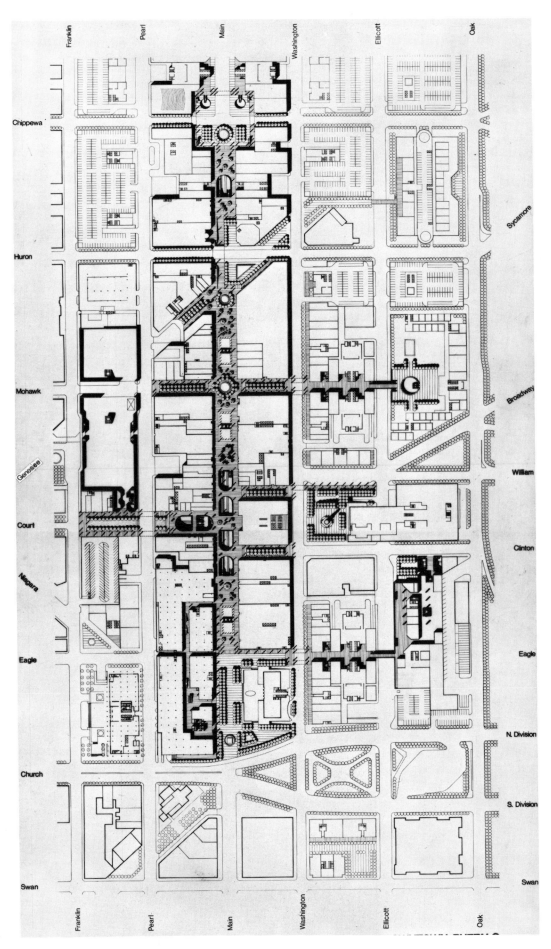

Plan of Main Street Mall.

This "anatomical" sketch shows the station levels at Lafayette Square. The buildings and ground have been cut away to reveal the relationship between the mall, elevator lobbies, stores and the two station levels. Elevators appear as vertical towers. The structure of the roof is shown at the upper left end of the mall; the roadways for the fire truck have been stripped away to reveal the girders necessary to carry the roadway. Lafayette Square, now only a traffic island, is shown as the site for a new department store and office building. The mall would eliminate the need for subway mezzanines and permit the station platforms to be at minimum depth below grade. This will reduce the length of stairs and allow a closer, more open relationship to the mall. It also provides a safer environment for the rider at significantly lower cost to the taxpayer.

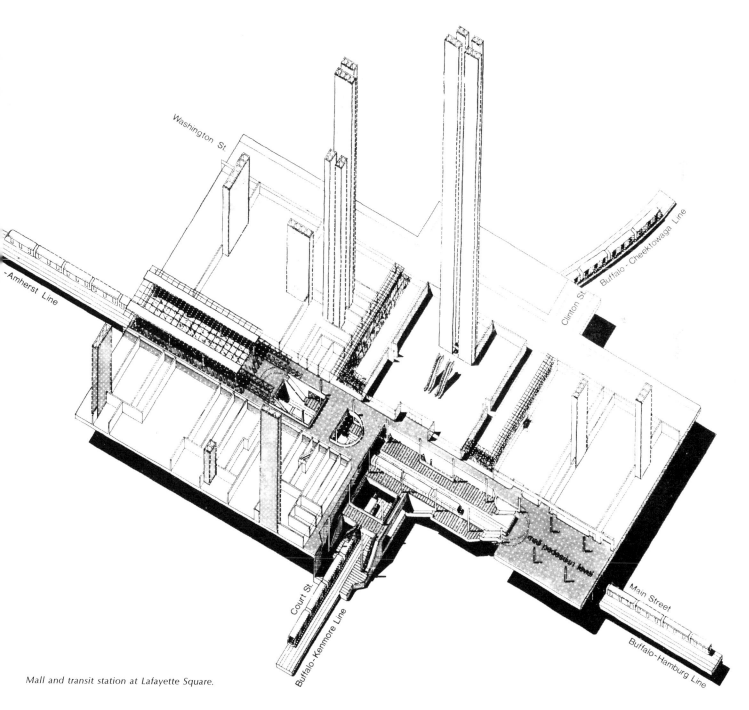

Mall and transit station at Lafayette Square.

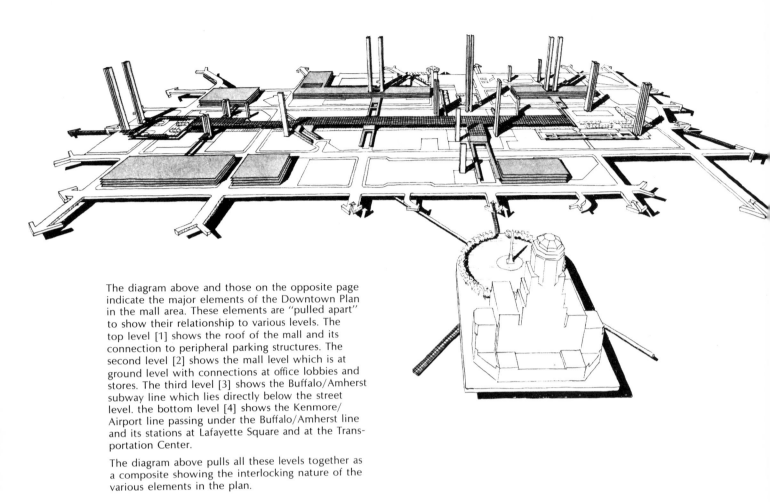

The diagram above and those on the opposite page indicate the major elements of the Downtown Plan in the mall area. These elements are "pulled apart" to show their relationship to various levels. The top level [1] shows the roof of the mall and its connection to peripheral parking structures. The second level [2] shows the mall level which is at ground level with connections at office lobbies and stores. The third level [3] shows the Buffalo/Amherst subway line which lies directly below the street level. the bottom level [4] shows the Kenmore/ Airport line passing under the Buffalo/Amherst line and its stations at Lafayette Square and at the Transportation Center.

The diagram above pulls all these levels together as a composite showing the interlocking nature of the various elements in the plan.

Composite diagrams of all major levels in the Main Street mall area.

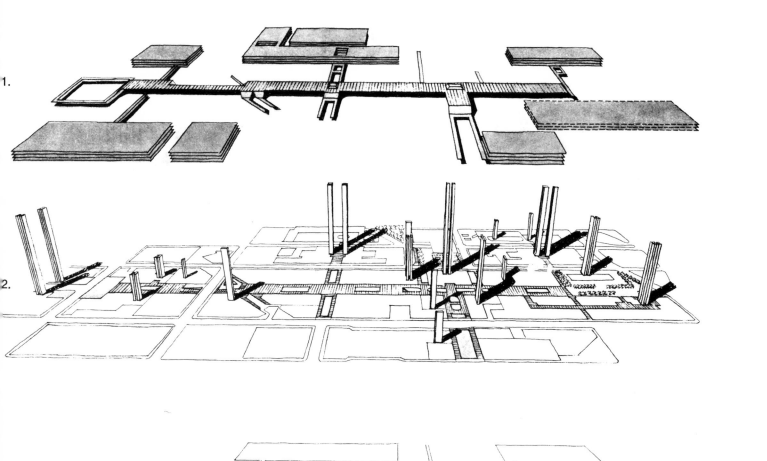

1. Parking Structures and the Roof of the Mall
2. The Mall Level Showing Vertical Elevator Towers, Lobbies and Stores
3. Buffalo/Amherst Subway Line Under the Main Street Mall
4. Kenmore/Airport Line Under Court Street

Composite diagrams of all major levels in the
Main Street mall area, showing individual elements.

4.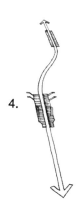

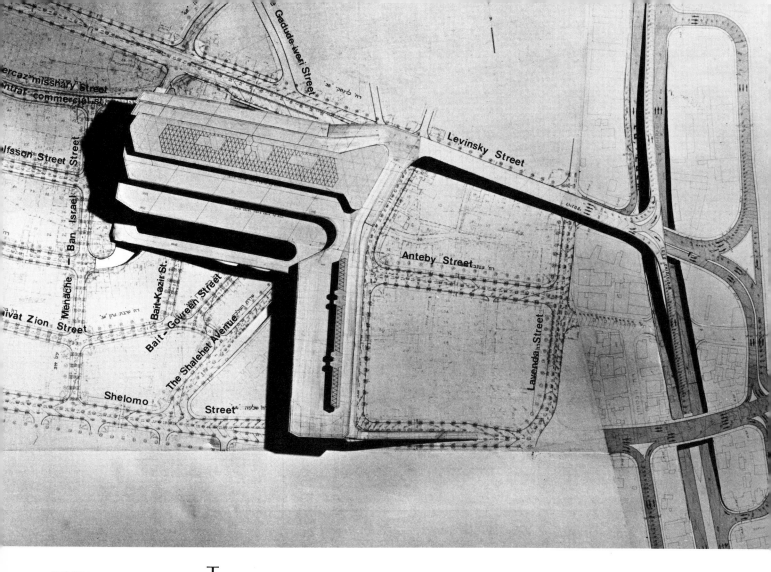

The Shalehet Avenue

Bait - Gouveen Street

Levinsky Street

Anteby Street

Lawenda Street

Shelomo Street

CENTRAL BUS TERMINAL AND SHOPPING CENTER

Tel Aviv, Israel

ARCHITECTS: Karmi & Associates

Tel Aviv's new Central Bus Terminal and Shopping Center is being built on a site of about 360,000 square feet, extending over three streets—Levinsky, Tzemach David, and Shalama.

The project comprises a seven-floor building on an area of about 1.8 million square feet, containing, in addition to the Central Terminal, a large commercial center, a recreation area, public offices, a supermarket, a department store, and numerous other facilities.

With the opening of the new Central Terminal at the end of 1976, the present terminal will cease functioning, and all public transportation—both urban and interurban—will be transferred to the new location. Calculations show that about 450,000 to 500,000 persons will pass through the new terminal daily.

The rapid development and continuing growth of Tel Aviv's population were taken into account in planning the new terminal so that it will be possible to expand its capacity as required.

The building itself will be seven stories high. The two top floors of the L-shaped structure will be devoted to interurban transport services, with one leg of the "L" serving incoming buses, and the other serving outgoing buses. The entrances to the various floor levels will be through an elevated passage which will connect the terminal to a main artery that will distribute all incoming and outgoing traffic. The two lower levels are intended for the urban traffic of the greater Tel Aviv area. Here, too, the floors are divided and subdivided for specific functions—the second floor for incoming traffic, and the first for outgoing.

Dividing the traffic into incoming and outgoing sections has the following advantages: maximum dispersal of passengers throughout the area, safety of pedestrians as a result of absolute separation between them and traffic, and directing of pedestrians through the commercial centers.

The terminal will contain an extensive commercial center on five floors with an area of 360,000 square feet.

OPPOSITE PAGE: *Site plan.* (Photographer: *Paul Gross Ltd.*) BELOW: *Section showing distribution of functions.*

TOWER CITY
Cleveland, Ohio

ARCHITECTS: Dalton·Dalton·Little·Newport

Tower City, in Cleveland, Ohio, is an imaginative renewal concept, planned to be constructed behind the existing terminal, above the now-unused railroad tracks owned by Cleveland Union Terminals Company. The complex, as proposed, will include a three-level shopping mall, a 1,000-room hotel, several office buildings, underground parking to accommodate 6,500 cars, and an underground air cargo terminal. The shopping concourse serves as a link connecting the public square from north to south and to the various parts of the complex.

The developer is Sheldon B. Guren, president of U.S. Realty Company.

126

100

85

72

52

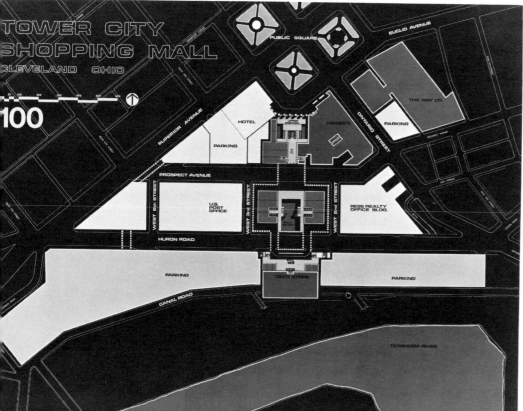

TOWER CITY SHOPPING MALL
CLEVELAND OHIO

100

OPPOSITE PAGE: *Site location.*
ABOVE: *Interior of mall—view to the south.*
LEFT: *Proposed site plan.*

WEST END REDEVELOPMENT
Washington, D.C.

ARCHITECTURE AND URBAN DESIGN: The Office of
Angelos C. Demetriou, AIA
URBAN PLANNERS: Richard W. Carr and
Lawrence D. Goldstein

The West End, comprising an area of over 80 acres, is one of the important underdeveloped land resources in central Washington, D.C., and is located between the central business district and historic Georgetown.

The West End plan is sponsored by West End Planning, Inc., a nonprofit group of property owners, tenants, and other individuals with a personal interest in the neighborhood. The primary objective of this organization was to complete a master plan which would provide for the redevelopment of the area as an integrated urban neighborhood—a place to live, work, play, shop, and enjoy the delights of central-city living, all within walking distance.

West End Planning, Inc., headed by Oliver T. Carr, Jr., a Washington developer, brought together a team of legal, transportation, economic, environmental, and design consultants headed by Angelos C. Demetriou as chief project designer. At the culmination of this effort a new urban zoning formula was written and structured to permit updating standards of performance.

The new formula attempts to encourage massive urban redevelopment by the private sector. The new formula encourages the private sector, by a series of incentives and bonuses, to make public easements, pedestrian ways, plazas, and arcaded concourses feasible. Furthermore, the new zoning district proposed by the consultants would create a blending of commercial, residential, entertainment, and other supporting uses that would make West End a vibrant urban entity.

In contrast to the existing regulations, the proposed zoning model would produce many of the design elements currently missing from the Washington scene. Well-planned residential enclaves, tree-lined pedestrian ways, courtyards, and plazas are all integral elements of the proposed plan. One goal was to replace the automobile with the pedestrian and the bike rider. Equally important is the effort to place local services and jobs within walking distance of residents. At the time of this writing, the design concept is being reviewed by public authorities.

The designers first established the measures of a desirable environment, its urban form for central-city living, and the mechanics of its operation. Subsequently, the study team defined the legal tools, zoning regulations, and other controlling instruments that would secure such an environment. It remains for the zoning commission to recognize the opportunity represented by these efforts and to adopt regulations which will allow private development to proceed in a manner that produces a viable concept of design.

BELOW: *Existing zoning.* BELOW, RIGHT: *Proposed zoning.* KEY: *C-M-2: Industrial–office development. C-2-A: Medium-density residential with commercial development. C-2-B: High-rise residential development with some commercial. R-5-D: High-rise residential development. C-R-1: High-density residential except for first floors which may be commercial. C-R-2: Not less than 50 percent residential with height limitation 130 feet. R-5-C: Medium-density residential.*

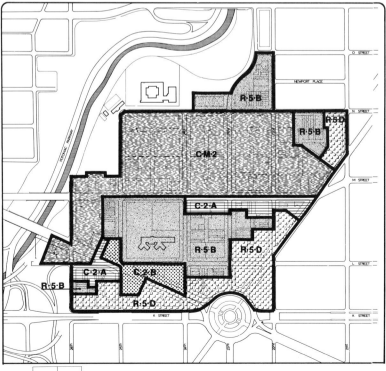

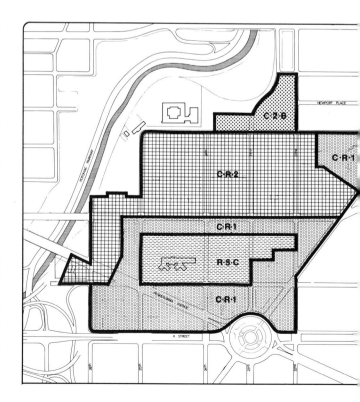

GRID OF ACRES

Master plan showing height restrictions.

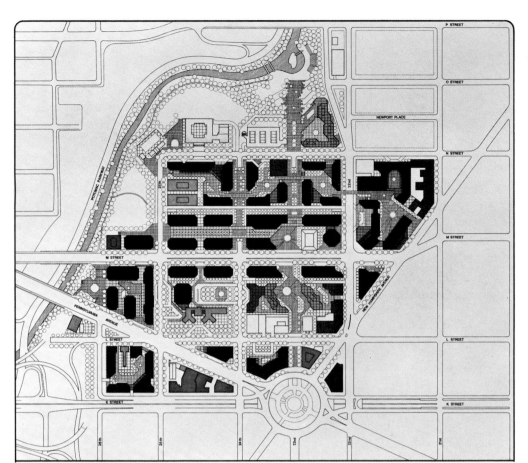

Bicycle and pedestrian ways.

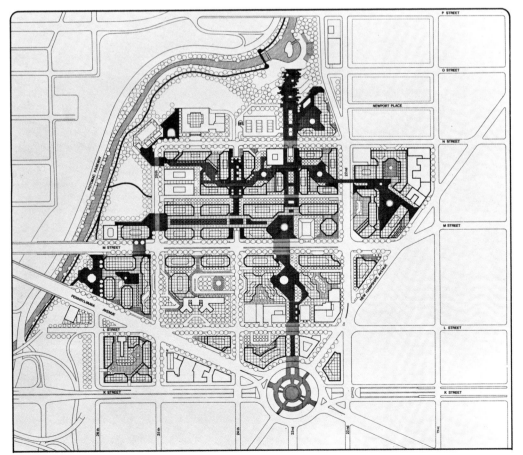

GRID OF ACRES

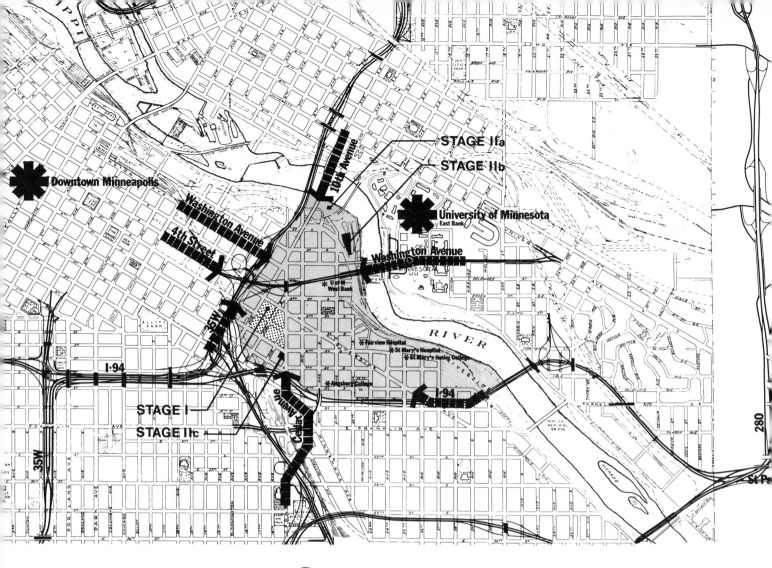

CEDAR-RIVERSIDE

Minneapolis, Minnesota

PROJECT ARCHITECT: Ralph Rapson & Associates, Inc.
DEVELOPER: Cedar-Riverside Associates, Inc.
PLANNING AND ENGINEERING: Barton-Aschman Assoc., Inc.
ENVIRONMENTAL PLANNING: Lawrence Halprin & Associates, Inc.
ENVIRONMENTAL DESIGN: Sasaki-Walker Associates, Inc.

Gloria M. Segal and Keith Heller, the initiators of this redevelopment project, envision its future as follows:

> Cedar-Riverside, on the west bank of the Mississippi River, 12 blocks from downtown Minneapolis, is America's first federally designated "New Town-In Town." One hundred acres of the 340 acre community will be redeveloped over the next 20 years into a highly urbanized community. Rich in history, culture and educational and medical facilities, Cedar-Riverside, by 1990 will house 30,000 persons of all ages, incomes and life styles in 12,500 apartments. Up to 60,000 will work or shop in the area each day or utilize the medical, educational and cultural resources of the community. River parkland will be extended and improved and open space will be emphasized for the enjoyment of the residents and visitors. The convenience of center-city living will be supplemented in Cedar-Riverside by high quality commercial, cultural and community facilities and services to create a balanced living, working and leisure time environment.*

At the time of this writing, Cedar Square West, the first phase (housing), was successfully under way. The total project is scheduled to be completed in stages covering a fifteen- to twenty-year development. An important feature of the development plan is a pedestrian and plaza walkway system which, vertically separated from automotive passageways, is intended to return the community to a pedestrian precinct.

The walkway system and plazas are a part of a large, diversified center which includes commercial, community, and cultural facilities, as well as a hotel, a theater, and specialty shops.

The centrum has still to undergo much negotiating with the various government, city, and citizen groups. While it has the conceptual support of the Housing and Redevelopment Authority and the city authorities, there are other groups opposed to this direction. Although the concept and flavor is there, the final centrum plan remains to be developed.

*Reprinted from *Northwest Architect*, July–August, September, October 1972.

OPPOSITE PAGE: *Location plan.*
BELOW: *Centrum redevelopment, phase one—master plan.*
BOTTOM: *Centrum court.*

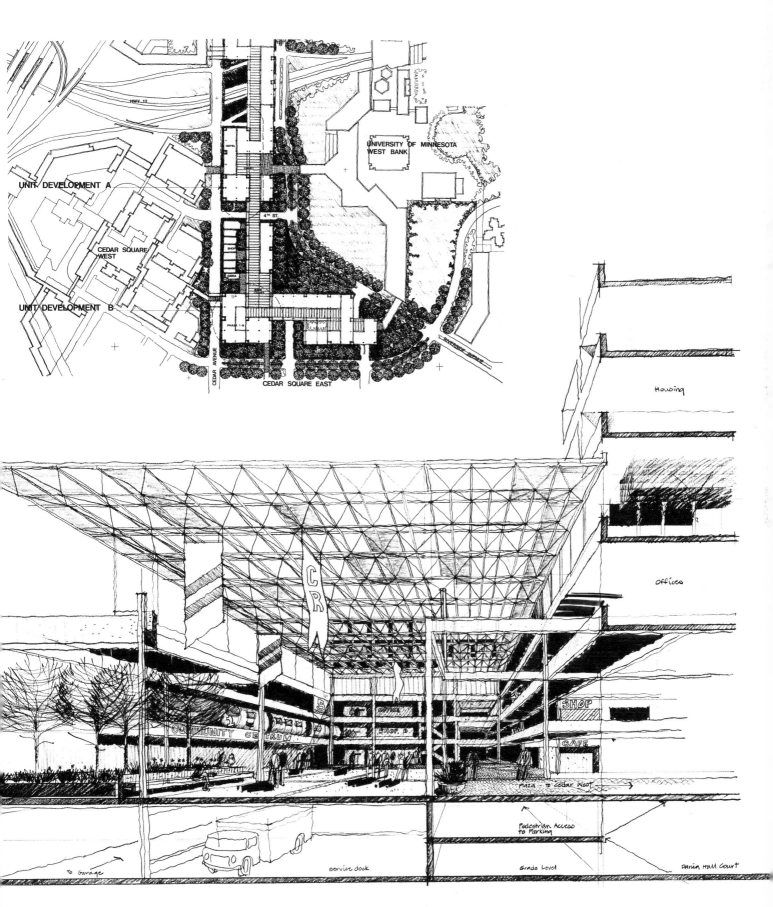

BELOW: *Centrum vehicular access.*
OPPOSITE PAGE, ABOVE: *Plaza and transit system.*
OPPOSITE PAGE, BELOW: *Section through Centrum, Third to Fourth Streets.*

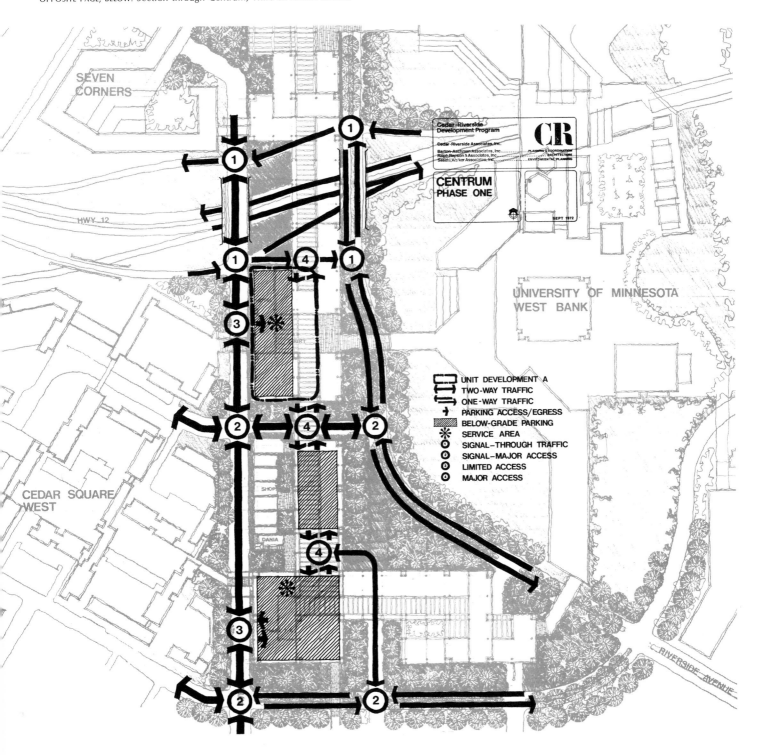

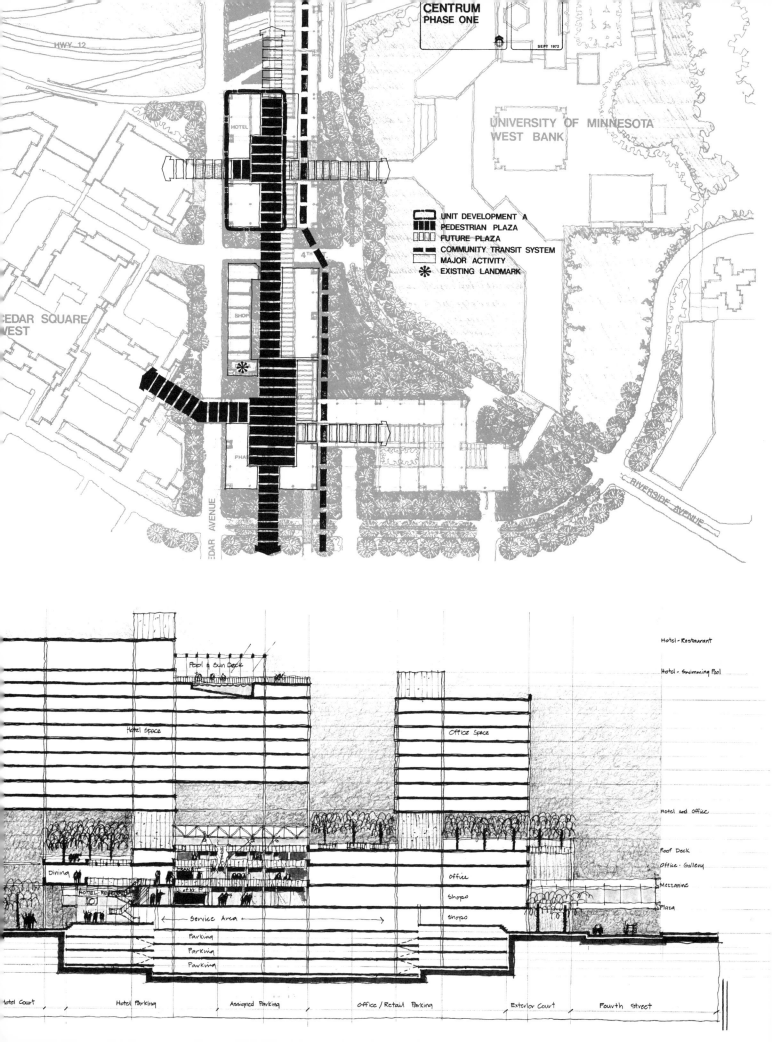

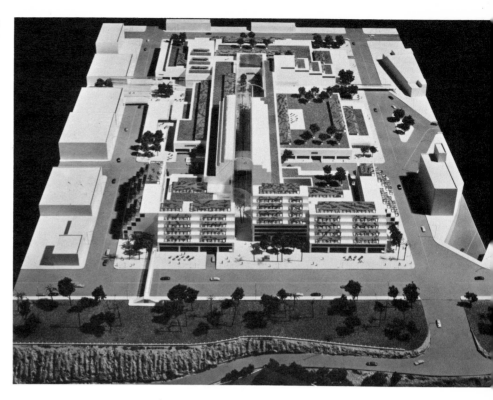

Model showing view from Ocean Avenue.

SANTA MONICA PLACE
Santa Monica, California
ARCHITECTS: Frank O. Gehry & Associates

The Santa Monica Mall will serve as a major gateway to a new retail complex proposed for a 10-acre site directly south of the mall. Two department stores and various retail shops are arranged around a two-level protected pedestrian shopping street, continuing the existing mall across Broadway by a pedestrian overpass into an active plaza space with small shops and places for people to sit. It will serve also as a major vehicular drop-off for passengers arriving by bus and car. The protected pedestrian street (along the Third Street right-of-way) funnels down through a bazaar-type shopping street leading into a central mall. There are department stores, shops, eating places, and entertainment areas, as well as trees and grass arranged on several levels within an air-conditioned glazed shopping arcade. The mall is envisioned as a multilevel hub connected by stairs and escalators to the parking levels below, with balconies overlooking the space. From the mall, facing west toward Palisades Park, the concept indicates a glass-roofed arcade, several stories high, which will extend west, crossing Second Street at the second level as a shopping bridge and then continuing through the 5-acre site flanking Ocean Avenue. Another overpass will extend across Ocean Avenue to Palisades Park itself. Constituting this multistory interior pedestrian spine on either side are two levels of office space and above that a hotel. Each room will look out on the city as well as on adjoining balconies.

The existing Sears, Roebuck store on Colorado will also be tied into the project by another pedestrian link leading again into a major open space facing Colorado with an arcade leading north into the mall. This plaza will be a major arrival point for people arriving by car from the Santa Monica freeway, via the Fourth Street off-ramp, as well as the civic center, to the south on Main Street.

Although the plan is organized around an interior pedestrian spine, it is designed so as not to turn its back on the adjoining streets. The department stores have major entrances along Fourth, Second, and Colorado Streets.

Parking for the project is mostly below grade. Above-grade parking has been indicated as terraces with landscaped edges. Lightwells are let into the parking levels, and escalators, stairs, and elevators will occur at these points, thus allowing some of the life and activity going on in the pedestrian area to penetrate, creating a consistent quality of experience that relates to parking as well as walking through the galleria.

The developers are The Rouse Company.

Interior perspective view
of the galleria.

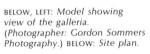

BELOW, LEFT: *Model showing
view of the galleria.
(Photographer: Gordon Sommers
Photography.)* BELOW: *Site plan.*

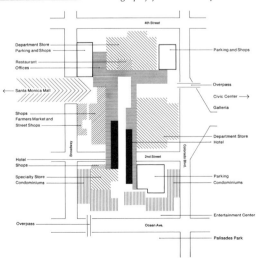

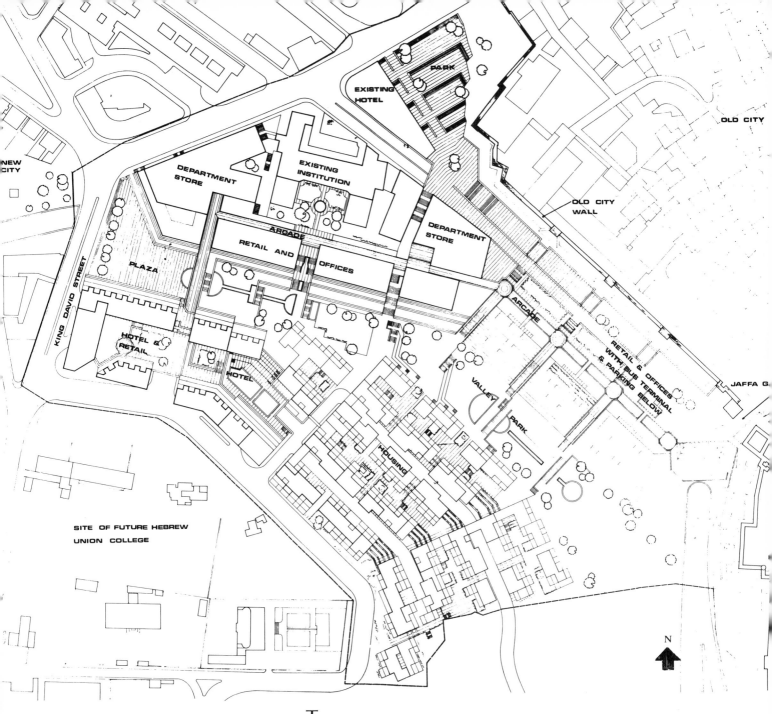

NEW
CITY

OLD CITY

OLD CITY
WALL

DEPARTMENT
STORE

EXISTING
INSTITUTION

EXISTING
HOTEL

PARK

DEPARTMENT
STORE

ARCADE
RETAIL AND   OFFICES

PLAZA

KING DAVID STREET

HOTEL &
RETAIL

HOTEL

ARCADE

RETAIL & OFFICES
WITH BUS TERMINAL
& PARKING BELOW

JAFFA G.

VALLEY
PARK

HOUSING

SITE OF FUTURE HEBREW
UNION COLLEGE

N

MAMILA QUARTER
Jerusalem, Israel
ARCHITECTS: Moshe Safdie & Associates

The site of Mamila forms the geographic center of the Jerusalem metropolitan region. Its location is unique inasmuch as it is surrounded by most of the major facilities of the city, i.e., the Old City with its markets, institutions and tourist attractions to the east; the fashionable residential area and hotel complexes to the south; the central business district with its retail and office facilities to the northwest; the expanding government district of the Russian Compound to the northeast.

Mamila is located between the Jewish and the Arab parts of the city; the Jewish new city, its central business district and institutional centers on one side and the eastern city with the neighborhoods of Sheik Gerach, the American Colony, the Arab central business district on the other side. It also connects the open space park system of the city, being surrounded by the National Park of the Valley of Ben Hinom, the National Park surrounding the Old City and Independence Park to the northeast.

By the very nature and character of its location, the redevelopment of Mamila has associated with it a number of objectives of critical significance to the future development of Jerusalem. As community goals of top priority, one must start with the adequate relocation of both the businesses and families presently in Mamila. The families housed in substandard slum conditions must be relocated and rehoused in a variety of neighborhoods where acceptable conditions and housing are available. In a similar way, the variety of businesses, primarily workshops and garages, should be relocated to light industrial areas presently being constructed on the outskirts of Jerusalem. Once this has taken place, the possibility will exist for the site of Mamila to be developed to its full potential to serve the city as a whole.

OPPOSITE PAGE: *Site layout.*

Mamila must achieve the following goals:

1. Mamila must be a service center for the Old City. Since its character is to be preserved and its streets are to remain pedestrian streets, and at the same time it must accommodate both the thousands living and working there as well as the hundreds of thousands of tourists who visit it every year, the Old City must be surrounded by adequate service centers. Foremost are the service facilities for parking, bus terminals, truck loading and unloading areas serving residents, businesses and visitors to the Old City. Hundreds of cars are involved at any given time in tourist traffic to the Old City, as well as tourist buses and regular buses. Hundreds of tons of merchandise are transported each day for the markets of the Old City. These must be unloaded from trucks and delivered to the Old City from its periphery. Mamila will form the major service center for the Old City adjacent and related to Jaffa Gate. This is the most important entrance to the Old City in relation to the central business district of the New City.

2. Of equal importance is the role of Mamila as a bridge between the Old and the New City. Many of the present structures in Mamila, built in the 1920s, were part of a concept for constructing a new commercial center that would bring about a meeting place for Arab and Jewish businessmen. Today, more so than ever in the past, Mamila has an important role to play as a live bridge between the Old City and the New City, between the Jewish and the Arab, between the secular and the holy. Mamila must act as a bridge at many levels and in many ways. Of greatest importance is its ability to act as a live bridge forming a continuous area for urban activity extending from the markets of the Old City to the commercial and retail streets of the New City. In that respect, Mamila is conceived both as an extension of the markets of the Old City and an extension of the retail area of the central business district. In other words, a connector formed of busy, attractive retail and recreational community activities. It will neither be similar to the markets of the Old City nor to the retail areas of downtown but will achieve its own unique commercial, retail and recreational character which will have the qualities of both, and will provide the opportunity to connect the two.

Mamila is also a throughway; it is a major pedestrian concourse for people coming from the downtown central business district to the Old City and for tourists coming from the hotel complexes along King David Street towards the Old City. In this respect also, Mamila must act as a connector and accommodate adequately the pedestrian traffic generated from and to the Old and the New Cities.

Mamila is the connector of the City's park system. It must complete the park system surrounding the city walls. It must also give continuity to and connect Independence Park with the National Park, presently separated by the existing Mamila structures and fill dumped in the valley over the past centuries.

But beyond being a connector between the Old and the New City, beyond being a throughway for pedestrian and vehicular traffic; beyond being a service center for the Old City, Mamila, by virtue of its location, by virtue of its position and by virtue of the deficiencies presently existing in the City of Jerusalem has a role to play in its own right. Mamila should become one of the major urban foci, a meeting place of metropolitan significance in the City of Jerusalem. This is an opportunity that must be acted upon because of its geographic location in the heart of Jerusalem and because Jerusalem today lacks the kind of urban meeting places and urban centers which a city of its size is worthy of.*

*From the architect's report to the City Council of Jerusalem, 1973.

Model of project, view from southeast.

Stamford's $250 million downtown redevelopment program is transforming a deteriorated 130-acre site in the heart of the city into a complex of commercial and residential structures. The focal point for this urban renewal project is the twenty-one-story Landmark Tower building. Six low-rise office, professional, and retail buildings surround the plaza of this office high-rise forming Landmark Square. Landmark Square includes over 100,000 square feet of office space and nearly 50,000 square feet of retail space, a twin cinema, two restaurants, and an ice rink for patrons and tenants.

The developers are F. D. Rich Company.

STAMFORD CENTER
Stamford, Connecticut

ARCHITECTS FOR MASTER PLAN: Moshe Safdie & Associa
ARCHITECTS FOR THE LANDMARK TOWER AND
GENERAL TELEPHONE AND ELECTRONICS BUILDING:
  Victor H. Bisharat
LANDSCAPE DESIGNER: Robert Killoran

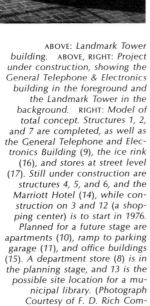

ABOVE: *Landmark Tower building.* ABOVE, RIGHT: *Project under construction, showing the General Telephone & Electronics building in the foreground and the Landmark Tower in the background.* RIGHT: *Model of total concept. Structures 1, 2, and 7 are completed, as well as the General Telephone and Electronics Building (9), the ice rink (16), and stores at street level (17). Still under construction are structures 4, 5, and 6, and the Marriott Hotel (14), while construction on 3 and 12 (a shopping center) is to start in 1976. Planned for a future stage are apartments (10), ramp to parking garage (11), and office buildings (15). A department store (8) is in the planning stage, and 13 is the possible site location for a municipal library. (Photograph Courtesy of F. D. Rich Company.)*

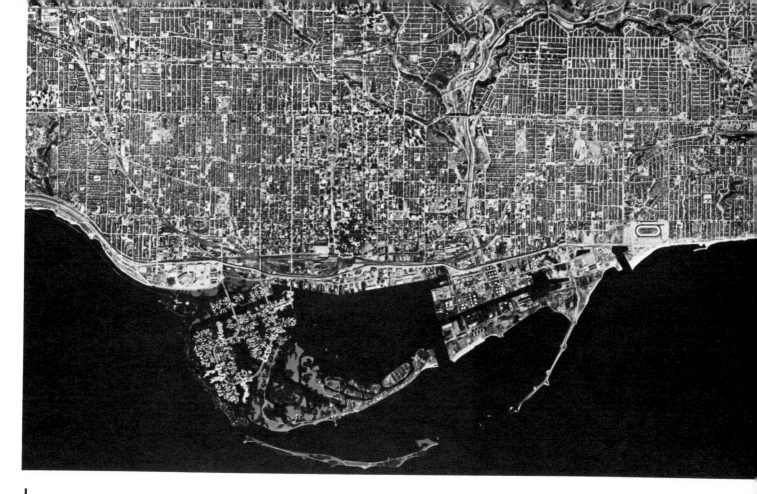

Involvement in the Harbour City concept goes back to early 1968, when the Metropolitan Toronto Waterfront plan was released. At this time, the Ministry of Trade and Development was introduced to the concept of developing the waterfront area, and it went about establishing that the land and water lots were in some form of public ownership and that this part was still vested in the province. At this point, a commission was set up for the purpose of determining the feasibility of a development project.

The architectural firm of Craig Zeidler & Strong, which designed Ontario Place, was commissioned to establish a program and study the possibilities of developing this harbor area further. The idea of creating Harbour City was made feasible through the experience of landfill gained at Ontario Place. The city is planned as a lively downtown urban residential and commercial area to be integrated with downtown Toronto; it is to provide a city environment with public plazas, restaurants, shops, studios, and private areas opening onto waterside walks. One of the basic elements of the concept is to integrate the commercial area with the residential area. Urban density is to be achieved by means of low buildings around intimate spaces.

Marinas and boatyards for general citywide use, along with space for boat fitters, sailing schools, and other marine facilities, are to create the character of Harbour City. Also, studios, workshops, small specialty shops, and other retail stores and water-oriented restaurants would be of interest to visitors as well as the local inhabitants.

The total complex will include some 510 acres of newly made islands and 220 acres of existing lands. A total of 280 acres of waterways between the islands and the new metropolitan parkland will provide lagoons and regatta courses as well as boating, skating, and scenic enjoyment.

The commercial areas will grow gradually over a period of development. They will be able to contract as well, because of the anticipated layout, in which commercial space no longer needed in a specific area can readily be transformed into residential use. Here, the planner sees the urban pattern of growth as "soft," lending itself to future change as orientations to the harbor develop in future years, meeting changing needs and lifestyles, and taking advantage of new opportunities.

HARBOUR CITY
Toronto, Ontario
ARCHITECTS: Craig Zeidler & Strong, Architects

ABOVE: *Metropolitan Toronto with superimposed view of Harbour City model showing the "texture" of the concept in relation to the "texture" of downtown Toronto.*

Aerial view from the southwest showing the park and water aspects of Harbour City in relation to the high-rise, high-density downtown core.

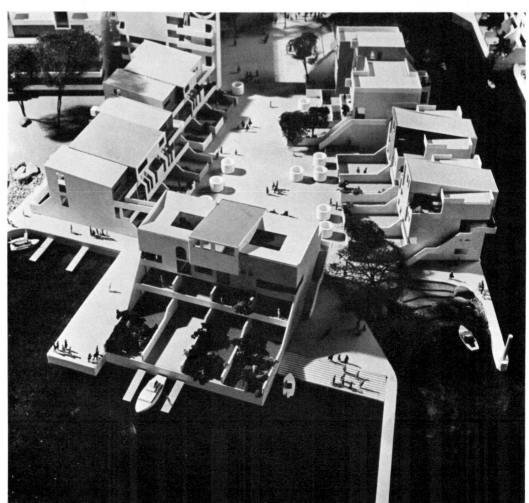

Aerial view of a Harbour City detail model showing the flexibility possible within the concept and demonstrating how recreational facilities can be combined with everyday living.

According to architect Eberhard Zeidler:

> The concept in itself is quite feasible, as it is based on the assumption that any money that would be put in by the government would be recovered in the sale of the condominium units. The leeway that this project had was that all land was owned by public institutions—namely, the provincial government, the city, and the harbor commission—and that by joint agreement, they would not be profit-making organizations. This allowed them to recapture sufficient capital to allow for the inclusion of items that usually will not find their way into a project of this size—such as the canals and social amenities—without taking the housing out of the general economic range.
>
> The project was brought to a final feasibility study stage in 1973. The key to the settlement would be an agreement between the provincial government, the city, and the harbor commission concerning the mutual ownership of the land.

Jane Jacobs, noted writer on urban affairs and recipient of the AIA Architecture Critic's Citation in 1975, had these comments to make at the Harbour City presentation at Queen's Park, Toronto (May 1970):

> The Harbour City scheme is urban in the best sense: full of surprises, contrasts and variety of all kinds, abounding with places for people to come together easily and naturally, full of scope for individual tastes and plans. It is conceived as a place for people to enjoy city life and make the most of its possibilities, instead of being bored, overwhelmed and imprisoned in it.
>
> The concept is liberated from the routine planning practices and clichés that have been making cities progressively more banal, sterile and inhuman. It discards the high-rise towers set in cold isolation, the deserts of parking lots, the commercial centers cordoned off, and the repetitive, meaningless buffer spaces.
>
> Instead, this concept is a return to enduring principles of lively and interesting city life. If certain views of Harbour City seem hauntingly like glimpses of famous cities beloved by artists and tourists, this is because Harbour City shares with them the underlying principles of urbanity. It is not at all because Harbour City is imitating other periods or employing superficial design tricks. For the other remarkable thing the designers of this concept have done is to re-think what lively urban life can offer in terms of today's leisure as well as work, and today's comforts as well as necessities. They have also re-interpreted, in terms of today's engineering and construction possibilities and economies, ways in which repetitive building elements can be employed to achieve variety of scene and use, instead of sameness. This is a most important technical achievement.
>
> This is the first time, as far as I know, that enduring urban qualities have been combined with today's ways and means in a whole new development. The implications are rather staggering: Harbour City is probably the most important advance in planning for cities that has been made this century.
>
> Harbour City's dwelling densities are urban, not suburban. The fact that they are not accommodated in high towers means that they cover the ground rather intensively. This, in turn, means that the concept can be infused with truly urban public places: intimate, interesting, varied, busy and surprising. Much is made of spaces for people to get together and take pleasure in the urban scene and its social contacts. The large Harbour City parklands, which are different in character, gain from this contrast.
>
> The intense, urban areas have a built-in flexibility. Their use is not rigid and frozen. The only fixed and pre-ordained elements are the frameworks of waterways, circulation and parks. Within these frameworks, the urban fabric can unfold in all kinds of patterns and combinations of uses. Furthermore, this flexibility need never be lost. Buildings can be converted from one use to another, even parts of buildings; adapted from this use to that, as the community's needs change or people want to try new possibilities. True urban life has scope for the plans of many, many people besides planners, and the flexibility and adaptability of this concept welcome that fact. Conformity or exclusiveness are not the aims. Because of the inherent flexibility of the buildings proposed, residents of all ages, families of all sizes, and people with wide ranges of income can all be accommodated without artificial isolation from each other. So can all manner of other things: shops, restaurants, workshops, small offices and many facilities shared with visitors to Harbour City from elsewhere in Metro.
>
> Well-loved city areas have unique characters. They are not anonymous places like a hundred others. Harbour City's physical character is both unique and delightful. But at least as important is the character it will gain from its uses and users. If the concept is carried out with the flexibility and diversity of use intended, Toronto will have one of the most interesting and remarkable city districts to be found anywhere in the world.

As imaginative as this concept is, it met with strong opposition from the environmentalists concerned with the negative effect on marine life and increased water pollution of the lake. Due to this opposition, as well as to economic factors at the time of this writing, the plans were held in abeyance.

Part Five

Preservation and Restoration of Historic Buildings in the Central Business District Area

The Train Station

PARKING 80 CARS

COVE STREET

SECOND STREET

HIGH STREET

STREET

Although city planning is an ancient profession, in the United States it was only in the early 1940s that widespread interest in the needs of replanning began to be evidenced. The schools of architecture started to offer courses in urban design, emphasizing the physical aspects, specifically the interrelations of buildings. Under the influence of these early planners, the basic approach to any redevelopment was the most direct—remove the old, existing structures to make way for their new concepts. In their convictions and enthusiasm that new, contemporary structures must replace the old, they did not take into account the historical significance of many buildings. The sociological factors of established neighborhoods and ethnic communities were also in many instances neglected.

We have seen, starting in the 1960s, a new generation of urban planners—the product of a broadened base of studies in the university curriculum. In addition to physical planning, courses covered the various sociological aspects, economics, regional history, and the psychological as well as the physical requirements of the individual and the group. At the same time, there was an increasing awareness on the part of the general public—bolstered by outspoken individuals, historical preservation groups, environmental groups, architects, professional organizations, and the federal government itself—of the importance of historic preservation and the conversion of old buildings in good repair into economically viable usage.

The reader at this point may ask how historic preservation will help the revival of the central business district. As explained in the Overview and in some of the case studies, one of the major attractions to any city is its individual character. Historic buildings, when properly adapted to functional uses, provide this special interest and stimulation, regarding the heritage and background of the city, for both local residents and out-of-town visitors. This positive approach to historic preservation is aptly expressed by Gerald E. Crane, chairman of the Department of Urban Planning, University of Michigan: "Adaptive reuse, as I interpret it, is more than preserving old buildings for the sake of sentiment and history, but is an attempt to incorporate and blend new buildings with older ones and to modify and use them to serve contemporary needs."

The importance of the preservation and conversion of old railroad stations is pointed out by Carleton Knight III, Assistant Editor of *Preservation News.*

> All across the country, railroad stations are being given new lives. The range of uses is as wide as the imaginations of the people they serve: Mt. Vernon, Ohio, is turning its station into a senior citizens center; Yuma, Arizona, an arts center; Woonsocket, Rhode Island, a commercial project; Montgomery, Alabama, a civic center. Restaurants seem to be popular—the Ann Arbor, Michigan station now houses the Gandy Dancer; Beverly, Massachusetts, the Depot; and Ithaca, New York, a facility that has additional seating space in several railroad cars. Countless numbers of stations have been turned into shops for books, dresses, gifts, antiques, toys —almost anything. Others have become offices for architects and lawyers, real estate and insurance companies.
>
> The best use would seem to be one where the railroads continue to use a portion of the space and the remainder is converted for other needs. This plan is being followed in a number of conversions—San Diego, New London, Connecticut; Indianapolis, and Little Rock, Arkansas. Amtrak is interested and willing to be a part of these projects and can be counted on by preservationists to help out by renting some space.*

*Excerpted from "Railroading: Saving America's Stations" by Carleton Knight, III, a supplement to *Preservation News,* April 1974, the monthly newspaper of the National Trust for Historic Preservation.

RIVER CORRIDOR
San Antonio, Texas

San Antonio stands out as a prime example of cities that have preserved their heritage by the restoration, renovation, and conversion of historic buildings. One of the highlights of restoration projects is the La Villita historical district, located just west of Hemisfair Plaza on the River corridor. The restoration is being financed by bond issue and federal dollars for a total cost of over one-half million dollars, to be shared equally. The project includes reconstruction of five houses in this historic area, preserving remnants of the same small village described by both French and Spanish travelers in the late 1700s.

An interesting example of the reconversion of wood structures is the old One Star Brewery, which was opened in 1884 at the Jones Avenue site. In 1900 construction was begun on the permanent buildings of pressed brick of the Romanesque revival style. This building has been purchased by the San Antonio Museum Association for redevelopment of the complex of buildings to provide a unique setting for an art museum and other compatible uses. The association raised $1 million in private money for redevelopment.

An example of reconstruction is Market Square, located about six blocks west of the Alamo Plaza project. It is currently undergoing reconstruction and expansion, including construction of a new $922,000 parking garage. The complex will continue to house produce and curio stalls, and it will preserve the atmosphere of a colorful municipal marketplace. The marketplace is a tradition in San Antonio, dating back to the first settlers, the Canary Islanders, who came there in 1731. The market moved to its present location from Military Plaza in 1874.

Another renovation project is the Ursuline Square complex. Originally a Catholic academy for girls, founded in 1851, it is now being renovated as a historic structure by the San Antonio Conservation Society.

Many homes of the Victorian period in Texas are being restored in this historic residential district in the central city. The King William District restoration is a good example.

An important element in the cultural heritage of San Antonio is the number of Spanish colonial missions and the roads and trails linking them. It is proposed that a missions advisory council be established to promote and implement a mission parkway, equally important in the high-quality standards achieved by the River Walk. The designation of a mission historic district is proposed as an interim measure, its main purpose being design control to prevent further visual deterioration and reduce uncontrolled conflicting development.

In general, historic structures have been identified and categorized as to "resource-type group" and "treatment group" in the 1972 *San Antonio Historic Survey, Historic Resource Data Cards and Instruction Manual,* prepared by the San Antonio Community Renewal Program, a division of city planning. The resource-type groups indicate the nature of the object of historic concern (for example, an individual building, landmark tree, or urban artifact). The treatment groups recommend a hierarchy of actions that are considered appropriate in regard to each resource.

Many locations identified by the historic survey are concentrated in the central city outside the protected King William and La Villita historic districts. Many more historic locations are scattered throughout the River corridor. The central-city staff planning (urban design) approach is to provide evaluation of historic conservation needs and the need for economic revitalization throughout the River corridor. The objective of this effort is the achievement of an economically dynamic central city, which at the same time will stand out as a unique example of the best of the nation's heritage. This exciting blend will occur because the reuse of historic structures will be made viable by the supportive upgrading and complementary new development within the area.

The proposed Alamo Plaza project will serve as an illustration to show that modern high-rise structures can be designed with sensitivity to the highly important historic buildings in the surrounding area. This new development will contribute to an urban mode of activity that will draw larger crowds to the historic Alamo and also create new opportunities for attractive reuse of less prominent, but valuable, historic structures now vacant or underutilized.

All the above-mentioned projects, in or near the central business district, emphasize again the importance of restoration and preservation to both residents and visitors.

CLOCKWISE, FROM TOP: *La Paloma del Rio Mexican restaurant with dining on the river and street levels (lower balcony); owner's apartment is on upper level. (Architects: E. B. Flowers.) The restaurant before development. (Photograph courtesy of the Department of Planning and Community Development.) La Sirena property following restoration. This shop, which deals in the arts and crafts of Mexico, is now located on another portion of the river. The building in the photograph is now occupied by the B'Wana Dik, an African motif nightclub. (Architects: Robert K. Winn.) The property before restoration.*

The Faneuil Hall Markets as they appeared shortly after their completion in 1826, as seen from Boston Harbor. Note the location of Faneuil Hall and the trees of Beacon Hill beyond.

The Faneuil Hall Markets as restored for Boston 200. The city's observance of the national Bicentennial includes sidewalk cafés and shops and retail and office space, with emphasis on pedestrian activities.

FANEUIL HALL MARKETS

Boston, Massachusetts

ARCHITECTS:
For the master plan: Benjamin Thompson
& Associates
For the restoration: F. A. Stahl & Associates

Famous Faneuil Hall and its three-block-long market annexes—Quincy, North, and South Markets—stand at the exact center of Boston's urban core. Once the heart of harbor activity and the city's wholesale food industry, the aging granite buildings have stood empty and neglected for almost a decade. Bostonians over the years have asked the questions that must haunt every historic building still standing: Could the old market buildings serve some useful purpose in a renewed downtown? Should antiquated low-rise buildings continue to occupy six acres of prime city real estate? If renovation were physically feasible, what purposes would make it economically viable? What new patterns of self-sustaining use, serving the changing needs and conditions of the city, could be found to save the treasures of our architectural past? Preservation, in the words of Ada Louise Huxtable, is finding ways of keeping those buildings which provide the city's character and continuity and of incorporating them into its living mainstream— original buildings on original sites that remember, but do not reenact, an earlier time and a different way of life. At the Faneuil Hall Markets, there will be no historical playacting, no costumed atmosphere, no phony old period pieces. These would only confuse and devalue authenticity. All that is usable and real will be kept and used, without denying the flow of the past into the present and the evolving future.

The Faneuil Hall Markets project is the name now given to the three-block area built by Josiah Quincy in 1825–1826 as extensions of Bullfinch's Faneuil Hall (which remains under city management). It is a larger landmark redevelopment than most in the country so far, but the principles of its rescue and rehabilitation are those which must affect most such historic projects in the future.

Basically, the issue is this: Among the old buildings hereafter worth saving, very few will or should be museums. In seeking a realistic future life, an old structure that is historically, socially, or architecturally interesting cannot become economically invalid, forever dependent on grants and doles, on government and personal largesse. Adaptive uses must be found which intrinsically provide means—and motive—for continued use and maintenance. Almost inevitably, this means that the uses must be vital ones, geared not to "pure preservation" but to the dynamic urban needs of communities. Buildings, to survive, must go on living.

To implement this philosophy, the architects, after numerous studies, evolved a master plan for the entire three-block area under which it would be used as a single marketplace, with maximum retail space on all three levels, assuring a full range of shops, restaurants, and entertainment. This concept is contrary to the usual approach of mass leasing to major institutional tenants, with heavy emphasis on office use. However, a limited area of office space will be available for professionals, organizations, service specialties, publishing, graphics design, and other tenants of limited size.

The key segments of the Faneuil Hall Markets plan are the Quincy Market building, North and South Market Streets, and the North and South Market Street buildings. Their uses are as follows:

1. Quincy Market, the central, domed building, is to be operated as a food bazaar, with the first floor kept open as a continuous "indoor street." Along this street, individual retail concessions will offer meat, fish, produce, dairy goods, specialty foods, and wines, while a variety of stalls—some open twenty-four hours a day—will create an enormous international buffet served by a central eating area. The present food retailers are encouraged to remain in the building as participants in the "bazaar."

Under the dome of Quincy Market, a special focal space is created by opening the building from the first floor to the roof. This unusual "rotunda" has the character of a large lobby or meeting place, where gatherings and informal entertainment occur continuously. On balconies around the rotunda, a special restaurant overlooks the activity at this crossroads of the marketplace.

2. Along the outside of Quincy Market on both North and South Market Streets, a wide canopy provides a cover where produce vendors can station their carts throughout the year and where pedestrians can walk the length of the marketplace. Cafés and eating places are to be found along these arcades, with outdoor tables and chairs extending into North and South Market Streets, as in a European piazza. These cafés continue to operate during the winter months, when the aisles are enclosed and heated.

3. The North and South Market Street buildings at ground level house a wide variety of stores, boutiques, services, restaurants, and nightclubs. All these face toward the traffic-free cobblestone streets, which with plantings, benches, kiosks, play areas, and mobile vendors, become busy pedestrian shopping malls, with people as the center of action.

Specific types of stores and shops will be sought as tenants to assure a genuine balance of offerings and price ranges. Thus restaurants will range from informal soup bars and coffee shops to elegant, first-class club restaurants. All are to be located in such a way as to create maximum variety of activity.

Areas of the market are organized into zones to create strong collective interest and drawing power to different points and to give visible contrast to the character of various parts of the complex. Thus one section might include a number of small "discovery" shops—art, craft, and print galleries—while a contrasting section would offer a range of quality stores—home furnishings, antiques, or boutiques.

Boston Exhibition Center, created on the second floor of the Quincy Market building, will serve as a focal point of *Boston 200* Bicentennial displays and information.

Outdoor activities and street fairs of many kinds are planned, including parades, local musical talent, children's theater, puppets, and special performers. Daily outdoor markets, including pushcart vendors from the Haymarket who may wish to relocate, as well as artists, craftsmen, and special retailers, will be located along the street malls and arcades.

Aerial perspective of proposed market area.

The original rooflines of the North and South Market Street row of buildings in the Faneuil Hall Markets are being restored, as are the granite building façades, which have been altered over the 150 years of the existence of the market complex.

Children's play areas, telephones, restrooms, and benches are accessible to the public using the outdoor spaces. Convenience kiosks provide centralized city information. There are also such outdoor features as individual bookstalls, news and tobacco kiosks, and stalls selling souvenirs, ice cream, and light lunches.

The malls are planned and surfaced so that they may be used by service vehicles on a schedule that does not disrupt other activities of the market. Trash-removal trucks, delivery trucks, and other vehicles will be able to reach specific service points at designated hours.

The Boston Redevelopment Authority designated The Rouse Company, a developer, to implement this project in March 1973. At that time the exterior restoration of the North and South Market Street buildings was under way, financed by a $2.2 million historic preservation grant from the Department of Housing and Urban Development. The architects for this restoration are F. A. Stahl & Associates.

According to the developers, the total cost is estimated at $18 million; this includes land utilities, mechanical and electrical facilities, interiors, street amenities, landscaping, and tenant improvements (prior to leasing). Also included is the operation budget for management insurance, promotion, tenant services, exterior lighting, security, and a special sum for the 1976 Bicentennial activities.

The Rouse Company also agreed to the following:

1. Payments to the city—guaranteed minimum, 20 percent of gross revenues or $600,000 per year, whichever is greater. This becomes effective after two years of operation, increasing during start-up from $200,000 to $400,000 annually to $600,000, in the third year and thereafter. This represents a guaranteed minimum payment to the city over the life of the lease of $58 million.

2. Probable maximums. On the basis of existing Rouse Company rent programs and records (minimum-plus-percentage rents), the growing success of the market retailers will produce increasing payments to the city well in excess of the guaranteed sum. The guarantee would be exceeded as rent payments reached $8 per square foot. As sales increase and rent payments (as a percentage of sales) also go up, the city's share could exceed $1 million in the coming decade. The city and its taxpayers thus become financial partners in the market's success during the entire life of the lease, based on the developer's expertise in the management of commercial projects of complexity and quality.

3. Financing sources—source of operating cash (equity). All funds for construction and operation of the project will be acquired by The Rouse Company on its own credit, prior to placement of long-term mortgages, which will be done by its subsidiary, Rouse-Boston, after the markets are in operation.

The Boston Redevelopment Authority now owns forty-two of the forty-five structures that make up North and South Market Streets. Quincy Market is owned by the city of Boston, and it is expected that The Rouse Company will negotiate a long-term lease on the building.

The three buildings not owned by the Boston Redevelopment Authority belong to the Durgin-Park Restaurant and are exempted from the BRA's waterfront renewal project. The owners of the buildings have, however, agreed to conform to the exterior restoration standards of the complex.

Faneuil Markets is the major link in the walk-to-the-sea that is included in the Boston Redevelopment Authority's waterfront renewal plan. It provides the pedestrian connector between Government Center and the waterfront at a pivotal point between these areas, the North End and the financial district.

A recent significant example of renovation and historical restoration is Trolley Square, in Salt Lake City, Utah. It is located on 13 acres, at Seventh Street East and Fifth Street South, and is only about five blocks from downtown. A complex of arch-designed vintage trolley barns forms the nucleus of the square. Built at the turn of the century as a home for the city's trolley system, the buildings today stand newly discovered after being hidden for decades beneath layers of grime and yellow paint. Antique cast-iron light fixtures that once adorned the downtown area have been obtained and fastened on the exteriors of several buildings. Inside, a colorful conglomeration of sprightly shops and galleries, fashion stores, services, an indoor farmer's market, several theaters, gourmet restaurants, sidewalk cafés, an oversized ice-cream store, and boutiques are interlaced along newly created brick streets.

An atmosphere of discovery pervades as shoppers, diners, browsers, and theater-goers wander through this multilevel indoor marketplace. Some of the attractions and services are situated appropriately in renovated Salt Lake City trolley cars. In a move to preserve the local flavor of the community, the square also has become a showplace for valuable antique artifacts rescued from local mansions just ahead of the bulldozers. Stained glass, hand-carved doors, and staircases have been used in a casual way as attraction accents for shops and restaurants throughout the complex.

The existing water tower, which is 97 feet high, has been redecorated in a Victorian theme as an observation platform and landmark for the square. Historians note that in the mid-1800s, this same site once served as Utah's first territorial fairgrounds. Today, Trolley Square has the distinction of being listed on the state's *Register of Historic Sites*.

Wallace A. Wright, Jr., developer of the project, offers the following suggestions:

Drive around any city—or, better still, walk—and take the time to study old hotels, warehouses, or groups of buildings. Some of the best ones are in the run-down sections of town. Consider the condition of the basic structure of the buildings and the mechanical elements—can they be brought up to date economically? Sometimes the most expensive part of renovating is tearing down portions that detract from the main structure. What you have to consider when you are looking for a building is how much "gutting" it will require. Normally, a building that is substantially remodeled will have to be brought up to the prevailing building codes, but in some cases it becomes impossible to modify the structure to comply fully, and so there will have to be exceptions.

Plan multilevel expansion wherever possible. We were fortunate in that the large carbarn building served as a natural enclosed mall with ceilings 33 feet high. We added a second level using concrete core-deck to increase the gross leasable area. Then when many of our second-level tenants requested an upstairs, there was room for a third level, again increasing the gross leasable area substantially. We are now planning a fifteen-story high-rise hotel to be constructed over a portion of the existing building.

Pool resources. Consider joint-venture partnerships in financing. A lot of financial institutions and insurance companies now are paying lip service to the value of preserving the environment. One might ask them to "put their mortgage where their mouth is."

Get the local press behind you. Trolley Square was situated in a declining area. Now there is an entire renaissance in action, accelerating surrounding property values, encouraging new developments, and stimulating other renovation projects. Environmental impact being the order of the day, the local news media have been most cooperative in reporting our progress, citing the project for "outstanding civic beautification."

TROLLEY SQUARE
Salt Lake City, Utah
ARCHITECTS: Albert L. Christensen of
Architects/Planners Alliance

CLOCKWISE, FROM TOP: *The center of attention in the mall is the stained-glass cupola. Furnishings were collected from antique shops. Water tower serves as a landmark and observation tower. Aerial view of square in 1972, nearing completion.*

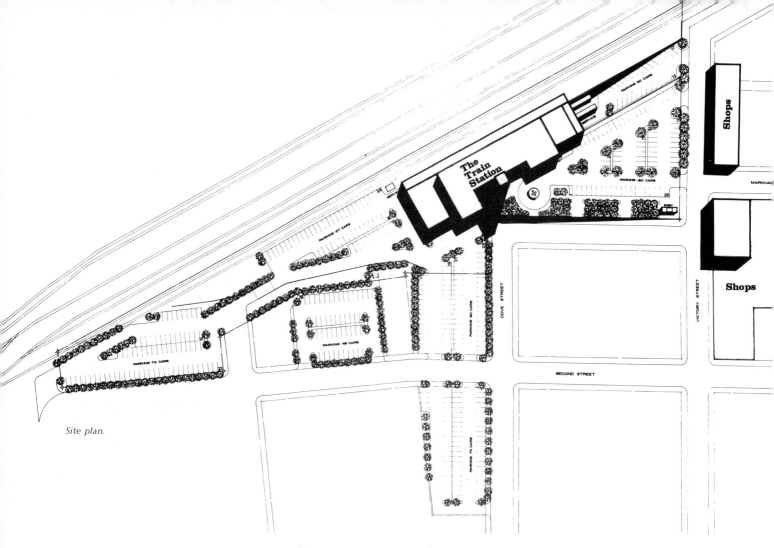

Site plan.

THE TRAIN STATION
Little Rock, Arkansas
ARCHITECTS: Wilkins/Griffin/Sims

The old Missouri-Pacific Union Station, located in the historic part of Little Rock's downtown, is the heart of a 56-acre renovation project developed by the Sierra Corporation. Renovated from the old Union Station and surrounded by old hotels and bars and turn-of-the-century homes, the Train Station includes exclusive specialty shops, fine restaurants, entertainment spots, and office space, designed with early-1900 decor.

The location adjoins the state capitol grounds, is within walking distance of the new downtown convention complex, and is easily accessible from the city's thoroughfares and interstate highways.

The success of the Train Station has been sparked by the great attraction of the Tracks Inn Restaurant, considered one of the busiest in Arkansas. As Train Station president Dan Fowler said:

> All over the country there is a rising tide of interest in saving old structures which are no longer suited, or needed for their original uses. Putting new businesses and commercial activities into renovated old buildings has many advantages. It preserves architecturally interesting buildings; it allows developers to utilize sound buildings which have detailing and decoration impossible to reproduce; and it puts modern activity in a building with "character" that is a refreshing change from strictly functional building styles.*

The next stage of the redevelopment will include the conversion of adjacent properties into additional retail complexes. Said Fowler:

> The Train Station's presence should revitalize this whole part of town. In recent years, many of us have been distressed to see the deterioration of this location which, in turn, has pulled down with it the surrounding blocks. The area is so near the State Capitol complex, the downtown area and the major traffic arteries that it is ideal for many uses. We also feel the Train Station complex will encourage the increasing interest of young couples and families to buy older houses convenient to the downtown area so that it can blossom into a once-again prime residential section.†

*Excerpted from *Quapaw Quarter Chronicle*, Little Rock, Ark., May–June 1974.
†Ibid.

ABOVE: *Perspective view showing the proposed renovation of adjacent buildings.* LEFT: *View of renovated façade.*

Plaza level.

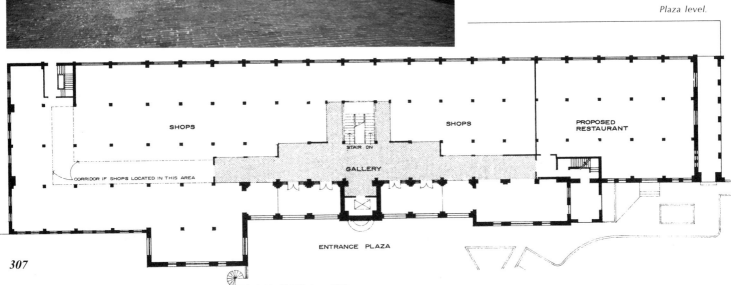

In July, 1960, the German Village Commission was formed to guide the general restoration of properties within the boundaries of the German Village area so that a uniformity of restoration would be pursued. In April, 1963, the Columbus City Council, by City Ordinance, established legal boundaries for German Village and declared it a historical area. This area includes approximately 233 acres, situated a few blocks south of where Broad and High Streets cross in the heart of downtown Columbus. Familiar landmarks in the Village are headquarters of the German Village Society, Inc., St. Mary's Church, Schiller Park, and Beck Square.

The restoration of Engine House #5 in the German Village is a successful accomplishment in preserving a historical building in the heart of a growing, fast-moving city where land is at a premium for redevelopment. It was converted from a fire station built in the late 1800's to a seafood restaurant of national reputation. The design problem was to retain the existing features of the basic space, while utilizing authentic firefighting equipment as a part of the overall decor. This, together with the interesting graphics, has created an atmosphere which made this building a magnet in the Village for both residents and tourists.

William Scheurer, director of the German Village Society, makes a good case for preservation of this historic area, "Why save an old area of the city? Why not tear down the old and make way for the new? We save it because we love it; because it says, this is our basis; our beginning. It was here on this spot that our forefathers lived, worked and worshipped. We save it because of our need to learn from the past, to remember our ancestors, and to be proud of our heritage."*

The owner-developer of Engine House #5 restaurant is C. A. Muer Corporation.

*Parts excerpted from *Visitors Guide to German Village.*

GERMAN VILLAGE
Columbus, Ohio
DESIGNERS: Jack Green and Roger Sherman
GRAPHICS: Chris Pohl

Engine House #5 restaurant exterior. (Photograph courtesy of C. A. Muer Corporation.)

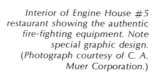

Interior of Engine House #5 restaurant showing the authentic fire-fighting equipment. Note special graphic design. (Photograph courtesy of C. A. Muer Corporation.)

Although the city of Northville, Michigan (located 20 miles from Detroit), started its renewal of the central business area by building a modern, enclosed-mall shopping center (see Part 3), it was aware of the great potential of preserving its historically worthwhile buildings in the vicinity. An 1885 vacated Methodist church building was converted into a fine and successful restaurant, The Drawbridge. The core of the Gothic design was retained, and the interior exposed trusses and beams were made into a design feature. On the exterior, the castle-like image was emphasized by a moat and a drawbridge.

The owner-manager is Leopold Schaeli.

DRAWBRIDGE
Northville, Michigan

Conversion of a historic church into a restaurant. ABOVE: *View after conversion.* RIGHT: *View before conversion.*

Flair House, a three-story brick mansion built in 1883 and located in the northwest neighborhood adjacent to the Chicago Loop area, is a success story of renovation and readaptation for business usage. The dilapidated building, which stands at 214 West Eric Street, was crumbling, and the owner wished to either sell or destroy it. Lee Flaherty, owner and president of the Flair Merchandising Agency, which he had started in the building in 1964, bought it for $35,000 in 1965.

Renovation of the original building cost $250,000, and construction of an adjoining building at the rear in 1970 cost another $511,000. This also included the alteration of the exterior of the original building and installation of a sloped ceiling to accommodate a gift of three Tiffany-signed stained-glass windows from an old brewery.

The two buildings, connected by a unique oval handcrafted staircase, are furnished with antiques collected by antique dealer Fred Lowman from famous old Chicago mansions long since razed. The items include a black marble mantelpiece, a nineteenth-century armoire, a marble-lined commode, stained-glass windows, a nineteenth-century French baccarat chandelier suspended above the main entrance, an 1850 Waterford cut-glass chandelier and special glass candle holders, a Sèvres vase, seventeenth-century carved Don Quixote figures, bronze statuettes, spooled latticework, and hand-carved wood oak paneling.

The advantages of restoration for the Flair Merchandising Agency have been many. Flair House is a good place for the staff to work, presents an excellent "image" to the client, and affords a good business arrangement for the owner.

Based on a ten-year amortization, the cost of approximately $10 per square foot is way below that of rentals in Chicago's high-rise buildings. The value of Flair House increases as time goes on, whereas conventional office buildings may depreciate.

Probably the most important advantage has been the stimulation of new interest in this block along Erie Street. Trees have been planted, neighboring building exteriors have been renovated, and the sidewalks are kept clean and free of debris.

In 1972 Flair House received the Chicago Beautification Award. The headquarters of a well-known interior designer has been established across the street, adding to the prestige of the location. A block away, developers have been successfully restoring old houses and converting them to desirable apartments. It is expected that the restoration of the area will result in a neighborhood of carefully maintained buildings that will be beneficial for all. The near north side is generally defined as the area between Lake Michigan and Dearborn Street. It varies in quality, improving as it continues north and blending into expensive residential areas consisting of restored houses and high-rises.

FLAIR HOUSE
Chicago, Illinois
ARCHITECT FOR THE RESTORATION AND ADDITION:
John Page of Page Midwest

ABOVE, LEFT: *Exterior before restoration. (Photography courtesy of Ruth L. Ratny, Flair Merchandising Agency.)* ABOVE, RIGHT: *Exterior after restoration. (Photographer: Photo Ideas Inc.)*

An inspiring element in the Detroit uphill battle for revival of the citizens' positive attitudes is seen in the special work of the Mayor's Merchants Assistance Program (MMAT). Most of the work consists of designing and painting murals on individual commercial buildings near downtown run-down areas. The design service is furnished free by the city to the merchant who pays for the materials used and for the contractor. These murals are quickly implemented because they are based on a one-to-one relationship—one merchant, one designer, one contractor, and, at the most, one city department!

In the case of the city-owned Eastern Farmers Market, built in 1881, which the long-range master plan had scheduled for removal, the murals resulted in a complete turnabout. The fact that the farmers who used the public sheds contributed toward the cost of the murals is a good indication of their desire for a stimulating and exciting atmosphere which they anticipated would also increase sales. Since the murals have been installed and modern improvements have been made in lighting, paving and curbing, new windows all financed from a three-year increase in stall rentals, business has increased 30 percent, and thousands of city dwellers and suburbanites come every weekend. The encouraging results from this inexpensive, innovative, and creative approach are bringing numerous new requests for murals from other merchants and businessmen. Jack Pryor is the deputy director of this special program. The city planner and designer staff is composed of Kenneth Bean, Alex Pollock, and Joe Orloff.

Projects like this one—the brainchild of Alex Pollock, who was loaned from the Detroit City Planning Commission—have stimulated so much enthusiasm that a second Farmers Market, at Chene and Ferry in the near downtown area, was rededicated in July 1974.

Also of importance is the commissioning by the Detroit Renaissance of talented local artists of national repute to paint outdoor murals on a number of buildings in various parts of the center city. The most recent is a 48- by 96-foot mural by John Egner for the Park Shelton apartment building at the entrance to the cultural center. Another is by Alvin Loving, Jr., a Detroit-born black artist, for the First National building in downtown Detroit. It is twenty floors high. This project and the one by Aris Koutroulis, which is a mural covering 2,400 square feet, designed for a wall of the Broadway Capitol building, were commissioned by a private volunteer group, Art for Detroit, with funds from Detroit Renaissance in 1971.

MAYOR'S MERCHANTS ASSISTANCE PROGRAM and DETROIT RENAISSANCE
Detroit, Michigan

CLOCKWISE, FROM TOP: *Eastern Farmers Market.* (*Artist: Alex Pollock.*) *Park Shelton apartment building, outdoor mural, 48' wide by 96' high.* (*Artist: John Egner. Commissioned by Detroit Renaissance. Photograph courtesy of Johnson Johnson & Roy, Inc.*) *The Everfresh building with painted mural.* (*Artist: Joe Orloff.*) *Mural on exterior of Eastern Farmers Market.* (*Artist: Alex Pollock.*)

BEDFORD-STUYVESANT COMMERCIAL CENTER

Brooklyn, New York

ARCHITECTS: Arthur Cotton Moore/Associates

This program was to provide the Bedford-Stuyvesant community with the needed commercial uses now precluded because of blight, crime, and general deterioration; to provide recreational amenities and community facilities; and to provide other uses so that the center would be economically self-sustaining and would act as a catalyst for a private commercial comeback in adjacent areas. To the special needs—such as a supermarket, a Health Maintenance Organization Clinic, a drugstore, and a skating rink—were added rent-producing office space, shops, a cafeteria and café, a restaurant and nightclub, three movie theaters, and craft-type retail industries.

To implement the above program, it was decided to break up the narrow block-long project into three interconnected yet different squares. The first square responds to the open feeling of Marcy Place (see the accompanying plan) and is also oriented to Fulton Street, the main commercial street and access. This first square contains the needed commercial and community uses. Five row-type buildings were removed to make room for the square and new construction, but the unique wall of three burned-out tenements was retained as a screen (conveying a sense of enclosure and allowing circulation to the second commercial level) and as a billboard upon which merchants can get signage through banners right out on the main street, Fulton. The buildings which surround the square are a mixture of old (deemed worth saving for both cost and aesthetic reasons) and new, with the new tying the old together for flexibility of leasing and the integration of new cores.

The 45-degree orientation is to bring people from Fulton visually through the first square to a fountain in the second square, which is mainly recreational, and to relate to the future new apartment house diagonally across Herkimer Street. The second square is itself subdivided into two areas: The first area is devoted to passive recreation and outside dining, with fountain and trees, and the second area stresses active recreation focused on the skating rink. The skating rink has

OPPOSITE PAGE: *Elevation—Fulton Street.*
LEFT: *Inner court looking toward skating rink.*

Plan at street level.

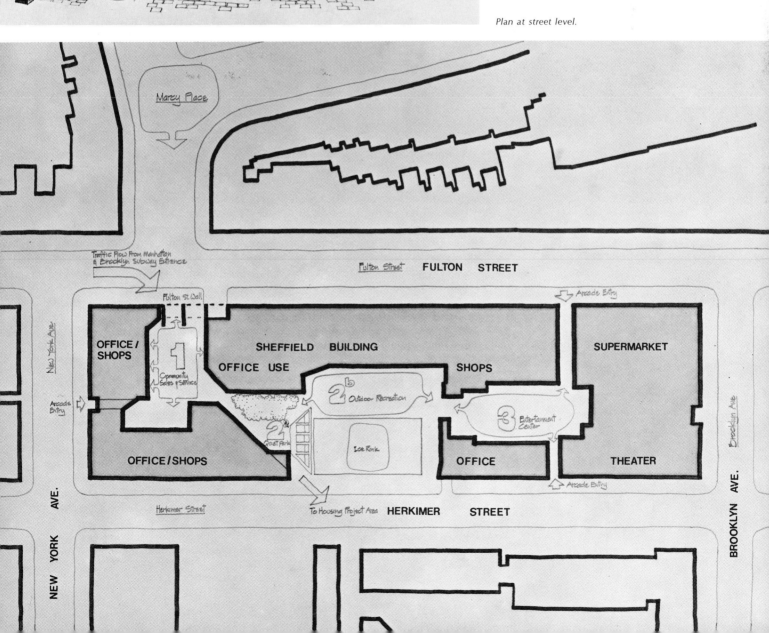

Section aa

Section through project.

been "dished in" so as to provide a natural amphitheater for community activities, such as dances, shows, exhibits, and concerts, as well as skating. The large building along Fulton has also been remodeled for office use and shops (architects for this building are Sancho, Kennedy.)

The third square is an existing court in a manufacturing building whose unique qualities have been exploited to create a more "swinging" atmosphere. The entertainment idea of this square is to broaden the appeal of the development beyond Bedford-Stuyvesant in order to import needed money for the project as a whole. Consequently, three piggyback theaters and a restaurant and nightclub are included; through their volume patronage, exposure will be given to the mixture of craft workshops, which, it is hoped, will outgrow this location and become job-producing local industries. A second level is designed as a mart where prospective purchasers can observe the actual making of goods; the top floor will be a film studio. Through raised plaza levels and other means of separation, an attempt is made to give a sense of patrolled security so that people from other areas will feel free to come here, walk around, and visit the shops and entertainment facilities in an enclave that is secure and yet is free of actual gates, fences, or real barriers to the ebb and flow of people from the neighborhood.

As to the general character of the project, the design approach is to leave old brick as is, except for occasional paint removal. New brick is of a similar dark color and is also used as pavers in the plaza and floors for the public areas. In the old warehouse structures, interior finishes are sandblasted old brick and existing heavy timber beams, ceilings, and columns. In general, most exposed surfaces are brick; new buildings are unadorned to accentuate the texture and ornament of the old structures. Heavy timbers salvaged from demolition are used for benches, bulletin boards, and sign space for the individual shops.

The developer-owner is James Shipp, of the Bedford-Stuyvesant Restoration Corporation. The center opened on October 2, 1975.

Plan at third level.

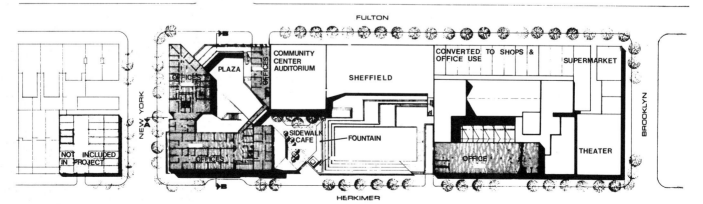

Like many of North America's older cities, historic Halifax (population 125,000) is suffering growing pains. The old seaport's enthusiastic endorsement of the trend toward urban renewal is being aggravated by the city's location on a narrow peninsula.

With land at a premium, the temptation was to cover the landscape with high-rises. However, a unique experiment in one three-acre site in the heart of the city proved that it is not necessary to tear down the old to make way for the new and that old and new commercial properties not only can stand "cheek by jowl" but also can compete with one another for income. The project result—a rare blend of private capital and know-how and public funding—is officially known as the "Restoration of Historic Waterfront Buildings." The project is known locally as the "Privateer's Wharf," after the long, low, rough-cut gray stone building forming the solid core of the complex.

This building, dating from the end of the eighteenth century, along with six other buildings all built in the early or mid-nineteenth century, is being restored to its original design. This is part of phase two of the overall project (phase one involved restoration of a group of nearby historic buildings). The balance of phase two is the construction of three new buildings in similar architectural style, plus a wharf and marina.

Work was completed in 1975, just five years from the time an aroused citizenry saved the buildings from what seemed like certain destruction to make way for a four-lane expressway.

Responding to the public outcry, the city of Halifax called for proposals from private developers to preserve the buildings, not as derelict reminders of the past, but as functional and historically authentic structures.

The proposal of Historic Properties Limited—a Halifax corporation—was eventually accepted, and with the agreement of the city and the Central Mortgage and Housing Corporation, a unique partnership was worked out between the company and the federal Department of Indian Affairs and Northern Development (Historic Sites Division).

Under this partnership, the federal government agreed to pay 50 percent of the costs of restoring the exteriors of the designated buildings. It also granted the developers a seventy-five-year lease on the properties.

HALIFAX, NOVA SCOTIA
ARCHITECTS FOR PRIVATEER'S WHARF:
Duffus, Romans, Kundzins, Rounsefell
PROJECT ARCHITECT: David Forsythe

ABOVE: *Scotia Square complex, 1974 construction photograph. In the foreground a new tower rises on the 17-acre Scotia Square complex. Behind the old buildings of Hollis and Granville Streets (to be restored by Durham Leaseholds), the Privateer's Wharf can be clearly seen in the background (being developed by Historic Properties Ltd.)*

Privateer's Wharf. Interior detail of the enclosed mall showing how effective use has been made of the original structure—much of it more than 100 years old.

As the next step, Historic Properties Limited then assembled a team of architects, engineers, construction men, and historical consultants. Their task was to find a way to restore the exterior of the buildings to as close to their original state as possible and to create interiors which would retain the spirit of the past and, at the same time, serve the needs of today and be economically viable.

According to project architect David Forsythe, the key to the successful realization of their plans was the massive strength of the structures as they stood, combined with the fact that they were virtually empty shells, so that little or no demolition work had to be done. The walls of the oldest building, the Privateer's Warehouse, are of rough stone blocks more than 2 feet thick. The only effect that time had had on them was to bulge them out of plumb in some sections. Where this had happened, masons carefully cut out the blocks and replaced them in their proper position.

The massive hand-hewn timbers and roof beams, joined by huge wooden "knees," are all in perfect shape, and the interior design will leave them uncovered.

When completed, the project will offer 123,000 square feet of space for leasing and will include a hotel, thirty retail stores, four restaurants, a bar, and office accommodations. Also, the Nova Scotia College of Art and Design will lease 19,000 square feet for studios and lecture rooms.

Just across the street from the waterfront site are two blocks of early-nineteenth-century shops and warehouses. These are owned by Historic Properties Limited. Here the character of an age has been recovered by revealing the handmade bricks and rough stone which are utilized for mall street material.

The malls are bordered by fifteen retail stores, many specializing in handcrafted ware.

The historic character of the low-rise restoration project contrasts with the high-rise contemporary towers of the 17-acre Scotia Square rising behind it.

According to C. E. Babb, director of planning, the start of the $65 million project in 1967 marked the beginning of the rebirth of downtown Halifax, which in turn led to the reconstruction of the historic waterfront properties. Already completed, this includes a mix of residential areas, a two-level shopping mall, and commercial facilities.

Privateer's Wharf—site plan.

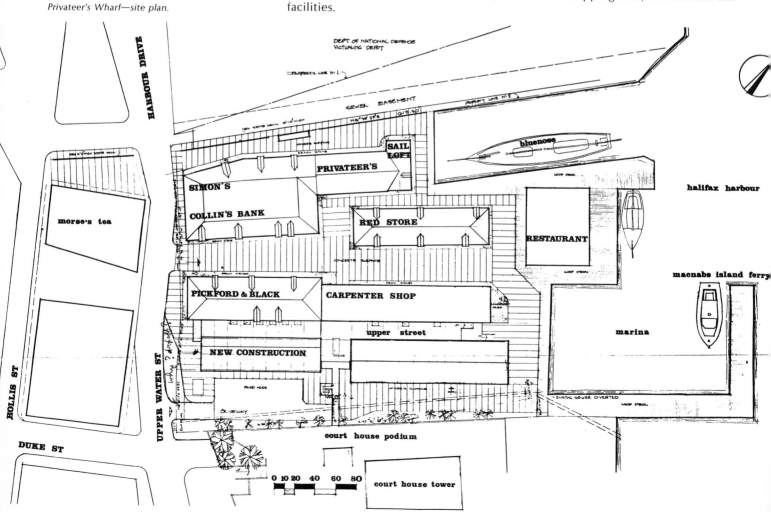

Index